Studies in Eighteenth-Century Culture

VOLUME 30

Studies in Eighteenth-Century Culture

VOLUME 30

Edited by

Timothy Erwin
University of Nevada, Las Vegas

and

Ourida Mostefai
Boston College

Published by The Johns Hopkins University Press for the
American Society for Eighteenth-Century Studies

The Johns Hopkins University Press
Baltimore and London

 Published 2001
Printed in the United States of America on recycled acid-free paper
9 8 7 6 5 4 3 2 1

The Johns Hopkins University Press
2715 North Charles Street
Baltimore, Maryland 21218-4363
www.press.jhu.edu

ISBN 0-8018-6674-X
ISSN 0360-2370

Articles appearing in this annual series are abstracted and
indexed in *Historical Abstracts* and *America: History and Life*.

Editorial Readers for Volume Thirty

JANET E. AIKINS / English / University of New Hampshire
BEATE ALLERT / Foreign Languages / Purdue University
BRIGITTE BAILEY / English / University of New Hampshire
JANINE G. BARCHAS / English / University of Auckland, New Zealand
JOSEPH BARTOLOMEO / English / University of Massachusetts
BARBARA BENEDICT / English / Trinity College
KEVIN BERLAND / English / Pennsylvania State University, Shenango
ANN BERMINGHAM / Art History / University of California, Santa Barbara
MURRAY L. BROWN / English / Georgia State University
RALPH BUECHLER / Foreign Languages / University of Nevada, Las Vegas
HELEN BURKE / English / Florida State University
LORNA CLYMER / English / California State University, Bakersfield
LEON COBURN / English / University of Nevada, Las Vegas
ALISON CONWAY / English / University of Western Ontario
THOMAS CURLEY / English / Bridgewater State University
JUDITH DORN / English / St. Cloud State University
HARRIS FAIRBANKS / English / University of Connecticut
KARL J. FINK / German / St. Olaf College
CARL FISHER / English / Austin Peay State University
CAROL HOULIHAN FLYNN / English / Tufts University
ROBERT FOLKENFLIK / English / University of California, Irvine
BETH FOWKES-TOBIN / English / University of Hawaii
CHRISTOPHER FOX / English / University of Notre Dame
LUIS GAMEZ / English / Western Michigan University
DANIEL GORDON / History / Stanford University
TASSIE GWILLIAM / English / University of Miami
CLEMENT HAWES / English / Pennsylvania State University
JULIE CANDLER HAYES / Modern Languages / University of Richmond
DAVID C. HENSLEY / English / McGill University
MARIE-FRANCE HILGAR / Foreign Languages / University of Nevada, Las Vegas
J. PAUL HUNTER / English / University of Chicago
CATHERINE INGRASSIA / English / Virginia Commonwealth University
LINDA LANG-PERALTA / English / Metropolitan State College

Contents

Editor's Note

The intellectual landscape of eighteenth-century culture has never appeared more varied or inviting in its physical aspect than it does today. Hence the geography of the Enlightenment provides a point of departure for several of the essays gathered in this volume. Their interest in physical geography reflects not so much the expected influence of military, national, and political centers, as the unexpected significance that living in a land apart may confer on writing. Set in a variety of local habitations, and moving with a purposeful discursiveness across the grounds of argument, they explore the way a sense of place affects literary creation as well as interpretation. One distinguished contributor even goes so far as to argue that it was the expansive geography of American space, as opposed to the more centralized spaces of Europe, which helped to shape one of the earliest and most important documents of American democracy. Why geographical space should have arrived at the forefront of study is a question well worth asking, certainly, even if any answer must remain speculative. The postcolonial decentering of early modern studies has taken a toll on outdated accounts of heroic nationalism, for one thing. It is partly because we recognize the nationalist politics of an earlier globalizing history that we seek to practice the interpretive geopolitics of planetary caretakers instead. For another, there is greater awareness of the possibility of researching topics that once may well have gone without an audience. The wide distribution of scholarship among several national, regional, and single-figure societies, many of them sponsoring journals, publication series, or newsletters, has created a community of interest in fields formerly considered arcane or rarefied, local geography among them. A yet more practical explanation for the ever-widening scope of interest is the relative ease of entering into electronic communication with that distant fellow scholar whose paper you heard at a conference or whose footnote suddenly cast new light on your work.

The four essays we begin with range in their geography from Scandinavia to Dutch Suriname, from the European periphery to the South American frontier. An initial study explores the narrative intersection of geological space and the newly discovered deep prehistoric time of scientific inquiry.

Above ground the earth revealed a weathered masculinity, it seemed, while mysteriously creative forces deemed feminine lay hidden underground. Just as the earth was gendered above and below, time's vector could likewise be configured as either female cycle or male arrow. Once plotted along these gendered axes of space and time, several narratives from the age of Goethe are understood to reflect the expanding chronotope of Enlightenment science in novel and exciting ways. Two of the essays that follow extend the envelope of generic description in order to make a postcolonial critical lexicon more accommodating of narrative variety. One of them argues cogently that an unknown drama written in Dutch Suriname by one Pieter Van Dyk has as much right to be called a captivity narrative as do the better known, histories of Mary Rowlandson or Olive Oatman. In the other what it means to write a conquest narrative is ingeniously enlarged on behalf of Mary Wollstonecraft to include the romantic conquest of a lover as well as the imperial conquest of a territory, and then to signify the comparative management of the first by the second, and at last to embrace the overcoming of any personal rhetoric of conquest and discovery altogether. Finally, a learned reading of the 1800 Irish Act of Union takes up a lesser known novel by Maria Edgeworth to demonstrate how thoroughly her writing reveals a responsive yet evenhanded politics of suffering nationhood.

Although included in this volume simply on the basis of their excellence, several other essays share related concerns. In the first a prime document of the United States is analyzed for the sake of redrawing the international political horizon against which it first appeared. John Adams staunchly defended his preference for a bicameral legislature against Turgot on the basis of the sheer vastness of American space as well as on the greater equity of bicameral as opposed to unicameral representation, it is argued. In another essay the actions of a cross-dressing heroine are displaced from the days just following the French Revolution, the time of the narrative, toward a German wartime context of decades later, the time of its publication. Two other contributions are linked by a highly developed sense of place even as they follow separate paths of argument. The representative manner of Eliza Haywood's spectatorial fiction, a composite of seeing and writing, is well suited to self-display among the *beau monde* in Bath, it is suggested, but the same manner inevitably undermines the feminine authority of the writer. A second essay shows that the unusual religious culture of Lancashire offers scholars a rare historical opportunity to observe more vividly than elsewhere paradigm shifts in eighteenth-century spiritual beliefs taking place across Britain, notably the shift from belief in divine intervention to an emphasis on the internal reform of character.

One of the great pleasures of the study of the Enlightenment is the tacit dimension of historical difference it continues to reveal. Here a straightforward scholarly study painstakingly demonstrates that during the third quarter of the eighteenth century—for reasons that can only be guessed at, the most likely of them being the availability of other consumer goods—an enormously significant decline in book advertising occurs all across literary London. Or an essay shows clearly how Samuel Richardson's familiarity with seventeenth-century religious lyric poetry inflects the most intensely personal emotional moments of *Clarissa*. Yet another fully elaborated essay asks us to consider how the terms *livery* and *hypocrisy* are linked in Swift's satirical vocabulary to an almost unthinkable discourse of class distinction, while a scholar of dance history pushes the perceived effeminacy of the male dancer back across the centuries to argue that the perception originates in the ridicule attached to the French noble style of dance during the Restoration. The concept that more than any other distinguishes British aesthetics is Addison's middle category of the novel, as opposed to the beautiful and strange, and not, as was once thought, the sublime. Two complementary essays explore the aesthetics of novelty in Addison and Sterne. In the first the major term is critically located in Ovid as the appropriation of desire. In the second, the novel and even strange text of Sterne is playfully applied to Barthes' postmodern text of bliss or *jouissance*. Readers will agree that there is much to enjoy in both.

All the essays in this volume were presented at meetings sponsored by the American Society for Eighteenth-Century Studies, were revised for submission against an annual midsummer deadline, and were afterwards revised again for publication. With this volume I pass the editorial pencil to *ma chère collegue* Ourida Mostefai and her board. Let me wish them every joy and success, and also thank departing board members Janet Aikins and Daniel Gordon for their care and dedication. It has been an honor and a pleasure.

Timothy Erwin
University of Nevada, Las Vegas

Studies in Eighteenth-Century Culture

VOLUME 30

Ruins and the Construction of Time: Geological and Literary Perspectives in the Age of Goethe

HEATHER I. SULLIVAN

In his 1778 text, *An Inquiry into the Original State and Formation of the Earth*, John Whitehurst writes of the "terraqueous globe" that having been "burst into millions of fragments . . . must certainly be thrown into strange heaps of ruins . . . ."[1] Whitehurst is not alone in extending the eighteenth-century fascination with ideas of ruins into early geology. In the rapidly proliferating texts analyzing the history of the earth during the Age of Goethe, when geology was just gaining a foothold as a field in its own right,[2] scientists like Whitehurst, Johann G. Wallerius, and Johann R. Forster describe the entire surface of the earth as a conglomeration of ruins of previous worlds. This vision of devastation is the basis for two queries I address here: whether the narrative describing how these ruins are created is a linear development of progress or a vision of ongoing cycles (as Stephen J. Gould calls it, "time's arrow or time's cycle");[3] and what the authors believe lies beyond the ruins, below the surface of the earth. Both of these questions are integral parts of theories describing the earth's history and structure, and the driving forces behind them. The first question regarding the construction of narratives and their relationship to time is the basis for fierce scientific and theological controversy in early geology.[4] The answer to the second question concerning the realm beyond the ruins is, on the other hand, something many thinkers in the late eighteenth and early nineteenth century agree upon. Whether they emphasize field observations or readings of Genesis, whether they construct time as arrow or cycle, these writers use metaphors of the feminine world below the ruins as the foundation for their narratives. They imagine a sexualized and "feminine" space, one that is "soft and moist," below the surface of the earth. There, natural structures are formed, pushed upwards and destroyed in ongoing processes of fluid creation. The construction of time in these texts thus occurs on a stage dominated by "heaps of ruins" above and lurking feminine forces below.

In this essay, I examine the construction of time in both scientific and literary narratives written during the Age of Goethe. That is the era when scientists begin to realize that the earth has a very long history—a defining moment for the entrance into scientific modernity.[5] This early anticipation of a greatly expanded temporal vista, what we now term "deep time," is a part of the more general revolution in understanding concepts of time and history taking place during and after the Enlightenment. While the full implications of this revolution only become widely recognized in the mid-nineteenth century, early indicators of its significance begin to appear already in the eighteenth century. Jonathan Z. Smith writes:

> In the mid-nineteenth century, European thought underwent a revolution with respect to time comparable to the revolution with respect to space that resulted from the Age of Exploration (or better, the Age of Reconnaissance) in the fifteenth through seventeenth centuries. Both revolutions produced a series of cognitive shocks to European thought and sensibility. The history of the prior, spatial revolution—above all the encounter with "other" cultures—and its effects on the human sciences has been insistently told. *The history of the temporal revolution has yet to be fully written.*[6]

This is my goal here: to contribute to the early history of the "temporal revolution" through an investigation of geological and literary depictions of ruins in the Age of Goethe.[7] In order to do that, I focus on how narratives of the earth and its ruins in this era depict time, how the term ruins ("Ruinen" or "Trümmer") in this context differs from the more traditional understanding of architectural ruins, and how these narratives relate to two German novellas from the same era, Ludwig Tieck's *The Rune Mountain* (1802) and Joseph von Eichendorff's *The Marble Statue* (1819). These novellas both have a central image of a ruined palace inside of which there lives an alluring and yet ancient woman whose character is defined by the cycles of nature. *The Rune Mountain* and *The Marble Statue* share with the geologists the contrast between what are termed ruins and the metaphor of an interior, feminized space—one associated with cyclical birth and decay. The novellas present uneasy reactions to the changing notions of time's arrow and cycle, reactions and feelings reflecting very closely those of the scientists Whitehurst, Wallerius, and Forster.

My analysis of time and ruins in the literary and scientific texts has three parts. First, I consider Whitehurst and Eichendorff together as examples of a more conservative vision of the dangerous flux of "feminine" nature. In their texts, the ruins (both geological and cultural) remind the viewer that the physical world, with its seasonal changes marking time, is a moral quagmire.[8] In both authors, natural cycles are associated with threatening feminine forces that must be overcome so that humankind can (re)align itself with the divine plan of linear human progress. The idea of natural cycles is thus associated with dangerous, "pagan" powers. Part two, in contrast, is a discussion of Wallerius, Forster, and Tieck, who approach the idea of nature's cycles with a more neutral attitude.[9] For them, the ruins standing above the "feminine" interior are less indicators of moral decay than fascinating (but not entirely lacking in peril) fragments of other worlds whose mystery hints, as Tieck says, at the "wonders from the ancient time."[10] Their accounts focus on sustained processes whose awesome powers are more important than origins and endings. Whether the cycles are defined "neutrally" or feared, the stretching of time geologically produces insights empirically based yet often sharing with theological treatises and literary texts the same metaphors and images, of ruins above and a feminine realm below.

The third part of this essay looks more closely at how these geological and literary narratives at the brink of modernity present the expanded scope of time in conjunction with nature's self-sufficient and "self-reflexive" forces (needing neither deity nor moral significance).[11] While the construction of time as a progressive, linear path often depicts nature's changes as part of an overall plan, constructions based on endless cycles with no clear beginning and no prospect of an end render nature rather more free of teleology and of the necessity of existing for anything but itself. Thus the eighteenth- and nineteenth-century idea that many ancient or "primitive" peoples describe nature in terms of ongoing cycles was opposed to an "enlightened" sense of human progress with a clear beginning and optimistic hope for continued, rational development.[12] Yet modern geology's growth out of eighteenth-century theology and natural history (typically, James Hutton and Charles Lyell are given credit for this development)[13] is actually characterized by theories based on earth's cycles driven entirely by nature's self-reflexive, physical laws. The narratives of the earth first become "modern" when they reject the linear structure of the scientific revolution and the enlightenment in favor of empirical descriptions of self-driven natural cycles. Gould and others have discussed this development in geology at length;[14] I analyze here the depictions of, and reactions to, this changing sense of the earth's history, particularly the scientific embrace of natural cycles whose relationship to the "primitive" sense of cycles remains decidedly ambiguous. The arrow/cycle dichotomy in the Age of Goethe is built upon an undifferentiated and yet assumed contrast between these types of cycles, and it is this morass of deepening and discordant time that geological thinking contributes to the beginnings of modernity.

I. Whitehurst and Eichendorff: The Peril of Seasonal Cycles

Whitehurst's *Formation of the Earth* initially assumes a heavenly hand guiding nature's workings and then moves towards a more self-driven world—but not without a sense of horror. Many aspects of his story are more traditional in nature than those of the other authors discussed here, as Whitehurst focuses primarily on the effect of the one great flood and presents a linear development based on Genesis. His narrative of the earth's history is rather typical for the eighteenth century in that it starts with a world "in a state of fluidity," one that eventually solidifies. Once solid, the earth's primary features in its peaceful, antediluvian phase, are a center of melted matter heated by the inner fire and the external ocean floating on the thin surface layer. These are separate until the "expansive force of the subterraneous fire" finally comes into contact with the water covering the entire surface. This produces steam which then explodes in a massive eruption, bursting the entire crust of the earth into pieces and leaving behind only the "strange heaps of ruins." This destruction is, according to Whitehurst, the "first convulsion of nature."[15] The surface water rushes into the interstices created in the explosion and leaves behind greatly reduced seas and, most troubling, terrain exposed for the first time to an unmediated gaze: "[M]uch of the terrestrial surface would be left naked and exposed, with all its horrid gulphs, craggy rocks, mountains and other disorderly appearances."[16] Below this disturbingly naked surface are "an infinite number of subterraneous caverns" now filled with water. Caverns had a much more central role in older theories of the earth, and many authors of the eighteenth century believed that there were vast systems of them just under the surface of the entire earth.[17] As Hartmut Böhme, Carolyn Merchant and others have discussed, such pictures of caves—and there was a vast proliferation of them during the Age of Goethe—created the sense that there is a subterranean world that is feminine and whose mysterious openings can be penetrated and explored.[18] Whitehurst adds to the image of the earth's womb with his "tremendous convulsions" giving birth to future geological features. Below his "heaps of ruins" is a series of immense caverns flowing with water and occasionally convulsing to produce new structures.

Whitehurst's feminized realm below the surface ruins has a pronounced reliance on theological authority, as do many geological treatises of the era.[19] This helps explain his attribution of a troubling quality to the earth's body once it has been ravaged by the flood. His vision arises out of his understanding of the great deluge punishing humanity, and it is solidly grounded in a linear narrative describing a series of singular events. Whitehurst starts at the beginning, at creation, continues with the solidification of the planet, followed by a description of the paradisiacal antediluvian world and its "universal temperature," smooth and harmonious features, and "the succulent state of its surface." All of this is tragically destroyed by the deluge, which leaves the earth in the state as we now know it: with mountains, seasons and thus ongoing changes: "But alas! the production of mountains and continents at the time of the deluge, put a final period to that universal harmony which prevailed over the antediluvian world. The burning heats of the torrid zone, and feverities of the frigid zone, were then brought forth . . . ."[20] The alteration after the flood brought about differing environments and, worst of all, seasonal change. Whitehurst discusses in this in chapter 13, titled: "Of the Temperatures of the Air, and Seasons of the Year, arising from the Production of Mountains and Continents at the Time of the Deluge." After the deluge, the tidy, linear progress guided by the deity has been transformed into a process of natural fluctuations, of constant change rather than "universal harmony." The geological ruins are, "alas," physical reminders of our fall, a fall into seasonal cycles. Whitehurst's "feminine" realm of productivity below the surface participates in these cycles; indeed, one can read as feminine the cycles themselves as well as the postdiluvian terrestrial surface whose decency has been disturbed when it was "left naked and exposed, with all its horrid gulphs, craggy rocks, mountains and other disorderly appearances." His cycles arise as a result of human sin and they embody nature's departure from Christian harmony.

Whitehurst shares a negative vision of earth's frightening, feminine cycles leaving ruins in their wake with Eichendorff's *The Marble Statue*. Eichendorff's novella, while not scientific in nature (although he did attend courses in mining as a part of his cameral studies in Halle),[21] presents a very similar conflict between an orderly sense of linear development and harmony threatened by an underground feminine force that actively participates in seasonal rhythms.[22] The tale is framed by Florio's educational journey, beginning as he arrives in Lucca during his travels through Italy, and ending as he finally disassociates himself from Venus and her ruins and heads "through the shining pastures down into blooming Milan."[23] This interruption of the linear progress of his journey represents a significant and potentially fatal interlude from his educational advancement.

The first encounter with Venus occurs when Florio cannot sleep after his exciting evening of revelry in Lucca. He had just made the acquaintance of the pretty Bianka, and the memory of her kiss keeps him awake. Taking his guitar with him, he heads out into the many gardens and wanders about, singing and dreaming, until he discovers a small pond with an enchanting marble statue of Venus. This statue seems briefly to come to life as he gazes at it, but then its luster fades and its stony silence shocks Florio. One important clue about the statue's significance emerges from the scenery: her form gleams in the bright moonlight, "The moon, which was just peering over the treetops, sharply lit up a marble statue of Venus . . .",[24] and it is only when the moon goes behind the clouds that Florio is shocked by the empty, deathly pale eye sockets of the marble statue. The moon is more than an expected part of any night scene, it is also a prime symbol for nature's cycles. It is this very symbol for months and planetary rotations which first shines so brightly, highlighting Venus's attractions. In addition to the moon, as Lothar Pikulik notes, Eichendorff emphasizes Venus's realm as one of endless cycles by including a description of the monotonous circling of the swans around the statue: "Several swans quietly made circles around the statue."[25] The motion of the swans and the moon draw Florio into this world of perilous attractions and cyclical systems ruled by Venus.

Florio's other encounters with Venus include the infamous confusion occurring at the masked ball, where the overtly ambiguous disguise of Greek costume attires both the cheery young Bianka and the goddess herself. While the two females are set up in opposition (this is discussed in greater detail below), it becomes clear at this central moment in the text that all women present a potential danger of seductive distraction. Bianka later regains her purity and piousness for Florio when she hides her gender under male clothing, whereas Venus becomes evermore unclothed in the text when the young man encounters her at her lavish palace. It is her palace that I focus on here, for this is the site of the "ruins." That is, once Florio has been "freed" from Venus's influence, he perceives the palace where he had visited her as "the old ruins on the mountain" where there lay an "old, deteriorated wall around beautiful columns half-buried in the earth and gracefully carved stones, all of which were surrounded by a voluptuous and blooming wilderness wrapped with green vines and covered by bushes and tall weeds."[26] The poet Fortunato offers to sing a song of clarification about the nature of the peril into which Florio had fallen during his brief interlude in the "ruins." This song describes how Venus reawakens from her slumber every year during spring, called up out of her grave by thoughts of earthly pleasures. It is here that we are told directly that she is a part of nature's cycles:

When the winds of spring waft,
Gently across the green plain,
A quiet resurrection
Arises in the valleys.

. . .

And beneath a perfumed veil,
As often as spring awakens,
The old magical power
Weaves its secret celebration.

Lady Venus hears the call,
Of the birds' mirthful chorus,
And rises gaily startled
Up out of the flowers.[27]

As the perfumed winds of spring return, they reawaken the restless Venus. She appears again in the lush wilderness and begins to seek out love—a danger for the young men who come across her. The endless repetition of Venus's reappearance is interrupted, however, when her power is finally conquered, indeed, when she is turned to stone, by the appearance of Mother Maria with the baby Jesus in her arms. The transformation presented in the poem is one where endless, natural cycles are altered in a singular moment in history, with the appearance of a unique mother and her child announcing the dawn of a universal, Christian harmony:

Venus stands and ponders,
So pale in the light of spring,
her eyes slowly sink,
Her lovely figure turns to stone.

For over the land and water,
Another woman appears,
So still and mild,
Enthroned on the rainbow.

The wondrous lady holds
A small child in her arms,
And heavenly compassion
Permeates the (entire) world.[28]

The appearance of Christianity in the world, with its specific story of universal harmony and Eichendorffian celebrated stasis, overcomes the heathen cycles so threatening to naïve young men. Eichendorff makes clear his view of Christianity's nature in his essay, "On the Results of the Eradication of the Sovereignty of the Bishops and Monasteries in Germany," where he writes that: "The innermost essence of Christianity is, in contrast [to religions of antiquity], always and throughout one and the same; there is no "becoming" [*Werden*] . . . ."[29] Venus's cycles are thus contrasted both to Christianity's inherent consonance and to the linear development of human history out of "pagan" religions (similar to the sort of development each individual undergoes in *his* progress towards personal enlightenment).

Eichendorff further accentuates Venus's intimate connection with the seasonal fluctuations—in contrast to the eternal harmony of Christianity—by describing her existence in terms of an uneasy restlessness, an uncontrolled desire to appear to young men every spring and draw them into her power. When she succeeds, they exist in a realm that is neither life nor death, where they must wander endlessly, aimlessly about. Venus thus embodies the opposite of Florio's linear progress towards Christianity's wisdom: "It is also said that the spirit of the beautiful heathen goddess never found peace. From the horrible silence of the grave she is drawn by thoughts of earthly pleasures every spring so that she appears over and over again in the green solitude of her ruined house. Through devilish deception, she practices her seduction on young, innocent souls. . . .[30] Contact with Venus tears the young men away from progressive development and into a place between realms where they roam lost and without purpose. They "depart from life and yet are not taken up by the peace of the dead. Instead, they exist between wild lust and horrific regret, and, lost in body and soul, they wander aimlessly about, consuming themselves with the most gruesome deception."[31] Venus's ruins are remnants of ancient beliefs that the "modern" individual, in Eichendorff's early nineteenth-century, Catholic view, must leave behind *him*self in order to find illumination. As Eichendorff writes in "History of Germany's Poetic Literature," sounding as if he were writing a short summary the central thesis of *The Marble Statue*: "In [classical literature of antiquity], the beauty of the human figure is petrified, with the dead eye, in [romantic literature there is], the mysterious play of light in wonderful colors, and the living eye through which one looks into the secret depths of the soul. Truth is in antiquity as in the romantic, but in the former it is material and mortal, in the latter it is immaterial and supernatural."[32] This dichotomy runs through much of Eichendorff's works, with the petrified and yet so very seductive eye and body of Venus contrasted to the living eye and truth of Maria and Christianity.

The novella ends with a self-satisfied Florio rediscovering the passive and pretty Bianka while they ride away from Lucca and into the blooming Milan and its promise of sunshine and harmony, the path towards Eichendorff's vision of supernatural truth:[33]

> They had now come upon a breezy height, behind them sank the city Lucca with its dark towers in the glowing air. Florio turned to Bianka and then said, 'I am as if born again. . . .' The morning light shone in long, golden beams shooting over the surface directly towards them. . . . And so the happy travelers rode joyfully through the shining pastures down into blooming Milan.[34]

United, Florio and Bianka leave the dark city behind them and continue their journey directly into the welcoming sunshine—a light that is "shooting straight" at them. In his essay on "The Nature-Religion" Eichendorff emphasizes the light of Christianity as the beacon towards truth: "There is surely nothing so natural, honorable and Christian as the human striving towards light, a reformative use of reason. . . ."[35] He makes multiple references to the association of Christianity and light in his other essays as well, saying, for example: "Yet life on earth was not closed in its heart but rather greatly broadened beyond the grave by the portentous and hopeful shimmering of the dawn of Christianity, and, as a shining [*überglänzt*—the same term used in describing the light of Milan in *The Marble Statue*] interlude, taken up into eternity."[36] Hence the closing scene of *The Marble Statue* and its description of Florio and Bianka heading off into the light is a clear reference to their direct entrance into enlightenment and, one must surmise, an indication of a "masculine" path of reason and linear progress as opposed to Venus's threatening revolutions.

Eichendorff, like Whitehurst, attributes a negative moral sense to nature's cycles as they represent a force opposite to Christianity. In Whitehurst's narrative of the earth, nature's cycles begin after the punishing flood and should remind us of our sins, elements which are represented by the geological ruins on the surface of the earth. In Eichendorff's novella, Florio must learn to turn away from the seductive attraction of Venus and her cyclical appearances from within the ruins in favor of a linear path of personal growth, Christian harmony, and a pious young bride. He must pursue his goal of educational development by continuing his journey through life, one that can only be properly accomplished with the help of turning to Christianity as a historical development out of nature's ominous flux. These natural cycles differ most radically from the linear path of enlightenment in that they occur in a space devoid of clear guidance and teleology. Both Eichendorff's Venus, whose reappearance is brought about by seasonal change, and Whitehurst's postdiluvian earth, which is also ruled by seasons, are independent forces threatening in their absence of a clear and focused progression. The feminine forces erupting out of the ruins in these two texts are portentously threatening and thus relegated as much as possible to the "underground." Yet what becomes clear in both Whitehurst's and Eichendorff's fearful vision of time's cycle is that it actually is not overcome once and for all by Christianity. Whitehurst's disruptive seasons destroying the face of the earth continue, even though he predicts an eventual divine intervention. Similarly, Venus may be a "pagan" force turned to stone in *The Marble Statue*, but the forced historical development out of her powerful sway into harmonious Christianity brought about by the arrival of Mother Maria is undermined by the fact that the goddess will return every year with spring. The apprehension these two authors feel regarding the inevitable continuation of the cycles (which are described more in terms of their "pagan" implications than their empirical qualities) contributes to their unsatisfied longing for a linear, "arrow" view of time.

II. Wallerius, Forster, Tieck: The Ongoing Processes of Nature's Cycles

In contrast to Eichendorff and Whitehurst, the authors Wallerius, Forster and Tieck maintain a more neutral attitude towards the earth's cycles. In addition, their cycles are not as clearly associated with "pagan" threats to morality. Wallerius, like Whitehurst, presents a watery origin of the world in his *Physical-Chemical Observations on the Origin of the World, especially our Earth and its Changes* (originally published in 1776). His fluid earth eventually takes form as solid particles begin to settle and "coagulate," gradually forming the earth's surface. Wallerius writes: "The earth was at one time fluid, and owes its origin to water."[37] The solid structures like the mountains and the stones are formed with "fermentation of the water" and "through coagulation."[38] The great fluidity then continues to act on the "still soft and moist rocks," forming and crumbling them into new shapes. This is an amorphous and productive force, a seemingly feminine soup where a fermentation of form takes place. In the fluidity are innumerable particles, as if a sort of masculine seeds,[39] that react in the warmth to bring about the gradual settling and the beginnings of solid shapes.

The earth solidifies by degrees, but even then the changes are not over, for the great flood eventually comes and wreaks havoc on the earth's surface, leaving ruins in its wake.

In answer to the inevitable query about the source of the water for this deluge, Wallerius, again like Whitehurst, speaks of vast caverns deep within the mountains that formed as the moist stones originally dried out. He claims that "We do not yet know the innermost secrets of nature,"[40] but that we can assume that is filled with water in which there forms a "light and thin consolidation of earth." Wallerius's earth is thus covered by a solid surface—littered with remnants from previous formations—yet underneath and inside that layer of ruins are caves "still soft and moist."[41] In this description, he comes very close to Whitehurst. Yet Wallerius condemns neither the "feminine" quality of the earth nor the mountains as evidence of the fall from grace. Instead, he sees them as part of the overall scheme of natural occurrences. For example, he does not believe that all mountains arose together after the flood to punish humanity with seasonal and climatic differences as does Whitehurst, but instead that some mountains were created at the beginning along with the earth, and others were formed by the ongoing action of solidifying particles in the sloshing waters of the earth.[42] While these "particles" are often derived from the original mountains that are "smashed into fragments and carried off," and are hence similar to Whitehurst's ruins, Wallerius emphasizes above all the "ongoing driving and drifting about" of all materials on earth.[43] Hence while he also maintains that there was a different environment on earth before the great flood, one, in fact, without rain, he is finally most interested in the continuing processes that move around pieces of the earth's surface. Wallerius is an intermediate of sorts between Whitehurst's primarily theological treatise and Forster's more empirical analysis of geological processes.

Forster, in his *Materials for a Future Model of a Theory of the Earth* (1798), describes a world much like Wallerius's where the inner fluidity is driven by a fermentation that leads to the solidification of an external layer he calls "the general cover or clothing."[44] He describes how the soft, flexible surface of the earth is formed and shaped by the movement of expanding steam: "and then ever more quantities of expanding vapors accumulated and expanded the still soft and malleable mass of the earth's surface into all kinds of large, irregular elevations or mountains, some linked, others isolated."[45] Common to all of the geological narratives discussed here is the "feminine" quality of the world beneath the surface "clothing," feminine in its emphasis on the openings and their moisture, the fluidity out of which the earth's surface is born. This fluid power both creates and then reduces even the most enormous and seemingly impervious features, the mountains, to mere rubble and ruins ("Trümmer" is Forster's term). Both Forster's and Wallerius's ruins form the earth's surface, but they hide beneath them a greater power of amorphous potential.

Forster's study is distinctly more empirical than both Wallerius's and Whitehurst's due perhaps to the information he gathered during his famous travels around the world with Captain Cook from 1772 to 1775.[46] In his journals from this voyage, he makes lengthy comments on the possible formation of islands in the sea and glacial ice, i.e., always presenting theories of long, slow processes that continue today. In *Materials*, Forster mostly avoids mention of biblical authority when questioning the formation of the planet, but this is not to say that he lacks fascinating speculation. His explanation for the obvious changes to the surface of the planet, for example, is the arrival of various comets whose long, watery tails brought excess moisture to the earth and flooded its surface. Forster does attribute all original planning to God, but he focuses his book on the general laws of nature that could have shaped the earth and that continue to do so in a manner that has "overall the same cause." While he still accepts the theory of the great flood, he explains its occurrence with the comet's contact with earth and goes on to discuss the impact of other comets in our planet's history. He also speculates on the future arrival of additional comets in continuing cycles.[47] With this emphasis on cycles, Forster marks a general shift away from theological pronouncements about the status of the earth's surface today, and a more neutral fascination with ongoing processes that may have been created by God, but that are not taking place as a heavenly response to human shortfall. He still presents a narrative starting at the beginning and moving through time today, but the greater part of the text is dedicated to overall cycles of nature including comets, wind, water, earthquakes, mountain formation and destruction. Forster's ruins evoke images of the ongoing processes of the earth's history rather than those directed by human history, a difference indicative of a more modern perception of the physical world. Its modernity is partially due to the fact that such narratives about nature focus on long-term processes and simultaneously attain an independence from theological or moral precepts. This independence requires that any explanation of earth's history should, in Forster's words, follow "logic" and "not a deus ex machina."[48]

Forster may exhort the necessity of logic for understanding natural history, but his world system is still founded on an image of ruins below which there is a hot and steamy inner space. His vision of the earth relates to Tieck's vision of nature in *The Rune Mountain* in much the same way that

Whitehurst's narrative does to Eichendorff's novella. Unlike Whitehurst and Eichendorff, who see directional, progressive history as divine and nature's seasonal cycles as troublingly pagan as well as feminine, both Forster and Tieck emphasize instead the many different kinds of cycles in the world as essential aspects of life on earth. In Tieck's case, this means a rather ambiguous tale of a young man trying to find inspiration in either his father's gardens or the minerals of the mountains, each represented by a different female.

Like Eichendorff's novella, the *Rune Mountain* begins and ends with the travels of its young protagonist. Yet Christian's journey is not interrupted by an exploration of nature's cycles as in Florio's encounter with Venus; instead, Tieck's character does the opposite. He tries and succeeds in obtaining social and financial prosperity and yet he finally abandons it in favor of the woman of the minerals (or the "Waldweib"), who, like Venus, represents nature's cycles existing outside the parameters of social law.[49] Christian first encounters the woman of the minerals on the Rune mountain late one night. He and the strange miner climb upwards towards the rugged peaks, where they see: "cloven mountain ranges in front of them, in the background was a steep mountain on which ancient, decaying ruins eerily revealed themselves in white light."[50] Clambering along a narrow precipice in the darkness, he comes to the end of the path and suddenly sees a window above him. There he witnesses a most magnificent sight: a beautiful woman in a glittery chamber filled with minerals. Like Florio's encounter with Venus, Christian's first encounter with the woman of the minerals takes place in the moonlight. The waning of the moon, as in *The Marble Statue*, plays an important role in establishing the connection between the female figure and nature's flux. Christian, in fact, refers to the moon when trying to explain to his father at a later point in the novella how important the *Waldweib* and her minerals are to him. He claims that he can forget his inner self for awhile and lead a normal life in the village, yet this life feels alien to him: "But then suddenly, like a new moon, there arises in my heart the ruling star that I myself am, and this star conquers the alien power."[51] His vision of himself after his contact with the woman of the minerals is one driven by forces like a new moon and its revolutions.

Like Venus, the *Waldweib* represents nature's cycles, and yet more of the minerals than of the plants. That is Tieck's more radical presentation of the overall fluidity of nature, one more "geological" than organic. Christian first sees the woman of the minerals as "a large female figure . . . who walks thoughtfully back and forth in the chamber. She seemed not to belong to the mortals as her limbs were so large and powerful, her face so stern, yet nevertheless it felt to the young man as if he had never seen or even imagined such beauty."[52] Her provocative song to "the ancient ones" establishes her participation in the mineral world, the realm of lengthy regeneration taking place at great depths of the earth:

Where are the ancient ones waiting,
That they do not appear?
The crystals weep and
From diamond columns
There flow streams of tears,
Tones ringing within;
. . . .[53]

Her description of the mineral world is based on the weeping crystals and diamond columns, in other words, a liquid/mineral world of flow and transformation which is reminiscent of the underworld of moist minerals in the cavernous depths described in the geological texts. The woman of the minerals ends her plea to the "ancient ones" with a call for them to raise themselves up, much like Venus herself does in Eichendorff's novella:

Come all ye spirits,
To the golden hall,
Raise from the dark depths
Your sparkling crowns![54]

Her spirits living deep in the earth are representatives of geological processes occurring in the great depths of the earth, a realm containing secret powers awakened by the call of the *Waldweib*. Christian is transfixed by this vision of mineral wealth and all that it promises, and he later condemns the world of plants for its short-lived moments of glory, its life that is merely a quick death: "I remember quite precisely that it was a plant that first made clear to me the misery of the entire planet . . . ; in the plants, herbs, flowers and trees there painfully stirs only a terrible wound, they are the corpses of former wondrous worlds of stone. They present our eyes with the most horrific decay."[55] Unlike Whitehurst and Eichendorff, Tieck does not portray linear human history and its progress in conflict with nature's cycles, instead, he portrays two aspects of nature's cycles, the one, the plants, being short and associated with death and decay, and the other, Christian's preferred type, the minerals and their "lofty, eternal happiness." Of course, this distinction between plant and minerals is subsumed by the conclusion where all of nature becomes "geological" including Christian and his companion, the *Waldweib*.[56]

In Christian's mind, the minerals partake in expansive time, something he hints at again in his statement to his father before finally leaving the village to join the *Waldweib*: "The *Waldweib* called me, I am heading off to look for her. Nearby here is an old, deteriorating mine shaft that was dug centuries ago by a miner; perhaps I will find her there!"[57] The *Waldweib* is associated with century-old mines and minerals, with the "ancient ones" instead of the ephemeral human and plant lives. While Tieck himself was no geologist, he was close friends with two geologists, Henrich Steffens (who claimed that his stories of collecting minerals in Norway inspired Tieck's writing of *The Rune Mountain*)[58] and Novalis (whose collected works, including his many geological writings, were published by Tieck and Friedrich Schlegel during the same time as Tieck wrote this novella). I would therefore like to suggest that the end of the novella is perhaps not simply a sketch of a madman whose heart has turned to stone; instead, as such authors as Maria M. Tatar and Marianne Thalmann have asserted, Christian may have discovered a new insight.[59] This insight, I believe, is one relating to the significance of the mineral world as a metaphor for systems of nature and its association with expanded time.

Christian not only celebrates the minerals' association with vast epochs, but also the fact that they are not merely lifeless, static bodies.[60] In his final speech to Elisabeth, when he returns for a last visit before departing forever, Christian demonstrates how the rocks contain sparks within them and so the potential for transformation. Defending their lackluster external appearance, he explains that they are simply not yet polished: "Thus they are still missing their eye and glance; the exterior fire and its glowing are still too deeply buried in their inner hearts. But one only has to beat it out of them so that they are afraid and so that no further pretence helps them; then one can finally see of which spirit they are born."[61] Having proclaimed their potential for fiery transformation, he then demonstrates it by smashing together two stones and producing a spark, a release of their inner "fire and light." Tieck presents a scientist intent on convincing his skeptical family of the fluid character, indeed the life and soul, at the core of what seems to be the most solid material on earth, the minerals.[62] The ruins in Tieck's *Rune Mountain*, with their seductive occupant who awakens the minerals, personify nature's fluid change, and thus the hidden potential within each and every rock.

III. The Flux of Nature: The Ruins as Signs of Self-Reflexivity

Tieck is not alone in his emphasis on nature's flux in the Age of Goethe. Indeed, many scientists in the eighteenth and early nineteenth century begin to understand all of nature as being composed of manifold processes still ongoing, and hence all of the structures on the earth's surface as fragments created by and then destroyed by these same forces. This is an essential part of modernity's temporal revolution; time expands simultaneous to the earth's becoming ever more fluid. As another geologist, G. H. Toulmin, says in 1780: "These immutable truths should never be forgot: That animals and vegetables flourish and decay; that earths are formed by slow degrees; that they too change by time; that stone is formed, is decomposed or altered in its composition; that mountains now are elevated, now depressed;—that nature lives in motion."[63] And Tieck's friend, Henrich Steffens, says in 1821: "All of nature is eternally changing, ever different, ever differentiated and change is itself the only constant."[64] For geologists like Steffens, Wallerius and Forster, the "ruins" no longer indicate God's wrath that brought about the one great deluge but rather the constant changes which the earth has been undergoing during its long history. This implies that solidity of the earth is a mere illusion; geology begins to recognize the long-term *Werden* of our planet.

Early geologists assert, in fact, that even the most vast and sublime geological features, the mountains, once considered to be as old as the planet itself, are themselves mere heaps of ruins, reduced to rubble by the ongoing processes occurring deep below the surface. Here we find another link to the literary texts, in the association of ruins with mountains. In both the novellas the cryptic ruins appear atop mountains and are thus linked to the powerful and terrifying quality of the vast ranges. In many of the geological texts, mountains are both central to the discussion of how the earth was formed and yet are somewhat reduced in stature as they, themselves, are defined as "ruins." Steffens puts it most succinctly: "All mountains are ruins. Mountain chains that have built up in regular and constant connections show only the rubble of the ancient connections."[65] The idea that the towering mountains are actually ruins is particularly intriguing and seemingly rather paradoxical during this era when explorers around the world like Alexander von Humboldt are often better known for their mountain-climbing adventures than for their scientifically significant collections of exotic flora and fauna or their ground-breaking geographical maps. They are most celebrated for their climbing of dizzying heights and thereby "conquering" the vast mountains.[66] For all the massive size and lofty heights of mountains—which add an undeniable sense of mystery to the ruins in both the geological discussions and in Tieck's and Eichendorff's presentations of them—they, too, are merely pieces left over in nature's recycling of materials.

The solidity of the earth has thus been transformed into a series of remnants from past worlds that are formed, destroyed and reshaped, and not just in a single, devastating deluge as held by Whitehurst and some of the older geologists. The planet's surface becomes as fluid as language in the construction of geological narratives about time. The earth is not just a text—better yet, not just a palimpsest presenting a jumble of inscriptions from the earth's many cycles and long historical changes—but also a conglomeration of metamorphosing and self-referential forces left without any teleological function. Nature is complete in itself and yet its very completeness is characterized by its fragmentary quality of ongoing change. Furthermore, the driving force of both production and destruction is presented with metaphors ominously feminine, a female body clothed in the fragments left over by her own processes. Whitehurst's horrid gulfs and craggy protrusions express a sense of awe and fear regarding a nature that is turned on itself, its self-reflexive acts creating ruins that have nothing to do with human efforts.

The broken fragments of "former worlds" in the geological texts and the ruined palaces' decaying walls in the novellas make all the more vivid the fecund femininity existing within or below the surface, but not, I assert, simply as a re-inscription of the decaying material body always contained within nature's voluptuous life-cycles. Instead this paradoxical vision marks the entry into a modern sensibility such that time and space themselves become solidly material (rather than a godly construct), hence bounded by laws of physics and geology, and yet are exploded out into dimensions of deep time and space that were previously unimaginable.[67] This context for the term "ruins" undermines more traditional understandings of decaying architectural structures whose significance is based on a simple clash between nature and culture.[68] For example, In Georg Simmel's paradigmatic essay "The Ruin," the decay of architectural structures displays the inevitable victory of nature over all humanly-created objects.[69] Inherent in this definition of ruins is the nature/culture dichotomy, one dependent upon the tension between work of the "spirit" and natural forces. Yet the term ruins appearing in the geological texts cannot be understood in Simmel's terms of a battle of nature against culture. Instead, the geological "ruins," all that exists on the surface of the earth, are themselves natural structures formed by, and in turn, destroyed by, nature in its ongoing processes. In this geological understanding of ruins, the tension between nature and culture exists not as such; instead, nature exists without reference to culture and devoid of an external administrator. It takes on a "self-reflexive" quality in the sense that its processes need no external reference.

This independence and self-reflexivity find a close parallel in Tieck's and Eichendorff's novellas. Both Venus and the woman of the minerals, as representative of nature's cycles, are far more focused on themselves than on the young men whom they seduce. This characteristic, more than anything else, is the true danger of these females as they defy standard expectations of femininity as a passive mirror for male subjectivity. Eichendorff's Florio experiences Venus as an enticing but eerie statue whose eyes, radiating the moonlight, dominate the scene. When his gaze is the active one, she is magnificently alluring, a mirroring of his inner desires. But this short moment of rapture passes when the moonlight fades, and the statue suddenly appears: "terribly white and motionless." In fact, it suddenly seems to stare *at him* out of frighteningly empty eye sockets in the stillness. Venus takes the active position and gazes at the now uncomfortable Florio. The alteration from beauty and life to threatening coldness and death is marked by the switch from active seeing to being seen. As long as Florio is the active viewer, he is overwhelmed by its charms, so much so that he shuts his eyes and looks with his mind's eye, for the object is less important than his perception of it. When he becomes the object being observed in turn, the passive one, however, the magical moment dissolves into horror.

Nevertheless, Florio is intrigued and seeks out Venus once again. This time her power is in full bloom. She lives with many beautiful maidens in the magnificent marble palace surrounded by gardens and fountains (later, of course, this is the "ruin"). Here is a key moment in the novella: Venus's most definitive act. She gazes into the mirror at her own beauty—a gesture of pure self-reference: "Florio's glances swept as if blinded across the colorful pictures, returning always with new drunkenness to the beautiful mistress of the castle. She didn't allow herself to be distracted from her graceful little tasks. Now improving something on her dark, perfumed braids, now glancing again into the mirror and contemplating herself, she continued to speak to the young man . . . ."[70] Eichendorff openly condemns such acts of self-reflection as Venus's mirror gazing because they lead, he states in his essay on "The Nature-Religion," to self-aggrandizement: "Then, because human beings soon became aware of the fact that they are the peak, indeed, *the eye*, of nature, it could only happen that they also soon considered themselves to be the actual master and law-giver of this world, thus first worshipping nature and then themselves."[71] Intense self-reflection and self-appreciation, particularly as an "eye" are hence blasphemous acts equivalent to placing oneself above the great works of God.

Such moments of feminine self-focus as Venus demonstrates are contrasted in *The Marble Statue* with the behavior of the innocent young girl, Bianka. Bianka is always passive when it comes to the act of seeing. She doesn't stare at Florio but rather, "draws Florio's eyes to her,"[72] making his the active gaze, or else she hides her eyes altogether only to glance up briefly with a shy request of being spared further pain: "Only occasionally did she look up from beneath her long, black eyelashes to him with her entire soul open in her glance as if to beg him 'not to deceive me again.'"[73] Thus Bianka's humility and down-turned eyes present the young man with a selfless, undemanding angel, indeed, an "Engelsbild" as a clear contrast to the "Marmorbild" whose powers he finally overcomes. At the end of *The Marble Statue*, Venus and her self-referential behavior sink back underground while Florio "enters the light" both literally (the rays of the morning sun) and figuratively with his spoken contract of marriage with Bianka. He has firmly taken on the role of the active male gaze no longer threatened by the feminine gaze that either frightened him, or even worse, focused primarily on itself.

Similarly, Tieck's woman of the minerals exists as a marked example of self-reliance and independence, contrasting sharply with the pious Elisabeth. There are three indications of the *Waldweib*'s self-reflexivity. First, she lives alone in the ruins atop the Rune Mountain. Second, the woman's beauty is akin to that of the minerals, stones and crystals surrounding her and reflecting in the light she carries like a miner in the depths of the earth. As the representative of the mineral world, she speaks to her own kind, the "ancient ones," calling them up from the earth. She carefully contemplates the tablet laden with jewels before turning, naked, to the startled young man and handing him this treasure: "that shone from the many inlaid stones, rubies, diamonds and all the jewels."[74] Christian's reaction to this sight, before she hands the tablet to him is, like her own behavior, one of self-absorbed fantasies. Inspired by her act of deep contemplation, Christian "stood, intensely observing the objects with his glances and at the same time deeply absorbed in himself."[75] It is, perhaps, not a coincidence, that Tieck uses terms borrowed from the forces of nature to describe Christian's feelings at this moment: "he saw a world of pain and hope open up inside of himself, *towering wonder-cliffs* of trust and defiant confidence, *vast currents of water* flowing as if from melancholy."[76] Christian's inner world becomes much like the earth as described by the geologists. Third, as these feelings wash over him, the magical female turns to him and makes a clearly self-referential gesture (like Venus with her mirror), saying: "Take this in my memory (Angedenken)" much as Christ says of the bread and wine. It is she, however, whom he should remember.[77] As with Eichendorff's Venus, Tieck's *Waldweib* is here the active figure, drawing Christian's eyes and mind into her self-reflexive world, a world of natural forces and minerals.

This scene ends then as Christian gapes at the tablet reflecting the light of the "sinking moon." Once again, the moon's motion and its reflective powers are combined to suggest nature's fluctuations. Immediately thereafter, Christian tumbles down the mountain and then encounters the *Waldweib*'s foil, Elisabeth, in the church on the next morning. She is quietly captivated as a passive viewer in the service, and "devotion and attentiveness"[78] are the words that occur to the young man as he watches her.

Like Bianka, she is the passive and pious young woman in this text, existing within the structures of social law and in opposition to the wild woman of the minerals. Elisabeth's reverence of Christian values, her father and society are thus clearly contrasted to the self-absorbed character of the woman of the minerals, who appears remarkably independent if not blasphemous in her actions. Whereas Elisabeth is a daughter, wife and, finally, mother, the *Waldweib* lives alone in the mountains or together with Christian on his travels. Both she and Venus represent nature's cycles and fertility yet without child-bearing, a troubling feminine power remaining as the overall potential deep in the earth and not a part of the social system.

The Rune Mountain closes with an emphasis both on the cycles of the rocks and their processes continuing outside of human systems. Christian's joining of forces with them has relegated him in the minds of most readers to madness, yet he has joined the early geologists and mineralogists in an elusive search for the key to the mineral world. He has chosen to live in this world, one characterized by ruins on the surface and a practically unclassifiable manner of "feminine" powers underneath it in the caverns and mines he explores. Whereas Eichendorff pushes Venus back underground at least temporarily, Tieck allows the power of nature's cycles to prevail over his young protagonist. The surface embodiment of the action of earth's processes, the ruins, fade at least temporarily behind the overwhelming light of Christianity in *The Marble Statue*, but they erupt with geological force into Christian's consciousness and become a permanent part of his persona in *The Rune Mountain*. Indeed, he himself, the male "Christian," enacts a cycle as he makes a "return" in the end, a reappearance with the *Waldweib*. What remains unanswered in this ambiguous scene is whether Christian has simply embraced the mythological significance of the ongoing cycles of nature throughout time, or whether he is attempting to appropriate their power in a manner prescient of scientific modernity.[79] In either case, he has enthusiastically entered the world of ruins, a world eschewed by Eichendorff and Whitehurst, and celebrated by the early geologists who established the foundation for the science of geology as we know it today.

The fascination of the ruins in these two novellas and the geological texts in the Age of Goethe goes beyond the general interest in the vacillation of human history as revealed in architectural fragments or the obsession with material decay. With the shared image of crumbling palaces and fragmented mountains, beneath or within which there lives a powerful feminine force driven by cyclical rhythms, all of these works portray ruins as signs that our entire world is in flux and that all that exists now will be the materials for future cycles (despite the attempt to push the evidence of the driving forces into the underground). The transformations of nature are thus not limited to the organic realm but rather are also aspects of the inorganic as well. This indicates that the minerals themselves have an apparent "life cycle," one that implies a certain vitality while simultaneously a mortality of sorts. Carolyn Merchant's proclaimed "death of nature" in the wake of the scientific revolution may, in the context of early geology in the Age of Goethe at least, be better termed the "mineralization of nature" or, perhaps, the "moving underground of nature's life force," as we see in these texts presenting an image of "dead" ruins on the surface covering, oh so lightly, nature's cyclical forces.[80]

The fact that the assumed potential of this energy is relegated to the underground, existing only beyond the ruins, may have something to do with the circumstance that narratives of the earth's history in the Age of Goethe feature the globe itself as the protagonist undergoing a historical development. The construction of earth's timeline was a vast enterprise that could be visualized in toto only with the aid of much imagination and thus, for all its empirical content, it often remained infused with mythological references. The images of ruins and a female earth or nature are themselves not new; what has changed here is their implications for the construction of time in certain narratives. This alteration in the meaning of ruins, from an inevitable decay of the material body and/or a sign of God's wrath into the sense of recycled materiality partaking in practically eternal yet nevertheless potentially measurable processes of nature, is part of the temporal revolution characterizing the entrance into scientific modernity.

Emerging from both the geological texts and the two novellas discussed here is the anxious response to such constructions of time based on a planet in flux. This anxiety is typically modern, and it has significant implications for modern constructions of human subjectivity formed through reflection on an "other." In this case, the other is the earth as representative of natural processes. If the earth in the Age of Goethe gains a long history marked by deep time and existing beyond human (his)story, indeed, a history characterized not so much by linear, rational progress as by fluid cycles of creation and destruction represented in these texts by the ruins, then the human being in turn takes on a similar, ever more fluid, shifting sense of the self and its relationship to its physical environment. This plays out in the nineteenth century in both biological and psychological constructions: Darwin's explanation of evolution indicates that the human body is itself in historical flux, much like the earth's body; and the human psyche is perceived as if it had a "geological depth" with a fragmented surface, a heap of ruins from the past, below which powerful forces seethe in their production of personal narratives. The temporal revolution at the threshold of modernity reveals new vistas of time, an expanded scope for the history of the earth whose breathtaking length is rendered both more human and tangible by images of ruins from previous worlds.

NOTES

1. John Whitehurst, *An Inquiry into the Original State and Formation of the Earth; Deduced from Facts and the Laws of Nature* (London: Cooper, 1778), 89.

2. Of the broader significance of the burgeoning new science of geology in the late eighteenth and early nineteenth century, Elinor S. Shaffer writes: "Geology, then a controversial new science, seen as presenting a challenge to traditional theological explanations of the formation of the earth, provided a meeting-ground for writers, painters, explorers, climbers and amateur naturalists, and served as a focus of discussion of the claims and role of science in general questions affecting all of science." *The Third Culture: Literature and Science* (Berlin: Walter de Gruyter, 1998), 9.

3. Stephen J. Gould, *Time's Arrow, Time's Cycle* (Cambridge, MA: Harvard University Press, 1987), defines these terms as follows: "At one end of the dichotomy—I shall call it time's arrow—history is an irreversible sequence of unrepeatable events. Each moment occupies its own distinct position in a temporal series, and all moments, considered in a proper sequence, tell a story of linked events moving in a direction. . . . At the other end—I shall call it time's cycle—events have no meaning as distinct episodes with causal impact upon a contingent history. Fundamental states are immanent in time, always present and never changing. Apparent motions are parts of repeating cycles, and differences of the past will be realities of the future" (10–11).

4. The debate includes questions about the precise age of the earth; the cause of the changes to the earth's surface: whether fire or water, as in the controversy between the vulcanists and the neptunists; and whether these causes were long and slow processes that we can view still today (uniformitarianism) or radical bursts of sudden change (catastrophism). All of these questions contribute to discussions regarding conformity (or lack thereof) to the description in Genesis of the formation of the earth and the influence of Noah's flood. See also J. M. I. Klaver's *Geology and Religious Sentiment* (Leiden: Brill, 1997).

5. John Bender and David E. Wellbery, the editors of *Chronotypes: The Construction of Time* (Stanford: Stanford University Press, 1991), write that "[T]ime is the *a priori* of the modern world. One need only think of the philosophical centrality of time (subjectively conceived) from Kant to Heidegger; *of the reconceptualization of geological history, whose temporal parameters have been studied by Stephen J. Gould*; of the introduction into physics, through the second law of thermodynamics, of a concept of irreversible time" (1–2, emphasis mine).

6. Jonathan Z. Smith, "A Slip in Time Saves Nine: Prestigious Origins Again," in *Chronotypes*, ed. Bender and Wellbery, 67–68, emphasis mine.

7. The widely varying versions of the earth's ruins in geology relate to the increasing interest in writing about the earth's physical history. The texts of early geology emerged out of a convergence of many fields including travel literature, mineralogy, natural history (in the older sense of a detailed description of natural phenomena), natural theology, and Biblical exegesis. If ruins were celebrated as physical evidence of the passing of time in history, whether of family, land or empire, they were also cause for awe and a discomfiting sense that everything human and/or physical will eventually crumble and fall into decay. What better way for authors writing in Germany, France and England between 1776 and 1819 (the parameters of the texts I consider here) to create a tangible sense of earth's immense history than to refer to its entire surface as a heap of ruins, fragments of previous worlds that have been formed, destroyed, and reshaped into new structures, thus creating an association with the more general discussion of ruins as markers of the past and of the inevitable changes occurring over time.

8. Older texts, both literary and scientific, understand the surface of the earth as "ruins" as well; the key difference, however, is the explanation for how the ruins come about. During the baroque era and early eighteenth century, philosophers understand the earth's "ruins" primarily in religious terms, that is, that they were the result of the one great flood and singular devastation of God's original creation. They thus indicate both the physical and moral decay of both the world and humanity. As John Dennis wrote in 1693 after crossing the Alps, for example, mountains "are not only vast, but horrid, hideous, ghastly Ruins," and are not part of the "original creation." Thomas Burnet also writes in his famous 1681 *Sacred Theory of the Earth* that the earth is "a gigantic and hideous ruin;" both Dennis and Burnet are quoted in Gordon L. Davies, *The Earth in Decay: A History of British Geomorphology, 1578–1878* (New York: American Elsevier, 1969), 36 and 71. In contrast, the authors in the age of Goethe begin to see the ruins as the result of ongoing processes still in place today, hence as part of an overall system of flux without such significant moral overtones.

9. The difference between the two sets of texts I examine here is not one of temporal sequence (Whitehurst writes in 1778, Eichendorff in 1819; Wallerius in 1776, Forster in 1798; and Tieck publishes his text in 1802) but rather one based on different approaches to narratives about the forces producing ruins, whether natural or cultural.

10. Ludwig Tieck, "Wunder aus der alten Zeit," *Der Runenberg* in *Phantasus* (Frankfurt am Main: Klassiker, 1985), 190. All translations here from the German texts are mine, unless otherwise indicated.

11. For discussions of nature's "self-sufficiency" and cycles, see Jacques Roger's essay "The Living World" in *The Ferment of Knowledge: Studies in the Historiography of Eighteenth-Century Science*, ed. G. S. Rousseau and Roy Porter (Cambridge: Cambridge University Press, 1980), 255–83.

12. Smith, "A Slip in Time Saves Nine," discusses the falsity of this idea that other cultures represent nature in terms of endless, meaningless cycles that present a clear opposition to the "rational" and "Christian" notion of linear time.

13. Hutton and Lyell are usually considered the "fathers" of geology in the English-speaking world. Both were more interested in ongoing cycles than a singular

development with a clear beginning and ending. As R. H. Dott says of Hutton: "Hutton's theory postulated a continued, cyclic decay and resurrection of land with 'no vestige of a beginning and no prospect of an end'; thus, in effect, he argued that the earth's interior always had been structurally dynamic." "James Hutton and the Concept of a Dynamic Earth," in *Toward a History of Geology*, ed. Cecil J. Schneer (Cambridge: M.I.T. Press, 1969), 137.

14. See, for example, Gould, *Time's Arrow, Time's Cycle*, Schneer, *Toward a History*, and Gabriel Gohau, *A History of Geology* (New Brunswick: Rutgers University Press, 1990).

15. Whitehurst, *An Inquiry*, 89.

16. Ibid, 89.

17. Whitehurst was one of many authors emphasizing the significance of caves. As Nicholas Rupke explains in "Caves, Fossils and the History of the Earth," *Romanticism and the Sciences*, ed. Andrew Cunningham and Nicholas Jardine (Cambridge: Cambridge University Press, 1990), 241–59: "At the time [the late eighteenth century], caves occupied a much more central position in geological theory than they do today. They were not regarded as minor and accidental perforations in the uppermost skin of the earth, as we regard them now, but they were believed to be persuasive and primordial features, present since the birth of the earth as a planet, providing essential information as to the manner of its origin. Caves were imagined as corridors to the deep recesses of our globe in which the archives of history were stored, and where the secrets of its past could be discovered . . ." (242).

18. See Hartmut Böhme, *Natur und Subjekt* (Frankfurt am Main: Suhrkamp, 1988), esp. "Geheime Macht im Schoß der Erde," 67–144; and Carolyn Merchant, *The Death of Nature: Women, Ecology, and the Scientific Revolution* (New York: HarperCollins, 1990), esp. "Nature as Female," 1–41.

19. Whitehurst is by no means an exception with his continued emphasis on biblical authority in matters geological. As Rachel Laudan states: "Cosmogonists took human testimony about the history of the earth quite seriously. The most important testimony was to be found in the first five chapters of Genesis. Most seventeenth-century scientists treated Scripture as history, as an empirical record. As such, it offered direct access to the earth's past." *From Mineralogy to Geology: The Foundations of a Science, 1650–1830* (Chicago: The University of Chicago Press, 1987), 37. This emphasis continues throughout the seventeenth and eighteenth centuries and only begins to decrease in the early nineteenth century.

20. Whitehurst, *An Inquiry*, 132–33.

21. See Theodore Ziolkowski, *German Romanticism and Its Institutions* (Princeton: Princeton University Press, 1990), esp. chap. 2: "The Mine: Image of the Soul."

22. See also Egon Schwartz for a discussion of these rhythms in *The Marble Statue* as an allegory for spring and a dialectic of regeneration and petrification in *Joseph von Eichendorff* (New York: Twayne, 1972).

23. Joseph von Eichendorff, "[D]urch die überglänzten Auen in das blühende Mailand hinunter." *Das Marmorbild* in *Ahnung und Gegenwart; Erzählungen* (Frankfurt am Main: Klassiker, 1985), 428.

24. "Der Mond, der eben über die Wipfel trat, beleuchtete scharf ein marmornes Venusbild . . . ." Ibid., 397.

25. "Einige Schwäne beschrieben still ihre einförmigen Kreise um das Bild . . . ." Ibid., 397. Lothar Pikulik writes in *Romantik als Ungenügen an der Normalität* (Frankfurt am Main: Suhrkamp, 1979): "Sehr bezeichnend, daß auch hier [in *Das Marmorbild*] warnend die Figur des Kreises beschworen wird. Auf dem Weiher, an dem die marmorne Statue der Venus steht, beschreiben einige Schwäne 'still ihre einförmigen Kreise um das Bild.' Noch bezeichnender, daß der Venusgarten bei Eichendorff fast immer die Züge des geometrischen Gartens, d.h. die Merkmale der Wiederholung und der Leere, trägt" (275).

26. They see "das Zwielicht über dem Gesteine der alten Ruine auf dem Berge" and there were lying an "altes, verfallenes Gemäuer umher, schöne, halb in die Erde versunkene Säulen und künstlich gehauene Steine, alles von einer üppig blühenden Wildnis grünverschlungener Ranken, Hecken und hohen Unkrautes überdeckt." Eichendorff, *The Marble Statue*, 422–23.

27. "Wenn Frühlingslüfte wehen / Hold überm grünen Plan, / Ein leises Auferstehen / Hebt in den Tälern an. / . . . . / Und unterm duft'gen Schleier / Sooft der Lenz erwacht, / Webt in geheimer Feier / Die alte Zaubermacht. / Frau Venus hört das Locken, / Der Vögel heitern Chor, / Und richtet froh erschrocken / Aus Blumen sich empor." Ibid., 423–24. Translation of the last stanza is by Egon Schwartz in *Joseph von Eichendorff*.

28. "Sie [Venus] selbst muß sinnend stehen / so bleich im Frühlingsschein, / Die Augen untergehen, / Der schöne Leib wird Stein. / Denn über Land und Wogen / Erscheint, so still und mild, Hoch auf dem Regenbogen / Ein ander Frauenbild. / Ein Kindlein in den Armen / Die Wunderbare hält, / Und himmlisches Erbarmen / Durchdringt die ganze Welt." Ibid., 424–25; translation by Schwartz.

29. Joseph von Eichendorff, "Über die Folgen von der Aufhebung der Landeshoheit der Bischöfe und der Klöster in Deutschland," in *Werke*, vol. 5 (Frankfurt am Main: Klassiker, 1993), 455–510. "Das innerste Wesen des Christentums dagegen ist immer und überall durchaus eins und dasselbe, es ist kein Werden . . ." (463).

30. "Auch sagt man, der Geist der schönen Heidengöttin habe keine Ruhe gefunden. Aus der erschrecklichen Stille des Grabes heißt sie das Andenken an die irdische Lust jeden Frühling immer wieder in die grüne Einsamkeit ihres verfallenen Hauses heraufsteigen und durch teuflisches Blendwerk die alte Verführung üben an jungen, sorglosen Gemütern." Eichendorff, *The Marble Statue,* 425.

31. "[D]ie dann vom Leben abgeschieden, und doch auch nicht aufgenommen in den Frieden der Toten, zwischen wilder Lust und schrecklicher Reue, an Leib und Seele verloren, umherirren und in der entsetzlichsten Täuschung sich selber verzehren." Ibid., 425–26.

32. Joseph von Eichendorff, "Geschichte der poetischen Literatur Deutschlands" in *Werke*, vol. 6 (Frankfurt am Main: Klassiker, 1990), 805–1074. "[Die sogenannte klassische Poesie der Alten hat] die Schönheit der menschlichen Gestalt versteinert, und das tote Auge; [die romantische hat] das rätselhafte Spiel des Lichts in wunderbaren Farben, und das lebendige Auge, durch das man in die geheimnisvollen Abgründe der Seele schaut. Wahrheit ist in der alten wie in der romantischen Poesie,

aber dort die sinnliche, endliche; hier eine übersinnliche, überirdische Wahrheit" (838).

33. In the poem "Die zwei Gesellen," Eichendorff presents a similar vision of Florio's choices with the description of two young men who set out to seek their fortune. The first one finds a lovely wife, settles down with his in-laws and is described as sitting with his baby looking out contentedly over his fields. The second young man, on the other hand, is drawn in by the voices from the deep. He enters the abyss or depths (*den Schlund*), following the seductive voices of the sirens, only to return to the surface of the earth and discover he is old, tired, alone and empty-handed.

34. "Sie waren unterdes auf einer luftigen Höhe angelangt, hinter ihnen versank die Stadt Lucca mit ihren dunkeln Türmen in dem schimmerden Duft. Da sagte Florio, zu Bianka gewendet: 'Ich bin wie neugeboren . . . .' Der Morgen schien ihnen, in langen, goldenen Strahlen über die Fläche schießend, gerade entgegen. . . . Und so zogen die Glücklichen fröhlich durch die überglänzten Auen in das blühende Mailand hinunter." Eichendorff, *The Marble Statue*, 428.

35. Joseph von Eichendorff, "Die Naturreligion" in *Werke*, vol. 6 (Frankfurt am Main: Klassiker, 1990), 453–74. "Es ist gewiß nichts so natürlich, edel und christlich, als das menschliche Streben nach Licht, ein reformatischer Gebrauch der Vernunft . . . " (453).

36. In Eichendorff's "Über die Folgen der Aufhebung der Landeshoheit. . .": "Aber das irdische Leben war nicht engherzig abgeschlossen, sondern durch das einbrechende Morgenrot des Christentums eben über das Grab hinaus heiter und ahndungsreich erweitert und, als ein überglänztes Zwischenspiel, in die Ewigkeit aufgenommen" (457).

37. Johann Gottschalk Wallerius, *Physisch-Chemische Betrachtungen über den Ursprung der Welt besonders der Erdwelt und ihrer Veränderung* [originally published 1776 in Stockholm], trans. D. Christian Friedrich Keller (Erfurt: Keyser, 1782). "Die Erde war mal flüßig und verdankt ihren Ursprung dem Wasser" (161).

38. "Gärung des Wassers," and "durch Gerinnung." Ibid., 242.

39. Wallerius uses the term "Teilchen" and elsewhere, "Saamen".

40. "Die Geheimnisse des Innersten der Natur kennen wir noch nicht." Ibid., 319.

41. There are "Höhlen in den Bergen," inside which everything is still "weich und feucht." Ibid., 298.

42. Wallerius describes this process as following: "[S]o können wir uns gewiß von der Entstehung der Berge keine andere Vorstellung machen, als daß sie aus großen zusammengeronnenen oder verwachsenden Massen oder abgetrennten weichen und fast flüßig im Wasser schwimmenden, hernach aber sich zu Boden gesenkten und über einen Haufen gegangenen Bergstücken bestehen." Ibid., 259.

43. The "fortwährende Umtreibung und Umwälzung" that forms "neue Berge" as "Theile sammeln sich am Ende des Flusses." Ibid., 298.

44. "Die allgemeine Bekleidung," Johann Reinhold Forster, whose actual book title is *Beobachtungen und Wahrheiten nebst einigen Lehrsätzen die einen hohen Grad von Wahrscheinlichkeit erhalten haben als: Stoff zur künftigen Entwerfung einer Theorie der Erde* (Leipzig: Breitkopf and Härtel, 1798), 12.

45. As Forster describes it: "[U]nd da immer neue Zuschüsse von expansiven Dünsten sich anhäuften, die noch weich und daher nachgebende Masse der Erdenoberfläche, in allerley große, unregelmäßig scheidende, theils einzelne isolierte Erhöhungen oder Berge aufblähen . . . ." Ibid., 9.

46. From this trip, Forster wrote extensive journals that were long denied publication because of his political battles in England. His son, Georg Forster, who accompanied his father on the entire journey, was allowed to publish his version, the famous text *A Voyage Around the World,* in 1777 (translated into German in 1778–1780). See Michael E. Hoare's edition of these journals: *The 'Resolution' Journal by Johann Reinhold Forster, 1772–1775* (London: Hakluyt Society, 1982), vols. 1–4.

47. Regarding other comets, Forster writes: "Es kann vielleicht bald in der Zukunft ein neuer Komet, alle die Elements darbieten, daß man seine ehemalige große Annäherung an die Erde daraus berechnen könnte." Forster, *Materials*, 67.

48. Ibid., 80.

49. Richard W. Kimpel describes the *Waldweib* as a more "natural" than "human" being. See his "Nature, Quest and Reality in Tieck's *Der blonde Eckbert* and *Der Runenberg*," *Studies in Romanticism* 9:3 (1970): 177–92, esp. 171.

50. "[D]as gepaltene Gebirge [lag] vor ihnen, im Hintergrund ein steiler Berg, auf welchem uralte verwitterte Ruinen schauerlich im weißen Lichte sich zeigten." Tieck, *Rune Mountain*, 189.

51. "[D]ann geht aber plötzlich wie ein neuer Mond das regierende Gestirn, welches ich selber bin, in meinem Herzen auf und besiegt die fremde Macht." Ibid., 201.

52. He saw "eine große weibliche Gestalt . . . , die sinnend im Gemache auf und nieder ging. Sie schien nicht den Sterblichen anzugehören, so groß, so mächtig waren ihre Glieder, so streng ihr Gesicht, aber doch dünkte dem entzückten Jünglinge, daß er noch niemals solche Schönheit gesehn [sic] oder geahndet habe." Ibid., 191.

53. "Wo die Alten weilen, / Daß sie nicht erscheinen? / Die Kristallen weinen, / Von demantnen Säulen / Fließen Tränenquellen, / Töne klingen drein; . . . ." Ibid., 191.

54. "Kommt, ihr Geister alle, / Zu der goldnen Halle, / Hebt aus tiefen Dunkeln / Häupter, welche funkeln!" Ibid., 191. For additional discussion of the significance of this poem, particularly in relationship to the two other poems in *The Rune Mountain*, see my: "The Three Poems in *Der Runenberg*," *The Intercontextuality of Self and Nature in Ludwig Tieck's Early Works* (New York: Lang, 1997), 111–34.

55. "[I]ch erinnere mich ganz deutlich, daß mir eine Pflanze zuerst das Unglück der ganzen Erde bekanntgemacht hat . . . ; in den Pflanzen, Kräutern, Blumen und Bäumen regt und bewegt sich schmerzhaft nur eine große Wunde, sie sind der Leichnam vormaliger herrlicher Steinwelten, sie bieten unserm Auge die schrecklichste Verwesung dar." Tieck, *Rune Mountain*, 202. Ziolkowski understands this statement as a "curious inversion of the usual theory," in that "Christian explains that the organic world of plants is nothing but 'the corpse of former splendid realms of stone' . . . and that the garden world of his father is hostile to him because of his

love for the magnificent symbols of the mineral kingdom." Ziolkowski, *Romanticism and Its Institutions*, 52. I would argue that this "inversion" is logical here, considering the geological treatment of nature in this text and the ambiguous presentation of time's cycle represented by the mineral woman or *Waldweib*.

56. Her name itself indicates this merging; she is both the representative of the minerals and the geological forces as well as the "forest wench" or woman living in the forest while seeking ancient mines.

57. "Das Waldweib hat mich gerufen, ich gehe sie zu suchen. Hier nebenan ist ein alter verfallener Schacht, schon vor Jahrhunderten von einem Bergmanne aufgegraben; vielleicht, daß ich sie dort finde!" Tieck, *Rune Mountain*, 205–206.

58. Manfred Frank discusses Steffens' influence on Tieck at length, quoting Steffens himself: "Henrich Steffens, the romantic natural philosopher who was born in Scandanavia, remembers having told Tieck . . . about the discovery of a stone that moved him deeply. During his travels through the Norwegian mountains, he came across a wonderful piece of Labradorian sienna containing zircon: 'An artist who seeks the Roman treasures cannot have been more intensely moved than I was. Tears poured out of my eyes; its seemed to me that the innermost part of the earth had opened its most secret workshop for me; as if the fecund earth, with its flowers and forests, were a chaste but light covering that hid unfathomable treasures, as if this covering were pulled back, cast away, in order to pull me down into the wondrous depths which had opened up. The impression was a thoroughly fantastic one and it may have been a lively presentation of this impression that inspired Tieck to write his novella, *The Rune Mountain*. . . . Tieck admitted that he thought of me with this novella.'" Manfred Frank, "Steinherz und Geldseele: Ein Symbol im Kontext," *Das kalte Herz* (Frankfurt am Main: Insel, 1978), 12.

59. See Maria M. Tatar, "Deracination and Alienation in Ludwig Tieck's *Der Runenberg*," *The German Quarterly* 51 (1978): 285–304; and Marianne Thalmann, *Das Märchen und die Moderne* (Stuttgart: Kohlhammer, 1961).

60. For discussion of the "generation of rocks," see Ziolkowski, *Romanticism and Its Institutions*.

61. "[D]arum fehlt es ihnen noch an Auge und Blick; das äußerliche Feuer mit seinem Glanze ist noch zu sehr in ihren inwendigen Herzen begraben, aber man muß es nur herausschlagen, daß sie sich fürchten, daß keine Verstellung ihnen mehr nützt, so sieht man wohl, wes Geistes Kind sie sind." Tieck, *Rune Mountain*, 207.

62. See also my essay, "Collecting the Rocks of Time: Goethe, the Romantics and Early Geology" *European Romantic Review* 10:3 (1999): 341–70, for a discussion of this final scene and its relationship to geology, particularly an analysis of the significance of the two materials Tieck mentions in Christian's hands: quartz and "Kiesel."

63. G. H. Toulmin, *The Antiquity and Duration of the World* (London: Cadell, 1780), 172.

64. "Die ganze Natur ist ein ewig Wechselndes, immer Veränderliches, immer Verändertes und der Wechsel selbst das einzige Beharrende" in: Henrich Steffens, "Beurtheilung dreier naturphilosophischer Schriften Schellings," *Schriften: Alt und Neu* (Breslau: Josef Mar, 1821), 8–9.

65. Henrich Steffens, "Alle Gebirge sind Ruinen. Gebirgsmassen, die sich regelmäßig und in stetem Zusammenhang gebildet haben, zeigen nur noch Trümmer des uralten Zusammenhanges." "Geologische Ansichten zur Erklärung der späteren Veränderungen der Erdoberfläche" *Schriften: Alt und Neu,* 219.

66. During his travels through South America, Humboldt mapped many previously unexplored (by Europeans) areas, made an impressive number of measurements of air pressure, temperature and humidity, and collected a wide assortment of plants and animals. Yet he was most celebrated upon his return to Paris in 1804 because of his impressive climb of the mountain Chimborazo in Columbia in 1802. Robert H. Brown refers to this general trend as a "colonization of Alpine nature space." *Nature's Hidden Terror: Violent Nature Imagery in Eighteenth-Century Germany* (Columbia: Camden, 1991), 7.

67. As Michel Foucault says about this emergence of time into natural history in *The Order of Things* (New York: Vintage, 1973): "It is in this classified time, in this squared and spatialized development, that the historians of the nineteenth century were to undertake the creation of a history that could at last be 'true'—in other words, liberated from Classical rationality, from its ordering and theodicy: a history restored to the irruptive violence of time" (132). See also Rogers, "The Living World," and Wolf Lepenies *Das Ende der Naturgeschichte: Wandel kultureller Selbstverständlichkeit in den Wissenschaften des 18. und 19. Jahrhunderts* (Munich: Hanser, 1976).

68. For discussions of the association of such architectural ruins with nation and history, see, for example, Anne Janowitz, *England's Ruins: Poetic Purpose and National Landscape* (Cambridge: Blackwell, 1990).

69. Georg Simmel, "The Ruin," *Georg Simmel, 1858–1918*, ed. Kurt H. Wolff (Columbus: Ohio State University Press, 1990).

70. "Florios Blicke schweiften wie geblendet über die bunten Bilder, immer mit neuer Trunkenheit wieder zu der schönen Herrin des Schlosses zurückkehrend. Diese ließ sich in ihrem kleinen, anmutigen Geschäft nicht stören. Bald etwas an ihrem dunkeln, duftenden Lockengeflechte verbessernd, bald wieder im Spiegel sich betrachtend, sprach sie dabei fortwährend zu dem Jüngling . . . ." Eichendorff, *The Marble Statue*, 416–17.

71. Eichendorff, "Die Naturreligion": "Da aber der Mensch sehr bald gewahr wurde, daß er die Spitze, gleichsam *das Auge* der Natur sei, so konnte es nicht fehlen, daß er sich auch ebenso bald als den eigentlichen Herrn und Gesetzgeber dieser Welt betrachten mußte, also erst die Natur und dann sich selbst vergötterte" (456, emphasis mine).

72. "Besonders zog die eine durch ihre zierliche, fast noch kindliche Gestalt . . . Florios Augen auf sich." Eichendorff, *The Marble Statue*, 387.

73. The contrast between active and passive viewing is made clear in this penultimate paragraph of the novella, where Florio gazes at the lovely and humble Bianka. Not only is his gaze the active one, but he consciously recognizes how he now can see clearly: "Mit Wohlgefallen ruhten Florios Blicke auf der lieblichen Gestalt. Eine seltsame Verblendung hatte bisher seine Augen wie mit einem Zaubernebel umfangen. Nun erstaunte er ordentlich, wie schön sie war! . . . Da ritt sie, ganz überrascht von dem unverhofften Glück, und in freudiger Demut, als

verdiene sie solche Gnade nicht, mit niedergeschlagenen Augen, schweigend neben ihm her. Nur manchmal blickte sie unter den langen, schwarzen Augenwimpern nach ihm hinauf, die ganze klare Seele lag in dem Blick, als wollte sie bittend sagen: 'Täusche mich nicht wieder!'" Ibid., 427.

74. "[D]ie von vielen eingelegten Steinen, Rubinen, Diamanten und allen Juwelen glänzte . . . ." Tieck, *Rune Mountain*, 192.

75. Christian "aber stand, die Gegenstände mit seinen Blicken verschlingend und zugleich tief in sich selbst versunken." Ibid., 192.

76. "[E]r sah eine Welt von Schmerz und Hoffnung in sich aufgehen, *mächtige Wunderfelsen* von Vertrauen und trotzender Zuversicht, *große Wasserströme* wie von Wehmut fließend." Ibid., 192, emphasis mine.

77. In her article, "'The Crystal Revenge': The Hypertrophy of the Visual in Novalis and Tieck," Alice Kuzniar speaks of the active gaze of the *Waldweib* and her "glistening tablet" overwhelming Christian: "[W]hat captures and displaces his attention is the compensatory fetish, the magic, glistening tablet. The polymorphosis of the mysterious Other gives him/her [the *Waldweib*, whose gender is ambiguous, according to Kuzniar] a certain omnipotence that evades all efforts of the studious eye. It also grants omnipresence, for Christian always fears the gaze upon him in one form or another. . . . Christian's scopophilic, enthralled look is thus halted once the gaze is thrown back at him." *The Germanic Review* 74:3 (1999): 224–25.

78. "Andacht und Aufmerksamkeit. . . . " Tieck, *Rune Mountain*, 194.

79. In my article, "Collecting the Rocks of Time," I suggest that Christian is a devious depiction of an early geologist and rock collector—one of so many collectors in the Age of Goethe.

80. See Merchant, *The Death of Nature*.

Constructing the Subaltern: White Creole Culture and Raced Captivity in Eighteenth-Century Dutch Suriname

LAURA LAFFRADO

Recent expansion and revision of studies of colonial discursive production have significantly extended the generic boundaries of the early American captivity narrative beyond the seventeenth-century Puritan New England prototype established with Mary Rowlandson's narrative, *The Soveraignty and Goodness of God* (1682).[1] Consideration of previously understudied texts, some written in languages other than English, that represent diverse geographical American locations reshapes our views of captivity and suggests the complicated context of captivity in the Americas. In the process, those constructed as captors have been refigured to include men of European descent as well as Native Americans, while representations of captives now include men, African-Americans, Mexicans, and others,[2] in addition to the white New England female, whose "passive innocence reinforce[d] white values" and "decoy[ed] attention away from the militaristic thrust of European culture into Native America."[3] Among those whose accounts of captivity have recently emerged from the broad New World contact zone, are captives whose voices are muted or silenced. As Walter Mignolo writes, "If scholarship cannot represent the colonized faithfully or allow the subaltern to speak, it can at least break up a monolithic notion of the subaltern and maintain an alternative discursive practice."[4] It is within this current dialogue concerning captivity in the early

Americas that I position my discussion of Pieter Van Dyk's *The Life and Business of a Suriname Plantation Manager, With the Slaves, on a Coffee Plantation* (c. 1765), a 66-page play written and set in eighteenth-century Suriname, a flourishing early American Dutch plantation colony on the northern coast of South America.

Collaboration by linguists in Surinamese Creole studies has resulted in the recovery from Dutch archives and 1995 publication of several texts from eighteenth-century Dutch Suriname, among them Van Dyk's play.[5] Originally published in Amsterdam in both Dutch and Sranan (the English-based creole language of slaves and many whites in eighteenth-century Suriname), *Life and Business* was "readily available in Suriname in the 1770s."[6] The editors, Jacques Arends and Matthias Perl, frame Van Dyk's play in a linguistics context to further "the reconstruction of creolization processes, thus contributing to better insights into problems of language genesis and language change."[7] While Van Dyk's text is indeed valuable for linguistic study, it also has much to offer eighteenth-century literary and cultural studies. The supporting roles of five black female plantation slaves mark an intersection of captivity, gender, and race which serves as the site of the play's investigation of unprofitable slave treatment on Suriname plantations. I suggest Van Dyk's *Life and Business* as a textual location for examination of intercultural and interracial issues of captivity in imperial realms, black female scripts, and continuing expansion and revision of our notions of captivity in the Americas.

Life and Business charts tensions on an eighteenth-century Suriname coffee plantation among an abusive white manager; Hendrik, a practical white overseer; and the African slaves who work the plantation. Thirty-two characters have speaking roles in the play: eight white Dutch creoles and twenty-four slaves. Among these thirty-two characters, there are nine African women and one Dutch creole woman, fifteen African men and seven white Dutch creole men. The majority of the characters have minor roles, some with as few as three or four lines of dialogue. The central characters are the white plantation manager, whose name we are never told; Hendrik, the sympathetic white overseer; Filida, a female slave who works in the coffee fields; and Lukresia, a female slave who works in the kitchen. Additionally, in the second half of the play, the plantation's white Dutch creole absentee owner has a significant supporting role.

The development and tension of the play, which takes place over the course of several days, is located in the white manager's transgressive actions. The play begins with his asking "'Why don't those black devils bring my coffee?,'" which leads to his ordering whippings of over one hundred lashes each for Lukresia and Aurora, two female kitchen slaves who are late with his coffee.[8] Throughout the play, the manager orders harsh, sometimes fatal, slave whippings for equally trivial reasons. Additionally, because he underfeeds the slaves and resists providing medical care for them, they are weak and sickly and so cannot work as hard as he wishes them to. Repeatedly violating what Van Dyk's footnotes tell us are prevailing standards of plantation slave labor, the manager dictates too many baskets of coffee beans be picked each day, punishes slaves when coffee beans are not yet ripe, and demands the digging of trenches far longer than can be completed in a day. He forbids slaves from singing while they work and denies them customary periodic celebrations. He also makes a practice of raping female slaves ("'Since he's been at the plantation, he's had over thirty women and as many young girls on top of that,'" Filida says [185]), particularly disrupting slave culture stability on the plantation by raping married female slaves. These harsh conditions provoke slave escape, suicide, and rebellion. In the course of the play, the manager's actions result in seven severe whippings, three deaths, and over twenty slave escapes. The slaves not only fear him ("'Don't let him hear, he'll kill you,'" [167]), but recognize and disapprove of how his actions weaken plantation productivity. As the slave Kupido later tells the plantation owner, "'[. . .] the manager's ruining the plantation,'" because he isn't "'knowledgeable about it,'" (208).

Hendrik, the sensible white overseer who is the manager's counterpart in the play, resists carrying out the manager's abusive orders and contests the manager's actions. Hendrik is rational and reasonable in response to the manager's arbitrary orders, dignified where the manager is vulgar ("'Don't curse me, I'm not one of your slaves'"[172]). He criticizes the manager's excessively abusive slave treatment as bad business leading to loss of plantation profits: "'The slaves must work hard all day long, but there's not enough food on the plantation. Sir, if you let them have more food then they won't steal anymore and they'll work harder too'"(175). In response, the manager accuses Hendrik of "'too much sympathy for the slaves'"(171), exclaims that he must be "'good friends'" with the slaves (171), and predicts that "'When you become a manager, I believe you'll almost be their brother'" (175). In Van Dyk's construction of the white overseer, normative treatment of slaves is good business, not, as the manager charges, pandering. Van Dyk's footnote makes this explicit: "Those in Suriname who deal well with their slaves, are immediately called 'Negro kings,' for which there is no reason. What does an owner wish except good products and no complaints from his slaves?" (222). Abolition of slavery is unrecognized in *Life and Business* and slave conditions are remarked on only in connection with plantation economic stability.

In the second half of the play, a group of white men visit the plantation and begin drinking wine with the manager. The manager summons Quassi, the slave who serves as the game hunter, who tells him, "'I didn't shoot anything, master, because it's the rainy season'"(202).[9] Van Dyk glosses this statement with a footnote that confirms the difficulty of hunting at this time of year ("In the rainy season the water in the bush is three, four or five feet high, and the game stays on the high hills; it's sheer luck when one shoots something" [202]). In a rage at what he regards as Quassi's disrespectful excuses ("'You talk back to me like that, in front of all these whites?'" [202]), the manager shoots Quassi in the head and kills him, horrifying his white visitors. Their response is less concerned with Quassi's arbitrary murder than it is with fear of justified slave rebellion: "'Oh, good Lord, you shot the slave right in his head! He's stone-dead. I wish none of us were here [. . . .] We won't report you, but the slaves of the plantation, they will tell the owner that we were all there when you killed the slave. This will come to no good'"(202–203). In this key scene, the manager's actions violate and exceed presumptive colonial interactions. When the slaves learn of the arbitrary killing of Quassi, they send a fellow slave, Kupido, as their representative to plead their case with the absentee plantation owner.

In response to Kupido's information and in order to protect his investment, the owner makes a surprise visit to the plantation. When the manager objects to the owner's inspection, the owner confronts him: "'Do you mind me doing that? Is the plantation yours or mine? You ruined the whole plantation, you killed my slaves, you drove more than twenty of them into the bush, and I can't inspect my property?'" (220). The owner explicitly links slave escape with the manager's excessive abuses. Here slaves do not flee into the bush in order to live freely, but are 'driven' to flee by disruptively harsh conditions. The owner forces the manager to resign, who leaves immediately and in disgrace. The slaves praise the owner ("'Thank you, my good master. Live long with God's help'" [226]), aligning themselves with prevailing forms of slave abuse and economic productivity. Van Dyk constructs slaves in *Life and Business* as hard workers, not normally given to escape or rebellion, invested in the success of the plantation. With order, profit, and the stability of slave culture restored, the play ends with the slaves given permission to honor and bury a female slave.

We know little of Pieter Van Dyk, the play's author. In *Life and Business,* as in many North American captivity narratives, authorship is complicated and unreliable. Given the sympathetic characterization of the play's white overseer, Van Dyk may himself have been a white overseer on a Suriname plantation; or the name he uses may be a pseudonym.[10] Linguistic study indicates Sranan was most likely Van Dyk's primary language, suggesting he was born in the colony and may have been second generation creole.[11] Whatever the particulars of Van Dyk's background, his play emerges from what Ralph Bauer has called "the creolized social environments of the colonial Americas."[12]

Further, little is known of the play's history. We do not know why the play was written; if it was ever performed or, if not, why not; if Van Dyk might have hoped to have it performed. The absence of stage directions in the play suggests that it was never performed[13] and Ingrid Van Trier-Guicherit has labeled *Life and Business* a *leesdrama*, that is, a "reading drama," suggesting that it may never have been meant for performance.[14] Additionally, as the play is part of a language manual intended for colonists and potential colonists, its purpose may have been to provide instruction in the language and culture of Suriname plantations. Yet fairly consistent linguistic differences in how the manager and the owner are addressed by Africans and whites throughout the play suggest that Van Dyk "wished to maintain a distinction in the forms of address for the manager and the owner when both are 'on stage.'"[15]

Some background on eighteenth-century Dutch Suriname theater may provide useful context here. In 1773, eight years after "Life and Business" was published, the first dramatic performance in Suriname mentioned in documents took place. In 1775, the first theater in Suriname was opened. Because the theater excluded Jews, the latter opened their own theater the next year. For the rest of the century (and well into the nineteenth century), free blacks and those of mixed race were admitted to the theater, but slaves were not. (Slaves were, however, allowed to physically reserve seats for their owners.) Many theater companies were subsequently formed, suggesting a thriving dramatic community. Plays were performed in Dutch for a white Dutch creole audience. As this suggests, theater in eighteenth-century Dutch Suriname served as a colonial site of Dutch cultural narratives, much as eighteenth-century theater did for English culture in Jamaica and Barbados.[16]

The production of Van Dyk's narrative in the form of a slave drama foregrounds links among excessive slave abuse, plantation profits, and social order. Written during an unstable cultural moment of escalating slave escapes and rebellion in Suriname, the play relies on dialogue to articulate and enact both effective and disruptive colonial interactions. The performativity of the play marks raced relations of power through its dramatic representations of cultural boundaries on the imperial frontier.

By way of contrast, Aphra Behn's *Oroonoko; or, The Royal Slave* (1688) set in seventeenth-century Suriname, and its dramatic adaptations by Thomas Southerne and John Hawkesworth, provided eighteenth-century European audiences with an Edenic Suriname; African slaves as princes, warriors, and chiefs; and "Imoinda, a black African female [in later adaptations converted to a white European woman] who embodies the ideal of white European womanhood."[17] *Oroonoko*'s popularity in the first half of the eighteenth century, when it was probably the most produced of all post-Shakespearean tragedies, signals its narratives of race, romance, and drama. In comparison, Van Dyk's *Life and Business* mutes many of the subjects magnified in *Oroonoko*. For example, the bush exists because slaves escape into it, the river because a boat arrives, and the plantation fields because slaves work them, but *Life and Business* offers no description or appreciation of the natural world in Suriname. Likewise, as I will argue later, the African origins of Surinamese slaves, while significant, appear only implicitly in *Life and Business*. No character development in the play is tied to any kind of past—royal, African, or otherwise. Further, while Van Dyk's character development of women in his play is not extensive, none of the African women reflect a white European female model. It is only in the potential for slave rebellion—which occurs in *Oroonoko* and remains a possibility in *Life and Business*—that the two texts are similar. While Dutch readers and colonists may have been familiar with a version of *Oroonoko*, Van Dyk's play appears largely uninformed by recognition of that text. However, Behn's *Oroonoko* and its dramatic adaptations are written from a European perspective and directed toward European racial narratives. *Life and Business* is written from a creole perspective on the periphery of imperial territories and was intended in part for a creole audience.

Life and Business was written at a moment in white Dutch Surinamese culture that privileged related concerns of commerce, wealth, and slavery. Thus, texts such as linguistic grammars were published in Dutch and Sranan as aids to help whites communicate with the slaves and natives, who were instrumental in the amassing of colonial wealth. John Gabriel Stedman's *Narrative of a Five Years Expedition Against the Revolted Negroes of Surinam* (1790), perhaps the most well-known contemporary work on eighteenth-century Dutch Suriname, provided a European outsider's perspective on Surinamese slavery and colonialism. Stedman's accounts of military action, travel, and, in general, "the narrative of a man of sensibility encountering a brutal and corrupt plantation society founded on the spectacular torment of slave bodies"[18] signal that his subject position is not that of a white Dutch Surinamese creole invested in and committed to that culture. Neither a grammar nor a Eurocentric commentary on Suriname, Van Dyk's *Life and Business* has, for the moment, reemerged with limited direct historical/literary context.

The current absence of materials that might provide literary/historical context related to *Life and Business* should not suggest that such materials do not exist or may not at some point be recovered. Americanist literary scholars have done very little work with eighteenth-century Dutch Surinamese archival materials. Van Dyk's play was recovered by linguists for linguistic purposes, not by or for literary scholars. Richard Price and Sally Price's impressive work in Dutch archives, which has resulted in the translation and publication of various letters, diaries, and other documents, along with their work in Suriname collecting and publishing native Suriname oral texts has compellingly reconstructed Suriname history and slave rebellion, but their project has not been to view such materials through a literary lens.

The very limited historical/literary context available signals the play's location outside eighteenth-century British or Dutch materials (for which there would be more context), and marks its New World creole location. A text such as Hans Staden's *Captivity of Hans Staden of Hesse, 1547–55: Among the Wild Tribes of Eastern Brazil*, for instance, while relating New World captivity, was written from and directed toward not a creole, but a wholly European audience, reinforcing imperial motives and establishing the construction of cannibalistic native captors. Examining *Life and Business* through the lens of narratives of captivity in the early Americas usefully brings into focus the play's New World markers of intercultural and interracial colonial tensions, creole economic concerns, and distance from European literary and cultural scripts.

Van Dyk's dramatization of this New World captivity of women originally from the west coast of Africa coincides with and yet is removed from racial/colonial early American captivities of white women of European descent. My classification of Van Dyk's text as a captivity narrative corresponds with similar generic contours of many North American Indian captivity narratives that partake of fact, fiction, and propaganda. Additionally, the generic lens Van Dyk selects—the play—would, later in the nineteenth-century, become a popular location in the United States for dramatic accounts of early American female captivity by Indians.[19] However, Van Dyk does not write across the play's boundaries into the sermon, (auto)biography, or religious account, all common strategies of captivity narratives. Indeed, the religious discourse typically dominant in the captivity narrative is entirely absent from Van Dyk's text, perhaps largely due to the secular nature of a portion of his audience, the notoriously decadent eighteenth-century Suriname plantocracy.

Van Dyk's text is more extensively compromised than the familiar, fact-based North American captivity narratives (for instance, narratives of Elizabeth Hanson and Mary Rowlandson). We know of no historical account of the women in Van Dyk's play, who may be individual women, composites of various women, or Van Dyk's fictional constructs.[20] The captive African women described in Van Dyk's play left no self-composed written or dictated record of their voices. Their female, African, enslaved voices come to us solely through the filter of Van Dyk's literate Dutch colonial voice.

Though Van Dyk may have been white or of mixed race, he is a man like Increase Mather, Cotton Mather, representatives of the Pennsylvania Quaker church, Jesuit editors, and others,[21] who appropriates and revises female captivity in his text. Like other male editors, too, he incorporates his female constructs into scripts designed to serve the dominant ideological order, in this case the Dutch colonized plantation slave system in Suriname. Van Dyk's text thus corresponds with the female subject/male editor generic paradigm of many North American captivity narratives. However, unlike the male editors of such captivity narratives, Van Dyk is not a husband or minister of the captive black women whose narratives he appropriates. He is distanced from them by his status and detached association. Rhetorically complicit as he is in the raced captivity of black women like those in *Life and Business,* Van Dyk is both editor and captor. In the absence of other historical information, the personhood of the colonized black women is rendered contingent on his male, colonial surveillance.

Though a colony of imperialist Holland, Suriname, like other distant colonial spaces, was not necessarily fully representative of Eurocentric cultures.[22] As Richard Price writes, a "long-simmering conflict between the office of the Governor (as representative of the Directors of the Society of Suriname in the Netherlands) and the local plantocracy became, during the late 1740s, a vicious personal battle."[23] The governor wrote that the planters "had no Dutch heart and consequently no patriotic sentiment, since they do not consider the Netherlands as their Fatherland."[24] Colonial white creole culture as seen in *Life and Business* reflects this diminished concern for Holland, its reputation, and its imperial rivalry with other European countries. Dominant white Suriname culture is portrayed as economically invested in a functional and efficient plantation slave system, criticizing "excessive" cruelty to slaves only insofar as it disrupted that local system.

The preface and dedication of *Life and Business* promote Van Dyk's creole authority to speak. In his preface, Van Dyk notes his "many years of trial and experience" (95) on Suriname plantations as qualification to instruct his early modern readers "how to make oneself respected and loved, without committing the inhuman cruelties . . . which serve absolutely no purpose but to make good slaves into bad ones, to the inevitable detriment of interested parties" (93). His chastisement of whites whose violent and sadistic abuse of slaves had disrupted the profitable plantation economy and threatened social order marks Van Dyk's engagement of this chaotic historical moment in the Surinamese mid-eighteenth-century slave plantation system.

The conciliatory nature of Van Dyk's 1765 text emerges with renewed significance when informed by the Djuka treaty of 1760 and the Saramaka treaty of 1762, which granted independence to the largest groups of organized escaped slaves (known then as maroons or Bush Negroes). Van Dyk's criticism of continued abuses by the Dutch plantocracy must be read both in the context of the Suriname government's maroon treaties (which did not address the brutal conditions of slavery that had contributed to maroon rebellion), as well as in terms of how the irresponsible actions of Suriname slaveholders could threaten Holland's position as a colonizing power. While England was celebrating its decisive victory over France (in the Seven Years War, 1754–63, known in America as the French and Indian War) that added valuable Caribbean sugar islands to its empire, Holland was recruiting eight hundred professional European soldiers to Suriname in a violent imperial attempt to hunt down rebellious ex-slaves and restore stability to the colony's plantation economy.

Eighteenth-century Dutch Suriname constitutes a heightened example of imperial agency and domination. Its corruption and harsh slave treatment rivaled the notorious reputations of Jamaica and Saint Domingue.[25] In what Richard and Sally Price have called "a maximally polarized society," the ratio of Africans to Europeans was 25:1 and as high as 65:1 in plantation areas.[26] (Jamaica's ratio, the highest in the British West Indies, was 10:1.)[27] In short, "some three thousand whites . . . liv[ed] in grotesque luxury off the forced labor of some fifty thousand brutally exploited African slaves."[28] As *Life and Business* was being written and published, "a tremendous increase in the extension of credits by Amsterdam bankers [occurred], as Suriname planters mortgaged their estates" to further finance their lavish lifestyles.[29]

Eighteenth-century Suriname was correspondingly marked by nearly a century of guerrilla war against colonists by maroons. Eric Sundquist, in a commentary on the cultural contours of maroon communities, classifies them as

> one of the most significant threats to planters—simply by encouraging other slaves to run away, by staging periodic raids on plantation supplies and robbing whites, or by more openly engaging in violent uprising. Cases of arson, attack, and plunder were common in areas with significant maroon communities, and assaults by white militia were typically met with harsh resistance.[30]

Decades of expensive military expeditions against the Suriname maroons by the Dutch had resulted in little more than increased marronage (desertions by slaves), a consequence of such expeditions making "known to the slaves both the escape routes from the plantations and the locations of maroon villages."[31] As Herbert Klein writes, "Between invasions and slave uprisings, some 6,000 ex-slaves had escaped into the interior of the colony by the early eighteenth century."[32] By mid-century, Dutch Suriname leaders had strategized to control rebellion by making peace with some, but not all maroons, with the central condition that the chosen maroon groups committed themselves to returning newly escaped slaves. The government thus hoped to divide the various maroon groups against each other. That this approach was marked by a refusal to recognize the collapsing of the Suriname plantation slave system is suggested by the treaties being issued a full century before general emancipation (July 1, 1863) in Suriname.

Both the Djuka treaty of 1760 and the Saramaka treaty of 1762 included controversial annual "presents" or supplies from the Suriname government, which, as Richard Price writes, were subject to interpretation: "The symbolic meaning of these 'goods' differed sharply for colonists and Saramakas. Were they 'presents,' freely given by the whites out of generosity to needy subjects, or were they 'tribute,' exacted by the victorious Saramakas as a kind of war damages?"[33] Planters criticized "the weakness of the Government of Suriname when they offered them [the Saramakas] freedom . . . and submitted to conditions so humiliating for us and so glorious for them."[34] and feared further maroon rebellions would be encouraged by the terms of the treaties. In fact, the treaties not only failed to halt further marronage and attacks by ex-slaves that continued to threaten to collapse the plantation economy, the agreement to return escaped slaves was repeatedly subverted by the Djuka and the Saramaka.[35]

In his study of captivity narratives, Christopher Castiglia writes, "since confinement (within bodies constructed by white, patriarchal discourse, and hence by language itself) cannot be finally escaped . . . [we] must read critically in order to revise the terms of those discourses."[36] In *Life and Business,* Van Dyk's male, creole perspective constructs and confines the play's black characters. His creole subject position in particular helps determine the nature of the captivity he scripts, just as the maroon rebellions and their consequences inflect his criticism of violence toward slaves. His slaves are not the rebellious maroons of the Djuka and Saramaka treaties, but peaceful, hard workers who rebel or escape only under disruptively harsh conditions. Van Dyk reinscribes plantation culture in his portrayal of willing, obedient slaves for whom marronage is a desperate resort, captivity their accepted condition.

Both the preface and dedication of *Life and Business* mark Van Dyk's creole focus on the business of plantation (and thus slave) management. This perspective is in contrast to that seen in the texts of European professional soldier John Gabriel Stedman, who refers to Suriname as "this Blood Spilling Colony"[37] and writes in his journal, "Those planters who dare so inhumanely to persecute theyr Slaves without a Cause deserve in my opinion no better treatment [than to have their slaves revolt]."[38] Though Stedman was by no means an anti-slavery advocate, his position as a European outsider enables him to see the cruel and arbitrary nature of slave abuse in Surinamese plantation society.[39] Van Dyk's creole position shapes his view of such violence differently. Unlike Stedman, Van Dyk locates the primary problem with brutal slave treatment in its interference with the efficient management and economic success of a coffee plantation.

The text's dedication further signals Van Dyk's status as an agent of Surinamese colonial culture as he praises managers (whites managing plantations for non-resident owners) who limit their uses of physical punishment: "There are managers who do not use the whip even once a year, but they are practical. The trick is to make oneself feared and loved and to be just to the slaves as well as to oneself" (95). The text's promotion of measured physical violence and calculated emotional effect to maintain a stable slave plantation economy in Dutch Suriname corresponds with the use of anti-Indian rhetoric and propaganda in North American captivity narratives to justify oppression of Native American tribes. Many Indian captivity narratives "were shaped by [early American] publishers exploiting a mass market that thrived on sensationalism, in a natural alliance with land speculators who wanted to implement a policy of Indian extermination in the interest of real estate development."[40] Van Dyk's text partakes of a colonialist model that Rafael Pérez-Torres has described as "a reliance on well-scripted roles [. . . that] leads again and again to a reinscription of asymmetrical power relations"[41] and, in this case, to the sustaining of a profitable economic order.

The significant presence of five of the black female plantation slaves—Aminba, Aurora, Kato, Lucresia, and, especially, Filida—mark a raced gendering of the play's economic focus. While this is not to suggest that *Life and Business* focuses on black women, we may infer much about the captive black female role in eighteenth-century white creole plantation culture in Suriname from a critical reading of their suggestive performative presence in this text. The black women of *Life and Business* may have been creoles, like Van Dyk, or more newly arrived Africans.[42] Variously characterized in the text as sisters, virgins, wives, or expectant mothers, they are primarily represented through the black female body. In an early emblematic moment, Hendrik, the white overseer, refuses to obey the manager's order to flog women who lag behind, explaining that "'women that are pregnant can't work like the others'" (176). The scene gestures toward both whipping and rape, the primary female slave body violations in the text.

The play's most explicit spectacles of colonial violence concern whipping of the black female body and use ritualistic dialogue of sadistic flogging. Frantic black female pleas for mercy ("'Please, master, it's enough, my buttocks are in pieces'" [179]) are responded to with orders for further punishment. Scenes of whipping are frequently glossed by Van Dyk's detailed footnotes ("Means that the slashes of the whip cut deeply into her naked skin" [166]; "A Spanish buck is carried out with thin rods on the naked buttocks, until pieces of the skin fall off" [168]).[43] Aminba's attempt to ease her sister Kato's flogging is met with the threat of further violence—"You come back one more time to put in a good word for your sister and you'll get some too" (179). The text explicitly condemns the manager's cruelty, yet the play's repeated, nuanced flogging descriptions signal that corporal punishment is being sexualized. Though no evidence has yet been uncovered that suggests that *Life and Business* was performed, its series of floggings may have been intended to titillate a white creole or European audience with eroticized images of the female African body.

Deborah E. McDowell, considering Frederick Douglass's claim that "the slave master derives pleasure from the repeated act of whipping," argues that, correspondingly, Douglass himself "derive[s] a vicarious pleasure from the repeated narration of the act."[44] Following McDowell, I would argue that Van Dyk, too, derives pleasure from his repeated narration of the flogging of black women. Like Douglass, Van Dyk repeatedly describes such scenes in detail. Van Dyk does include dialogue condemning frequent whipping because it adversely affects slave labor (demoralizes, injures or kills slaves) and results in a less efficient and profitable functioning of the plantation. However, his detailed reinscriptions of whipping scenes gesture toward his conflicted responses. Such scenes in *Life and Business* mark the tension between Van Dyk's effort to condemn poor business practices and his participation—for himself, for his imagined audience—in the dominant white culture's eroticizing of violence, gender, and race.

As opposed to explicit representations of flogging the black female body, the frequent rape of the body occurs in gaps in the narrative. Though rape occurs offstage, it is repeatedly a subject of condemning dialogue, particularly in terms of a distinction made between married and unmarried black female bodies, with the rape of a married woman the more transgressive act.[45] As one male slave complains to the plantation owner, "'[The manager] takes women by force who have a husband. Aren't there enough young girls at the plantation?'" (206). Indeed, the play's climax occurs with the manager's rape of married Filida and the subsequent suicide of Diki, her husband. Afterward, when Filida weeps in grief, the manager threatens to kill her if she "'open[s] [her] mouth once again'" (198). So traumatized that she cannot silence herself, Filida's response to sexual abuse becomes what Alfred Hunt, in another context, has called a "refusal to accept the white colonists' world":[46] "'I can't keep my mouth shut, master. You've done me too much harm. You killed my husband so I could be your whore'" (198). Filida's transgressive outburst is located in "the overwhelming physical and psychic violence of colonial Suriname."[47] Immediately after this confrontation, Filida runs off to the bush: her rape and the death of her husband force her, in Van Dyk's construction, to at least temporarily join the rebellious ex-slave communities and continue the maroon tradition of black defiance.[48]

Despite the "notorious sexual license of white men in the Caribbean that all contemporary commentators noted,"[49] rape of the black female body, unlike whipping, may not be explicitly represented in *Life and Business* for generic reasons. The locating of explicit sexual violence offstage may have been a dramatic choice on the part of Van Dyk as playwright. Additionally, rape may be unseen in the play because the consequences of the rape of black women by white men have the potential to significantly destabilize the plantation's social order. The rape of Filida results in loss of two slaves (Diki, Filida's dead husband, and escaped Filida herself) and in the colonizing manager's diminished agency. Transgressive mistreatment by the colonizer engenders agency to speak and to escape captivity for the colonized black woman. The rape of Filida's married body and its consequences mark the manager's poor business practices, of which there have been many examples, but they also signal a cultural boundary in white creole arrangements regarding slave treatment. In *Life and Business,* frequent whipping of a female slave, though detrimental to the plantation economy, is not transgressive; it can be represented and condemned, even if it is, at the same time, eroticized. Rape of a married woman slave, however, is unrepresentable and significantly disruptive. Black female scripts are central to a critical reading of this text: they reveal that violations of the slave body are integral to the white creole slave system; and that violations of the captive black woman's body that exceed the normative system of abuse have potential to result in redemption and liberation, thus threatening the stability of the slave-dependent plantation economy.

In the final scenes of the play, the owner dismisses the manager and the plantation returns to prevailing forms of slave abuse and economic stability. The slave community, represented as satisfied now that order has been restored, asks for and receives permission to bury an unnamed black woman who has died offstage. The black female body is celebrated as slaves affectionately bid their "sister" and "sweetheart" a safe journey home to Africa. Van Dyk's footnote to this scene—"The slaves believe that, when one of them has died, he'll resurrect in his own land"(237)—indirectly marks his knowledge that the majority of slaves in the West Indies, Caribbean, and South America were African born and knew Africa as their homeland. The combination of disease, climate, and harsh conditions that gave these locations a higher death rate than the North American mainland resulted in the "continuing introduction of Africans," that, together with "traditions nourished by the maroon bands meant that black Caribbean societies remained more African than did their counterparts on the mainland, particularly in Britain's North American colonies."[50] Most of Dutch Suriname's slaves had experienced part of their lives in Africa, as well as a high slave death rate and knowledge of an Afrocentric maroon culture in Suriname.

The tacit classification of slaves in Suriname as natives of Africa is seen in Van Dyk's definition of Africa as a slave's "own land," which implicitly acknowledges the slave diasporic experience: an African is enslaved, shipped to Suriname, and, when freed by death, returns home to Africa. Van Dyk scripts slavery as a liminal and temporary captivity, situating both the Americas and slaves in Suriname in a larger geographic context. The play's final image is located in the silent testimony of the African female body in Suriname, lifeless but no longer captive, redeemed by death and, in the belief system of her subaltern community culture, on her way to freedom.

Pieter Van Dyk's *Life and Business* emerges from cultural and national narratives of Dutch imperialist and Surinamese creole tensions, eighteenth-century maroon peace treaties, and the Afrocentric nature of slavery in Suriname. Van Dyk's generic choice of the play may well have been determined by its central features of drama and tragedy, as they resonated with the unfolding global conflicts of this critical moment. Van Dyk's text, as it charts complications of raced and gendered captivity in eighteenth-century Dutch Suriname's white creole plantation culture, contributes to a more nuanced understanding of studies of colonial discursive production and of our notions of captivity in the Americas.

NOTES

A much earlier version of this article was presented at the Northeast American Society for Eighteenth-Century Studies meeting at Williams College, September 1998. I am grateful to Marlyse Baptista who introduced me to Van Dyk's text and to Zabelle Stodola for her encouragement. I am especially indebted to Jacques Arends for his generosity in sharing his knowledge of *Life and Business* and of eighteenth-century Dutch Suriname.

1. For a summary of this wider consideration, see Ralph Bauer, "Creole Identities in Colonial Space: The Narratives of Mary White Rowlandson and Francisco Nùñez de Pineda y Bascuñán," *American Literature* 69 (1997):665–67. I borrow the term "colonial discursive production" from Peter Hulme, *Colonial encounters: Europe and the Native Caribbean, 1492–1797* (New York: Methuen, 1986), passim. See also Walter Mignolo's discussion of the term in *The Darker Side of the Renaissance: Literacy, Territoriality, and Colonization* (Ann Arbor: University of Michigan Press, 1995), 7.
2. Kathryn Zabelle Derounian-Stodola and James Arthur Levernier, *The Indian Captivity Narrative, 1550–1900* (New York: Twayne, 1993), xi.
3. Bauer, "Creole Identities," 687.
4. Mignolo, *Darker Side*, 5.
5. An extract from *Life and Business* had previously been published in 1958 in Ursy Lichtveld and Jan Voorhoeve, *Suriname: spiegel der vaderlandse kooplieden* (Zwolle: W.E.J. Tjeenk Willink, 1958).
6. Jacques Arends, introduction, *Early Suriname Creole Texts: A Collection of Eighteenth-Century Sranan and Saramaccan Documents*, ed. and trans. by Jacques Arends and Matthias Perl (Frankfurt: Bibliotheca Ibero-Americana, 1995), 20.
7. Ibid., preface, 9.
8. Pieter Van Dyk, *The Life and Business of a Suriname Plantation Manager, with the Slaves, on a Coffee Plantation*, in *Early Suriname Creole Texts: A Collection of 18th-Century Sranan and Saramaccan Documents*, ed. and trans. Jacques Arends and Matthias Perl (Frankfurt: Bibliotheca Ibero-Americana, 1995), 165. All subsequent references will be from this edition and will be noted in the text.
9. "Quassie" was a common African (Ghana) name for a slave in Suriname. For a discussion of a well-known Suriname slave called Quassie or Kwasi, see Richard Price, introduction, *To Slay the Hydra: Dutch Colonial Perspectives on the Saramaka Wars* (Ann Arbor: Karoma, 1983), 26–34.
10. Arends, *Early Suriname Creole Texts*, 19.
11. Ibid., 64.
12. Bauer, "Creole Identities," 667.
13. See Arends, *Early Suriname Creole Texts*, 22.
14. Ibid., 67. Also see Ingrid Van Trier-Guicherit, "De eerste taalgids Sranan-Netherlands," *OSO* 10 (1991): 31–47.

15. As Arends and Perl explain,

> The forms of address *mastra* and *mynheer* are translated as 'master' and 'Sir,' respectively[. . . .] The manager is addressed as *mastra* both by the slaves and the black overseer, and as *mynheer* by the white overseer. The owner is addressed as *(gran)mastra* in his house in Paramaribo by the slave Kupido, but as *mynheer* by everyone, including the slaves and the black overseer, from the moment he has arrived at the plantation. (Van Dyk, 240, n. 8)

16. For information in this section regarding eighteenth-century Dutch theater in Suriname, I am indebted to Jacques Arends's generous research and translations. See C. F. A. Bruijning and Jan Voorhoeve (eds.), *Encyclopedie van Suriname* (Amsterdam: Elsevier, 1977), 611; H. D. Benjamins and Johannes F. Snelleman, *Encyclopaedie van Nederlandsch West-Indie* (Gravenhage, 1914–1917), 683; Gabbi Mesters, "Historische, theaterwetenschappelijke analyse van het Koloniale Surinaamse theater tussen 1773 en 1900" (Faculty of Humanities, 1998); R. A. J. Van Lier, *Frontier Society: A Social Analysis of the History of Surinam* (The Hague: Martinus Nijhoff, 1971), 82–83; H. Zoutendijk, "Toneel: een wederopbloei," *Cultureel mozaiek van Suriname* ed. Albert Helman (Zutphen: Walburg Pers, 1977).

17. Stephanie Athey and Daniel Cooper Alarcon, "*Oroonoko*'s Gendered Economies of Honor/Horror: Reframing Colonial Discourse Studies in the Americas," *American Literature* 65 (1993): 415–43.

18. Tassie Gwilliam, "'Scenes of Horror,' Scenes of Sensibility: Sentimentality and Slavery in John Gabriel Stedman's *Narrative of a Five Years Expedition against the Revolted Negroes of Surinam,*" *ELH* 65 (1998): 653–73.

19. Derounian-Stodola and Levernier, *Indian Captivity Narrative*, 37.

20. The male and female plantation slaves in Van Dyk's play are given names that seem to have been common slave names, some with classical resonance, coined by what Richard Price terms "ironic" masters. See Price, *To Slay the Hydra*, 57. For partial slave name lists, see Price 107, 110.

21. Derounian-Stodola and Levernier, *Indian Captivity Narrative*, 21.

22. For a thorough discussion of the history of Suriname, see Van Lier, *Frontier Society*.

23. Price, *To Slay the Hydra*, 14.

24. Ibid.

25. For commentary on the San Domingo revolution, see Alfred N. Hunt, *Haiti's Influence on Antebellum America,* (Baton Rouge: Louisiana State University Press, 1988); and Eric Sundquist, *To Wake the Nations* (Cambridge: Harvard University Press, 1993).

26. Richard Price and Sally Price, introduction, *Narrative of a Five Years Expedition against the Revolted Negroes of Surinam,* by John Gabriel Stedman, ed. Richard Price and Sally Price (Baltimore: Johns Hopkins University Press, 1988), xiv.

27. Price and Price, *Narrative*, xiv.

28. Ibid.

29. Ibid.

30. Sundquist, *To Wake the Nations*, 195–96.

31. Price, *To Slay the Hydra*, 12.

32. Herbert S. Klein, *African Slavery in Latin America and the Caribbean* (Oxford: Oxford University Press, 1986), 133.

33. Price, *To Slay the Hydra*, 38.

34. Ibid.

35. See Price, *To Slay the Hydra*, 40. The Dutch Surinamese government attempted to legislate maroon reluctance to return escaped slaves who claimed excessive abuse by their owners; the Saramaka treaty of 1762 asserted that "the government has the exclusive prerogative of finding out about this [mistreatment of slaves by masters] and punishing their masters" (Price, *To Slay the Hydra*, 160).

36. Christopher Castiglia, *Bound and Determined: Captivity, Culture-Crossing, and White Womanhood from Mary Rowlandson to Patty Hearst* (Chicago: University of Chicago Press, 1996), 5.

37. Price and Price, *Narrative*, xiv.

38. Ibid., lxiii–lxiv. This passage, along with many other explicit antislavery remarks, was omitted from the first published version (1796) of Stedman's *Narrative of a Five Years Expedition against the Revolted Negroes of Surinam* (original manuscript 1790) and all subsequent editions until the 1988 Richard and Sally Price edition. For a fascinating discussion of the editing of Stedman's manuscript, see the Price and Price introduction.

39. Stedman's descriptions of slave abuse were both sufficiently graphic and condemning for ardent abolitionist Thomas Wentworth Higginson, who, in his essay "The Maroons of Surinam" read the Surinamese slave rebellions through the lens of Stedman's writings on Suriname. (Though the essay does relate the history of Surinamese slave revolts, Higginson primarily retells and further romanticizes Stedman's experiences in Suriname.) See Thomas Wentworth Higginson, *Black Rebellions: Five Slave Revolts* (New York: Da Capo Press, 1998).

40. Derounian-Stodola and Levernier, *Indian Captivity Narrative*, 31.

41. Rafael Pérez-Torres, "Chicano Ethnicity, Cultural Hybridity, and the Mestizo Voice," *American Literature* 70 (1998): 158.

42. "Suriname's slave population . . . contained an unusually high ratio of Africans to Creoles, and of recently arrived Africans to seasoned slaves" (Price and Price, *Narrative*, xiv).

43. For another eighteenth-century account of the "Spanish buck" (also known as the "Spanish whip" and "Spaanse bok"), see Price, *To Slay the Hydra*, 7–8.

44. Deborah E. McDowell, "In the First Place: Making Frederick Douglass and the Afro-American Narrative Tradition," *Critical Essays on Frederick Douglass*, ed. William L. Andrews (Boston: Prentice Hall, 1991), 203.

45. Historically, the rape of a virgin has been characterized as the more transgressive act of female rape. However, in *Life and Business* the subaltern community repeatedly ranks rape of a married woman as the greater offense.

46. Hunt, *Haiti's Influence*, 20.

47. Gwilliam, "Scenes of Horror," 654.

48. Escape from a plantation did not necessarily entail permanently joining a maroon group. In many cases, marronage was temporary (hence the term *petit marronage*). I am grateful to Jacques Arends for providing me with this detail.

49. Maaja A. Stewart, "Inexhaustible Generosity: The Fictions of Eighteenth-Century British Imperialism in Richard Cumberland's *The West Indian*," *The Eighteenth Century: Theory and Interpretation* 37 (1996): 46.

50. Hunt, *Haiti's Influence*, 15–16.

Gendering the "Union of Hearts": Irish Politics between the Public and Private Spheres

MITZI MYERS

Who fears to speak of Ninety-Eight?
Who blushes at the name?

It is much less significant that men's History is made of wars than that men's wars are made of stories.

No one can write about Ireland without getting into trouble.[1]

The three epigraphs above are most obviously related to the gendering of 1798, the bloody events that precipitated the passage of the Irish Act of Union in 1800, but they apply just as readily to the Union itself.[2] The larger issues, as my title indicates, involve gender and politics. They raise the much vexed and contentious subjects of how the so-called public and private spheres interconnect (or, as some still argue, fail to) and of how women do politics, if indeed they do. In an Irish context, some might still argue that they do not. Gender concerns are arriving late to Irish studies but as the title of a recent collection—*Women and Irish History*—announces, they are arriving nonetheless. At the same time, that handy and noncommital *and* of my title yokes two discrete subjects ambiguously. Who can help recalling Virginia Woolf's musings on her similarly tricky title, "Women and Fiction"? In translating her terms to an alternative dyad, we might ask whether "Irish history" should mean what women were really like (as opposed to the feminine stereotypes of the past, perhaps); or should the phrase refer to the history that Irish women actually wrote (and, indeed, one essay in this new collection does concern women historians in Ireland); or should it call into question women and the history that is written about them? Or should it finally encompass all three concerns: an accurate portrayal of Irish women, their right to pen their own historiography, and also to correct the historiographical record? In putting the question to the phrase "women and fiction" Woolf recognized the interconnections of concerns like these, and also the difficulty of arriving at a conclusion about them in a brief essay.[3]

In situating notions past and present of a gendered Irish Union within this context of public and private spheres, of "women and fiction," of "women and Irish history," I want also to argue for a broadening of our understandings of what the Union meant, to factor genre as well as gender into the rethinking of the civil imaginary that bicentennial conferences necessitate. Wars, rebellions, and risings are not just records of military battles won or lost. Acts of Union are not just political documents enacted through men's public speech making or private bribe taking. One might parenthetically remark that David Wilkinson's recent work on massive and organized Secret Service expenditures seeks to undercut G. C. Bolton's classic on the passing of the Act of Union as a study in parliamentary politics—more or less corrupt Irish business as usual—in much the same way that the ongoing flurries of essays, monographs, and anthologies underlining United Irish organizing and propaganda seek to revise older orthodoxies on undisciplined and incoherent radical politics.[4] The explanatory paradigm of a spontaneous peasant *jacquerie* fueled by sectarian hatreds rather than radical ideologies taken for granted in mid-twentieth-century scholarship has been under sustained siege for some time, with new work appearing almost weekly.

Bicentenary reconsiderations of Ireland in 1798, like those of Revolutionary France that began almost a decade ago, bid fair to rethink not just one historical period or event, but the whole question of how history is constituted and represented. But we have scarcely begun to consider what women were doing behind the lines or behind the scenes, as in Lady Londonderry's intercession for the government scapegoat William Orr or Lady Moira's warnings to Catholic leaders like Denys Scully who, she thought (quite rightly, as it turned out), seemed too sanguine about the emancipatory potential of Union with English partnership.[5] We still don't quite know how to deal with what conduct book writers notoriously called "female influence" and modern scholars are beginning to read as informal political activity.[6] We still don't quite know how to decode the gendered formal structures and multilayered allusive strategies that authoritatively transform many women's tales into political commentary. Having addressed the general issues of gendered politics, historical agency, and representation via several exemplary Irish women, I'll conclude by analyzing one instance. A puzzling sequence in Maria Edgeworth's *Ennui* (1809) that has been read as artistic lapse when noticed at all looks very different when contextualized within the political discourses generated by the revolutionary 1790's. It suggests how a woman writer's narrative layering might query and reconstitute national political identity, how tale telling is telltale, encoding a performative political act within a fictional product. In Ireland as elsewhere narration and nation travel together; questions generated by narrative strategies are also questions about national identity.[7]

If it is now much in fashion to read Irish history as myth, as fiction, as some sort of narrative or tale, as competing and contentious stories about a past that won't stay still long enough to get depoliticized, perhaps we also need to repoliticize women's kinds of storying, their mix of fiction and history, as another gendering of Union.[8] It is quite insufficient to trot out Burke's "little platoon" as a reactionary explanation for women's overtly familial fictions or to *cherchez la femme* only in explicit representations of Irish public politics as conventionally and masculinely defined: the military maneuvers that men undertake, the Parliamentary speeches that men deliver.[9] Although recent overviews of English women's political participation and influence are beginning to query the conventional paradigm of dichotomous public and private spheres, much new Irish scholarship does not.[10] It is noteworthy and regrettable that emergent archival investigation concerning Irish women and 1798 too often reproduces the "rigid distinction between male and female roles" that is said to refuse women's admission to the "political process." Because rebellion was "perceived as men's work," women could be "symbol or model or victim but . . . the role of actor, activist or combatant—*in a political context*—was denied them."[11] Ironically, in arguing that "if the recent progressive trend of social, cultural and political re-evaluation of 1798 is to advance, other aspects of the experience must be addressed," Ruan O'Donnell's exemplary "other"—treacherous "Croppy Biddy" Dolan of Wicklow—is nevertheless situated within the familiar framework of proactive participation in rebellion and its aftermath.[12]

Although I will be citing specific genderings of the Irish Act of Union, epecially those by men past and present, I will also be thinking more globally about gender and multiple acts of union, arguing that writing is cultural work, that literature both reflects and effects social change and that "literature" as conceptualized at the time of the Union cannot be segregated tidily into "fiction" and "history." Nor—as the cases of feminocentric novels of sensibility and "political" tracts by Mary Wollstonecraft, anti-union political pamphlets by her pupil Margaret King, Lady Mount Cashell, later "Mrs. Mason," and especially Irish regional (and "English") novels for adults by Maria Edgeworth demonstrate—can women writers' grownup productions be severed from supposedly "minor" genres such as stories for the young and manuals for parents.[13] How is it that developmental narratives constituting human subjectivity and developmental narratives of national identity have been so long disunited, anyway? Like the public record offices, Rebellion papers, and politicians' manuscripts so revealingly plundered of late, women's fictions deserve the archival attention necessary to disclose the layerings of textual and social complexity, of ideological sophistication, that have been too long overlooked. And so do their interventionist actions as writers and makers of history.[14]

When historians of an earlier period talked about women's part in Irish politics, as in Mrs. Thomas Concannon's *Women of Ninety-Eight* (1919), they knew their subjects' place in relation to public events: "The Mothers of 'Ninety-Eight,'" "The Wives of 'Ninety-Eight,'" the sisters, the romantic partners, and, in a brief concluding section, obscure heroines of the "White Terror" that was the Rebellion's aftermath. Alternatively, of course, as in one 1968 male writer's pop recycling, war's women can be sentimentally privatized as *Sweethearts of the Irish Rebels*, thrilling models for today's young women to emulate because "They Lived and Loved in the Shadow of the Gallows."[15] Perhaps most striking among Concannon's more dignified pantheon is Mrs. Denis Downey, whose bloody prophetic dreams of her husband's death are of course realized. Having turned over two hundred corpses, she wraps her man in a sheet and must consign him to a mass grave; she sells the wrecked family farm and retreats elsewhere. For Concannon, her story is synecdoche, presenting "to our imagination the tragedy of the 'Widows of the Massacre' in concrete form." Although "the story of only one woman," we must "think of it as multiplied by the number of all the women who were left desolate. . . . and estimate these contributions to the sum of woman's misery—if our hearts dare." No wonder Concannon's epigraph for her highly dramatic histories comes from William Drennan's "Lament of the Women after the Battle": "Alas! how sad by Shannon's flood, / The blush of morning sun appears! / To men who gave for us their blood, / Ah! what can women give but tears!"—verses that might be read as a translation of Drennan's Latin epigraph for his famous elegy on the Protestant martyr William Orr, the "Wake" of 1797, "Feminis lugere, honestum est: viris, meminisse," a borrowing from Tacitus that counsels "It is right for men to mourn and women to remember." Even when men witness, as Drennan's elegy continues, "Monstrous and unhappy sight! / Brothers' blood will not unite. / Holy oil and holy water, / Mix—and fill the earth with slaughter," they must not weep, but watch for the Enlightening dawn, the "morning light" that prefigures a true union of brothers.[16]

And presumably sisters, for, as every reader of Drennan's correspondence knows, his sister and the female kin of the rebels whom Concannon's history lauds, kept their sturdy radical politics, richly contextualized and documented by more recent historians of Antrim and Down.[17] Citing Mary Wollstonecraft (whose Irish ancestry and pivotal Irish experiences often go unemphasized), these women energetically devoted themselves to philanthropy, pedagogy, and the public good.[18] Indeed, Drennan himself, whose role as the initiator of a United Irish brotherhood is still popularly elided in favor of Wolfe Tone's dashing bravado and tragic death, worked for decades after the political Union he opposed to effect a different kind of union through education. Emulating Mary Wollstonecraft, her former pupil Margaret King—whose fictional prototype Mary in her governess's *Original Stories from Real Life: With Conversations, Calculated to Regulate the Affections, and Form the Mind to Truth and Goodness* (1788) "wish[es] to be a woman . . . and to be like Mrs. Mason"—assumed that name from Wollstonecraft's idealized teacher (and self-portrait) in the tales. The student "Mary" of the *Stories* became a real-life "Mrs. Mason" after she abandoned her husband Lord Mount Cashell in 1805 for George Tighe.[19] Daughter to one of Ireland's largest landowners and sister to Lord Kingsborough, reputed popularizer of pitchcapping the peasantry and leader of the murderous North Cork Militia, scourges of the Wexford insurgents, Margaret Jane King Moore, wife of Stephen Moore, the second Earl of Mount Cashell, called herself a United Irishwoman, was suspected by the government as an associate of Lord Edward Fitzgerald, and twenty years later wrote Wollstonecraft's daughter, Mary Shelley, that her "nerves have never recovered the shake" from the rebellion and its tragic aftermath: "since my country sank never to rise again, I have been a cool politician; but I cannot forget how I once felt, and can still sympathize with those capable of similar feelings."[20]

Attributed with three pamphlets against the Union by scholars of the Shelleys and their circle, Margaret King refigured as "Mrs. Mason" lived an active philanthropic life abroad, producing children's books for William Godwin's Juvenile Library and the guide to the physical management of infants that Mary Wollstonecraft projected but never lived to write. Before and after the official Act of Union, her cultural activities for the public good strikingly contrast with those of her brother, "Big George," notorious not only for his wanton killings but also for his sexual exploitation of the female petitioners who tried to ransom their kin from governmental clutches. Whether involved with Lord Edward and other Dublin radicals, visiting the 1794 treason trials in London, or impersonating "Old Daniel" for William Godwin's Juvenile Library from her Italian exile, Margaret King's war and peace work form a continuum. For Big George, gendering the Union meant torturing men and raping women's bodies, complaining all the while that he took so few maidenheads among the poor women he abused.[21] It's worth recalling that when Wollstonecraft was updating the second edition of *Original Stories* (the 1791 text that first included Blake's famous illustrations), she was also composing the *Vindication of the Rights of Woman* (1792). The first is shunted aside as literature for the nursery; the second is historicized as public female political activism, even though it was intended, read, and favorably reviewed as a revisionary work of education. It mentions votes for women just once, as a distant possibility.[22] So how do we categorize what is "public" and what is "private"; what counts as "history" and what belongs to "fiction"?

To return for a moment to Helena Concannon, discussed in Mary O'Dowd's "From Morgan to MacCurtain: Women Historians in Ireland from the 1790s to the 1990s," which starts with citing generically diverse late eighteenth- and early nineteenth-century writers like Maria Edgeworth (especially for the antiquarian notes to *Castle Rackrent*) and Sydney Owenson, Lady Morgan, and with noting that for women writers in Ireland, historical experience both lived and literary is mapped onto a number of generic forms (including biography and personal narrative), thus blurring binaries of fiction and history, and I would add, of public and private spheres. Uniting recurrent motifs that O'Dowd identifies, Concannon, perhaps the most prolific author to date on the history of Irish women, conflates the female role model of heroic kin to politicized men with the valorization of Catholic womanhood and Irish nationalism. As O'Dowd notes, she was nominated for a Senate seat by de Valera in the 1930s and probably shaped his views on Irish women and their place in society, so that female history writing had direct political consequences. Thus Concannon, whose dramatic narratives of woman as heroic and usually grieving accessory to man's political acts seem at first to be comfortably legible, turns out to be indicatively problematic. Before we can think concretely about the gendering of the Act of Union and of representations thereof, we might hazard a redefinition of traditional historical assumptions about what constitutes politics and what counts as female citizenship, active playership in the political narrative. Women were busy on the hustings, in bread riots, in benevolent and educational associations; without unduly glamorizing female

Whiteboys, Masons, United Irish adjuncts, or women warriors, we might more broadly conceive of politics, as Maria Luddy suggests in her work on nineteenth-century organizations like the early anti-slavery societies and the later Ladies' Land League, as including individual or group actions that formally or informally seek to affect or alter government policy or the beliefs and behaviors of more local persons or communities, for the benefit of a certain group or constituency.[23] An individual working for individual ends does not qualify; a "didactic" novelist intervening in the public literary sphere to reshape the civic polity surely does.

The eighteenth century's naughty fiction-reading misses know, as George Colman's Polly Honeycombe famously announces in Garrick's 1760 Epilogue, that "novels will teach us all the art of war." But female readers and writers also show that novels can step outside the usual courtship plots and marital unions to teach all the arts of peace as well.[24] By way of illustrating the interpenetration of fiction and history, the lengthy Extract (presumably of Polly's reading repertoire) preceding Colman's "Dramatick Novel" contains an extraordinary number of "histories," "adventures," "lives," and "memoirs," although most critique of female reading pays more attention to lubricious single entries like "Fair Adultress." It's important to notice that, even if Polly was not, later eighteenth-century women were intellectually interested in the production and reception of historical knowledge, not just steered toward it because it was safer than romances.[25] Anyone reading about gender, Ireland, and women writers can be certain that Maria Edgeworth will turn up. And she does turn up, rather surprisingly, in what looks like odd company at first glance, for *Castle Rackrent* (1800) is C3 among the entries labeled "An Annotated Alphabetical Title-List of the Pamphlets with Call Numbers for Copies Preserved in the Major Libraries of the British Isles," which makes up most of W. J. McCormack's *The Pamphlet Debate on the Union Between Great Britain and Ireland, 1797–1800*.[26]

Although many of the polemicists are anonymous, there are at least two other women among them and perhaps many more who remain unrecognized (despite attributions elsewhere). Take, for example, Mrs. Mason, whose three anti-union pamphlets can be identified in McCormack's list only by consulting scholarship on the Shelley circle, even though these works are ascribed to her in the National Library.[27] There are apparently no other novels besides that of Edgeworth that properly belong to this pamphlet debate. Bill McCormack, who has also edited Edgeworth, does not elaborate on *Castle Rackrent*'s anomalous inclusion. Nor am I going to digress on what position in the Union controversy that enigmatic and emblematic tale might occupy. Literary historians invariably note that 1800 marks both the passage of the Act of Union, the statute making Great Britain and Ireland legally one nation, and the publication of *Castle Rackrent*, the narrative conventionally designated as the originary Anglo-Irish fiction and canonically located as the first "regional" novel. Because Maria Edgeworth's earliest tale published for an adult market self-consciously constructs its real world readers as well as its fictional subjects as polyglot, it's not surprising that no critic has yet succeeded in imposing a unitary reading on the story's ironic dialogue of variant Celt and Saxon voices, neither of which is univocal. Even the title—*An Hibernian Tale Taken From Facts, and From the Manners of the Irish Squires, Before the Year 1782*—veers in different directions, and the story and its multiple layers of apparatus have been variantly interpreted as to genre, gender, ethnicity, and Unionism. It was initially published anonymously and widely thought to be by a man until the vexed author claimed her work, so that it exemplifies the blurred boundaries and multiple unions this essay thematizes. It would require many pages of notes on its notes to demonstrate the history in its fictions and the fictions in its history, not to mention its imbrications in public and private politics.

Unlike McCormack's earlier, highly argumentative *Dublin Paper War of 1786–1788: A Bibliographical and Critical Inquiry Including An Account of the Origins of Protestant Ascendancy and its "Baptism" in 1792*, this bibliography on the Union has minimal apparatus, and readers can use it as they will. McCormack revealingly remarks, however, that except for the Glorious Revolution, "no earlier event in Anglo-Irish relations had been so self-consciously historical than [*sic*] the union," because the intervening period "had witnessed a revolution in intellectual activity, with history increasingly influential not so much as the hand-maid but as the fairy-godmother of politics"—or, as the obsessively anti-Catholic rebellion historian Richard Musgrave might read Clio, as the wicked witch of Rome.[28] At the same time that it feminizes "history," McCormack's list implicitly genders the controversy over the Union as masculine and conventionally "political," a matter of print culture and debate in the public sphere that Terry Eagleton argues Ireland did not develop (hence all the violence).[29] How the individual polemicists typically gender union and translate their political positions into narrative mode is nicely illustrated by the title of a pamphlet that Richard Lovell Edgeworth happened to own, now in the Royal Irish Academy. We know from various catalogues of the family's extensive library that this is only one of many pamphlets that they acquired, although the shelf lists unfortunately do not give full titles as does McCormack.

This title, W2 in his collection, is T. Canning's *The Wedding and Bedding, or John Bull and His Bride Fast Asleep, A Satirical Poem Containing an History of the Happy Pair from Their Infancy to the Present Period, with*

Reasons for and Means Used to Accomplish Their Union; Also The Matchmakers Matched, with their Rueful Lamentation for the Loss of the Bride-Cake! That's a lot of narrative modes to pack into only fifty-six pages, and it neatly demonstrates the masculine "historical" text as gendered literary artifact. Or consider two of the pithy "bulls" on the Union produced by Sir Boyle Roche, notorious for his verbal entanglements: "'Sir, there is no Levitical degrees between nations, and on this occasion I can see neither sin nor shame in *marrying our own sister*'"—or, again, "England, it must be allowed, is the mother country, and therefore, I advise them (England and Ireland) to live in filial affection together like sisters, as they are, and ought to be." Reviewing John O'Driscol's *The History of Ireland* for the *Edinburgh Review* in October 1827, Francis Jeffrey genders a more jaundiced view of contemplated divorce: "Two such countries, after all that has passed between them, could no more live in quiet and comfort beside each other, than a wife who had deserted her husband's house could live again in his society and that of his family, as a friend or visitor." By now, "the sister island" has become "an exasperated matron, whose domestic grievances had led her to contemplate such a fatal step."[30] Readers at this point are invited to identify two more quotations—the one in the title (along with its source) and this reflection on "History, [that] when divested of the graces of eloquence, and of that veil which the imagination is taught to throw over antiquity, presents a disgusting, terrible list of crimes and calamities; murders, assassinations, battles, revolutions, are the memorable events of history." If it is surmised that the "union of hearts" derives from private female sentiment and the indictment of history from a masculine public author (say, Edward Gibbon or William Godwin), the assumptions are incorrect. The first is Ireland's elder statesman, Henry Grattan, in national political debate; the second is Maria Edgeworth, representing men's standard histories from the private child reader's perspective.[31]

Introducing an anthology tellingly entitled *Ideology and the Historians*, Ciaran Brady observes that "Historical writing is always conducted by means of synecdoche . . . one set of details . . . selected from the mass of evidence to represent the whole of the phenomenon described. But because such a selection can never be replicated . . . historical argument can never be 'falsified' in scientific terms. Thus . . . historical controversies have generally displayed strikingly closed formal structures."[32] French historian Robert Gildea, seeking a more inclusive story of the past, argues that no "objective, universally agreed history" is possible and that "what matters is myth, not in the sense of fiction, but in the sense of a construction of the past elaborated by a political community for its own ends. Similarly there are only histories, mediated by different cultures, providing a multitude of viewpoints on the same events or historical figures, for the benefit of political communities, and reconstructed over time to meet their needs."[33] Yet neither noted historian considers the literary. What this essay suggests is that we direct the parturient labors that a bicentenary calls forth and devote some archival energy to locales hitherto unmapped in Irish studies, that we look for elusive political traces elsewhere than men's official records or even celebrated female Irish fictions like Edgeworth's *Castle Rackrent*, that we open out Brady's closed forms to include literary genres from novels to parent manuals and children's tales and that we devote sufficient contextualizing energies to these to see how they signify.

Maria Edgeworth is just one example, but an especially noteworthy one because politics are everywhere in her oeuvre, in the "British" novels, in the tales for children and adolescents, in the manual *Practical Education* for parents published in 1798, but only if we're as clever as the decoders in the highly political "English" novel, *Patronage* (1814). Learned and witty, subtle and sly, urbane and extraordinarily allusive, Edgeworth solicits readers with minds as alert and agile as her own. Almost always, however, critics and interpreters arrive impenetrably armed with preconceptions and ready-to-wear interpretations. What they expect, they find: that Edgeworth didn't take herself seriously as an artist, that she wasted too much time on educational writing and children's stories (which can of course be conveniently ignored when postcolonializing her Irish, Jamaican, or Oriental tales), and that her authorship dribbled away into insignificance after her father's death. Richard Lovell Edgeworth's adoring daughter supposedly reproduces his experiences, ventriloquizes his opinions on improving landlordism, political economy and practical education, and produces moral tales labeled transparently sociological when they work and awkwardly allegorical when literary mechanics obtrude on the reader's attention.

Edgeworth is not Jane Austen. Well-wrought courtship plots are not her forte, and her work resists the aestheticizing and extrahistoricity still available to Janeites, despite much recent contentious scholarship that demonstrates and contextualizes Austen's implication in multiple wars of ideas. Nor is Edgeworth an Irish Walter Scott. She does not, like her Scottish admirer, distance past gore and package colonialist politics within exfoliating prefaces and afterwords that foreground literary conventions and marketplace economics. Thus her tales have not fueled the endless debates on the problematics of fiction and history or on the relation between gender and a putatively remasculinized and thereby respectable novel that characterize Scott scholarship. Edgeworth can write like a man. She is fond of male narrators, as in Glenthorn of *Ennui*, and ghosted much of her father's publication, including official addresses to the Irish Lord Lieutenant; and she was reviewed with the same respect accorded Scott, the serious "manly" author. But Edgeworth is too ironic and Enlightened, too much of the interventionist educator and the philosophical Whig, to be romanticized into a Jacobite storyteller whose plots and treasons are safely past. Around 1867, Jane Austen's niece Caroline Austen recorded that "A very warm admirer of my Aunt's writing but a stranger in England, lately made the observation that it would be most interesting to know what had been Miss Austen's opinion on the great public events of her time. . . . anyone *might* naturally desire to know what part such a mind as her's [*sic*] had taken in the great strifes of war and policy which so disquieted Europe for more than 20 years—and yet, it was a question that had never before presented itself to me—and tho' I have *now* retraced my steps on *this* track, I have found absolutely nothing!"[34] Given the proliferation of late-twentieth-century studies on Austen as politically and ideologically aware (however contradictorily scholars read those encoded politics), we can only express amazement at what Caroline Austen did not see. Before we amuse ourselves at her expense, however, we might better ask what we do not yet see—and why so much work considering the novel and political economy, the novel and disciplinarity, the novel and literary history, and a dozen other subjects continues to see Jane Austen as the only woman writer who counts in mounting a large historical argument. Is it because she is familiar territory instantly available for remapping, already nicely footnoted, much discussed and much annotated, a way to do politics, to read the history in fiction and the fiction in history without descending into the messiness of archives?

What has not yet been noticed about that odd chapter midway through *Ennui* briefly illustrates how political commentary is interpolated within Edgeworth's fictional genres, and, more broadly, how historical archives help excavate literary structures, making visible women writers' oblique political engagement. In the thirteenth chapter, Glenthorn takes a tour, an odd gap between the tale's layered narratives of overt and subterranean rebellion.[35] The preceding chapters show the pseudo-aristocrat anti-hero beginning to stir from the lethargy that will plague him until he finally discovers he is really an Irish peasant, an impostor switched at birth for the real heir by his foster nurse and true mother, Ellinor. Through the revelations of Ellinor, the chapters following the enigmatic thirteenth dramatically uncover the hidden plots surrounding Glenthorn in the aftermath of 1798, a private "White Terror" in which his own servants turn outlaws who seek him first as leader and ultimately as prey to slaughter when he has served their purposes. The confessions of Ellinor that follow hard upon the squelching of these guerrilla warriors movingly reveal the secret identity that turns the wastrel wimp into a courageous individual who can then educate and ready himself for an emblematic final marital union that brings together multiple Irish identities. What do we make of Glenthorn's relapse into "my former inactivity" after the stir of the Rising, seeking but not finding solace in tourism, as he visits "the only things I had ever heard mentioned as worth seeing in Ireland": the already hackneyed sites of the Giant's Causeway and the Lake of Killarney, along with the latter's obligatory stag hunt on the water (245, 248). The hero is too listless to care as the guidebooks say he should, and his dawdling travels don't advance the plot. What is Edgeworth up to? What connections and inferences might be available to earlier readers that must be laboriously mapped to document the author's public awareness and revisionary narrative moves? What can we learn from history that makes this fiction make sense?

Setting aside the literary intertextualities and coded politics that link the Giant's Causeway visit with the Killarney stag hunt, I shall look only at the very long footnote that takes up virtually all of two pages (251–52), almost a record even for Edgeworth, who achieves much political referentiality through such encrypted messages. Glenthorn says that he relies on a "Guide to the Lakes" not further specified. The Penguin edition remarks that this odd interpolation is "apparently a parody of Carr's overwritten description of the Killarney stag-hunt," referring to John Carr's 1806 *The Stranger in Ireland: Or, A Tour in the Southern and Western Parts of That Country, in the Year 1805*, recently critiqued for the *Edinbugh Review* by Edgeworth and her father. But there is no stag hunt in Carr's travelogue, because inclement weather often made the long chase, cornering, and killing of the baffled deer impossible.[36] Edgeworth does not to my knowledge make up any footnotes, but she really knows how to make footnotes count for alert readers. Following hard upon the description of the Rising that some critics of *Ennui* have found bland or evasive is the deer's bloody murder, graphically detailed from the shouting crowds about the lake through the desperate animal's entrapment and plunge into the lake as "the hounds roar with redoubled fury at the sight of their victim." But the prey just exchanges "one merciless enemy" for another, the boatmen who finish off the majestic stag, haltered and dragged to shore "while the big tears roll down his face, and his heaving sides and panting flanks speak his agonies, the keen searching knife drinks his blood, and savages exult at his expiring groan" (251).

Although Glenthorn's travel guide warns him that the hunt after the frantic stag is so exciting that "in his raptures and ecstasies he may forget himself, and jump out of the boat," he does not have that much energy. He is at least "kept awake this whole morning" by a spectacle he himself compares to the decadent Roman contests between gladiators and wild beasts, but he cannot yet articulate the analogies that the author expects from her audience (252–53). The woman writer and the politically aware reader are collaborators who share an investment in the rational public sphere of discourse from which the effeminized pseudo-aristocrat Glenthorn is at this point debarred. He cannot say or see what the writer and reader notice. Edgeworth has real sources, and the two very popular travel books she draws from are overlaid here with a Shakespearean reference to one of the most famous scenes from *As You Like It.* Exiled to the Forest of Arden, even the Duke who can find "good in every thing" stumbles over the wretched stag left mutilated and weeping, one of the "native burghers of this desert city" gored by transgressive intruders in "their own confines." The readers who did not recognize John Bush's and Philip Luckombe's descriptions of the Killarney stag's ritualized death would surely recall Jaques's invective against colonizers of Arden, including even the good Duke as "mere usurpers, tyrants" killing the local animals "In their assign'd and native dwelling-place." As the mordant Jaques moralizes, there are, despite the good Duke's pronouncement, no lives "exempt from public haunt" in Arden (II.ii).[37] Edgeworth's allusive lamination cross-writes history and fiction, implicating all, "Orange" or "Green," who resort to war instead of working for Enlightened peace and a reparative union that might heal the hurts of Irish history.

Only when the fictive Glenthorn recognizes himself as an Irish child can he learn and progress, and for Edgeworth real Irish children are still more important. Key to the positive remaking of Irish identity that Edgeworth envisions are the young, who must be educated to reform the nation. Having failed to convince the bellicose Ascendancy Parliament that nondenominational state education for every Irish child deserved priority over hanging, shooting, and burning, Richard Lovell Edgeworth took his eldest daughter and fourth wife on a belated honeymoon trip while the first round of post-Rebellion debates over the proposed Union between Great Britain and Ireland was still going on. "Tell Sneyd that there is a political print just come out, of a woman, meant for Hibernia, dressed in orange and green, and holding a pistol in her hand to oppose the Union," Maria Edgeworth wrote on 2 April 1799.[38] Scribbled en route to England, Edgeworth's tidbit for her much younger half-brother provocatively juxtaposes national iconography and themes perhaps even more crucial to her achievement than the acclaimed *Castle Rackrent*: children as agents in and audiences for both juvenile and adult fictions, the 1798 Rebellion and the unreadable Hibernia produced by civil war, her father's radical "Education Bill" and the revisionary tales for and about the Irish young added to the expanded edition of her *Parent's Assistant* (1800). Discordantly garbed in reactionary Orange and revolutionary green, conventionally feminized as "Hibernia," yet martially (or suicidally) armed: how can this illegible image of home make sense for young Sneyd?

Shelley proclaimed poets the great unacknowledged legislators of the world. As only full contextualization can reveal, Maria Edgeworth put her faith elsewhere, in the new cultural space opened out by vernacular education and her own penchant for densely allusive cross-writing. Multivocal by virtue of her ambiguous national situation and class sympathies, her dual status as a rational public authority and a feeling private daughter, her generic experiments and innovation, and, above all, by virtue of her ongoing engagement with educational and juvenile writing, she merits rethinking from the variety of current theoretical perspectives—feminist, historical, postmodern, postcolonial—that position female authors as border crossers, as literary unionists who bridge public and private spheres. Only when the Pickering and Chatto annotated edition does for Maria Edgeworth what the contextualized works have done for Mary Shelley can we begin to understand how children brawling over cherries, Irish orphans achieving a house and business of their own, and the white pigeon that makes a little boy's fortune are, for Edgeworth, the thoroughly politicized creatures of 1798, bespeaking unionist positions continuous with the emblematically "Irish" *Castle Rackrent* or the dazzlingly allusive "English" *Belinda* (1801). Instead of looking at women only in the context of their supportive relationships with men, we need also to re-view female literary work within the context of male political actions, seeing each as equally engaged in the discursive public sphere. When Martha McTier, Mary Ann McCracken, and Mary Leadbeater undertake educational work and highly intellectual private writings and discussions, when Margaret Bond (whose husband Oliver was a member of the Leinster directory of United Irishmen) smuggles forbidden writing tools and secret communications into Kilmainham Jail inside a pie crust, when Maria Edgeworth evokes assassination and rebellion by way of her hero's tourism to the Giant's Causeway and the Killarney stag hunt, we should be seeing more than a schoolroom, a dessert, and a bloody deer. Concannon's terrible vignette of the young girl murdered by yeomen and buried so shallowly where she fell that her long hair waved enigmatically in the breeze aboveground can also figure other facts about women from the period yet awaiting the scholar's unearthing.[39]

NOTES

1. The sources of the epigraphs are John Kells Ingram, "The Memory of the Dead," in Georges-Denis Zimmermann, *Songs of Irish Rebellion: Political Street Ballads and Rebel Songs 1780–1900* (Hatboro, PA: Folklore Associates, 1967), 226–27; Nancy Huston, "Tales of War and Tears of Women," *Women and Men's Wars*, ed. Judith Hicks Stiehm, *Women's Studies International Forum* 5.3–4 (1982): 271; and Halliday Sullivan, *Irish Journey* (London: Geoffrey Bles, 1956), 1. Ingram's 1843 Young Ireland product is said to have been composed following a convivial Trinity College discussion of the Rising: the man who "hangs his head for shame" at slaughter is no man, but "a true man, like you, man, Will fill your glass with us." Even though Ingram later became a Unionist opposed to violence, he still included the song in his 1900 works.

2. The Act took effect 1 January 1801, coincidentally the birthday (in 1768) of Maria Edgeworth.

3. See Mary O'Dowd, "From Morgan to MacCurtain: Women Historians in Ireland from the 1790s to the 1990s," in *Women and Irish History: Essays in Honour of Margaret MacCurtain*, ed. Maryann Gilanella Valiulis and Mary O'Dowd (Dublin: Wolfhound Press, 1997), 38–58; Virginia Woolf, *A Room of One's Own*, 1929, Harbinger Books (New York: Harcourt, Brace, and World, 1957), 3.

4. See David Wilkinson, "'How Did They Pass the Union?' Secret Service Expenditure in Ireland, 1799–1804," *History* 82.266 (April 1997): 224–51; and G. C. Bolton, *The Passing of the Irish Act of Union: A Study in Parliamentary Politics* (Oxford: Oxford Univ. Press, 1966).

5. Alexander Haliday informs Lord Charlemont during the notoriously repressive Armagh troubles that "our dear countess [Londonderry's second wife and Earl Camden's sister] has done all it was possible for her to do" to forestall the execution and martyrdom of Orr (6 October 1797), in James Caulfeild, *The Manuscripts and Correspondence of James, First Earl of Charlemont: Vol. 2 1784–1799*, Historical Manuscripts Commission, Thirteenth Report, Appendix, Part 7 (London: Eyre and Spottiswoode, 1894), 306; for a succinct account of Orr's framed case, see A. T. Q. Stewart, *The Summer Soldiers: The 1798 Rebellion in Antrim and Down* (Belfast: Blackstaff Press, 1995), 45–53. "It seems to me singular to approve of a measure before your religious persuasion know what you are to get by it. If you are put upon the footing with the Roman Catholics in England you will [be] worse off than you are at present. . . . Ireland has made speedy advances in its welfare since America has made itself independent—Its own Parliament must as that increases favor the majority of the nation, but the Roman Catholics when united to England will not be the majority of the British Empire—Sound policy prompts your persuasion therefore to keep yourselves as a political majority," writes Lady Moira on 13 September 1799, *The Catholic Question in Ireland and England, 1798–1822: The Papers of Denys Scully*, ed. Brian MacDermot (Dublin: Irish Academic Press, 1988), 40.

6. See, for example, Linda Colley, *Britons: Forging the Nation, 1707–1837* (New Haven: Yale Univ. Press, 1992), ch. 6, "Womanpower," citing Mitzi Myers, "Reform or Ruin: 'A Revolution in Female Manners,'" *Studies in Eighteenth-Century Culture*, ed. Harry C. Payne (Madison: Univ. of Wisconsin Press, 1982), 11: 119–216, reprinted in the revised Norton Critical Edition of Mary Wollstonecraft's *A Vindication of the Rights of Woman*, ed. Carol H. Poston (New York: W. W. Norton, 1988).

7. Twentieth-century postcolonial fiction and criticism cast revealing lights on much earlier narrative strategies. Consider, for example, the counterhegemonic and pedagogic, even didactic, function of many African narratives. Chinua Achebe, among others, frankly considers himself a teacher, who helps readers bring into being "an alternative world beyond the realities imprisoned in colonial and postcolonial relations of power," Simon Gikandi, *Reading Chinua Achebe: Language and Ideology in Fiction* (London: James Currey; Portsmouth, N.H.: Heinemann, 1991), 3.

8. R[oy] F. Foster, *The Story of Ireland: An Inaugural Lecture Delivered before the University of Oxford on 1 December 1994* (Oxford: Clarendon Press, 1995), typifies the storying approach to Irish studies. As Kevin Whelan observes, in what is becoming the most widely quoted passage on variant interpretations of 1798, "the rebellion never passed into history, because it never passed out of politics." Thus 1798 is still being refought in words, because to control war's meaning is to obtain political legitimacy, so that interpretations of 1798 from the "high drama of the Union debate" to the present seek to mold public opinion and to influence policy formation. Despite his having written on the power of alternative literary forms in shaping political attitudes, however, Whelan hews closely to standard historical genres in his influential "'98 After '98: The Politics of Memory," *The Tree of Liberty: Radicalism, Catholicism, and the Construction of Irish Identity, 1760–1830* (Notre Dame, Ind: Univ. of Notre Dame Press in association with Field Day, 1996), 133–75, quoted at 133.

9. "To be attached to the subdivision, to love the little platoon we belong to in society, is the first principle (the germ as it were) of public affections. It is the first link in the series by which we proceed towards a love to our country and to mankind," Edmund Burke, *Reflections on the Revolution in France and on the Proceedings in Certain Societies in London Relative to that Event*, ed. Conor Cruise O'Brien, 1790 (Harmondsworth, Eng.: Penguin Books, 1969), 135. Burke's linkage between the family and the state, the private and the public, has a long lineage. If it is exploited by conservatives of the 1790's to valorize the domestic woman, it is equally available for reformist rethinking of the continuity and inseparability of the "private" and "public" spheres.

10. Karl Von Den Steinen's pioneering "The Discovery of Women in Eighteenth-Century English Political Life," *The Women of England From Anglo-Saxon Times to the Present: Interpretive Bibliographical Essays*, ed. Barbara Kanner (Hamden, Conn.: Archon Books, 1979), 229–58, is applicable to both elite and middling women's works. For representative examples, see Elaine Chalus, "'That Epidemical Madness': Women and Electoral Politics in the Late Eighteenth Century"; and

Amanda Foreman, "A Politician's Politician: Georgiana, Duchess of Devonshire, and the Whig Party," both in *Gender in Eighteenth-Century England: Roles, Representations, and Responsibilities*, ed. Hannah Barker and Elaine Chalus (London and New York: Longman, 1997), 151–78; 179–204; and Mitzi Myers, "'A Peculiar Protection': Hannah More and the Cultural Politics of the Blagdon Controversy," *History, Gender, and Eighteenth-Century Literature*, ed. Beth F. Tobin (Athens: Univ. of Georgia Press, 1994), 227–57. Even as they argue for women's inclusion, however, historians' facts and interpretations may be at odds, as in P. J. Jupp, "The Roles of Royal and Aristocratic Women in British Politics, c. 1782–1832," *Chattel, Servant, or Citizen: Women's Status in Church, State, and Society*, ed. Mary O'Dowd and Sabine Wichert, Historical Studies 29 (Belfast, Queen's Univ. of Belfast Institute of Irish Studies, 1995), 103–13. Also, scholars who are seemingly mutually involved in the needed reconfiguration of past politics may disagree as to the shape of emergent female agency: see, for example, Linda Colley, reviewing Foreman's *Georgiana: Duchess of Devonshire* (London: HarperCollins, 1998), in "An Icon of Fashion," *TLS* 4965 (29 May 1998): 15–16.

11. Quotations in the text are, respectively, from the otherwise exciting essays by Dáire Keogh, "The Women of 1798: Representations and Realities," *1798, 200 Years of Resonance: Essays and Contributions on the History and Relevance of the United Irishmen and the 1798 Revolution*, ed. Mary Cullen (Dublin: Irish Reporter Publications, 1998), 64–65; and Thomas Bartlett, "Bearing Witness: Female Evidences in Courts Martial Convened to Suppress the 1798 Rebellion," *The Women of 1798*, ed. Dáire Keogh and Nicholas Furlong (Dublin: Four Courts Press, 1998), 65, 67 (italics in original). The latter collection will be supplemented by John D. Beatty, ed., *The Rebellion Remembered: Protestant Women's Narratives of the Irish Rebellion of 1798* (Fort Wayne, Ind.: Round Tower Books, forthcoming). Another recent overview is Mary Cullen, "Partners in Struggle: The Women of 1798," in *The Great Irish Rebellion of 1798*, ed. Cathal Póirtéir, The Thomas Davis Lecture Series (Dublin: Mercier Press; Boulder, Colorado: Irish American Book Company, 1998), 146–59.

12. Ruan O'Donnell, "Bridget 'Croppy Biddy' Dolan: Wicklow's Anti-Heroine of 1798," in *The Women of 1798*, ed. Keogh and Furlong, quoted at 87. As Jim Smyth notes in his omnibus review of recent work, "Interpreting the 1790s," *1798 Rebellion Special Issue, History Ireland* 6.2 (Summer 1998): 55, these essays must be taken as "an introduction to, rather than a comprehensive treatment of, the gendering of late eighteenth-century Ireland," for although "the usual suspects are included," many others, including "the prime suspect, Maria Edgesworth [*sic*]" are missing. He might have added that certain genres, as well as certain people, have gone missing. For analyses of "the prime suspect" with comprehensive notes on contemporary critiques of the public-private sphere dichotomy, see Mitzi Myers, "'Completing the Union': Critical *Ennui*, the Politics of Narrative, and the Reformation of Irish Cultural Identity," *The Intersections of the Public and Private Spheres*, ed. Paula R. Backscheider and Timothy Dykstal, *Prose Studies: History, Theory, Criticism* 18.3 (December 1995): 41–77; "'Like the Pictures in a Magic Lantern': Gender, History, and Edgeworth's Rebellion Narratives," *Special Issue:*

Writing Women/Writing Power, Nineteenth-Century Contexts 19.4 (1996): 373–412; and "War Correspondence: Edgeworth and the En-Gendering of Revolution, Rebellion, and Union," *Special Issue: Ireland, 1798–1998: From Revolution to Revisionism and Beyond*, ed. Mitzi Myers and Robert P. Maccubbin, *Eighteenth-Century Life* 22 n.s. 3 (November 1998): 74–91, especially the updated references in n. 14.

13. These are but a few of the notable women writers who have produced work for young readers and not just to turn a penny. Supposedly innocuous tales for children may also function as carriers of radical ideologies, as can educational treatises.

14. Representative examples of current trends in cultural studies that rethink the symbiotic relationship between history and fiction and that query conventional classificatory enterprises differentiating "history" from "literature" include Deidre Lynch and William B. Warner, ed., *Cultural Institutions of the Novel* (Durham and London: Duke Univ. Press, 1996); Clifford Siskin, *The Work of Writing: Literature and Social Change in Britain, 1700–1830* (Baltimore: Johns Hopkins Univ. Press, 1998); and *Pierre Bourdieu and Literary History*, a special issue of *Modern Language Quarterly* 48.4 (December 1997).

15. The front and back matter for Seamus G. O'Kelly, *Sweethearts of the Irish Rebels* (Dublin: A1 Books, 1968), incongruously published at the start of Anglo-American feminism's last wave, solicits young female readers "to be true to their Great Traditions" of loving doomed revolutionaries.

16. Mrs. Thomas [Helena] Concannon, *Women of Ninety-Eight*, 1919, 4th impression (Dublin: M. H. Gill, 1930), 315 (Mrs. Downey), ix (epigraph); William Drennan, *Glendalloch, and Other Poems, By the Late Dr. Drennan, with Additional Verses by His Sons*, 2nd ed. (Dublin: William Robertson, 1859), 45–47.

17. See William Drennan, *The Drennan Letters*, ed. D. A. Chart (Belfast: H. M. Stationery Office, 1931); Mary McNeill, *The Life and Times of Mary Ann McCracken 1770–1866: A Belfast Panorama*, 1960 (Belfast: Blackstaff Press, 1988); John Gray, "Mary Anne McCracken: Belfast Revolutionary and Pioneer of Feminism," *The Women of 1798*, ed. Keogh and Furlong, 47–63; and Nancy J. Curtin, "Women and Eighteenth-Century Irish Republicanism," *Women in Early Modern Ireland*, ed. Margaret MacCurtain and Mary O'Dowd (Edinburgh: Edinburgh Univ. Press, 1991), 133–44. In seeking to reinforce McCracken's credentials as a "wholehearted revolutionary," not just "a doer of good works," Gray (quoted at 49) inadvertently reveals his and history's difficulties in recognizing the latter as "real" politics.

18. For recent work contextualizing Wollstonecraft, see N. F. Lowe, "James Barry, Mary Wollstonecraft, and 1798," *Eighteenth-Century Ireland*, ed. Thomas Bartlett and Kevin Barry, 12 (1997): 60–76; and Lowe's "Mary Wollstonecraft and the Kingsborough Scandal," *Eighteenth-Century Ireland*, ed. Alan Harrison and Ian Campbell Ross, 9 (1994): 44–56. Lowe does not notice that the daughter was the third girl, not one of the two older children specifically designated as Wollstonecraft's pupils. The runaway girl's relative-seducer was tracked and shot by her enraged father. His heavily symbolic but nominal trial as Earl Kingston before the Irish House of Lords in late May 1798 was at one point targeted for a

bloody attack that would initiate the rebellion. For the latest version of the assassination plans for the trial on the 18th, see Stella Tillyard, *Citizen Lord: Edward Fitzgerald, 1763–1798*, 1997 (London: Vintage, 1998), 266–67, 316–17. The first wave of insurrection began instead on the 23rd, when Lord Edward had already been captured.

19. Quoted at 52 in the first edition (London: J[oseph] Johnson, 1788).

20. The quondam Lady Mount Cashell's letter of January 1820 is quoted in Edward C. McAleer, *The Sensitive Plant: A Life of Lady Mount Cashell* (Chapel Hill: Univ. of North Carolina Press, 1958), 138–39. Not always reliable, McAleer can be supplemented by *Shelley and His Circle 1773–1822*, vol. 8, ed. Donald H. Reiman and Doucet Devin Fischer (Cambridge: Harvard Univ. Press, 1986), 908–15; *The Journals of Mary Shelley 1814–1844*, ed. Paula R. Feldman and Diana Scott-Kilvert, 2 vols. (Oxford: Clarendon Press, 1987), 1: 309–10n; 2: 585–88; *The Journals of Claire Clairmont 1814–1827*, ed. Marion Kingston Stocking (Cambridge: Harvard Univ. Press, 1968), 119n; *The Clairmont Correspondence: Letters of Claire Clairmont, Charles Clairmont, and Fanny Imlay Godwin*, ed. Marion Kingston Stocking, 2 vols. (Baltimore: Johns Hopkins Univ. Press, 1995), 1: 134–35n; C. Kegan Paul, *William Godwin: His Friends and Contemporaries*, 2 vols. (London: Henry S. King, 1876), 1: 369–70; and Catherine Wilmot, *An Irish Peer on the Continent (1801–1803), Being a Narrative of the Tour of Stephen, 2nd Earl Mount Cashell, Through France, Italy, etc.*, ed. Thomas U. Sadleir, 2nd ed. (London: Williams and Norgate, 1924). Wilmot records an impressive array of political acquaintances abroad, including Talleyrand, Lafayette, the painter David, Charles James Fox, Tom Paine, Thomas Holcroft, and Helen Maria Williams. Lady Mount Cashell had Fitzgerald, Moira, and Granard connections, and evidently knew more of Lord Edward's doings just before his arrest than his biographer Thomas Moore, for her copy of Moore, *The Life and Death of Lord Edward Fitzgerald*, 2 vols. (London: Longman, Rees, Orme, Brown, and Green, 1831), queries his account of the citizen-lord's last movements; she sent her servants to Lady Pamela Fitzgerald, staying at Moira House, which was, ironically, not far from where her husband had just been seized. Mrs. Mason's then-husband, Lord Mount Cashell, was one of the twenty Irish peers to vote against the Union. For the later career of "Mrs. Mason" and her involvement with the Shelleys, see also Claire Tomalin's introduction to the recently rediscovered story dedicated by Mary Shelley in 1820 to Laurette, the elder of Mrs. Mason's two daughters by George Tighe, for whom she left her husband. Like much writing for the young at this period, that of Mary Shelley and Mrs. Mason has both personal and political implications. In Mary Shelley's *Maurice, or the Fisher's Cot: A Tale* (New York: Alfred A. Knopf, 1998), for example, the lost child is symbolically reunited with his parents, but the harmonious union does not make him forget his humbler past and democratic sympathies. Like Mary Wollstonecraft and Maria Edgeworth, Mrs. Mason wrote progressive guides for parents as well as children's tales.

21. The North Cork cuts a lurid figure in most histories of the period: see especially the anecdotes of local historian Courtenay Moore, "An Incident of 1798," *Journal of the Cork Historical and Archaeological Society*, 2nd series 9 (1903):

229–32; and "Some Account of the North Cork Regiment of Militia . . . Especially with Reference to Its Services in the Year 1798," *Journal of the Cork Historical and Archaeological Society*, 2nd series 4 (1898): 222–41. One English officer wrote indignantly of Big George as a "worthless wretch," citing Lord Kingsborough as among the worst of the Irish oppressors, deserving government punishment for his flogging victims and throwing salt on the wounds; routinely bartering female petitioners' bodies for promises to help their husbands, fathers, and brothers; and even offering a loyal soldier a pass and promotion if the man would prostitute his sister, Public Record Office of Northern Ireland, *Eighteenth-Century Irish Official Papers in Great Britain: Private Collections*, vol. 1. (Belfast: Her Majesty's Stationery Office, 1973), 187.

22. For the symbiosis between Wollstonecraft's 1792 *Rights of Woman* and the revised second edition (1791) of *Original Stories*, see Mitzi Myers, "Impeccable Governesses, Rational Dames, and Moral Mothers: Mary Wollstonecraft and the Female Tradition in Georgian Children's Books," *Children's Literature*, ed. Margaret Higonnet and Barbara Rosen (New Haven: Yale Univ. Press, 1986), 14: 31–59.

23. Maria Luddy, "Women and Politics in Nineteenth-Century Ireland," in *Women and Irish History*, ed. Valiulis and O'Dowd, 89–108.

24. George Colman, "Polly Honeycombe: A Dramatick Novel," 1760, *The Dramatick Works of George Colman* (London: T. Becket, 1777), 4: 1–60, quoted at 60. Interestingly, recent award-winning representations of later Irish rebellions and wars, whether authored by men or women, are notably anti-heroic and anti-war, as well as thoroughly politicized. Jimmy Conway, for example, the young protagonist of Gerard Whelan's *The Guns of Easter*, recognizes the glamour of 1916, but his odyssey of survival ends by affirming his mother's point of view: "Let men fight each other if they must: they always had. . . . She could see no sense in it herself. She too had a war to fight, but it was a war that made sense: the fight to feed her children and keep her family whole and safe. It was a secret war without any glory attached, a war just as old and just as dangerous as any fought by men, and the results of losing in that war were just as terrible." In braving the war zone to feed his family, Jimmy has achieved true heroism (Dublin: O'Brien Press, 1996).

25. A recent overview from a historian with no particular feminist agenda, published in the house organ of the American Historical Association, usefully counters condescending representations of this period's woman reader that are still being perpetuated: see D. R. Woolf, "A Feminine Past? Gender, Genre, and Historical Knowledge in England, 1500–1800," *American Historical Review* 102.3 (June 1997): 645–79. For another take on late eighteenth-century shifts in female reading styles, see Mark Salber Phillips, "'If Mrs. Mure be not sorry for poor King Charles': History, the Novel, and the Sentimental Reader," *History Workshop Journal* 43 (Spring 1997): 111–31.

26. For strictures on the arrangement and methodology of McCormack's *The Pamphlet Debate on the Union Between Great Britain and Ireland, 1797–1800* (Dublin: Irish Academic Press, 1996), see James Kelly, *Eighteenth-Century Ireland*, ed. Thomas Bartlett and Kevin Barry, 12 (1997): 166–67.

27. See *The Journals of Claire Clairmont* (available since 1968), 119n. They are McCormack's F4, R8, and H5; apparently read and discussed by the Shelleys, these gendered works can be assumed to have influenced the political views of other major writers, but, because McCormack cites TCD copies for some works and NLI for others in his alphabetized list, there is no way they could be discovered unless the reader already knew what they were.

28. (Dublin: Irish Academic Press, 1993), 8. Sir Richard Musgrave's construction of 1798 as merely the latest in a series of popish plots, *Memoirs of the Different Rebellions in Ireland. . . .*, 2nd ed. (Dublin: Milliken; London: Stockdale, 1801), went through three editions in a year, adding to the revisions considerations on the means of extending the Reformation's benefits in Ireland. Musgrave's importance as a rebellion historian, often surprisingly accurate despite his biases and omissions, is attested by the recent reprint of the 4th edition, ed. Steven W. Myers and Delores E. McKnight (Fort Wayne, Ind: Round Tower Books, 1995).

29. Terry Eagleton, *Heathcliff and the Great Hunger: Studies in Irish Culture* (London: Verso, 1995), 73, claims that "what Ireland lacks is a public sphere of discourse and dialogue, an enlightened space in which conflicts may be peaceably resolved."

30. Roche is quoted from Sir Jonah Barrington, *Personal Sketches of His Own Times*, 2 vols. (London: Henry Colburn, 1827), 1: 214; and G. R. Neilson, ed., *The Book of Bulls: Being A Very Complete and Entertaining Essay on the Evolution of the Irish and Other Bulls* (London: Simpkin, Marshall, Hamilton, Kent, and Tucker, [1898?]), 150; Jeffrey, *Contributions to the* Edinburgh Review, 4 vols. (London: Longman, Brown, Green, and Longmans, 1844), 4: 133–50, quoted at 144.

31. The "union of hearts" is from *The Select Speeches of the Right Hon. Henry Grattan; to Which Is Added His Letter on the Union, with a Commentary on His Career and Character*, ed. Daniel Owen Madden (London: Bohn, 1847). Grattan's nuanced terminology in his speech of 26 May 1800 resists binarization of the Union debate into pro and con: "Connexion is a wise and a profound policy; but connexion without an Irish Parliament, is connexion without its own principle. . . . Identification is a solid and imperial maxim, necessary for the preservation of freedom, necessary for that of empire; but, without union of hearts—with a separate government, and without a separate parliament, identification is extinction, is conquest—not identification" (292–93). The unsparing critique of history from the child's view comes from Maria Edgeworth, with Richard Lovell Edgeworth, *Practical Education*, 2 vols. consecutively paged (London: J[oseph] Johnson, 1798), 351. In recent years, *Practical Education* has been misrepresented as a conduct book, a conservative work, a text dictated by a father, and so on. In fact, it began as a pioneering child observation log initiated by Maria Edgeworth's first stepmother, Honora Sneyd Edgeworth, in the late 1770's. The project to write a guidebook from real anecdotes of how children actually learn languished from her death until it was taken up by Maria Edgeworth in the early 1790's, and the manual is largely the daughter's work, as letters of the period indicate. The book itself gives Honora full credit in the Appendix.

32. Ciaran Brady, Introduction, *Ideology and the Historians, Historical Studies 17*, ed. Ciaran Brady (Dublin: Lilliput Press, 1991), 9.

33. Robert Gildea, *The Past in French History* (New Haven and London: Yale Univ. Press, 1994), 12.

34. Caroline Austen, *My Aunt Jane Austen: A Memoir* (London and Colchester: Spottiswoode, Ballantyne for The Jane Austen Society, 1952), 9.

35. Edgeworth's tale has twenty-two chapters in the third of the 1809 editions from which I quote, *Ennui* in *Tales of Fashionable Life*, 3rd ed., vol. 1 of 3 vols. (London: J[oseph] Johnson, 1809); page references in the text refer to this edition. The tale is also currently available in *Castle Rackrent and Ennui*, ed. Marilyn Butler (London: Penguin, 1992). Butler's introduction and my two articles cited in n. 12 are being supplemented by many conference papers and forthcoming essays. The political points that Edgeworth's layered allusions reveal are developed extensively in my forthcoming literary life and other work; much more is going on in this single chapter than I have space to discuss here.

36. See 359 n. 72 of the Penguin edition, which also reprints the Edgeworths' review of Carr. The edition of Carr I have checked was printed in America (Philadelphia: Bradford et al., 1806).

37. Edgeworth's footnote is almost verbatim from J[ohn] Bush, *Hibernia Curiosa: A Letter from a Gentleman in Dublin, to his Friend at Dover in Kent: Giving a General View of the Manners, Customs, Dispositions, &c. of the Inhabitants of Ireland* (London: W. Flexney, 1769), 104–108, with inflections from Philip Luckombe, whose *A Tour Through Ireland Wherein The Present State of That Kingdom Is Considered; and the Most Noted Cities, Towns, Seats, Buildings, Loughs, &c. Described: Interspersed with Observations on the Manners, Customs, Antiquities, Curiosities, and Natural History, of that Country, To Which Is Prefixed A General Description of the Kingdom; with the Distances Between the Ports, &c. on the Coast of Great Britain, and Those on That of Ireland* (Dublin: Whitestone et al., 1780), cannibalizes the popular Bush and others too; see 232–44. These earlier authors exemplify the discursive revaluation of things Irish from the mid-eighteenth century on. Like Arthur Young, another travel writer Edgeworth favors, Bush is notably liberal in denouncing absenteeism, rackrenting, religious tithes, and greedy middlemen; he feels with the peasants, not the representatives of his own class; his overview of Ireland, used by Edgeworth elsewhere as well, is as much social critique as topographical description. For further discussion of these attitudinal shifts, see Joseph Th. Leerssen, *Mere Irish and Fíor-Ghael: Studies in the Idea of Irish Nationality, Its Development, and Literary Expression Prior to the Nineteenth Century*, Utrecht Publications in General and Comparative Literature vol. 22 (Amstersdam: John Benjamins, 1986), chap. 2.

38. *A Memoir of Maria Edgeworth, with a Selection from Her Letters by the Late Mrs. [Frances] Edgeworth*, ed. by Her Children, 3 vols. (London: Privately printed, Joseph Masters and Son, 1867), 3: 96.

39. Concannon, *Women of Ninety-Eight*, 311.

Fair Trade: The Language of Love and Commerce in Mary Wollstonecraft's *Letters Written during a Short Residence in Sweden, Norway, and Denmark*

CYNTHIA RICHARDS

If we know Mary Wollstonecraft's *Letters Written during a Short Residence in Sweden, Norway, and Denmark*, we know it largely through reputation. It is the book that won William Godwin's heart. Godwin himself endows it with this status: "If ever there was a book calculated to make a man in love with its author," he writes in the *Memoirs*, "this appears to be the book."[1] And apparently, Godwin was not alone in succumbing to its charms. As Marilyn Butler and Janet Todd note in the introduction to *The Works of Mary Wollstonecraft,* the book "moved and haunted the leading men writers of her generation. . . . and several of the women too."[2] Thomas Holcroft purportedly proposes after reading the *Letters Written in Sweden,* and although Robert Southey does not go that far, the language of his praise suggests an equally strong response: upon reading the *Letters* he proclaims no woman her equal and professes: "She has made me in love with a cold climate, and frost and snow with a northern moonlight."[3]

Thus, through reputation, this book has become a "conquest narrative," of the amorous sort, famous not so much for what it says, but for how it was received. We can't help but read the letters looking for some clue as to why Godwin fell in love (and did so, after finding Wollstonecraft rather unpleasant company upon their first meeting) and how Wollstonecraft, with apparently no calculation, managed to accomplish this considerable end. In other words, we read it looking for some power, aesthetic or perhaps purely sentimental, that transcends the particularities of its composition and which models an ideal union between writer and reader or subject and object of address. For when the reader falls in love, the text's power is figured as absolute yet non-coercive, the writer remains exposed, vulnerable even in this feat of total persuasion.

The critical reception of the *Letters Written in Sweden* has, by and large, continued in this romantic vein. Ralph Wardle calls the *Letters* "Mary's most mature and most delightful book," showing "how truly charming she could be when relaxed."[4] Indeed, her biographers are uniform in their praise, finding in this text the most appealing, and not incidentally the most true, representation of Wollstonecraft, "the whole person."[5] Gary Kelly, in his intellectual biography *Revolutionary Feminism: The Mind and Career of Mary Wollstonecraft*, speaks of this work's merits in less "intimate" terms than Wardle, but still distinguishes it for its effective synthesis of object[ive] and subject[ive] knowledge: for Kelly, the *Letters* bring the "arguments and experience together in one text," offering up a portrait of the "female philosopher" in her most compelling pose.[6] Yet the *Letters* are persuasive, Mary Poovey argues, precisely because they are so seemingly without design: her plot remains largely unrevealed in the work itself, her emotional development instead taking precedence.[7] As Syndy Conger succinctly explains, "There is a sense of the narrator's mind—emotion and intellection—wholly shared."[8] Thus, in our expressions of admiration for this last and most successful of Wollstonecraft's "authorized" texts, we remain indebted to a language of romantic correspondence. In the *Letters,* we find Wollstonecraft most affecting because most unaffected, our own reactions paying implicit homage to Godwin's personal feelings about the book.

Yet any discussion of this book's public reception necessarily evokes its private (and far more tragic) one. For, of course, the text has become almost as famous for being a *failed* conquest narrative, of the amorous sort. The letters written during this short residence in Sweden, Norway and Denmark (both those which remained "private" and those which assumed this curious semi-personal form) we now know to have had little or no effect on their intended reader—Gilbert Imlay, Wollstonecraft's lover and the father of her illegitimate child, Fanny. Once again, it appears we have Godwin to thank for the public perception of the text's ultimate "failure." Upon its publication, readers would certainly have been intrigued by the mysterious references to a muddled love affair, but they would not have known the identity of the addressee, the exact circumstances of their relationship, nor the ultimate outcome of both her travels and these lovesick missives.[9] It was not until the publication of *Memoirs of Mary Wollstonecraft*, to which Godwin appended his own edited *Letters to Imlay*, that these details would have been known.[10] Godwin intended the publication of these private letters to verify his own enraptured response to those already offered up as "private" by Wollstonecraft herself in *Letters Written in Sweden;* but, as we all now know, his efforts did not have this desired effect. Recast as a blazon of his love, Wollstonecraft's complex romantic history becomes one too easily caricatured, and thus, at least temporarily, dismissed.

This reception should not have been surprising, for the "private" letters tell a quite different story. They suggest not her inevitable "conquest" of a disinterested reader, but rather record the growing indifference of her "intended," Imlay. In these letters, Wollstonecraft becomes the generic, seduced and abandoned heroine of eighteenth-century amatory fiction. Like the familiar figure of the Portuguese nun, she awaits letters that never come and when they do, they always disappoint.[11] Indeed, one such letter appears to have precipitated her return home and the seemingly just as hasty re-emergence of her suicidal thoughts. When *calculated* to win back Imlay's love, the letters fail miserably: Wollstonecraft returns to find Imlay living with another, herself resolved to raise Fanny alone.

Thus, strangely enough, the private reception of these letters to Imlay stands in direct inverse relationship to its public one. The letters did not win back Imlay's love; their power proves far from absolute and only temporarily persuasive. Moreover, the frank vulnerability of her truly personal letters gets read as merely emotionally coercive, lost on an audience all too familiar with the language of abandonment. If we are to understand the power of the *Letters Written in Sweden* then, can we fully comprehend it if we read them only in the sentimental, romantic terms laid out by Godwin? In order to understand their power, perhaps we must read the letters as a conquest narrative of a somewhat different sort.

II

For if we return to the particularities of its composition and to some extent its genre, *Letters Written in Sweden* emerges as a conquest narrative of a more historical and seemingly impersonal kind: the conquest narrative of the sixteenth-century explorer and consummate trader. The letters are a travel log, the journey a business trip, the writer an agent of the addressee, her purpose to seek treasure, and implicitly (although no less certainly) her own self-promotion. To be more specific, Wollstonecraft, on her Northern journey, has been appointed by Imlay himself as his legal representative in an attempt to recover a stolen ship containing a large amount of silver and plate. Her charge, according to Richard Holmes, is "to discover the fate of the ship, the attitude of all parties concerned, and to reach some financial agreement on an out of court basis."[12] No small charge, and one that requires Imlay—at a time in which he is otherwise pursuing a public distance from her—to make her his official "agent." In the terms of their official contract, Wollstonecraft—as his agent—is granted "sufficient power, enabling her to receive all the money that may be recovered."[13] Thus, we have these particulars: a woman heading into what was generally perceived as an unknown region, commissioned by her legal sovereign (Imlay is identified as her husband in their official agreement), instructed to seek treasure and, in the process, to rectify any imbalances in his search for absolute power over his own financial destiny. Moreover, as Mary Favret is right to emphasize, this text becomes Wollstonecraft's most successful act of self-promotion.[14] The *Letters Written in Sweden* prove a commercial success, her loyalty to Imlay's cause ultimately furthering her own economic interests.

Despite these compelling parallels to the typical structure and motives of the sixteenth-century conquest narrative, this comparison—hinged as it is upon a ready pun—suggests, at first, an anachronistic reading of Wollstonecraft's *Letters.* As Charles Batten notes in *Pleasurable Instruction*, eighteenth-century practitioners of the travel narrative were eager to distinguish themselves from their Renaissance predecessors, "rebelling" against its mercenary, and hence often hyperbolic, form. "A thirst for knowledge," he explains, "joined a lust for gold in motivating the typical traveler in his search through foreign lands."[15] Yet as is often true with rebellions, this new form of the travel narrative borrowed as much as it rejected from its Renaissance ancestors. The purpose of the travel narrative remained acquisitive, with knowledge being easily substituted for gold in the above equation, and possession—here figured as that of new experience rather than a new world—remaining its ultimate goal. In *Imperial Eyes*, Mary Louise Pratt famously terms this newly disguised form of the Renaissance travel log "the anti-conquest narrative." For Pratt, any difference between the openly hegemonic Renaissance travel text and the more sentimentalized late eighteenth-century one lies in its implicit strategy, certainly not in its purpose. Both narratives participate, she argues, in a commodifying gaze—those "imperial eyes" which "look out and possess." But in this later form, this gaze is masked in a new rhetoric of seeming passivity or innocence.[16] In some of the more radical examples of the "anti-conquest narrative" (specifically abolitionist literature), this imperial vision can even assume the guise of idealized, reciprocal love—an unchallenged right of possession proving central to both the language of love and commerce.[17] Within Pratt's rubric then, to call Wollstonecraft's *Letters Written in Sweden* a "conquest narrative" might obscure the new strategic qualities of the form, but it would not misrepresent the extent to which a Renaissance tradition of travel literature continued to influence the more sentimental narratives of the late eighteenth century.[18] The ready assimilation of this new rhetoric of imperialism with a language of love easily suggests its attractiveness to an "explorer" with Wollstonecraft's dual interests.

Moreover, for Wollstonecraft the influence of the "conquest narrative" would not have been so remote nor so insidious. She would have had to go no further than the work of Imlay himself, her addressee and lover, to find a model for this form. Indeed, Imlay is first known to her as the celebrated author of *A Topographical Description of the Western Territory of North America*, a series of letters detailing "the soil, climate, natural history, population, etc" of the recently chartered state of Kentucky with the primary purpose of promoting emigration to this newly opened territory.[19] In both purpose and structure, the topographical genre was clearly the literary successor of the sixteenth-century conquest narrative.[20] Written to a distant reader—in the sixteenth-century form, the explorer's "sovereign" and/or benefactor, in the eighteenth-century form, the prospective emigrant—both narratives promised to make that reader prosperous if only he or she would take possession of this new land. Flamboyant descriptions of abundance and of a vast and largely welcoming emptiness were used to buttress these claims even as these narratives paradoxically detailed the native inhabitants in all their diversity and plenitude. On a more practical side, much attention was given in both forms to the logistics of conquest and/or settlement, with Imlay, for example, including in the *Topographical Description* a comparative analysis of the various routes of entry to this new, and still largely unexplored, territory of Kentucky. Also like the sixteenth-century form, the topographical genre relied heavily on lists and inventories to make real its promises of riches, with the eighteenth-century narratives focusing more on plant life and other sustainable resources than on exportable gold and silver. Finally, the ultimate goal for both narratives was typically the self-promotion of the explorer himself. Although this purpose is more veiled in this later form, it was clearly still apparent to most readers. Imlay himself was accused of speculation schemes, his penning of the *Topographical Description* known to be far from disinterested.[21]

Imlay's fame, however, arose from his ability to fuse successfully a radical agenda, with its emphasis on natural rights and the leveling of opportunities, with the practical and conquest-oriented dictates of the topographical genre. Imlay achieved this end, in part, because he wrote as an insider rather than as a speculator, able to claim unquestioned sympathy with the people and interests of this fledgling state by virtue of his status as a native son. Moreover, his economic observations gained greater moral weight as they were filtered through the language of lost innocence. In what was most likely a self-penned introduction, the "editor" describes the author as one "accustomed to that simplicity of manner natural to a people in a state of innocence," but who now resides in a kind of fallen state, "powerfully stricken with the very great difference" between the sincerity of the new world and the more scripted behavior of the old.[22] The personal letter format further allowed him to register this shock of difference even as he remained focused on his immediate goal of promoting emigration. It is for his success in masking his speculation schemes within this rhetoric of egalitarian politics, natural sympathy, and native simplicity that he ultimately gained entry into Wollstonecraft's circle.

Given her own fallen status as well as her new role as Imlay's "agent," it is hard to imagine then that Wollstonecraft did not have his *Topographical Description* in mind when she set out to explore what were still the relatively unknown territories of Scandinavia. She certainly does not let Imlay forget how similar their experiences are. Repeatedly, she will remind him of the likenesses between their ventures, at times even suggesting that her own experience, although occurring after his and at his request, is more "original": "You have probably made similar reflections in America, where the face of the country, I suppose, resembles the wilds of Norway."[23] And although, as many critics have noted, she offers little information about the business at hand, she does provide a rather exhaustive survey of the land, detailing its climate, population, and natural history, and even making some brief references to its soil.

Such detail was far from typical for a writer more noted for her philosophical abstractions, yet its inclusion was certainly consistent with the new world fictions which had fueled Imlay's and her relationship. Imlay's second and less successful book, *The Emigrants* (published only a few months after the beginning of their affair), reworked his *Topographical Description* as an epistolary romance, recasting his travel narrative as a rambling love story between two political progressives, Ar——ton and Caroline. The two ultimately marry and establish a home in an utopian community on the banks of the Ohio, but only after they are forced apart from one another by a combination of domestic and political trials.[24] Apparently, it was this story that Wollstonecraft and Imlay took as their own: at the height of their relationship, they both dreamed of moving to America and beginning anew in a pastoral land.[25] Thus, the romantic drama so explicit to this work—that of winning back Imlay's love—was not disconnected from the commercial one she chose to keep largely hidden from view.

Indeed, one wonders to what extent their shared fantasies shaped this work. In order to flatter him, would she become him—to win back his love, assume his guise as explorer and speculator? Would such an impersonation, in turn, suggest a capitulation to the romantic fictions that had led to her own exploitation or just possibly a sustainable independence from them? In assuming his position, she would necessarily inherit his acquisitive gaze, as his agent, function as his "imperial eyes." But would she also gain license to rewrite this one-sided narrative, to re-imagine Imlay's empire-driven and commercial vision along lines that might have accommodated a wife and child, and the familiar politics through which she had already made a name for herself?

III

The work of Mary Favret in *Romantic Correspondences* and Karen Lawrence in *Penelope's Voyages* has already done much to wrest Wollstonecraft's *Letters* away from what Favret calls the "sentimental romance" of Godwin's reading and to restore it to the arena of public discourse.[26] Departing from earlier readings of this text, Favret emphasizes its status as savvy commercial enterprise rather than uncalculated emotional outpouring, and Lawrence locates it firmly with the highly "purposeful" and masculinist tradition of the travel narrative. For both critics, however, it is the "double[ness]" of Wollstonecraft's narrative that distinguishes it, its tense movement from "love story" to "social comment," from "lover's discourse" to "educational" travel guide.[27] In reading Wollstonecraft's *Letters* as "conquest narrative," I would not contest the significance of this doubleness within Wollstonecraft's narrative, but rather suggest that it arises *from* the historical/structural dictates of this form rather than in opposition to it. Moreover, I would argue that neither the success nor the failure of this text as a conquest narrative of the amorous sort can be viewed apart from its indebtedness to what Louis Montrose terms "the protocolonist discourse of discovery." In particular, I am intrigued by how this discourse—as outlined by Montrose in his article "The Work of Gender in the Discourse of Discovery"—could work to empower Wollstonecraft's narrative and make it as most critics, even her impartial ones agree, her most moving work. Citing Michel de Certeau, Montrose characterizes this discourse as "writing that conquers." "Authorized" by his sovereign to "discover" and "possess," the writing subject gains the power to name and even to inscribe upon an "unknown territory" its ultimate significance and fate.[28] Wollstonecraft appears to avail herself of such a power not only in her survey of these Northern lands, but also of her own inner territory as well—those romantic flights of self-discovery so admired by her nineteenth-century male devotees. If we detect a greater confidence, relaxation, or even seeming vulnerability here, to what extent is it enabled by the "imperialist" perspective she is required to adopt on her commercial commission?

In *Desire: Love Stories in Western Culture*, Catherine Belsey suggests a more substantial connection between the historical conquest narrative and the amorous one than that evoked by a mere play on words. She argues that the structure of the "colonial project" and that of love are directly parallel: "The colonial project is addressed to a Third Party: it offers up the indigenous culture to an Idea: civilization . . . salvation . . . God. Its aim is to be able to say to others of the colonial subject, who comes to reflect back the image of the colonizer, 'I am proud of you.'" As Belsey points out, love—in Julia Kristeva's psychoanalytic account—takes this same form: "Love is addressed to a third party. The auto-erotic mother-child dyad becomes love when it is offered to an Other."[29] In both cases, this "transaction" proves successful because of a necessary and enabling separation. As Kristeva explains, "'Isn't he beautiful,' or 'I am proud of you,' and so forth are statements of maternal love because they involve a Third Party; it is in the eyes of a Third Party that the baby the mother speaks to becomes a *he*."[30] For Certeau, the conquest narrative marks the beginning of not an individual, but a cultural identity for strikingly similar reasons: "From the moment of rupture between a subject and an object of operation, between a *will to write* and a *written body* (or a body to be written), this writing fabricates Western history."[31] In both love and conquest then, it is differentiation, and not total absorption, that marks the beginning of this new and ultimately quite consuming relationship.

Moreover, the parallels outlined by Belsey become quite literal in Wollstonecraft's case. She is both mother of Fanny and agent of Imlay on this trip. Even as she details these "unknown" Northern lands, their economic as well as their physical terrain, she rehearses the plight of her child and seeks to make her real in the eyes of the intended reader. Thus, we find appreciative comments for the pristine beauty of this land melding into statements of pride in the gratifying innocence of her daughter. She may embark on this journey to reclaim Imlay's stolen property (and at the same time, his love), but it is Fanny who she seeks to return to his loving possession. Hence, even in her most personal of entreaties, the language of love and commerce can never fully be disconnected.

Yet as the above discussion makes readily apparent, Wollstonecraft's appropriation of the discourse of conquest—even if to some extent it is forced upon her—would embroil her in a curious web of gender relations. As Montrose explains, "The tendency of such discursive representation [is] to assume a narrative form, to manifest itself as a 'historied body'—in particular, as a mode of symbolic action whose agent is gendered masculine and whose object is gendered feminine."[32] Indeed, Certeau pointedly takes as his inaugural scene for this "writing that conquers" Jan Van der Straet's highly sexualized representation of Vespucci's discovery of America—a 1619 etching in which der Straet portrays America as a reclining nude just awakened by the fully alert and still standing Vespucci. Thus, in assuming the role of the explorer, Wollstonecraft would at once gain a kind of agency—and indeed as pointed out earlier, this symbolic power is wonderfully concrete in this case, and even given legal sanction—but at the same, she, as a woman, and in particular as a fallen, cast-off woman—would remain its object.

A woman participating in trade, and necessarily trading upon her fairness, Wollstonecraft's position—to put it mildly—is a complex one, and one that might even suggest ways of explaining *The Letters'* contradictory status. The conquest narrative, as Certeau suggests in his chapter on "Ethno-Graphy," is by definition contradictory, for "at the same time that it creates a profit, the voyage creates a lost paradise relative to a body-object, to an erotic body."[33] In other words, even as the explorer reclaims this land as a means of production, its pleasures remain intact by their very excess and ephemerality outside the economy he represents. Thus, the enforced and imported economies of the explorer produce pleasure even as they insist on gain. That Wollstonecraft's own commercial venture produced such enraptured assurances of pleasure on the part of her contemporary readers then should not surprise us. What remains remarkable is that these moments of sublime excess could be orchestrated by the very body-object presumably yet awakened to the transgressive power of the business trip.

IV

In fact, Wollstonecraft—unlike her readers—appears acutely aware of how greatly her "business" has affected the very nature of her observations. In the appendix to the *Letters*, she goes so far as to apologize for its influence: "Private business and cares have frequently absorbed me as to prevent my obtaining all the information, during this journey, which the novelty of the scenes would have afforded, had my attention been continually awake to inquiry" (346). Of course, Wollstonecraft primarily intends "business" here to suggest an internal enterprise—the "lovesick" musings inspired by Imlay's betrayal and which, in spite of her denials, are generally read as attesting to her heightened rather than diminished consciousness. But what is significant here is that she also means "business." She is here on trade, and this term's double duty in this sentence suggests that the partialities arising from the private and the commercial strangely coincide.

Moreover, in the context of Certeau's inaugural scene of "writing that conquers," it is hard to miss the doubleness of Wollstonecraft's own pose here. Wollstonecraft remains the unawakened "America" in this apology: she accuses herself of not being "continually awake to inquiry" and strangely too "absorbed" to be attentive. Yet she is also the explorer herself—the alert Vespucci—who through implication is at least partially awake to these new scenes, but whose "business" has kept her too "absorbed" to be fully attuned to this land's simple "novelties" and hence unable to catalogue them.

Wollstonecraft maintains this kind of doubleness throughout the narrative. Richard Holmes, in fact, argues that it is Wollstonecraft's business itinerary that accounts for much of the "mystery" of the text, what other critics would connect to its more romantic qualities. With this itinerary concealed, we get hasty departures, sudden shifts in plans, unexplained detours, and other such significant, even haunting, gaps in the text. We even get one telling scene where Wollstonecraft steals ashore like an invader, taking a small boat to land when her ship overshoots her business destination.

The fact that Wollstonecraft chooses to conceal the cause of her adventuresome entry seems particularly remarkable. Of course, Imlay would be aware of why she is so determined to reach Arendal, but her general reader would not, and in the absence of such knowledge, this port takes on almost mythic status. And Wollstonecraft appears careful to cultivate that impression: "she watch[es] two long hours for a boat to emancipate [her]" and "every cloud that flitted on the horizon was hailed as a liberator" (243). Ultimately, however, she must "exert all [her] rhetoric to prevail on the captain to let me have the ship's boat" and she approaches land as her own liberator, even conquering lord. Approaching the "unwrought space" of the barrier island, she names it anew, claiming its rocks are made of the "rude materials of creation" (243). Indeed, even the threat of male aggression—represented by the lone cottage on shore—dissipates in the wake of her delayed recollection of this space's primitiveness, and her status as explorer rather than woman ultimately marks her essential difference from this place:

> Approaching a retreat where strangers, especially women, so seldom appeared, I wondered that curiosity did not bring the beings who inhabited it to the windows or the door. I did not immediately recollect that men who remain so near the brute creation, as only to exert themselves to find the food necessary to sustain life, have little or no imagination to call forth the curiosity necessary to fructify the faint glimmerings of mind which entitles [*sic*] them to rank as lords of creation. (245)

By taking this novel approach to her prescribed destination, Wollstonecraft begins her journey in full and singular possession of its significance. Moreover, by concealing her purpose, she only gives more weight to her words. She takes on the pose of the conquistador—in her role as agent she can feel fully entitled to this forced entry—but her silence on this issue keeps her comments intensely her own.

It is ultimately ironic then that the cottage is indeed occupied and then by a woman, but when Wollstonecraft makes this discovery, she has already shifted her position from subject of exploration to once again its object. Reminded by her daughter's nurse Marguerite of the threat of isolation represented by this new and unknown place, she takes comfort in the sight of another woman: "drawing near" the cottage, "I was not sorry to see a female figure" (245). Yet having made that admission, she quickly distinguishes her fears from those of the more womanish Marguerite, returning once again to the position of a traveler preoccupied with more pressing concerns. Throughout this passage, Wollstonecraft's own position—despite her more imperialistic posturings—remains a double one: she is both watcher and watched, uniquely attentive to the value of this "new" land yet ultimately caught unawares of its easily foreseeable dangers.

As is clear from this very first letter, Wollstonecraft's unconventional role on this journey and her attitude toward her business venture remain paramount both in her choice of details and in the comments that they elicit. In Letter Five, Wollstonecraft openly protests the force of business upon her travels, and accordingly upon the very nature of her discoveries: "Had I determined to travel in Sweden merely for pleasure, I should probably have chosen the road to Stockholm" (269). At first gently chiding Imlay for his inordinate influence on her destiny (and indeed even her pleasure), Wollstonecraft quickly turns this commercial-driven course, however, to her own advantage. Compelled by business to travel in the country and not the city, her observations—she argues—will prove more discriminating. The differences induced by climatic changes in the country will give her what amounts to a "first view," a truer estimate of this country because it will be unclouded by intimacy or repetition. Her business route, in other words, will allow her discovery and not merely observation. Notably, pleasure becomes the remainder in this equation: compelled by her business concerns, she no longer travels "mere[ly] for pleasure," these moments of personal delight become by design in excess of her goal. But as Certeau suggests, that very insistence on "profit" in her quest will necessarily produce a heightened sense of its pleasures.

Never again is Wollstonecraft so direct in mentioning the effect of business on her narrative, but it is clear from points she makes later in the same letter that "discovery" dictates her entire journey. In fact, she regards Sweden itself as though seen at "first view." She writes, "Every object seemed to remind me of the creation of things" (261). In her attempt to give Sweden (and her observations) this "original" flavor, she would even seem to rewrite history: "So far from thinking that the primitive inhabitants of the world lived in a southern climate, where Paradise spontaneous arose, I am led to infer . . . that the first dwelling of man happened to be a spot like this" (263). The result, however, of seeing this spot as more "original" is to make it more backward. Indeed, her descriptions of the Swedish often echo those provided by sixteenth-century explorers of the "new world": the people are sluggish, the women voluptuous, the heat—here provided by wood stoves and comforters—suffocating and detrimental to the health of the mind and body.

In fact, it is in the above remarks that Wollstonecraft sounds most like Imlay himself. With Imlay famous for having claimed Edenic stasis for the new and southern state of Kentucky, Wollstonecraft cannot be unaware of how such an assertion would both echo and undermine his authority. The gesture itself was actually quite conventional in the literature of emigration, and indeed by the time of the publication of the *Letters* would not have had the effect one would assume. Rather than suggesting a kind of disinterested, even fanciful appraisal of the land, this metaphor within the topographical essay format would have indicated a personal investment. The writer, eager to encourage emigration to a territory where he had a vested interest (at times actually owning large tracts of land), needed to represent this territory as both untouched and at the same time quite habitable. The image of Eden proved a convenient trope for these purposes. Yet once again, Wollstonecraft's use of this convention is double-edged. She echoes these mercantile interests—even partakes indirectly in the intense competitiveness of these emigration pamphlets—but she does so within a context of reflection, a seeming lull in her "plan." Indeed, the passage that precedes this observation is one of her most descriptive, the scene one she deliberately positions as sublime. Her "plan" (both determined by Imlay's own business interests and her own desire to capitalize on this opportunity) thus ultimately both produces this scene as pleasure (and a pleasure deliberately "read" as excessive), and at the same time re-establishes this moment of personal digression as belonging to a more profitable scheme.

But my point here is not to emphasize the negative—to show how Wollstonecraft resembles the clearly exploitive Imlay or to demonstrate how she herself could become guilty of a kind of national chauvinism—but rather to show how the fictions of discovery which she appropriates in this text and which are necessitated by her business venture act to give her—in the terms of her contract—"sufficient power." Envisioning these Northern lands as a "new world," she is allowed to name, and even to rewrite its history as to empower her own perspective. Significantly, Wollstonecraft herself seems most aware of this new-found power when she encounters the women of these new lands. Attracted by her "stranger" status—even the "solitariness of [her] situation"—they appear to woo her: "They gathered round me—sung to me—and one of the prettiest, to whom I gave my hand, with some degree of partiality, to meet the glance of her eyes, kissed me very affectionately" (282). Wollstonecraft's travels clearly place her in a "masculine" role, and she is not averse to reminding Imlay and her general reader of the effects of that new power. Yet the scene she stages here is more than that, one not of simple, but double conquest. She remains both the object, remarkably passive under the "glance of their eyes," yet by that very same gesture clearly in control of the event. The "some degree of partiality" which might connote mere coyness in a woman becomes the sign of healthy circumspection on the part of an explorer alone in a new world. For Imlay's sake, she both lays out the riches of this land, detailing the beauties of the Swedish women, and makes herself its dearest possession: "I was very much flattered when I was told, the next day, that they said it was a pleasure to look at me, I appeared so good-natured" (283).

Earlier in this same letter, Wollstonecraft gives that power more complex (and ultimately more revealing) representation. Describing the entrance at the bay of Tonsberg, she writes:

> Here I have frequently strayed, sovereign of the waste, I seldom met any human creature; and sometimes, reclining on the mossy down, under the shelter of a rock, the prattling of the sea amongst the pebbles has lulled me to sleep—no fear of any rude satyr's approaching to interrupt my repose. (279)

Remarkable in this passage is how Wollstonecraft at once evokes herself as the "object" of discovery—the threat of the satyr coming upon her unawares while sleeping that is implicit in this passage—and at the same time retains her own status as sovereign subject. For it is Wollstonecraft who remains in control here—the threat of the satyr can be revoked at the very moment it is implied. In this "new world," it is she who names the place, its significance, and even the parameters of her own "repose" there. Not incidentally then, this passage in which she surveys this "new world" from such a "sovereign" vantage point ultimately becomes a moment of Romantic self-discovery. She accomplishes this end by moving seamlessly between an evocation of her own body and the objects which surround her: the white sails, the cliffs, the islands. As she awakens, so do the pines "rise" on those like isolated bodies. She even moves to a language in which the act and its statement coincide: "I pause, again breathless, to trace, with renewed delight" (280). Breathlessness is enunciated through commas; her body both enacts and represents the proof of this new world's beauty. Finally, Wollstonecraft turns toward a recounting of her own soul, finding its vivacity mirrored in the prospect before her—the language of discovery empowering her own self-knowledge and even self-approbation. In this evocative passage, she becomes at once "sovereign of the waste" and the body-object of which it is composed.

Yet as should also be apparent, the above passage speaks to the complexities of gender in these fictions of discovery. For Wollstonecraft is at once conqueror and commodity in this passage. She is the one who imposes the threat and the one who can be violated. Discovery—even of the Romantic sort—cannot be accomplished without first evoking—to cite Montrose again—the "historied body"—specifically, the figure of a sleeping woman yet to be "awakened" by the if not "civilizing," certainly domesticating, influences of a classic world. Yet if Wollstonecraft's evocation of this "historied body" seems a by-product of her own excited state in the above passage, it is far more deliberate and even quite literal earlier in the *Letters*. In planning a side trip to Frederichshall, Wollstonecraft notes the special preparations she must make to insure the success of this excursion:

> There, and back again, was but a day's journey, and would not, I thought, interfere with my voyage. I agreed, and invited the eldest and prettiest of the girls to accompany us. I invited her, because I liked to see a beautiful face animated by pleasure, and to have an opportunity of regarding the country whilst the gentlemen were amusing themselves with her. (265)

Note again the doubleness of Wollstonecraft's pose in this passage. She is at once the explorer and the one who is always vulnerable to scrutiny. Without the "historied body" of the "eldest and prettiest of the girls," she fears she will lose her own "opportunity" for discovery, herself becoming the body for observation. By contrast, in bringing along this attractive and (presumably) unsuspecting woman, she can divert her fellow male travelers and provide space for own private reflection and exploration. Yet just previous to this admission, Wollstonecraft adds the more incongruous phrase: "I like to see a beautiful face animated by pleasure." Here, the woman becomes the vehicle for own pleasure, and, significantly, one represented as secondary to the serious business of even this short excursion. In order to profit from this short trip, she must reproduce (and even participate in) the very dynamics which would conventionally exclude women from this very experience. In other words, she must *become* Imlay, be his "imperial eyes," when ostensibly all she wants is for him to see and even claim her own (shared) "historied body." No wonder she meets with little success upon her return. Yet writing within this new context of discovery, Wollstonecraft's isolation becomes chosen, her alienation a source of strength rather than weakness. She can rewrite her abandonment by Imlay as a victory over space and the allotment of her own time.

But at what price?

IV

It is Wollstonecraft herself who raises such a question. Once her business is largely concluded and her journey becomes one of repetition rather than discovery (a recursive structure more reminiscent of the woman's story), Wollstonecraft's own "agency" begins to unravel.[34] Once Wollstonecraft is literally *retracing* her steps, returning to her daughter who has remained behind, her isolation becomes no longer chosen, but forced upon her. Entering Tonsberg, she "dread[s] the solitariness of [her] apartment" and in that dread, "wish[es] for night" and a return to sleepfulness—to "close my eyes on a world where I was destined to wander alone"(298). In this unbidden state of isolation, "self-applause" becomes a cold solitary feeling, one that cannot supply the place of disappointed affection" (298). Thus, if in the first half of her narrative, her isolation is controlled, plotted, even self-possessed, now it becomes merely a product of a society that would exclude her as different.

Within this more familiar domain, she becomes once again the object of discovery rather than its subject, and this time there is no enabling doubleness in this pose: "I drew near my old abode . . . Tonsberg was something like a home—yet I was to enter without lighting up pleasure in any eye"(298). Here, Wollstonecraft makes herself—unselfconsciously—the object to be surveyed and only laments that she has no such permanent status. Moreover, without business to direct her journey and her prose, Wollstonecraft loses much of her composure. Faced with her return to Imlay and a return to her status as a mere seduced and abandoned lover, she notes, "I cannot write composedly" (299).

Yet ultimately, what she abandons is not her own writing, but the language of discovery itself. She begins to question this "fair trade." By the end of the journey, she confesses, "I am weary of changing scene, and quitting people and places the moment they begin to interest me" (299) and connects explicitly this largely unsatisfying quest for the new with

Imlay's equally troubling insistence for novelty in women. She longs for the familiar, and in particular for Fanny, the reminder of her own affections and even her own "colonized" state—this daughter the product of a earlier transaction between herself and a noted profiteer. Wollstonecraft cannot sustain the rhetoric of discovery: she is too much its object, far more written upon than its writing subject.

It is the recollection of Fanny, her illegitimate child, that reminds her of this prior and prioritizing status. Catching sight of a peasant family—a father, boy, and "little girl . . . mounted a straddle on a shaggy horse"—as she journeys across land, she laments:

> My eyes followed them to the cottage, and an involuntary sigh whispered to my heart, that I envied the mother, much as I dislike cooking, who was preparing their pottage. I was returning to my babe, who may never experience a father's care or tenderness. The bosom that nurtured her, heaved with a pang at the thought which only an unhappy mother could feel. (315)

Remembering Fanny, Wollstonecraft remembers her own "discovered" status—her own heart and her own body already claimed by the now distant Imlay. At this point, she realizes that she and her daughter will always remain "other" to their sovereign, her own journey a return to that status rather than an exploration. As a result, she is no longer separate from the world she inspects, (indeed even overcoming her own dislike of cooking to make the above analogy), but far too visible within it. Yet even though she can now see her own plight in this new world, it no longer reflects back a image she can be proud of—as Belsey explained, the prerogative of the colonizer. And not incidentally, with this recognition comes the acknowledgment that Imlay cannot feel what she feels for Fanny, that her statements of pride in her daughter will have little currency within the now alien world of her intended reader.

The letter ends abruptly with this passage, and from this point on, her prose grows progressively more fragmentary, seemingly hasty, certainly less likely to "conquer" Imlay's heart, and, when one reads the private letters, shocking suicidal. Yet with this loss, she begins to break down the distance between herself and the people she surveys, to recover some of the affective possibilities of her more radical prose. She begins to re-imagine Imlay's commercial venture along the familiar plot lines of her own work and experience. Yet is it, one wonders, ultimately a "fair trade"?

NOTES

The author would like to thank Robin Inboden, Mimi Dixon, Susannah Mintz, and Adam Todd for their comments on previous versions of this essay.

1. The fact that until recently the most readily available edition of the *Letters Written in Sweden* included both this text and Godwin's *Memoirs* has further entrenched this status. As Godwin's *Memoirs* appear first in this edition, we learn of the *Letters'* reputation, then read the actual text. The significance of this work becomes, in effect, predetermined by Godwin's own reading. See Mary Wollstonecraft, *A Short Residence in Sweden, Norway, and Denmark.* With William Godwin, *Memoirs of the Author of "The Rights of Woman,"* ed. Richard Holmes (New York: Penguin, 1987).

2. Janet Todd and Marilyn Butler, introduction to *The Works of Mary Wollstonecraft*, 7 vols., by Mary Wollstonecraft (New York: New York University Press, 1989), 21.

3. Quoted in Ralph Wardle, *Mary Wollstonecraft: A Critical Biography* (Lincoln: University of Nebraska Press, 1951), 256.

4. Wardle, *Mary Wollstonecraft*, 256.

5. The five biographies of Mary Wollstonecraft published in the early 1970s, for all their varying degrees of approval of their subject, concur on this one point: this text is her most revealing and, not incidentally, her most successful. See Margaret George, *One Woman's "Situation": A Study of Mary Wollstonecraft* (Urbana: University of Illinois Press, 1970) and Edna Nixon, *Mary Wollstonecraft: Her Life and Times* (London: J.M. Dent & Sons, 1971). Emily Sunstein in *A Different Face: The Life of Mary Wollstonecraft* (New York: Harper & Row, 1975) gives fuller expression to this sentiment, finding the *Letters* a "vehicle through which she could display all her charm, personality, and intellect to convince the public of her distinction and value" (294). Claire Tomalin in *The Life and Death of Mary Wollstonecraft* (New York: Meridian, 1974) finds it a rare occasion of "harmony in a life and career more characteristically chaotic and shrill." Yet still, she argues, this work is Wollstonecraft's most natural: "There was no pretense of a systematic approach: Mary had simply allowed her eye for nature, her curiosity about mankind and her bent toward didacticism to run together in an oddly successful harmony" (185). Eleanor Flexner, however, in *Mary Wollstonecraft* (New York: Penguin, 1972), proves a bit more skeptical, wondering if Wollstonecraft in this work "displays a canniness worthy of old Edward Wollstonecraft, in turning her anguish to account" (222).

6. Gary Kelly, *Revolutionary Feminism: The Mind and Career of Mary Wollstonecraft* (New York: New York University Press), 177.

7. Mary Poovey, *The Proper Lady and the Woman Writer* (Chicago: University of Chicago Press, 1984), 82–113.

8. Syndy Conger, *Mary Wollstonecraft and the Language of Sensibility* (New Jersey: Associated University Presses, 1994), 153.

9. The review in *New Annual Register for 1796* (1796):248–49 mentions that there is a mysterious melancholy tone to this work, but offers no speculation upon

its cause other than it must result from some cruel disappointment. The review in *The British Critic* 7 (1796): 602–10 claims to have specific and "insider" knowledge of the source of Wollstonecraft's new-found feminine sensibilities, but offers no details to its readers.

10. Mary Wollstonecraft. "Letters to Imlay." In *The Works of Mary Wollstonecraft*, Vol. 6, 365–438.

11. Mariana Alcoforado, *The Portuguese Letters*, trans. Donald E. Ericson (New York: Crown Publishers, 1941). Also, see Linda Kauffman, *Discourses of Desire: Gender, Genre, and Epistolary Fiction* (Ithaca: Cornell University Press, 1986) for a description of the typical heroine of the seduction tale.

12. Holmes, introduction to *A Short Residence in Sweden, Norway, and Denmark*, 25.

13. Quoted in Holmes, introduction to *A Short Residence in Sweden, Norway, and Denmark*, 22.

14. Mary Favret, *Romantic Correspondence: Women, Politics, and the Fiction of Letters* (Cambridge: Cambridge University Press, 1993), 110.

15. Charles Batten, *Pleasurable Instruction: Form and Convention in Eighteenth-Century Travel Literature*. (Berkeley: University of Berkeley Press, 1978), 6. In the latter decades of the eighteenth century, Batten further explains, this "thirst for knowledge" took the form of more subjective reminiscences, with even the recounting of "trifling occurrences" becoming significant. The enumeration of such "trivial events" would certainly not lead to any profitable inventory of this "new world," but such "hints" could, as one theorist of the period argues, "lead the mind to exert it own activity" (77) and hence allow the reader to claim this travel experience as his or her own. Indeed, Wollstonecraft's advertisement for this work echoes this general sentiment: she notes in her preface that "the effect different objects had produced on my mind and feelings" will take precedence over simple "description" (241).

16. Mary Louise Pratt, *Imperial Eyes: Travel Writing and Transculturation* (London: Routledge, 1992), 7.

17. Pratt in *Imperial Eyes* draws this equation between "capitalist commerce" and "romantic love": "As an ideology, romantic love, like capitalist commerce, understands itself as reciprocal. Reciprocity, love requited between individuals worthy of each other, is its ideal state. The failure of reciprocity,or of equivalence between parties, is its central tragedy and scandal" (97).

18. Tzvetan Todorov in *The Morals of History*, trans. Alyson Waters (Minneapolis: University of Minnesota Press, 1995) would go even further in breaking down in the distinction between these forms, for Todorov all true travel narratives are by definition conquest narratives. He writes, "In order to ensure the tension necessary to the travel narrative, the specific position of the colonizer is required: curious about the other, and secure in his own position" (69).

19. Gilbert Imlay, *A Topographical Description of the Western Territory of North America* (London: J. Debrett, 1792).

20. For notable examples of this form, see Jonathan Carver, *Travels through the Interior Parts of North America* (London, 1778); Thomas Cooper, *Some Information*

Respecting America (London, 1794); John Filson, *The Discovery and Settlement of Kentuckee* (London, 1784); Thomas Hutchins, *A Topographical Description of Virginia, Pennsylvania, Maryland and North Carolina* (London, 1778); and Brissot de Warville, *New Travels in the United States* (London, 1792).

21. In its review of Thomas Cooper's topographical work *Some Information Respecting America, The British Critic* V (1795) accuses Imlay of being Cooper's "rival auctioneer," with Imlay "being an agent for the disposal of landed property in Kentucky" (27). *The British Critic* ultimately amends this statement in respect to Cooper's motives, but not in respect to Imlay's.

22. Gilbery Imlay, *A Topographical Description of the Western Territory of North America*, iv.

23. Mary Wollstonecraft, "Letters Written during a Short Residence in Sweden, Norway, and Denmark." In *The Works of Mary Wollstonecraft*, vol. 6, 288, and cited parenthetically hereafter in the text.

24. Gilbert Imlay, *The Emigrants*, ed. W. M. Verhoven and Amanda Gilroy (New York: Penguin, 1998).

25. John Hare in his 1964 reprint of *The Emigrants* (Gainesville, Fla: Scholars' Facsimiles and Reprints, 1964) makes it literally Wollstonecraft's own, attributing both the novel, with its strikingly feminist agenda and, more strangely, *A Topographical Description* to Wollstonecraft herself. For a depiction of their relationship as having this pretension to a new world romance, see Ralph Wardle, *Mary Wollstonecraft: A Critical Biography*, 215–57.

26. Also, see Elizabeth Bohls, *Women Travel Writers and The Language of Aesthetics, 1716–1818* (Cambridge: Cambridge University Press, 1995) for another recent and significant work which re-positions *The Letters* as public discourse.

27. Mary Favret, *Romantic Correspondences*, 97 and Karen Lawrence, *Penelope's Voyages: Women and Travel in the British Literary Tradition* (Ithaca: Cornell University Press, 1994), 74–79.

28. Louis Montrose, "The Work of Gender in the Discourse of Discovery." In *New World Encounters*, ed. Stephen Greenblatt (Berkeley: University of California Press, 1993), 182.

29. Catherine Belsey, *Desire: Love Stories in Western Culture* (Oxford: Blackwell Publishers, 1994), 138–39.

30. Quoted in Belsey, *Desire*, 138.

31. Michel de Certeau, *The Writing of History*, trans. Tom Conley (New York: Columbia University Press, 1995), xxvi.

32. Montrose, "The Work of Gender in the Discourse of Discovery," 182.

33. Certeau, *The Writing of History*, 227.

34. See Karen Lawrence, *Penelope's Voyages*, 79–85 for a thorough and excellent discussion of how this text borrows from the recursive structure of the seduction tale.

John Adams Confronts Turgot

A. OWEN ALDRIDGE

A recent scholar has described John Adams's *Defence of the Constitutions of the United States of America* (1787) as perhaps the most important work of American political thought prior to *The Federalist*.[1] It ranks in significance with three other eighteenth-century literary works published originally in Europe by eminent Americans, Benjamin Franklin's *Memoirs,* Thomas Paine's *Age of Reason,* and Thomas Jefferson's *Notes on Virginia.* According to a specialist on French-American relations, Durand Echeveria, John Adams "seems to have been the only diplomat besides Franklin to make a lasting impression on the French public."[2] A distinguished librarian, Zoltan Haraszti, has given a systematic description of Adams's *Defence*,[3] and a Belgian historian, Jean-Paul Goffinon, has given the work a penetrating analysis,[4] but American scholarship in general has neglected the work, probably because the *Defence of the Constitutions of the United States of America*, despite its title, has more to do with Europe than with America. It is composed essentially of quotations from European authors whose works were not at the time to be found in the United States, even in the best libraries.

Adams does not mention Turgot at all in the title of the first edition of his *Defence* in 1787, but the following year he added to the title page of an expanded edition of three volumes the phrase "against the attack of Mr.

Turgot." In a letter to John Trumbull four years later, 23 January 1791, he seems to defend himself for drawing attention to Turgot in this way: "If another edition should ever be published, I would insert in the titlepage: 'A defence, &c. against the attack of M. Turgot.' This, I apprehend, would cure all defects in point of title."[5] Presumably Adams believed that the addition of the symbol for *etcetera* to the title would serve to decrease the significance of Turgot and suggest the importance of other matters. The only change he made in a new edition in 1794, however, does not in the least detract attention from his French opponent: "*Against the Attack of M. Turgot in his Letter to Dr. Price Dated the Twenty-Second day of March 1784.*" In this succession of titles, Adams may have meant to convey the impression that Turgot's attack was delivered against the Constitution of the United States, but the final subtitle suggests that it had been directed against Adams himself. The latter was not in any sense true. Price published Turgot's letter in 1784, shortly after the latter's death, when he included it as an appendix to his own *Observations on the Importance of the American Revolution and the Means of Making it a Benefit to the World.* Readers of Adams's *Defence* three years later in 1787 would have had no reason to associate the work in any way with Turgot. They may well have considered it a reply to a similar study by the abbé Gabriel Bonnot de Mably. On the other hand, Mably's *Observations sur le gouvernement et les lois des Etats-Unis de l'Amérique* (1784) boldly states on its first page that it is addressed to Adams: "A Mr. ADAMS, Ministre Plénipotentiare des Etats-Unis en Holland & pour les Négotiations de la Paix." The title of an English translation in London was even more specific concerning the role of Adams: *Remarks concerning the Government and the Laws of the United States of America: in Four Letters Addressed to Mr. Adams* (London: Debrett, 1784).

Biographers have suggested that Adams wrote his *Defence* in order to prepare the way for his return to the United States. Because of his absence in Europe, he had dropped out of the public eye in America and needed to fortify his reputation.[6] The hypothesis does not explain why he selected the particular subject of the state constitutions, however. It may be that he had subconsciously felt the urge to reply to Mably's *Observations*, to which his *Defence* is slightly related, but had refrained from doing so, thinking that such an action could be condemned as ungracious if interpreted as censuring a work that he was thought to have encouraged. According to one of his own explanations, written many years later, during June 1809, his book was inspired by his perception of the seeds of the French Revolution in the sessions of the Assembly of Notables in 1787. He had predicted the carnage and desolation that was to ensue, he said: "I was determined to wash my hands of the blood that was about to be shed in France, Europe, and America, and show to the world that neither my sentiments nor actions should have any share in countenancing or encouraging any such pernicious, destructive, and fatal schemes."[7] But the explanation depends too much upon hindsight to be taken seriously, particularly since there is no warning of any French upheaval in the *Defence*.[8]

In a letter to Jefferson, 13 July 1813, Adams affirmed that he had originally decided to write about his theories of government after hearing Lafayette hold forth on the topic for an entire evening in the presence of Adams and his son John Quincy at Jefferson's residence in Paris. According to Adams, "I was astonished at the Grossness of his Ignorance of Government and History, as I had been for Years before at that of Turgot, Rochefaucault [*sic*], Condorcet and Franklin." Their "gross Ideology," as he went on to call it, gave him the notion of rebutting their theories, despite his lack of reputation in Europe, the pains he experienced through the exercise of writing, the negligence of his style, his risk of making enemies in both Europe and America, and the difficulty of finding documentary evidence.

> But when the French Assembly of Notables met, and I saw that Turgot's "Government in one Centre and that Centre the Nation" a sentence as misterious [*sic*] or as contradictory as the Athanasian Creed, was about to take place; and when I saw that Shaises [*sic*] Rebellion was breaking out in Massachusetts; and when I saw that even my obscure Name was often quoted in France as an Advocate for simple Democracy; and when I saw that the Sympathies in America had caught the French flame: I was determined to wash my own hands as clean as I could of all the foulness. I had then strong forebodings that I was sacrificing all the honours and Emoluments of this Life; and so it has happened: but not in so great a degree as I apprehended.[9]

He had written in essentially the same masochistic spirit on the eve of publication in a letter to James Warren, 9 January 1787. "Popularity was never my mistress, nor was I ever, or shall I ever be a popular Man. This Book will make me unpopular."[10] Six days later he gave some mundane details of publication in a letter to his brother-in-law, Richard Cranch, and there he traced the origins of his *Defence* directly to conversations on government with friends in Holland previous to his departure in September 1786. The expressed desire of these friends, who "were much employed in revolutions," to see his thoughts in writing together with "disturbances in New England" determined him to write.[11] In this communication there is no mention whatsoever of Turgot.

In a series of letters written in his old age to John Taylor, published under the date 15 April 1814, Adams joins Turgot and the state constitutions of America as twin motives for his *Defence*. He affirms that "the drift of my whole work was to vindicate the constitutions of New York, Massachusetts, and Maryland against the reproaches of that great statesman, philosopher, and really excellent man, whom I well knew, and to defend them against his attacks, and only upon those points on which he had assaulted them."[12] The Massachusetts constitution in particular was dear to Adams because he had exerted considerable influence in its framing, especially its provision for a bicameral legislature, which had been one of his favorite notions ever since 1776 when he had published his *Thoughts on Government* against Thomas Paine's advocacy of unicameralism for the Pennsylvania legislature. A farmers' rebellion led by Daniel Shays demanding easy credit and a halt to foreclosures had subsequently erupted in Massachusetts in August 1786. This movement led to support for a stronger central government on both the state and federal levels. Many of Adams's conservative views in the *Defence* could be read, therefore, not only as replies to Turgot, but as a reaction to the uprisings in Massachusetts and as recommendations for the federal consitution of the United States. The French statesman, however, did not mention the constitution of Massachusetts in his letter to Price nor did Adams accord it separate treatment in his *Defence*.

Adams was also uneasy about his association with Mably's 1784 publication *Observations on the Government of the United States*. He therefore included as a postscript to the first edition of his *Defence* a detailed account of their personal relations, including the text of a letter to the abbé indicating that if he had at one time in conversation seemed to have requested Mably to write upon American affairs, it "was a mere civility," and rather a desire that Mably would not expose himself by "attempting a history that he was altogether unprovided for, than any formal request that he should write at all."[13] Adams repeated the substance of this denial several times, most notably in a communication to the *North American Review* in November 1816 as a reply to a paragraph in the London *Daily Advertiser* suggesting that a review of the *Observations* in October 1789 by Melchior Grimm vindicates Mably's version of the affair.[14]

Adams had an excellent opportunity to repudiate Mably in October 1785, soon after their initial meeting, when Thomas Jefferson's protégé Fillipo Mazzei wrote to him from Amsterdam on the alleged harm being done to the American cause by French writers, particularly the abbé Raynal and the abbé Mably. Mazzei characterized the former as "an Angloman" and the latter as having written "for the mere sake of writing, probably in his dotage, without knowing what he was about." He then asked Adams whether he would like him to contradict Mably's assertion that Adams had "desired him to write on the several constitutions of the United States." Adams rejected the offer, however, on the grounds that no good result would come from "entering into the Fracasseries of the Men of Letters in France."[15] It therefore seems somewhat anomalous that two years later he would himself publish an extensive treatise allegedly designed as a reply to Turgot.

Adams's earliest association of Turgot with his *Defence* exists in a letter to Jefferson, 28 October 1787, shortly after the appearance of the book. He explains that he had chosen the title

> "a Defence of the American Constitution, because it is a resistance to an Attack of Turgot": The two volumes are confined to one point, and if a City is defended from an Attack made on the North Gate, it may be called a Defence of the City, although the other three Gates, the East, West and South Gates were so weak as to have been defenceless, if they had been attacked.—If a Warriour should arise to attack our Constitutions where they are not defencible, I'll not undertake to defend them. Two thirds of our States have made Constitutions, in no respect better than those of the Italian Republicks, and as sure as there is an Heaven and an Earth, if they are not altered they will produce Disorder and Confusion.[16]

Adams's metaphor of the city gates is not crystal clear. What he probably means is that he is using all his strength and efforts in regard to a single concept concerning the American constitutions, the one which, he believes, is the most fundamental, and the one which, he suggests, Turgot opposed and which, by means of his reputation, was tending to subvert the American system of government. According to Adams's metaphor, the single gate or point that needed to be protected against Turgot was that of a bicameral legislature. Adams was correct in affirming that the essence of Turgot's system lay in the concept of collecting all authority into one center, the nation. But Turgot did not equate this center entirely with a single branch of government; instead, he advocated what later scholars have summarized as 'one king, one nation, one house.' It was the concept of one house that upset Adams. For Massachusetts and the rest of the American nation, he advocated a legislative body of two houses rather than that of a single house embraced by Franklin in Pennsylvania and Turgot in France. At that time, however, the French single house, the Estates General, consisted of three groups, the clergy, the nobility, and the commoners. The arguments of Turgot and Adams, therefore, were based entirely on abstractions rather than on actual national governments.

Adams's letter to Trumbull already quoted strongly suggests that he realized that the use of Turgot's name on the title page would draw the attention of European readers. This was important to Adams, for his correspondence reveals that he hoped that French and German translations would follow. But his primary motivation was to promote in the United States the concept of a bicameral legislature. That the work was published early in 1787 or even in the year preceding the date on the title page is indicated by a complimentary letter from Thomas Jefferson of 23 February 1787, affirming that he had read it "with infinite satisfaction and improvement. It will do good in America. It's learning and it's good sense will I hope make it an institute for our politicians, old as well as young."[17] Jefferson's fellow Virginian, James Madison, however, predicted that in regard to the choice of a single or bicameral legislature, the *Defence* would probably "revive the predilections of this country for the British Constitution. Men of learning find nothing new in it, Men of taste many things to criticize, And men without either, not a few things, which they will not understand. . . . I wish many of the remarks in it, which are unfriendly to republicanism, may not receive fresh weight from the operations of our Government."[18]

During the following month, while Jefferson was on vacation in southern France, his secretary William Short sent him similar discouraging news:

> "Mazzei tells me that the men of letters here think very poorly of Mr. Adams [*sic*] book. It is easy to see that these are the disciples of M. Turgot. Mazzei asked me what I thought of it, taking great pains to impress well on my mind that he had not yet read it and of course had not been able to form his opinion. I had just finished it and of course was able to give him mine, which is that it shows Mr. Adams's profound researches on the subject he treats, that there are a great many valuable ideas developped [*sic*] in the work, and that it puts the reader in the plain way of developping others; but that it has neither order in its matter or taste in its style."[19]

In August 1787, Adams sent Jefferson a copy of his second volume along with a letter insisting that in it "every Tryal was intended and contrived to determine the Question whether Mr. Turgot's System would do. The Result you may read. It has cost me a good deal of Trouble and Expense to Search into Italian Rubbish and Ruins. But enough of pure Gold and Marble has been found to reward the Pains. I shall be Suspected of writing Romances to expose Mr. Turgot's theory. But I assure you, it is all genuine history."[20]

As soon as Jefferson finished reading his copy of the first volume, he sent it to the publisher Frouillé to be considered for a translation, assuring Adams that one would be "immediately announced." Short in his letter to Jefferson of 26 March 1787, however, informed Jefferson that he did not believe that a French translation would be successful and would not be generally read. The translator was of the same opinion but was still going on with the work. Adams himself also wrote to Mazzei, 12 June 1787, inquiring about the possibilities of a translation. When one finally came out in 1792, the publisher was Buisson, who had published Franklin's *Memoirs,* rather than Frouillé, whom Jefferson had unsuccessfully approached, but who had published instead an attack on Adams by John Stevens, treated later in this paper. Buisson's double-title encapsulates Adams's purpose: *Défense des Constitutions américaines, ou la Nécessité d'un balance dans les pouvoirs d'un gouvernement libre.* A notice in Grimm's *Correspondance littéraire* indicates that the translator, M. de La Croix, has added some notes attempting to counteract the unfavorable impressions Adams's system might inspire against the "sublime infallibility" of the new French constitution.[21] The editorial introduction to Adams's letter to the *North American Review* in 1816 observes that this French edition is the only one not containing Adams's Postscript which incorporates his letter to Mably.[22] More important, this French edition does not include the first part of the four parts of the first volume, the section that has the most direct criticism of Turgot.

On 30 April 1819, Adams reported incorrectly that the *Defence* had been translated into German. He was, therefore, somewhat amazed when someone subsequently told him that the work had become "rare."[23] He was delighted to learn in the next year, however, that many people, including the American publisher Mathew Carey, had acknowledged their error in condemning the *Defence.* What he found even "more surprising" was that Judge Cooper, "the learned and ingenious friend of Dr. Priestley," had recently published "a very handsome eulogium" of it in the *Portfolio.*[24] The three volumes of the enlarged *Defence* consist primarily of a history of European governments from ancient times through the seventeenth century, eighty per cent in the form of excerpts from writers of each period and twenty percent comprising Adams's own analysis. Adams undoubtedly chose this historical method of exposition because he had tenaciously advocated throughout his entire career the efficacy of history as a guide for political and social action. Early in the American revolution, he entreated his ten-year-old son John Quincy to study history with particular attention to revolutions resembling the one going on around him.[25] H. Trevor Colbourn has observed that by piling up examples of recorded experience in his *Defence* he believed that "he was showing his countrymen how to frame a foolproof constitution. The constitution-makers, meeting at Philadelphia a few months later in 1787, employed a similar technique, reviewing past constitutions for their flaws and weaknesses in an effort to discern the most stable composition for American national needs."[26] The text of Adams's

Defence could also be considered a reflection of his life-long fascination for the classics and for tradition. After chiding Mably on the need for exhaustive historical background, he felt obliged to demonstrate that his own preparation had not been neglected.

Despite his broad denunciation of Turgot, Adams has very little to say about him and even less about Massachusetts in his treatise, most of which is devoted to reprinting the words of celebrated political philosophers from Cicero to Harrington. Adams gives the impression, nevertheless, that he and Turgot were implacably hostile to each other, in large measure because of his objections to the unicameral legislature. In a letter in 1809 he complained, "Mr. Turgot, the Duke of la Rochefoucauld, and Mr. Condorcet and others admired Mr. Franklin's Constitution and reprobated mine."[27]

The essence of his opposition to Turgot is given in six introductory pages of the *Defence*, bearing the title, "Preliminary Observations."[28] Turgot had objected that the state constitutions followed the English system of king, council and legislature rather than a more simple system that would better suit their circumstances. Adams asks his readers to assume that the English "customs," using Turgot's word, are neither good nor evil in themselves, but merely indifferent. Since the American people are by their birth, education, and habits attached to these customs, this in itself would be a reason for their retaining them rather than endangering public tranquility and unanimity by rejection. If, in addition, these customs were "wise, just and good, and calculated to serve the liberty, property and safety of the people," Adams asks whether Turgot would maintain that they should be renounced merely because the people were "justly incensed against the English government." He affirms that Turgot has put forth only a single example of American retention of an allegedly evil custom, "that a body of representatives, a council, and a governor, have been established, because there is in England a house of commons, a house of lords, and a king." Denying that the system of three branches was due primarily to English influence, Adams maintains that it derived from the organization of the colonial assemblies. It was not so much habitual attachment as the influence of nature and reason that had led to the retention of this power structure.

Adams then suggests that Turgot's entire system rests upon a phrase in his letter, "collecting all authority into one centre, the nation." He grants that this could easily be brought about under a despot or a monarch, but otherwise finds it unworkable. "When a number of men, women, and children, are simply congregated together, there is no political authority among them; nor any natural authority but that of parents over their children." Adams then points out the obvious reason why a large body of people cannot form a pure democracy, that large numbers cannot all be gathered together at one time for deciding political issues. "A simple and perfect democracy never yet existed among men." Adams concludes that "M. Turgot intended that an assembly of representatives should be chosen by the nation, and vested with all the powers of government; and that his assembly should be the centre in which all the authority was to be collected, and should virtually be deemed the nation."[29] He then introduces the rest of his book as "placing this idea of M. Turgot in all its lights; in considering the consequences of it, and in collecting a variety of authorities against it." In pursuing this objective, he allowed the method of collecting historical authorities to dominate his entire composition, for in the rest of the work Turgot is almost entirely dropped out of the picture. Indeed his name reappears no more than half a dozen times. An unfriendly critic in the *Monthly Review* observed that except for a single passage quoted from Turgot, the reader of the *Defence* "scarcely acquires any information concerning the constitution of the American states."[30]

In chapter 1, Adams associates Turgot with Rousseau's statement that "a society of gods would govern themselves democratically" by affirming that anyone who accepts Turgot's views must "name the age, the country, and the people in which such an experiment has been tried."[31]

In chapter two he introduces Turgot by the almost obvious statement, "It is scarcely possible to believe that M. Turgot, by collecting all authority into one centre, could have intended an aristocratical assembly" (*Defence,* 4: 328). In a recapitulation at the end of the chapter, he seems to recognize that he cannot very well claim to have refuted Turgot's political system since the latter's letter to Price was not systematic and Adams was covering only one paragraph in it. "If M. Turgot had made any discovery which had escaped the penetration of all the legislators and philosophers who have lived before him, he ought at least to have communicated it to the world for their improvement, but as he has never hinted at any such invention, we may safely conclude that he had none; and therefore, that the Americans are not justly liable to censure for instituting *governors*" (*Defence,* 4: 379). Adams's next sentence merely repeats his major grievance concerning Turgot: "by collecting all authority into one centre he meant a single assembly of representatives of the people without a governor, and without a senate" and that the representatives would be chosen annually (*Defence,* 4: 389). He suggests, moreover, that Turgot derived his favorable opinion of the Pennsylvania constitution from Franklin. He proceeds to attack Turgot's vindication of a single assembly on the basis of "the equality of all citizens" by enumerating a number of inequalities—in wealth, in descent, in education, and in talents. Taking for granted that "property, family and merit" all influence public opinion and public deliberations, he accuses Turgot of inability to discover the exact quantity of each (*Defence,* 4: 389). He then argues that the great fault in a single assembly is that no "counterpoise, balance or equilibrium" exists to restrain it from making and enforcing tyrannical laws. The vigilance of the electorate is no protection, for it is illogical to suppose that the same person who casts a favorable vote for a candidate will immediately after the latter's election turn into a suspicious overseer (*Defence,* 4: 400). Adams does not object to Turgot's denial of the common notion "that liberty consists in being subject only to the laws," but he points out that the principle is true whether the laws are made by a single body or a multiplicity (*Defence,* 4: 401–2). He charges that Turgot should have realized that English political writers when they praised a government of laws and not of men intended the description of a commonwealth, not a definition of liberty (*Defence,* 4: 405). Adams insists that the whole controversy between Turgot and himself depends on whether a unicameral legislature would "compel the formation, impartial execution, and faithful interpretation of good and equal laws" (*Defence,* 4: 406). Here Adams is not far from the truth.

In chapter 6, he says that his purpose is more extensive than merely to show the imperfection of Turgot's ideas, which could be done in a few words (*Defence,* 4: 434). According to such a résumé, Turgot's entire system is based on a single assembly in which the more ambitious members as well as those with most wealth and fewest scruples would use their wealth and chicanery to gain power, thereby contaminating the assembly with rage and violence. The only remedy would be "to throw the rich and the proud into one group, in a separate assembly, and there tie their hands" (*Defence,* 4: 444). Adams concludes that the only way of realizing Turgot's system in America would be to follow the example of the Greek city-states by forming every town into a free and independent democracy and allowing them to go to war with each other. The population would be divided by lot into slaves and freemen, 80 percent and 20 percent respectively. The slaves would labor in agriculture and the mechanical arts, and the freemen would go to war and do nothing else (*Defence,* 4: 504).

Adams recognized that Turgot was a lover of liberty, but only of the kind that could be introduced into France and reconciled with a simple monarchy (*Defence,* 4: 559–60). Adams also granted that Turgot was an "enthusiast for the liberty of commerce, the liberty of religious sentiments, and the personal liberty of the subject," but insisted that he was not "an enthusiast for a free constitution of government" (*Defence,* 4: 560). This is the final mention of Turgot in the *Defence*. He does not appear at all in volumes 2 and 3. Adams was not really writing against Turgot, but against the theory of collecting all authority into one center.

One of Franklin's circle in Paris, the abbé André Morellet, reported sardonically to Franklin on the first appearance of the *Defence:*

> "Toute cette érudition sur les anciennes républiques me paroît de l'encre et du papier perdus. Je ne crois pas qu'on puisse en tirer une seule conseqence véritablement logique et qui puisse déterminer un homme d'état à faire ou à ne faire pas une seule démarche. C'est dans la raison et non dans faits tantôt unique[,] tantôt mal constatés et mal connus qu'il faut chercher les vrais principes d'une bonne constitution et d'une bonne législation."[32]

In a letter to William Petty, Marquis of Lansdowne, Morellet was even more caustic, describing Adams's work as "le bavardage le plus inlisible qu'on puisse voir. A propos de quatre mots de mr. Turgot[,] il verse l'encre sur le papier."[33]

One of Adams's political opponents in New York, John Stevens, published in that city in 1787 *Observations on Government, including some Animadversions on Mr. Adams's Defence,* calling Adams a "stale empiric," who prescribes one single remedy, "Order" and "Balance," for all illnesses. What brings Adams "to the highest pitch, is, that not a single sample of this universal and so much boasted political nostrum is to be found in any one of the governments of the United States." Denominating him "Doctor Adams," Stevens charges that amidst "all the rubbage [*sic*] which with *profound* and infinite pains he has collected from the storehouses and magazines of antiquity," not one single passage could be styled as a defense of American constitutions.[34] Adams realized that the general reception accorded to the *Defence* was not favorable. In his letter to John Taylor, 16 April 1814, he maintained that his book "has been misunderstood, misrepresented, and abused, more than any other, except the Bible, that I have ever read."[35]

Elsewhere Adams expressed himself more fully about Turgot by means of handwritten comments interlaced in his copy of Turgot's letter to Price as it is printed in the latter's *Observations on the Importance of the American Revolution.*[36] This private commentary constitutes no more of a rebuttal of Turgot's entire principles and system, however, than does the historical compilation of the *Defence*. His commentary is nevertheless thorough. He reacts to every idea in the letter, even dividing some of Turgot's sentences in order to comment separately on each part. Yet these comments are not by any means all attacks. Some express agreement, some are complimentary, some give additional information, and some express personal reactions. The hostile or unfavorable comments are by and large limited to the issues stressed also in the *Defence,* those which are linked in some way with collecting all authority into one center. On the limitations of Locke's principle of rule by law, not by men, Adams remarks, "Republican writers contend that liberty consists in being subject to equal laws only. If any have omitted the word equal, they have supposed that a free people would make no other but equal laws." Or again, on the possibility of individual rights being denied by the central authority, Adams remarks "Laws may be unjust, the public will is not infallible. But personal liberty must be restrained in some cases so must property."[37] On Turgot's charge that the American states copied English tradition by establishing three powers in their own governments, Adams pours forth his frustration: "What does he mean [by] collecting all authority into one center? What does he mean by the center of a nation? Where would he have the legislation placed? Where the execution? Where the decision of controversies? Emptier pieces of declamation, I never read: It is impossible to give a greater proof of ignorance."[38] Concerning the economic clashes arising from each state possessing the right to tax and regulate commerce, Adams recognizes that problems may occur. Although an "enemy to embargoes, prohibitions, exclusions" in general, he "cannot swear that they are always unlawful or impolitic."[39] On similar problems likely to arise from the diversities in laws, customs, and opinions in various states, Adams agrees with Turgot while seeming to oppose him. "Americans must consider more soberly than Mr. Turgot did what is practicable and what is not. One homogeneous body cannot be made out of such heterogeneous parts scattered over such an immense continent. The parts are too distant as well as unlike."[40] On American opposition to a standing army as opposed to a militia, Adams says bluntly, "This Letter is a mass of wild, inconsistent reveries and paradoxes."[41] On Turgot's description of the American people as "the hope of mankind," however, Adams says "Mr. Turgot is very good."[42]

Although these marginalia cover nearly all of Turgot's letter, with more emphasis on prediction of the future than analysis of the past, their opposition to Turgot is almost entirely limited to points connected with the central authority in the state. They are no more a blanket repudiation of Turgot than Turgot's letter to Price is a rude and insolent attack on the American constitutions. Likewise Adams's *Defence* is directed against Turgot but not primarily against the Turgot's letter to Price. If his opposition to Turgot was no more extensive than that against Mably, he had no incentive to reveal publicly his attitude toward the latter. Although he appreciated both men as individuals and dinner companions, classifying them together as "amiable, learned and ingenious," he did not believe that either one was competent to criticize the American constitutions—especially that of Massachusetts, to which he had assumed a proprietary right.[43]

NOTES

1. Johnson Kent Wright, *A Classical Republican in Eighteenth-Century France: The Political Thought of Mably* (Stanford: Stanford University Press, 1997), 179.

2. Durand Echeverria, *Mirage in the West: A History of the French Image of American Society to 1815,* with a foreword by Gilbert Chinard (Princeton: Princeton University Press, 1957), 45.

3. *John Adams and the Prophets of Progress* (Cambridge, MA: Harvard University Press, 1952).

4. *Aux origines de la Révolution américaine* (Bruxelles: Editions de l'Université de Bruxelles, 1996).

5. *The Works of John Adams*, ed. Charles Francis Adams, 10 vols. (Boston: Charles C. Little, 1856), 9: 573.

6. Thomas Ferling, *John Adams: A Life* (Knoxville: University of Tennessee Press, 1992), 287.

7. Adams, *Works*, 6: 623.

8. In a letter to Jefferson, 13 November 1815, Adams cites Price's biographer William Morgan as authority for his opinion. According to Morgan, Adams wrote a long letter to Price in which "he expresses himself in terms of contempt in regard to the French Revolution; and after asking rather too severely, what good was to be expected from a nation of atheists, he concludes with foretelling the destruction of a million human beings as a result of it" (Adams, *Works*, 10: 175). A letter from Adams to Thomas Brand Hollis dated 11 June 1790, however, at the very height of the revolution, indicates an attitude bordering on indifference: "We are in no more danger than the empire of China is. The great revolution in France is wonderful, but not supernatural. The hand of Providence is in it, I doubt not, working, however, by natural and ordinary means, such as produced the reformation in religion in the sixteenth century" (9: 570).

9. *The Adams-Jefferson Letters*, ed. Lester J. Cappon, 2 vols. (Chapel Hill: University of North Carolina Press, 1959), 2: 350–55.

10. *Warren-Adams Letters*, 2 vols. (Boston: Massachusetts Historical Society, 1917), 2: 281.

11. Adams, *Works*, 1: 432.

12. Ibid., 6: 486.

13. Ibid., 5: 492.

14. Ibid., 4: 48–50.

15. *The Papers of Thomas Jefferson*, ed. Julian P. Boyd and others, 27 vols. to date (Princeton: Princeton University Press, 1950–97) 8: 679, n.

16. Ibid., 12: 291.

17. Ibid., 11: 177.

18. Ibid., 11: 163.

19. Ibid., 11: 239–40.

20. Adams, *Works,* 8: 447–48.

21. Friedrich Melchior Grimm, *Correspondance littéraire*, ed. Maurice Tourneux, 16 vols. (Paris: Garnier frères), 1872–82.

22. Adams, *Works,* 4: 48.

23. Ibid., 10: 379

24. Ibid., 10: 39.

25. *Familiar Letters of John Adams and His Wife Abigail*, ed. Charles Francis Adams (New York: Hard and Houghton, 1876), 284.

26. *The Lamp of Experience* (Chapel Hill: University of North Carolina Press, 1965), 101.

27. Adams, *Works*, 9: 623.

28. Ibid., 4: 299–302.

29. Ibid., 4: 302.

30. John Adams, *Diary and Autobiography*, ed. L. H. Butterfield, 4 vols. (Cambridge, MA: Harvard University Press, 1961), 4: 74, n.7.

31. Adams, *Works,* 4: 303, and cited hereafter in the text as *Defence.*

32. André Morellet, *Lettres,* eds. Dorothy Medlin and Paul Leclerc, 2 vols. (Oxford: Voltaire Foundation, 1991), 2: 273.

33. Ibid., 2: 260.

34. (New York: W. Ross, 1787), 3. A translation of Stevens's work appeared two years later with the title *Examen du gouvernement d'Angleterre, Ou l'on réfute quelques assertions contenues dans l'ouvrage de M. Adams, intitulé* Apologie des Constitutions des Etats-Unis d'l'Amérique, *& dans celui de M. Delolme, intitulé:* De la Constitutions d'Angleterre ("A Londres"; Paris: Frouillé, 1789). The work appeared three years before a translation of the *Defence* was published. Its translator in a lengthy series of notes protects Adams's talents and integrity against Stevens's sarcasm, affirming that he was justified in his corrections, but also wishing that he had been less extreme in expressing them.

35. Adams, *Works*, 6: 447.

36. Zoltan Haraszti prints Turgot's text and Adams's corresponding commentary in dialogue form in his *John Adams and the Prophets of Progress* (Cambridge, MA: Harvard University Press, 1952), 142–53.

37. Haraszti, *Adams and the Prophets*, 144.

38. Ibid., 143.

39. Ibid., 147.

40. Ibid., 140.

41. Ibid., 151.

42. Ibid.

43. Adams, *Works,* 5: 4.

Swift's Servant Problem: Livery and Hypocrisy in the *Project for the Advancement of Religion* and the *Directions to Servants*

JENNY DAVIDSON

Very few people are willing to speak up for hypocrisy. As a rule, to use the word at all is to position oneself against it.[1] I am no more likely to identify myself as a hypocrite than I am to call myself a cannibal, although I may do either so long as I invoke a rhetoric of confession or conversion to separate my present identity from the past one I name and thereby disavow. Many defenses of hypocrisy begin by giving it an attractive alias: manners, civility, decorum, self-control, politeness. To defend hypocrisy under its own name means breaking a taboo, and a strong incentive is required to risk the outrage such a defense is likely to provoke. Not the least remarkable aspect of Jonathan Swift's defense of hypocrisy, the *Project for the Advancement of Religion* (1709), is the extent to which Swift foregrounds the very word *hypocrisy*.[2] The success of Swift's *Project* depends in a sense on his careful management of two words. One of these words is *hypocrisy*. The other is *livery*, a term whose signification in eighteenth-century discourse is curiously divided: used metaphorically, it offers a conventional analogy for surfaces or appearances, while its literal meaning is associated with an explosive set of arguments about the rights and duties of the servant class.

As Swift puts it in the *Project*, "Hypocrisy is much more eligible than open Infidelity and Vice: It wears the Livery of Religion, it acknowledgeth her Authority, and is cautious of giving Scandal" (2:59–60). The phrase "the Livery of Religion" momentarily undermines Swift's positive argument for hypocrisy as the best approximation of virtue, introducing into his metaphor a key word in contemporary attacks on the behavior and morals of servants in livery. Indeed, it is not just the extensive pamphlet literature on servants but Swift's own *Directions to Servants* (1745) that directs a battery of satire against servants in livery, identifying livery with not-so-secret insolence in a manner that would seem to subvert the *Project*'s case for wearing "the Livery of Religion." Yet once the *Project* and the *Directions* are situated in the context of early-eighteenth-century attacks on bad servants by Locke, Defoe, Mandeville and others, the structural underpinnings of Swift's argument in favor of hypocrisy become clear. The presence of bad servants in arguments about virtue turns out to be not accidental but essential, and the evidence suggests that successful defenses of hypocrisy depend on a strategy of exclusion. Swift is finally able to promote certain kinds of hypocrisy because he rejects what he identifies as the destructive and self-interested hypocrisy of the servant class.

On the surface, the *Directions to Servants* has little in common with the *Project*. The *Project* is difficult to identify generically, though it has been described on occasion as an unsuccessful prose satire, a political polemic or a radical moral treatise. The satire of the *Directions* is far more straightforward. Published posthumously, this compilation of mock-advice is formally related not to Swift's moral writings but to his other major compilation on manners, *A Complete Collection of Polite and Ingenious Conversation* (1738). Their mutual interest in livery, however, works as a hinge to connect the *Directions* to the *Project*. Johnson's *Dictionary* provides an eighteenth-century precedent for this cross-referencing of the word *livery* across Swift's career. To illustrate the word *hypocrisy* (defined as "dissimulation with regard to the moral or religious character"), Johnson cites Swift's *Project*: "*Hypocrisy* is much more eligible than open infidelity and vice: it wears the livery of religion, and is cautious of giving scandal: nay, continued disguises are too great a constraint: men would leave off their vices, rather than undergo the toil of practising them in private."[3] And though the term *livery* appears in this passage, Johnson chooses to illustrate the word "livery" under its own heading not by the metaphorical usage of the *Project* but by a literal example from the *Directions to Servants*: "If your dinner miscarries, you were teized by the footmen coming into the kitchen; and to prove it true, throw a ladleful of broth on one or two of their *liveries*."

Reading the *Project* alongside the *Directions*, then, offers a critical opportunity to illuminate Swift's main argument about hypocrisy by bringing back together his metaphorical and literal uses of the word livery. How does Swift's attack on liveried servants in the *Directions* inform his central argument for hypocrisy in the *Project*? Given the strong etymological connection between hypocrisy and part-playing—hypocrisy traditionally involves putting on a costume or a mask—and the existence of pairs of words like *custom* and *costume*, or *habit* (in the sense of a pattern of behavior) and *habit* (a suit of clothes), it seems plausible enough that the word *livery* should describe both a servant's dress and a habit that becomes a second nature. But even a quick survey of early-eighteenth-century writing on servants reveals that the connotations of livery are almost entirely negative. In fact, the rhetorical risk of giving the term *livery* a positive inflection corresponds quite precisely to that of using the word *hypocrisy* in a favorable sense. Swift's *Project* offers a version of the famous Liar's Paradox: the sincere defense of hypocrisy enacts a performative contradiction akin to the act of identifying oneself as a liar. Swift's defense of hypocrisy is hardly a simple argument about power and class, and the transgressive energy of the *Directions* is no more reducible to the terms of a patrician ideology than are the flexible positions of the *Project*. Yet to substitute the word *livery* for the word *hypocrisy* is to invoke a problematic discourse about deception and class relations, a discourse that I will explore here in order to map the limits of Swift's argument for hypocrisy.

In his book on the role of servants in the realist tradition, Bruce Robbins describes "the surprising and (to one trained as a historical critic) annoying sameness of these formal manifestations of literary service."[4] This observation applies equally to the employment of the topos of the bad servant in moral writing, and I do not mean to suggest either that the servant problem Swift describes is a new one or that his arguments about servants differ fundamentally from those of Mandeville, Defoe, Fielding and others. Yet it is important to account for the ways in which Swift finds servants both useful and problematic when he writes about virtue. Positive arguments for hypocrisy seem finally to be liable to a structural instability that Swift actually exploits when he claims that hypocrisy wears the livery of religion. In the context of the *Project*, Swift's livery metaphor pays deference to a related set of arguments against crudely self-interested forms of hypocrisy, allowing Swift very efficiently to acknowledge both the drawbacks and the advantages of his argument for hypocrisy. The success of the argument depends in turn on this act of rhetorical exclusion. Hypocrisy is allowed to be a good thing for certain elements of society only because servants are forbidden as a class to practice what might be called the good forms of hypocrisy; in other words, Swift is able to retain hypocrisy as an upper-class privilege because he denies it as a right to the servant class.

I

Swift's *Project for the Advancement of Religion* (1709) opens with a statement whose language is congruent with that of the projector. The con artist always promises that his own scheme is like no other, that it may be easily implemented and that he will remedy universal ills by means of a cure-all that is both obvious and completely original. "Among all the Schemes offered to the Publick in this projecting Age," Swift writes,

> I have observed, with some Displeasure, that there have never been any for the Improvement of Religion and Morals: Which, besides the Piety of the Design from the Consequences of such a Reformation in a future Life, would be the best natural Means for advancing the publick Felicity of the State, as well as the present Happiness of every Individual. For, as much as Faith and Morality are declined among us, I am altogether confident, they might, in a short Time, and with no very great Trouble be raised to as high a Perfection, as Numbers are capable of receiving. Indeed the Method is so easy and obvious, and some present Opportunities so good; that, in order to have this Project reduced to Practice, there seems to want nothing more than to put those in mind, who by their Honour, Duty, and Interest are chiefly concerned. (2:44–45)

Even a cursory glance at the closely contemporary *Argument against Abolishing Christianity* should alert readers to some dubious features of this argument. To claim that one's own project is exempt from the objections applying to schemes in general tends to elicit suspicion, not confidence. Moreover, rather than relying on the obvious benefits of his design in this world, Swift uses the distracting word "besides" to bracket a secondary argument about its payoff in the next. His parenthetical aside about "a future Life" thus undercuts the references that follow to "the publick Felicity of the State" and "the present Happiness of every Individual." The order of these claims is counterintuitive: a more persuasive argument would probably build from the immediate consequence of the individual's present happiness, through the public good, to one's long-term benefit in the afterlife. The sentence that follows is even more characteristic of the classic scam: this projector is "altogether confident" that "in a short Time, and with no very great Trouble," his "easy and obvious" method will transform both religion and morals. If the method be so easy and obvious, the reader may ask, why has it not already been adopted?

The symptoms of language that arouse the reader's suspicion can hardly be accounted for by the assumption that the *Project*'s primary mode is ironic, since critics have found it extremely difficult to sustain a reading of the *Project* as a straightforward satire. Their interpretations either emphasize the pamphlet's morality at the expense of its satire, or vice versa. Caught in this bind, Irvin Ehrenpreis calls the *Project* "both the finest and the flattest of Swift's essays on religion and morality" and suggests that it "reflects so shallow and banal an intellect that some acute scholars have thought it a parody."[5] Contemporary critical assessments were no less equivocal. While one of Swift's Tory colleagues thought that the *Project* might be "of very great use," the *Tatler* mentions nothing about the pamphlet's utility, calling attention instead to the author's "Good Breeding."[6] The list of apparently incompatible qualities attributed to the *Project* does not stop here. Samuel Johnson writes in the *Life of Swift* that the *Project* is "formed with great purity of intention."[7] But Thomas Sheridan notes that in spite of the fact that the pamphlet appears to be "written by some disinterested hand, from no other principle but a due regard to religion and morality," a closer examination reveals "that nothing could be more directly, though covertly, aimed at the destruction of the power of the Whigs."[8] The *Project* is accordingly supposed to be at once pure, disinterested and gentlemanly; partial, political and expedient; even, perhaps, tyrannical and totalitarian.[9] Can it possibly be all of these things at once?

Swift's main tactic in the *Project* is to perform a strategic displacement of morality into manners. The text substitutes the relative for the absolute in a rhetorical move that would subsequently become associated with Burke, whose writings allow manners to do the work of morals by means of habit, custom and prejudice. J. G. A. Pocock and others have shown the centrality of the concept of manners to eighteenth-century political writing, and a society that constitutes manners as a crucial term for understanding political virtue must almost of necessity celebrate hypocrisy as a leading value.[10] Many of the rhetorical oddities of the *Project* can be directly attributed to the tension between its all-or-nothing commitment to morality and its readiness to substitute manners for morals. The pamphlet is obliged to reconcile its own absolute condemnation of certain offenses with its qualified endorsement of a morality based on compromise. Elsewhere, Swift presents compromise in a less flattering aspect: the speaker of the *Argument against Abolishing Christianity* hopes that "no Reader imagines [him] so weak to stand up in the Defence of real Christianity. . . . since every candid Reader will easily understand my Discourse to be intended only in Defence of *nominal* Christianity; the other having been for some Time wholly laid aside by general Consent, as utterly inconsistent with our present Schemes of Wealth and Power" (*Works*, 2:27–28, original emphasis). The *Project*'s argument that the appearance of virtue is better than open vice also shares something with the clothes philosophy of *A Tale of a Tub*, whose narrator suggests that "Religion [is] a *Cloack*" and "the outward Dress must needs be the Soul" (*Works*, 1:47–48, original emphasis). In the *Tale*, of course, the narrator's belief that "so far preferable is that Wisdom, which converses about the Surface, to that pretended Philosophy which enters into the Depth of Things" implies a level of self-deception hardly preferable to the grotesque dissection of insides he claims to disavow (1:109).

What price must an argument that supports compromise pay for the sacrifice of integrity? In the opening section of the *Project*, Swift deplores the lack of decorum in contemporary society. Men "never go about, as in former Times, to hide or palliate their Vices," he says; "but expose them freely to View, like any other common Occurrences of Life, without the least Reproach from the World, or themselves" (2:45). The substitution of indifference for decorum is not confined to men: "Women of tainted Reputations find the same Countenance and Reception in all publick Places, with those of the nicest Virtue, who pay, and receive Visits from them, without any Manner of Scruple" (2:46). Swift takes this "to be of most pernicious Consequence":

> It looks like a Sort of compounding between Virtue and Vice; as if a Woman were allowed to be vicious, provided she be not profligate: As if there were a certain Point where Gallantry ends, and Infamy begins; or that an Hundred criminal Amours were not as pardonable as Half a Score.

Swift deplores the "Sort of compounding between Virtue and Vice" involved in the application of numbers to morality. Against this relative morality, Swift enforces an absolute equivalence of vice and profligacy. Gallantry and infamy cannot be separated, and in this case at the very least, "Half a Score" and "an Hundred" mean exactly the same thing.[11]

The problem here for Swift's main argument is that while the satirical animus of this passage is directed against compromise ("a Sort of compounding"), the *Project* as a whole endorses compromise as the next best thing to virtue. If "Virtue and Conduct" are primarily tools with which to preserve reputation, how can Swift assert an absolute distinction between virtue and vice? Swift attempts to contain the aftershock of this contradiction by returning to the essay's main purpose: the discovery of "an effectual Remedy" for the sad state of present affairs (2:47). Moral reform will become effective, he says, only when it adopts the standard of self-interest.[12] Even virtue may become fashionable once it is made a qualification for professional advancement:

> There is no Quality so contrary to any Nature, which Men cannot affect, and put on upon Occasion, in order to serve an Interest, or gratify a prevailing Passion: The proudest Man will personate Humility, the morosest

> learn to flatter, the laziest will be sedulous and active, where he is in pursuit of what he hath much at Heart: How ready therefore would most Men be to step into the Paths of Virtue and Piety, if they infallibly led to Favour and Fortune? (2:50)

The passage of the Corporation and Test Acts had already rendered public affirmations of orthodoxy necessary for many kinds of professional advancement.[13] In this context, Swift's argument for the impersonation of virtue looks considerably more controversial. Perhaps the most quixotic element of the passage, however, is its problematic use of the adverb "infallibly." How will this projector manage to reduce the vagaries of advancement to a regular set of steps?

Throughout this section of the *Project*, Swift emphasizes the practical nature of his plan, insisting that all his proposals "are such as come within the Reach of the Administration" (2:56). He also argues that the proposal is unanswerable, in a passage that becomes the crux of the *Project*:

> Neither am I aware of any Objections to be raised against what I have advanced; unless it should be thought, that the making Religion a necessary Step to Interest and Favour, might encrease Hypocrisy among us: And I readily believe it would. But if One in Twenty should be brought over to true Piety by this, or the like Methods, and the other Nineteen be only Hypocrites, the Advantage would still be great. Besides, Hypocrisy is much more eligible than open Infidelity and Vice: It wears the Livery of Religion, it acknowledgeth her Authority, and is cautious of giving Scandal. (2:56–57)

The persuasive force of this passage lies in Swift's provocative redefinition of hypocrisy. Swift allows the charge of hypocrisy, admitting it through the back door by putting it in the mouth of an imaginary opponent. He then defuses that charge by allowing hypocrisy to be "much more eligible" than the vices whose expression it suppresses. The obvious question here is whether Swift's redefinition of hypocrisy can be sustained. The "yes, but" formulation he uses to describe the benefits that will accrue from his proposal is traditionally a weak one. It also introduces a claim whose rhetorical pitch oscillates too fast. The presence of a specific number—here, "One in Twenty"—often signals in Swift's writing a turn towards satire, and while the intention here is evidently serious, the opposition between one virtuous man and nineteen hypocrites sets into play a certain comic effect.[14] Another potential problem for readers of the *Project* is that the methods Swift has already outlined include measures of censorship about which he is disastrously explicit (2:55–56). The inconspicuous phrase "by this, or the like Methods" (a phrase omitted by Johnson from his citation in the *Dictionary*) thus seems to threaten an ominous extension of power into the unspeakable.[15] If the phrase is euphemistic, how far might not these acts of repression extend?

Most important, what are we to make of the figure of hypocrisy as a servant in livery, the interests of religion close to its heart? Contemporary writing about servants suggests that Swift's use of this particular metaphor is extremely risky.[16] As soon as the phenomenon of the livery servant is born, writers of plays and pamphlets isolate the tendency of livery to mask insolence beneath subservience. In general, livery signifies not just a set of clothes, but a uniform that expresses the wearer's allegiance to a particular master. The French word *livrer* from which the English *livery* is derived, however, means both to entrust and to betray, and the contradictory tendency of servants in livery to represent both loyalty and treachery follows this double etymology.[17] The servant temporarily entrusted with his master's authority is all too likely to abuse, if not actively to betray it. The *OED* shows that as soon as the word *livery* becomes current, it picks up the connotation of hypocrisy in its crudest form: a self-interested duplicity on the part of both the individual servant and the class of servants in general that threatens what Defoe calls "the great law of subordination." As a symbol, livery is thus more effectively used by opponents of the system of masters and servants than by those who wish to maintain that system.[18] Opponents to servitude find in livery an extremely effective symbol of oppression, as when Frantz Fanon says (as late as 1952) that "Le nègre doit, qu'il le veuille ou non, endosser la livrée que lui a faite le Blanc."[19] In such a context, livery is simply a bad thing, an emblem of servitude whose negative connotations may be admitted precisely because servitude is about to be thrown off.

Even in a cultural context which accepts servitude with few reservations, however, the word *livery* retains a strong link to deception. In the *Directions to Servants*, Swift's satirical instructions about how to cause mayhem in a master's household, the narrator tells the groom that the latter is "the Servant upon whom Care of [his] Master's Honour in all Journies entirely depends": "Your Breast is the sole Repository of it," the narrator insists. Every penny spent on the road raises the master's character, and for this reason (if for no other) "his Reputation ought to be dear to you" (13:46). Furthermore, the groom should "deal with those who will be the most liberal" to him, "for Service being no Inheritance, you ought not to let slip any lawful and customary Perquisite."[20] Care for the master's reputation can be reduced, however, to care for one's own livery:

> A Master ought always to love his Groom, to put him into a handsome Livery, and to allow him a Silver-laced Hat. When you are in this Equipage, all the Honours he receives on the Road are owing to you alone: That he is not turned out of the Way by every Carrier, is caused by the Civility he receives at second Hand from the Respect paid to your Livery. (13:50–51)

The order of things here is turned upside down. From the servant's point of view, respect paid to his livery produces civility at second-hand for his master. Yet the most alarming thing about this reversal is that it exaggerates rather than subverts an existing norm. Footmen and grooms in handsome livery do in fact increase a master's standing in the world.[21] This passage reveals the extent to which servants in livery reduce honor to its lowest common denominator, exposing status as a crude matter of display. A primary concern of the *Directions* is to expose the monstrous and self-interested nature of servants' arguments for a morality of appearances. Yet how does the groom's concern for appearances ultimately differ from the *Project*'s plea for an interested hypocrisy?

II

One very different though closely contemporary discussion of livery may clarify what is at stake in both the *Project* and the *Directions*. Support for servitude is not expressed exclusively by members of the class of masters. Individual servants sometimes write to endorse this system of values as well; most prominent among these is the so-called footman poet, Robert Dodsley, whose *Servitude* was published in 1729. Dodsley represents a native informant, so to speak, from the servants' quarters. In light of the extraordinary volume of anti-servant polemic, he is concerned to redeem the word "livery" from its current debasement:

> Submission next must an Admittance find,
> The humble Liv'ry of a Servant's Mind;
> By which we ought to be distinguish'd more,
> Than by the Liveries on our Bodies wore.[22]

Dodsley's response to attacks on servants is to redefine their distinguishing characteristic. Servants in livery may sometimes be insubordinate, he admits. Yet submission should be the true livery of a servant's mind (his prescription sounds almost wistful, as though servants won't be distinguished by their humility any time soon). With the patronage of Pope and others, Dodsley became first a bookseller and then a publisher, and when the manuscript of the *Directions to Servants* surfaced after Swift's death, it was very naturally Dodsley who published it.

In a letter, Swift wrote of an earlier draft of the *Directions*, "I may call it the Whole Duty of Servants, in about twenty several Stations."[23] This mock title links the *Directions* to the popular Anglican devotional work *The Whole Duty of Man* (1657); the stations of servants are satirically equated here with the stations of the cross. How seriously does Swift take the text's didactic intentions? In a 1739 letter to Faulkner, he complains that "I cannot find a manuscript I wrote, called Directions for Servants, which I thought very useful, as well as humorous."[24] Useful for the servants? Or for their masters, alerted now to the destructive tactics of their employees and enabled thereby to circumvent them? The equivocal status of the *Directions* is illuminated by a quotation from Maria Edgeworth, who refers with surprising frequency to the *Directions to Servants*.[25] Edgeworth's treatise *Professional Education*, co-authored with her father, contains a long footnote on the tone and purpose of Swift's *Directions*. While it is difficult to imagine that anyone could have taken the *Directions* literally, this is exactly the charge against which the Edgeworths preemptively defend it. They link Swift's *Directions* with Machiavelli's *Prince*, identifying both as works of "sober irony" and suggesting that each text "may have done harm to some, and must have excited the indignation of others, who were so stupid as to understand it literally."[26] However useful the work may be to masters, in other words, it is only useful to those servants who contemplate acts of destruction.

Servants clearly benefit from the reputation of their masters in terms of increased prestige, and one subset of Swift's directions urges servants to manipulate the cant of the master's honor for ends that are both self-interested and interested on behalf of servants as a group. Servants who lay waste to their masters' property assert the interest of one class against another, barely troubling to conceal their insubordination beneath the false rhetoric of honor. The narrator of the *Directions* insists on the compatibility of these two conflicting obligations, but it is clear which really predominates:

> Take all Tradesmens Parts against your Master, and when you are sent to buy any Thing, never offer to cheapen it, but generously pay the full Demand. This is highly for your Master's Honour; and may be some Shillings in your Pocket; and you are to consider, if your Master hath paid too much, he can better afford the Loss than a poor Tradesman. (13:8–9)

First comes "your Master's Honour," and only then does the narrator mention the self-interested desire to put "some Shillings in your Pocket." The over-expenditure is always justified in advance, on the grounds that it furthers the master's honor.

Indeed, the master makes himself especially vulnerable when he allows servants cash in hand, with all the independence that confers on the servant, as another instruction shows:

> If you are sent with ready Money to buy any Thing at a Shop, and happen at that Time to be out of Pocket (which is very usual) sink the Money and take up the Goods on your Master's Account. This is for the Honour of your Master and yourself; for he becomes a Man of Credit at your Recommendation. (13:13)

The cant here is that the servant vouches for the master as "a Man of Credit." In this case, however, the argument is double-edged. The servant's power to make or break his master's reputation is a matter of fact as well as of satire, and would remain a source of considerable anxiety throughout the eighteenth century.[27] The footman is reminded here that his hold over his master continues even after employment is terminated:

> When you have a Mind to leave your Master, and are too bashful to break the Matter for fear of offending him, your best way is to grow rude and saucy of a sudden, and beyond your usual Behaviour, till he finds it necessary to turn you off; and when you are gone, to revenge yourself, give him and his Lady such a Character to all your Brother-servants, who are out of Place, that none will venture to offer their Service. (13:13)

This goes well beyond the aphorism that no man is a hero to his *valet de chambre*. The power to make or break a reputation is entirely in the hands of the servant, or so Swift suggests.

Under the heading *"The Rules that concern All Servants in general,"* Swift's narrator lays out the obligations of servants to their colleagues. "If you see your Master wronged by any of your Fellows-servants, be sure to conceal it, for fear of being called a Tell-tale," he says: "However, there is one Exception, in case of a favourite servant, who is justly hated by the whole Family; who therefore are bound in Prudence to lay all the Faults they can upon the Favourite" (13:7). The obligation to fellow servants overrides that to the master, and this exception only goes to prove the rule. A "favourite servant" implicitly rates the master over the other servants, and is thus "justly hated by the whole Family"—"Family" meaning neither the master's family, nor the household as a whole, but rather the family of servants. Prudence in turn prompts the colleagues of a favorite servant to undermine his or her privileged status. In fact, the hierarchy inside a household reproduces in miniature the social world outside the house; while Swift is careful never to reduce relations between master and servants to a simple metaphor, he variously uses the relationship as a synecdoche for the relations between king, court and country and as a way of writing more generally about England and Ireland, men and women or any other pair of groups whose interests seem diametrically opposed.

Servants are especially likely to share their masters' prejudices. "If an humble Companion, a Chaplain, a Tutor, or a dependent Cousin happen to be at Table, whom you find to be little regarded by the Master, and the Company," the butler is told, "it must be the Business of you and the Footman, to follow the Example of your Betters, by treating him many Degrees worse than any of the rest" (13:18). The master's wealthier guests, on the other hand, are of the utmost importance to the butler.

> If a Gentleman dines often with your Master, and gives you nothing when he goes away, you may use several Methods to shew him some Marks of your Displeasure, and quicken his Memory: If he calls for Bread or Drink you may pretend not to hear, or send it to another who called after him: If he asks for Wine, let him stay awhile, and then send him Small-beer; give him always foul Glasses; send him a Spoon when he wants a Knife; wink at the Footman to leave him without a Plate: By these, and the like Expedients, you may probably be a better Man by half a Crown before he leaves the House, provided you watch an Opportunity of standing by when he is going. (13:25)

While "vails" or tips formed a regular part of a servant's income, vails-giving would become increasingly unpopular with the employer class over the course of the century.[28] Livery servants who extorted contributions from guests in the form of vails were seen as disrupting social intercourse, especially when they insulted and mistreated those who refused to pay. Even worse, by allowing guests to supply vails, Jonas Hanway argued at the middle of the century, masters undercut their own authority and "[sowed] the seeds of contempt of superiors."[29] The cook and the butler are particularly likely to assume a debased version of aristocratic values, since they identify themselves as heads of the family. "If you live in a rich Family, roasting and boiling are below the Dignity of your Office, and which it becomes you to be ignorant of," the cook is told; "therefore leave that Work wholly to the Kitchen Wench, for fear of disgracing the Family you live in" (13:28). The cook is also encouraged to cut corners under the pretext of exaggerating the family's gentility: a "lump of Soot . . . will give the Soup a high *French* Taste," and butter melted into oil may be sent up without a qualm, "for Oil is a genteeler Sauce than Butter" (13:30).

The chapter giving directions to the footman is fuller than any of the others. "I have a true Veneration for your Office," says the narrator, "because I had once the Honour to be one of your Order, which I foolishly left by demeaning myself with accepting an Employment in the Custom-house" (13:34). Government office-holders are inferior types of the footman, who is "the fine Gentleman of the Family" and sometimes even "a Pattern of Dress to [his] Master" (13:33). The footman "understand[s] Men and Manners" and may rise readily by getting a good command in the army or by marrying the master's daughter. But he must not advance himself at the expense of his colleagues. As the narrator instructs the footman, "Be not proud in Prosperity": "Pay your Contributions only to your late Brothers the Cadets" (13:44). Neither should the footman be governed by ordinary moral scruples:

> When your Master and Lady are talking together in their Bed-chamber, and you have some Suspicion that you or your Fellow-servants are concerned in what they say, listen at the Door for the public Good of all the Servants, and join all to take proper Measures for preventing any Innovations that may hurt the Community. (13:43)

The vocabulary of "preventing . . . Innovations" for the sake of the "Community" once again alerts the reader's suspicion. The language of political theory is appropriated here by servants for self-interested and socially destructive motives. Moreover, it is not only male servants who perform this act of rhetorical hostility. Female servants also justify their abuses in the language of political obligation. If mistresses will insist on locking up their tea and sugar caddies, thereby blocking free access for servants, they must accept the consequences: servants have a right to "relieve" themselves, even to the extent of making "a false Key, which is a Point both difficult and dangerous to compass; but, as to the Circumstance of Honesty in procuring one, I am under no Doubt, when your Mistress gives you so just a Provocation, by refusing you an ancient and legal Perquisite" (13:57). The "ancient and legal Perquisite" must be retained by any means, so that the waiting-maid becomes in this case a Lockean apologist for revolution on a small scale, justifying her morally dubious actions in the language of rights. (In the *Drapier's Letters*, of course, Swift applies the subversive language of rights in a serious cause; to the extent that Swift applies the master-servant paradigm to relations between England and Ireland, moreover, it should be clear that he does not always speak for the master.)

The footman's two most prominent roles are those of labor organizer and sexual aggressor—because he apes the manners and dress of a gentleman, he threatens the chastity of the master's daughter and wife.[30] The footman has two ways to improve his condition; his solidarity with his colleagues in a prototype of the modern labor union is a companion strategy to the threat he poses to the sexual integrity of the upper-class household.[31] With a little care the footman may pass for a gentleman:

> Chuse a Service if you can, where your Livery Colours are least tawdry and distinguishing: Green and Yellow immediately betray your Office, and so do all Kinds of Lace, except Silver, which will hardly fall to your Share, unless with a Duke, or some Prodigal just come to his Estate. The Colours you ought to wish for, are Blue, or Filemot, turned up with Red; which with a borrowed Sword, a borrowed Air, your Master's Linen, and a natural and improved Confidence, will give you what Title you please, where you are not known. (13:41)

The footman's manners could take him as far as the army: "value not now and then a Kicking, or a Caning; for your Insolence will at last turn to good Account; and from wearing a Livery, you may probably soon carry a Pair of Colours" (13:42–43). The satirical point is that while footmen are morally despicable, the tactics they put to work in their calling are precisely the same qualities that procure advancement in the army or at court.

The introduction to *Polite Conversation* deals explicitly with the risks that face all conduct manuals, even parodic ones. Swift anticipates the objection that it may be dangerous to provide other classes with the secrets of upper-class conversation:

> It may be objected, that the Publication of my Book, may, in a long Course of Time, prostitute this noble Art to mean and vulgar People. But, I answer; that it is not so easily acquired, as a few ignorant Pretenders may imagine. A Footman can swear; but he cannot swear like a Lord. He can swear as often: But, can he swear with equal Delicacy, Propriety, and Judgment? No certainly; unless he be a Lad of superior Parts, of good Memory, a diligent Observer, one who hath a skilful Ear, some knowledge in Musick, and an Exact Taste; which hardly falls to the Share of one in a thousand among that Fraternity, in as high Favour as they now stand with their Ladies; neither, perhaps hath one Footman in six, so fine a Genius, as to relish and apply those exalted Sentences comprised in this Volume. (4:112)

The subversiveness of Swift's irony here results not just from his decision to make the manner in which one swears the criterion for social distinction, but from the critique of supposedly aristocratic manners this choice implies. A skilful footman *can* in fact "swear like a Lord. . . . with equal Delicacy, Propriety, and Judgment," insofar as neither lowly nor aristocratic swearing is at all proper in the first place. It is no more likely that anybody would use *Polite Conversation* as a witty manual of dinner-party repartee than that he or she should seize on the *Directions* as a training manual for servants, though the text might hold some useful ideas both for masters who wish to avert certain kinds of fraud and for servants who want to become household terrorists. The Edgeworths' anxiety about potential misreadings of Swift's *Directions* suggests that even an obviously satirical conduct book is in some danger of being taken seriously. In this sense, the possibility that the *Directions* might be appropriated by destructive servants is built into the text by Swift himself, who imagines servants as ruthlessly subverting or turning on its head the cant of aristocratic honor, a rhetoric thereby revealed to be as base, self-interested and class-bound as its parodic double below-stairs.

Swift wrote a number of directions to his own servants, all more or less serious. "The Duty of Servants at Inns" covers much the same ground as the *Directions to the Groom* and is just as precise in its instructions (13:163–65). "Laws for the Dean's Servants" enumerates the fines and forfeits exacted for various offenses: servants must not be drunk, must not leave the house without notice to the Dean and must not "be abroad together when the Dean is from home" or they shall pay a forfeit out of their wages (13:161–62). The rules are generally designed to keep the servants sober and under their master's surveillance. (I do not use the word *surveillance* lightly: Laetitia Pilkington's account of one dinner party at the Deanery describes Swift sitting "at the Head of his Table opposite to a great Pier-Glass, under which was a Marble Side-board, so that he could see in the Glass whatever the Servants did at it."[32]) The conclusion of Swift's "Laws" sounds almost desperate to rule out equivocation or exceptions: "Whatever other laws the Dean shall think fit to make, at any time to come, for the government of his servants, and forfeitures for neglect or disobedience, all the servants shall be bound to submit to" (13:162). Thus a body of "Laws," "Rules" or "Directions" is all that stands between order and chaos.

III

No doubt Swift enjoyed his skirmishes with the household help. Consider this testimonial, written by Swift for a former servant who asked him for a reference: "Whereas the bearer served me the space of one year, during which time he was an *idler* and a *drunkard*; I then discharged him as such; but how far his having been five years at sea may have mended his manners, I leave to the penetration of those who may hereafter chuse to employ him."[33] The tone of the *Directions* is also perversely exuberant. On a more serious note, there is a great deal of evidence for Swift's fondness for certain of his servants: the tablet he raised to his favorite servant Saunders

McGee in St. Patrick's Cathedral, for instance, or the fact of his servants' refusal to turn Swift in as author of the *Drapier's Letters* in spite of the bounty placed on his head by the government.[34]

In other words, Swift seems successfully to contain the local disruption which the problematic word *livery* introduces into his central argument for hypocrisy in the *Project for the Advancement of Religion*. What then is the servant problem of this essay's title? The servant problem (more fairly described as the problem masters perceived with regard to their servants) erupts into a great many eighteenth-century arguments about virtue. Swift is clearly not alone in his preoccupation with bad servants. Educational theorists from Locke to Edgeworth put on hold a main argument about virtue to indulge in diatribes against bad servants, digressions that are fascinating but often extremely distracting. In fact, many other arguments about virtue are rather less successful than Swift's at isolating hypocrisy within protective layers of paradox. In *Some Thoughts Concerning Education*, for instance, Locke insists that children are "wholly, if possible" to be kept from conversation with servants:

> For the contagion of these ill precedents, both in Civility and Vertue, horribly infects Children, as often as they come within reach of it. They frequently learn from unbred or debauched Servants such Language, untowardly Tricks and Vices, as otherwise they possibly would be ignorant of all their Lives.[35]

This is only the initial salvo against bad servants, who crop up to pose problems under many different headings in Locke's educational treatise. Mandeville's *Essay on Charity* is punctuated by exactly the same kinds of attack on servants that interrupt Locke's thoughts on education, digressions so conspicuous that one of Mandeville's more vituperative adversaries seized on them as a rhetorical peculiarity: "But how comes all this Severity on Footmen to make a Part of his *Essay upon Charity Schools*?"[36] The evidence of these texts suggests that a diatribe against servants is not merely an incidental digression from a tightly focused moral argument, but that servants pose for eighteenth-century moral writing a problem on the level of content. As servants enter the discussion at hand, the text often becomes troubled by fluctuations of rhetorical register. At the most basic level, the presence of all-too-real servants in a discourse about morality, virtue or education suggests a kind of rhetorical failure.

For Swift, servants continue to pose problems on the level of both argument and metaphor. The trope of the mismanaged household is prominent throughout Swift's political writings.[37] His arguments in favor of civility are often accompanied by diatribes against the irremediably uncouth, whose presence in society at once threatens and paradoxically secures ideals of social behavior. The momentary destabilization of the *Project*'s argument for hypocrisy by the introduction of the term *livery* is effectively arrested by the forward momentum of Swift's rhetoric. As it turns out, describing hypocrisy as "the Livery of Religion" is a private joke for those in the know (in this case, just about everybody, given the universal loathing for servants in livery). If hypocrisy is a bad thing, livery is even worse, and Swift will get away with hypocrisy because he casts off livery without any reservations once the metaphor has served his purpose. Swift thus successfully defends hypocrisy by a policy of strategic containment, excoriating the threat posed by the subversive and self-interested hypocrisy of the lower classes, even as he endorses the virtue of a society based on manners.

NOTES

A shorter version of this paper was presented under the title "'The Livery of Religion': Servants and Hypocrisy in Swift's *Project for the Advancement of Religion*," at the twenty-ninth annual meeting of the East-Central American Society for Eighteenth-Century Studies during October 1998 at Salisbury State University, Salisbury, MD. Another version was presented as "Swift's Servant Problem" to the Yale English Department's eighteenth- and nineteenth-century colloquium in December 1998. In addition to thanking the audience on both of these occasions for their helpful questions and comments, I am grateful for the suggestions of a number of people who read earlier drafts of this piece: Claude Rawson, David Bromwich, Alexander Welsh, Jill Campbell, Imraan Coovadia, Michele Martinez, and the two anonymous readers for *Studies in Eighteenth-Century Culture*.

1. Important discussions of hypocrisy include Hannah Arendt, *On Revolution* (1963; reprint, London: Penguin 1990), 97–98; and Arendt, *The Life of the Mind*, 2 vols. (New York: Harcourt Brace Jovanovich, 1978), 1:36–40; Judith N. Shklar, "Let Us Not Be Hypocritical," in *Ordinary Vices* (Cambridge and London: Belknap, 1984), 45–86; Stanley Cavell, "A Cover Letter to Molière's *Misanthrope*," in *Themes Out of School: Effects and Causes* (San Francisco: North Point Press, 1984), 97–105; and Ruth W. Grant, *Hypocrisy and Integrity: Machiavelli, Rousseau, and the Ethics of Politics* (Chicago and London: University of Chicago Press, 1997).

2. Swift's prose is quoted in the edition of Herbert Davis et al., *Prose Works*, 16 vols. (Oxford: Blackwell, 1939–74), 2:56–57. Subsequent references are cited in the text.

3. All citations are from Samuel Johnson, *A Dictionary of the English Language*, 4th ed., 2 vols. (London: W. Strahan. 1773), *s.v.*, original emphasis. Relevant citations in the first edition are substantially the same; see Johnson, *A Dictionary of the English Language*, 2 vols. (London: W. Strahan, 1755).

4. *The Servant's Hand: English Fiction from Below* (New York: Columbia University Press, 1986), x.

5. Irvin Ehrenpreis, *Swift: The Man, His Works, and the Age*, 3 vols. (Cambridge: Harvard University Press, 1967–1983), 2:276. For an eighteenth-century view corresponding to that of Ehrenpreis, see Lord Orrery, who suggests that Swift is here "writing in shackles": "The author appears in earnest. . . . But as the pamphlet is of the satirical kind, I am apt to imagine, that my friend the Dean put a violence upon himself, in chusing to appear candidly serious, rather than to smile under his usual mask of gravity," in *Remarks on the Life and Writing of Dr. Jonathan Swift* (London, 1752), 98–99. On the close relation between Swift's satirical projectors and the voice of the *Project*, see Claude Rawson, "The Character of Swift's Satire," in *Order From Confusion Sprung* (1985; reprint, Atlantic Highlands, NJ, and London: Humanities Press International, 1992), 32.

6. Letter of Apr. 1709 from the Earl of Berkeley to Swift, *Correspondence of Jonathan Swift*, vol. 1 (1680–1713), ed. Harold Williams (Oxford: Clarendon, 1963), 139; *The Tatler*, ed. Donald F. Bond, 3 vols. (Oxford: Clarendon, 1987), 1:47.

7. Samuel Johnson, *Lives of the Poets*, ed. G. B. Hill, 3 vols. (Oxford: Clarendon, 1905), 3:13.

8. Thomas Sheridan, *The Life of the Reverend Dr. Jonathan Swift* (London, 1784), 6. Swift supports this account in the "Memoirs relating to that Change which happened in the Queen's Ministry," where he identifies the *Project* as one of several tracts he wrote in opposition to the low-church party (*Works*, 8:122).

9. David Nokes charges with regard to the *Project* that "Robespierre himself could not have formulated a more thoroughgoing apparatus for ensuring the tyranny of virtue"; *Jonathan Swift: A Hypocrite Reversed* (Oxford: Oxford University Press, 1985), 97. For an interesting refutation of this argument, however, see Shelley Burtt, *Virtue Transformed: Political Argument in England, 1688–1740* (Cambridge: Cambridge University Press, 1992), 60.

10. See especially J. G. A. Pocock, "Virtues, rights, and manners," in *Virtue, Commerce, and History* (Cambridge: Cambridge University Press, 1985), 48.

11. Rawson contrasts Swift's position here with those of Fielding and Chesterfield, who value chastity without condemning criminal loves; see "The Character of Swift's Satire," 34–35.

12. Swift's friend and political ally Bolingbroke offers a very similar argument when he says that "by rendering publick Virtue and real Capacity, the sole Means of acquiring any degree of Power or Profit in the State, [the Patriot King] will set the Passions of their Hearts on the Side of Liberty and Government," in *The Idea of a Patriot King: With Respect to the Constitution of Great Britain* (London: T. C., n.d.), 63. On the passion of self-interest, see also Albert O. Hirschman, *The Passions and the Interests: Political Arguments for Capitalism Before Its Triumph* (Princeton: Princeton University Press, 1977), esp. 27, 43.

13. On Swift's strong support for the Test Acts, see "The Advantages Proposed by Repealing the Sacramental Test, Impartially Considered," in *Works*, 12: 243.

14. Jill Campbell has drawn my attention to Biblical precedents for this kind of accounting. Mandeville may also have this passage in mind when he writes in *An Enquiry Into the Origin of Honour and the Usefulness of Christianity in War* that "ever since the Notion of Honour has been receiv'd among Christians, there have always been, in the same Number of People, Twenty Men of real Honour to one of real Virtue" (London, 1732), 43–44.

15. On Johnson's practice of altering quotations to suit his purpose, see Allen Reddick, *The Making of Johnson's Dictionary, 1747–1773* (Cambridge: Cambridge University Press, 1990), 10.

16. For a representative contemporary attack on the behavior of servants in livery, see Daniel Defoe, *The Great Law of Subordination consider'd* (London, 1724), especially the section on footmen (191–209). Defoe's arguments are by no means original, and a minor pamphlet literature abusing servants had begun to appear in the years prior to the publication of the *Project*.

17. Johnson's citations in the *Dictionary* for the word *livery* display an interesting pattern of ambiguity. The Chadwyck-Healey English Poetry Database also confirms a strong connection between livery and hypocrisy; see in particular Samuel Speed, "On Hypocrisie," lines 1–7, *Prison-Pietie* (London, 1677). For the expression "virtue's livery," see Sir Philip Sidney, "Come Dorus, come, let songs thy sorowes signifie," line 137, in *Complete Works*, ed. Albert Feuillerat, 4 vols. (Cambridge: Cambridge University Press, 1912–26); John Oldham, "Imitation of Juvenal, Satire 13," lines 163–65, in *The Poems of John Oldham*, ed. Harold F. Brooks with Raman Selden (Oxford: Clarendon, 1987); and Matthew Green, *The Spleen* (London, 1737), line 701. And for Shakespeare's use of the word *livery* (7 instances of "liveries," 28 of "livery"), see Marvin Spevack, *The Harvard Concordance to Shakespeare* (Cambridge: Belknap, 1973), 729.

18. On the anxiety of eighteenth-century proponents of servitude to retain a positive valence for the word *livery* against the drift of contemporary usage, see J. Jean Hecht, *The Domestic Servant Class in Eighteenth-Century England* (London: Routledge & Kegan Paul, 1956), 74.

19. *Peau noire, masques blancs* (1952; reprint, Paris: Editions du Seuil, 1995), 27; "Willy-nilly, the Negro has to wear the livery that the white man has sewed for him," *Black Skin, White Masks*, trans. Charles Lam Markmann (New York: Grove, 1967), 34.

20. *Works*, 13:48. On Swift's use of the form of the proverb, see Pat Rogers, "Swift and the Reanimation of Cliché," in *The Character of Swift's Satire*, ed. Claude Rawson (Newark: University of Delaware Press; London and Toronto: Associated University Presses, 1983); and on working-class use of the proverb as a form of verbal resistance, see Pierre Bourdieu, *Distinction: A Social Critique of the Judgement of Taste* (1979), trans. Richard Nice (Cambridge: Harvard University Press, 1984), 461–62. Chesterfield identifies the use of proverbs and sayings as "proofs of having kept bad and low company," letter of 25 July 1741, in *The Letters of Philip Dormer Stanhope, 4th Earl of Chesterfield*, ed. Bonamy Dobrée, 6 vols. (London: Eyre and Spottiswoode, 1932), 2:461. And for other uses of the proverb

"Service is no Inheritance," see James Townley, *High Life Below Stairs* (Dublin, 1759), 7; and William Hazlitt, "Of the Knowledge of Character," in *The Complete Works of William Hazlitt*, ed. P. P. Howe, 21 vols. (1931; reprint, New York: AMS Press, 1967), 8:309.

21. Hecht shows that servants in livery offered a useful "symbol of wealth" for the *nouveau riche* as well as for the aristocracy; *Domestic Servant Class*, 2, 53.

22. [Robert Dodsley], *Servitude: a Poem. To which is prefix'd, An Introduction, humbly submitted to the Consideration of all* Noblemen, Gentlemen, *and* Ladies, *who keep many servants. Also a Postscript, Occasion'd by A late Trifling Pamphlet, entituled,* Every Body's Business, is no Body's *written by a Footman. In Behalf of* good *Servants, and to excite the* Bad *to their Duty* (London: T. Worrall, [1729]), 20. Defoe was the author of *Every Body's Business* and also wrote Dodsley's postscript; see Ralph Straus, *Robert Dodsley: Poet, Publisher and Playwright* (New York: Burt Franklin, 1910), 20–21. The poem was republished two years later as *The Footman's Friendly Advice To his Brethren of the Livery; And to all Servants in General* (London: T. Worrall, [1731]), a title that makes its similarity to Swift's *Directions* more evident, not least in that they both address servants rather than masters (although Dodsley's *Advice* differs from Swift's not just because it is more serious but because the material is divided under headings according to subject rather than job description).

23. Letter of 28 Aug. 1731, cited in *Works*, 13:vii.

24. Letter of 4 Dec. 1739, cited in *Works*, 13:viii.

25. See for instance Maria Edgeworth, *Patronage* (1814; reprint, London and New York: Pandora, 1986), 12.

26. R. L. Edgeworth [and Maria Edgeworth], *Essays on Professional Education* (London: J. Johnson, 1809), 421n.

27. Henry and John Fielding set up a Registry Office to regulate the relationship between servants and employers; much of their anxiety arose from the question of the "character" given a servant by his master, and vice versa. For a discussion of this phenomenon, see Robbins, *The Servant's Hand*, 35–36, 109.

28. See Hecht, *Domestic Servant Class*, 158–68.

29. Cited in ibid., 162.

30. On the sexual threat, see also Swift, *Works*, 13:59. Swift's language anticipates Burke's well-known attack on Rousseau's seduction plot in the *Letter to a Member of the National Assembly* (1791), in *The French Revolution (1790–1794)*, ed. L. G. Mitchell, vol. 8 of *The Writings and Speeches of Edmund Burke*, ed. Paul Langford (Oxford: Clarendon, 1989), 8:317. Rousseau's revolutionary followers, Burke says, "propagate principles by which every servant may think it, if not his duty, at least his privilege, to betray his master" (8:319).

31. See Hecht, *Domestic Servant Class*, 85–86 on footmen's formation of friendly societies or trade unions.

32. *Memoirs of Mrs. Laetitia Pilkington*, 2 vols. (London, 1748), 1:54–56.

33. Swift, "Certificate to a Discarded Servant" (1738), *Works*, 13:166.

34. See especially Ehrenpreis, *Swift*, 3:322–26. Ehrenpreis has a tendency to sentimentalize Swift's relations with his servants, mostly on evidence drawn from

Patrick Delany, *Observations upon Lord Orrery's Remarks on the Life and Writings of Dr. Jonathan Swift* (London, 1754), but the evidence speaks for itself.

35. John Locke, *Some Thoughts concerning Education*, ed. John W. Yolton and Jean S. Yolton (1693; reprint, Oxford: Clarendon, 1989), 127. Subsequent references are cited in the text; all emphasis is original. On the problem of servants in eighteenth-century pedagogy from Locke to Edgeworth, see also the excellent essay by Mitzi Myers, "'Servants as They Are Now Educated': Women Writers and Georgian Pedagogy," *Essays in Literature* 16 (1989): 51–59.

36. [Blewitt], *An Enquiry whether A general Practice of Virtue tends to the Wealth or Poverty, Benefit or Disadvantage of a People? With some Thoughts concerning a Toleration of the Publick Stews* (London, 1725), 205.

37. For one link between household and national abuses, see *Works*, 3:81–82; and for an analogy between the prime minister and an insolent footman, contributing to an argument that the king has a right to choose his own "servants," see *Works*, 5:116.

Clarissa's Relics and Lyric Community

G. GABRIELLE STARR

Samuel Richardson's *Clarissa* is, at core, a novel about the limits of emotional intimacy. From letter to letter, page to page, Richardson explores models of consensus—literally, of feeling together, the true correspondence of hearts and minds. From the beginning, however, *Clarissa* is a story of intimacy thwarted and correspondence violated. The novel records Richardson's attempts to mold a language that can make his heroine's inner experience available to those outside, a language of feeling composed of words and images, patterns of expression and of thought, ways of imagining emotional communication and its lapses. As other critics have demonstrated, the novel's crisis develops from the emotional and physical isolation of its heroine. She is deprived of direct communication, shut off from the presence of her father and mother, her aunt, her nurse, all those closest to her. Believing that if "they did but know [her] heart" all would be well, Clarissa attempts to create a complete correspondence with her family—as Lovelace's false etymology would have it, a union of the heart.[1] Desperate, afraid, she sends letters designed to show the extremity of her plight, to represent her emotional experience so that it can be felt and understood. But as the novel progresses, at moments of high emotional intensity, a true correspondence seems impossible. Letters fragment and are replaced by relics: the ten quasi-epistolary papers she writes in near-madness after being raped, the careful meditations written in her sorrow, the emblematic self-elegy she orders engraved on her coffin. These impassioned inscriptions participate in lyric models of emotional consensus, models taken from religious poetry like the book of Job and George Herbert's *The Temple*. Epistolary correspondence converges with or gives way to lyric attempts at community, and the novel is opened up to the lyric mode.

Richardson's attempt at exhaustive representation situates lyric within the novel's range of possibility, suggesting not only that the history of genre we apply to understanding the birth of the novel needs significant revision, but also that the story of the lyric involves a more complex tradition than is usually granted it. Making this case with regard to *Clarissa* will require some abbreviated discussion of the relations between texts and practices which contribute to the eighteenth-century history of genre, as well as detailed accounts of Richardson's aesthetic choices. My concerns here are two: *Clarissa* provides us with a case that challenges generic orthodoxies; in examining that challenge, in exploring Richardson's adaptation and modification of lyric, we are also given access to a new way of analyzing the connections and constraints which underlie the novel's emotional richness (and its version of the speaking subject).

While most analyses of the language of emotion in Clarissa have focused on the influence of the drama or earlier epistolary works, the emotional repertoire available to Richardson was much more varied.[2] Jocelyn Harris points out the breadth of Richardson's literary knowledge, noting that he published Sidney's sonnets in 1724 and knew (and quoted from) Herrick, Herbert, and Donne as well.[3] In fact, in the eighteenth century, there was a wide range of models for emotional intensity, models limited or affected by genre in complicated ways. First, generic and modal distinctions functioned on shifting axes. In addition to the classical drama-epic-lyric triptych, biblical models were of great importance. Lyric was subdivided by hymn, thanksgiving, epithalamium or lament in the Biblical scheme (largely relying on the Psalms, the Song of Songs, and the Book of Job), while in other formulations, pastoral, anacreontic, ode, or elegy were the privileged (and contested) groupings.

Genres seemed made for expansion and renewal. The late Renaissance and early eighteenth century are marked by an extraordinary amount of literary experimentation; whatever our preconceptions about neoclassicism might lead us to expect, there was a high degree of generic flexibility. Even distinctions between prose and poetry were complicated by developments in biblical scholarship that revealed poetry in sections of the Bible long read as prose (chief among these the greater part of the Book of Job).

Literary criticism both reflected and shaped the possibilities for generic cross-pollination. Not only do we find compendia like Bysshe's *Art of English Poetry* (1702), organized not by genre but by theme or emotion, but criticism in the era tended to revolve around the presentation of exempla, as any perusal of Johnson, Kames, Blair or Dryden will show. There existed a set of recognizable kinds, but they could be endlessly assorted and recombined. Models of emotional intensity ranged from drama to poetry both Biblical and contemporary, and all could be newly adopted based on rules of decorum and thematic affinities.[4]

Several studies have established the cultural and literary influence of the seventeenth-century Protestant poets in this regard over their contemporaries and their immediate heirs.[5] Poets like Herbert and Vaughan provided model constructions of powerful emotional experience to their readers. John Wesley's adaptations of Herbert for the hymnal (in the 1740s) brought a version of Herbert's sensibility to entire congregations—offering the poet's anguish or joy to men and women whose voices could merge with his, making his experience in a sense their own. Wesley's was not the first attempt to popularize Herbert, and an earlier anonymous hymnal, *Select Hymns, Taken out of Mr. Herbert's Temple*, and *Turn'd into the Common Metre* (1697), was, "before the hymns of Isaac Watts [,] . . . one of the most widely used collections of religious song 'either in private families, or Christian-assemblies.'"[6] In effect, as Anne Williams argues, poems by the Protestant poets made "a lyric voice of the minutest psychological verisimilitude . . . familiar" to eighteenth-century England (51), either through private reading or public devotions. Biblical poetry was still more important; Job, the Psalms, the Song of Songs, and other biblical sources were models of emotional expression and lyric speech, generating countless published poems of imitation or paraphrase, as well as being quoted in diaries, sermons, and everyday life. Given the generic complexities which characterize the period, it is not surprising that at the most emotionally intense moments of a novel like *Clarissa* we find traces of Protestant lyric traditions, figures not merely replicated, but expanded, renewed, and made to carry functional importance.

I will here trace the connections between *Clarissa* and four kinds (loosely speaking) or instances of religious lyric, first establishing Richardson's use of the lyric model offered by the Book of Job, and then focusing on representative lyrics by Herbert whose structural, rhetorical, and thematic characteristics make them particularly close kin to *Clarissa*: his Jobian laments (constructed in terms of fragmentation and self-division), lyrics of lapsed communication (or denial), variations on shaped verse, and emblem poems (specifically taken, as Herbert does, to unify conflicting aspects of personal experience). In all of these instances, lyrics provide models of emotional consensus imagined, lost, and ultimately reconstructed.

Richardson's story may be quickly summarized: barely eighteen, Clarissa Harlowe is tricked away from her father's house by Robert Lovelace, an infamous rake whose weak conscience cannot stand up to his appetites or his monomania. He keeps Clarissa prisoner in a brothel, then drugs and rapes her in a tale of prolonged and intense suffering. Clarissa appears as fortune's one-time favorite now brought intolerably low, and her history is told in terms remarkably similar to those of the Book of Job.[7] From her beginning as shining example of piety to her end as warning, as byword to the people, Clarissa's path parallels Job's: he is the "admired exclaimer" whose words she "often repeat[s]" (1114, L 359). The catalogue of similarities between her tale and Job's is long, including references to Clarissa's awe-inspiring presence (see Belford's description of her conversation with Lovelace's gang in letter 169), her isolation and ruin, the foolish counsels of her friends, and her longing for death. Clarissa's identification with Job goes up to and beyond her final moments: in the tableau she constructs to adorn her coffin, she quotes, slightly altered, from Job's third chapter, and Job dominates the meditations she writes in her sorrow. We certainly find in Job a partner narrative for *Clarissa*, but more importantly, it is also a stylistic analogue for Richardson's masterpiece.

While twentieth-century critics are apt to read Job as the proto-novel, Richardson's contemporaries saw it in another light. As Jonathan Lamb describes, Augustan critics were divided as to whether Job were allegory (the position of Warburton) or historical fact (that of Lowth et. al.); the possibilities for interpretation were not confined, however, to theology. While Lowth classes Job on the whole as a dramatic text, individual utterances within it can be, and were, read differently. As Job himself exclaims, "My harpe also is tuned to mourning, and my organe into the voyce of them that weepe" (30:31).[8] In fact, Job plays an important role both in the developing rhetoric of sublimity and in what would become the rhetoric of the lyric.[9]

Of the many contemporary paraphrases of Job, the majority are lyric, focusing on his lament.[10] Clarissa's use of Job follows this pattern as well: in her trials, Clarissa reads, copies and rereads the lament, finding in it a vocabulary and pattern of expression which suit her own troubled heart. Four "meditations" in the novel come from Clarissa's pen, and save one, they are transcriptions of biblical verses and rely exclusively on lyric sources: Job and the Psalms (one, in letter 399, combines Psalms with Ecclesiasticus).[11] Richardson combines these meditations with others supposed to be written by Clarissa in an almost apocryphal text, *Meditations*

Collected from the Sacred Books; and Adapted to the Different Stages of A Deep Distress; Gloriously surmounted by Patience, Piety, and Resignation (1750). Although Richardson printed the collection, he refused to publish the *Meditations* beyond a small circle of friends, reserving them for those who had been bereaved or were themselves in great distress.

In restricting the circulation of the *Meditations* as a separate work to people in pain, Richardson attempts to enforce an emotional congruity between readers and heroine or text. Clarissa herself, both in the novel and in her preface to the *Meditations*, emphasizes the foundational importance of emotion in her use of Job: "Indeed, at the first of my calamity, I had great grief, and, at times, had great impatience in my grief . . . : So that I could not help transcribing, as my first Mediation, the Curses of Job on the day of his birth."[12] She writes and meditates in accord with an emotional plot-line, so that if "perhaps too many of the first Meditations are *passionate exclamations*," then, "by degrees, more chearful prospects [i.e., of death] opening upon my benighted mind, I looked forward to the promises of divine pardon and reconciliation, which are every where to be met with in the Sacred Books . . . then the Mediations carry a more comfortable appearance," and "at length, my pen, as well, as my voice, could break out into *Praises* and *Thanksgivings*" (171, emphasis original).

In adapting the words of Job or the Psalms to her distress, in moving from one lyric genre (lament) to others (praises and thanksgivings), Clarissa is carrying out the reciprocal projects of lyric reader and writer as they come to be understood by contemporary theorists of religious poetry. Like the singer of a hymn, Clarissa enters the "I" of the poet (Job or David) and makes it her own, experiencing a profound emotional consensus, sharing her griefs and his in one boundless moment. The eighteenth century marks the point at which this kind of affective claim for lyric is codified in criticism.[13] Robert Lowth's *Lectures on the Sacred Poetry of the Hebrews* (Latin 1753, English 1787), a landmark text in this history, establishes the terms of the emotional relation embodied in Biblical poetry. He begins by arguing that "[t]he origin and first use of poetical language are undoubtedly to be traced into the vehement affections of the mind."[14] Hebrew poetry is both morally and aesthetically important for Lowth because of its "new and extraordinary forms of expression, which are indeed possessed of great force and efficacy in this respect especially, that they in some degree imitate or represent the present habit and state of the soul."[15]

Earlier in the century, the idea of an "imitation" of the inner self appears as an essential part of the concept of the religious lyric put forward by the popular hymn writer Isaac Watts. In his preface to the *Horae Lyricae* (1706), Watts lauds Job's emphasis on personal experience:

> How mournful and dejected is the language of [Job's] own sorrows: Terrors are turned upon him, they pursue his soul as the wind, and his welfare passes away as a cloud; his bones are pierced within him, and his soul is poured out; he goes mourning without the sun, a brother to dragons, and a companion to owls; while his harp and organ are turned into the voice of them that weep.[16]

For Watts, this kind of representation of emotion is so fundamental that he recommends it as a model for the Christian poet, emphasizing its affective potential: "our wonder and our love, our pity, delight, and sorrow, with the long train of hopes and fears, must needs be under the command of a harmonious pen whose every line makes a part of the reader's faith, and is the very life or death of his soul" (156). What is key in Watts's analysis is the way in which the expression of experience by a poet may lead us as readers to align ourselves with it, to experience a powerful form of emotional consensus. His own "Poems Sacred to Virtue" (printed in the *Horae Lyricae*) "were formed when the frame and humour of my soul was just suited to the subject of my verse. The image of my heart is painted in them, and if they meet with a reader whose soul is akin to mine, perhaps they may agreeably entertain him" (159). This is the complex of emotional response expected by Clarissa and Richardson in regard to the *Meditations*.

Job's and Clarissa's use of the lyric voice and lyric paradigms of emotional responsiveness differ strongly from those we encounter in the preponderance of early eighteenth-century poetry. Personal poetry about one's own emotions (especially in the first person), whether lyric or otherwise, is not common in the first half of the century. However, as Lowth notes,

> in Hebrew poetry, the case is different, in part at least if not in the whole. The free spirit is hurried along . . . . Frequently, instead of disguising the secret feelings of the author, it lays them quite open to public view, and, the veil being, as it were, suddenly removed, all the affections and emotions of the soul, its sudden impulses, its hasty sallies and irregularities, are conspicuously displayed. (Elledge 2:691)

Hebrew poetry like Job offers to reveal the self denuded, moving, so that its language (of hastiness, disruption, distress) becomes part of a complex of shared emotion, part of a lyric model of the experience of reading and writing.

Richardson's decision to model some of the most pivotal language of his novel on the language of Job takes on particular importance in this respect. As with the *Meditations*, in the ten fragments which Clarissa scribbles in near-madness after she has been raped, we find an intensely lyric use of biblical language. A passage from Job 29 is the model (with a shift in person) for her fifth paper:

> How art thou now humbled in the dust, thou proud Clarissa Harlowe! Thou that never steppedst out of thy father's house, but to be admired! Who wert wont to turn thine eye, sparkling with healthful life, and self-assurance, to different objects at once, as thou passedst, as if . . . to plume thyself upon the expected applauses of all that beheld thee! Thou that usedst to go to rest satisfied with the adulations paid thee in the past day, and couldst put off everything but thy vanity!— (891)

In Job 29, we see that Job's suffering casts him back to his own days of grace:

> When I went out to the gate, through the citie, when I prepared my seate in the street
> The yong men saw me, and hid themselves: and the aged arose, and stood up.
> The princes refrained talking, and laid their hand on their mouth.
> The Nobles held their peace, and their tongue cleaved to the roofe of their mouth.
> . . . .
> I put on righteousnesse, and it clothed me: my judgement was as a robe and a diademe.
> . . . .
> Unto me men gave eare, and waited, and kept silence at my counsell.
> After my words they spake not againe, and my speach dropped upon them,
> And they waited for me as for the raine. . . . (29:7–10; 14; 21–23)

Important parallels here include the reference to the glad clothing of the past as well as shared emphasis on the body, the adorations of the crowd, and the absence of peers: these form the substance of both lamentations.[17]

Richardson underlines the peculiarity of Clarissa's language in the frame which he gives the papers, fragments unique among the documents which comprise the novel: "Dorcas tells me that what she writes she tears, and throws the paper in fragments under the table, either as not knowing what she does, or disliking it: then gets up, wrings her hands, weeps, and shifts her seat all round the room: then returns to her table, sits down, and writes again" (L261, 889). Their history marks them from the outset as extraordinary, and within them we find neither Clarissa's normative language nor the novel's normative epistolary discourse. As Lovelace describes them, these are "poetical flights" (L261, 894). They are expressive of intense anguish and, as Lovelace complains to Belford, so moving that they draw even the author of Clarissa's griefs into sympathy with them. In line with Watts's description of Job or the *Horae Lyricae*, these passages work to create emotional consensus.

If the post-rape papers borrow the language of a lyric model in the Book of Job, they also draw on characteristics of lyrics more contemporary. Each paper carries with it the fiction of being a tiny, discrete document, a short manuscript. Punctuation works in these outbursts to enforce a kind of cadence, dividing sentences almost as line breaks and caesuras function in verse.[18] Papers V and VII are written with irregular line lengths that could not be further from the disciplined justification of printed prose. In most of the fragments, trochees and spondees litter the page, distancing the language from either the smoother, less differentiated tones of plain prose, or the formal regulation of much Augustan poetry.[19] Richardson attempts a kind of regulated disorder, something which we may assume is intended to imitate the processes of a mind where "thought, and grief, and confusion came crowding so thick" that all seems utterly lost (890):

> —And can you, my dear honored papa, resolve for ever to reprobate your poor child?—But I am sure you would not, if you knew what she has suffered since her unhappy—And will nobody plead for your poor suffering girl?—No one good body?—Why, then, dearest sir, let it be an act of your own innate goodness, which I have so much experienced, and so much abused—I don't presume to think you should receive me—no, indeed—my name is—I don't know what my name is!—I never dare to wish to come into your family again!—But your heavy curse, my dear papa—Yes, I will call you papa, and help yourself as you can—for you are my own dear papa, whether you will or not—And though I am an unworthy child—yet I am your child. (890)

This language is highly rhetorical, an index of the burden of emotional weight it is expected to carry. Like any stylized language, this had to be invented: it is neither natural nor plain (to take the descriptor usually associated with Richardson's style).[20] The language Clarissa uses with her father, that of a recalcitrant child attempting to do her duty but laboring under his displeasure, is remarkably close to what we encounter in Herbert's *Longing*: [21]

> My throat, my soul is hoarse;
> My heart is withered like a ground
> Which thou dost curse.
> My thoughts turn round,

And make me giddy; Lord I fall,
Yet call.
(ll. 7–12)

Thou tarriest, while I die,
And fall to nothing: thou dost reign,
And rule on high,
While I remain
In bitter grief: yet I am styled
Thy child.
(ll. 55–60)

Both texts, Richardson's and Herbert's, provide a Jobian lament. [22] There are evident similarities in diction and self-positioning between this poem and Clarissa's second paper: they share an emphasis on fragmentation, the possibilities of grace, and an insistence on the naming of father and child.[23] These similarities might be coincidental: Lawrence Stone notes that one of the characteristics of family life in Puritan England was an elevation of the father-child bond to a quasi-religious status.[24] Clarissa's use of such language might be merely another indication of the prevalence of this attitude, but the particular complex of issues which surrounds her writing links this speech firmly to the tradition of the lament.

As Helen Vendler points out of Shakespeare's sonnets: "Aesthetically speaking, it is what a lyric *does with* its borrowed social languages—i.e., how it casts them into new permutational and combinational forms—that is important."[25] What I wish to underline here is that both Herbert's and Clarissa's reconstructions of the Job lyric emphasize intimacy. For Herbert, the potential austerity of God's relationship to mankind is made personal by subsumption in a father-child model; for Clarissa, the language of authority and of absent grace (her father's "innate goodness") is made intimate by the powerful, if abject, statement with which she closes: "Yes, I *will* call you papa, and help yourself as you can . . . I *am* your child." The centripetal force of the speaker's voice pulls against the tendency of power to distance, to sterilize, and to estrange. The lyric subject draws addressee and readers into a close of intimacy, the hothouse atmosphere of personal experience which Coleridge found so distressing in Richardson.[26]

Clarissa's convergence with Herbert's lyrics is founded on a concern with ways that fragments can be made to speak (fragments of experience or of the self; divisions born of trauma or of conflicting desires and principles): both Richardson and Herbert are interested in discovering how self-alienation can become the building block of an aesthetic, experiential, and even lyric whole (this last claim will be most clear in the discussion of emblems with which I will close). In Clarissa's mad papers and in Herbert's poems, we are presented with minds wracked to such a vast extent that a coherent sense of self is on the verge of dissolution. In *Longing*, as we saw, the threatened absence of grace exerts incredible pressure:

> My heart is withered like a ground
> Which thou dost curse.
> My thoughts turn round,
> And make me giddy; Lord, I fall,
> Yet call.
> (148, ll. 7–12)

The promise of grace (withheld) is then balanced against internal fragmentation:

> Lord JESU, hear my heart,
> Which hath been broken now so long,
> That ev'ry part
> Hath got a tongue!
> (150, ll. 73–76)

Clarissa's experience of self-division is the result of rape (and the drugs used against her). As she says in her first mad paper:

> I sat down to say a great deal—my heart was full—I did not know what to say first—and thought, and grief, and confusion, and (Oh my poor head!) I cannot tell what—And thought, and grief, and confusion came crowding so thick upon me; one would be first, another would be first; so I can write nothing at all—only that, whatever they have done to me, I cannot tell; but I am no longer what I was in any one thing.—In any one thing did I say? Yes, but I am; for I am still, and I ever will be,
> Your true— (890)

This paper, torn in two pieces as Richardson points out, shows a strategy similar to Herbert's—the attempt to reconstruct a fragmented self by reinstating a set of lapsed relations ("I am your child" in Paper II; "I am still your true" here). I do not maintain that Herbert's poem is, strictly speaking, a source for the passage above, but rather point out that Richardson, as well as Herbert, is exploring a dilemma close to the heart of religious lyric. The first and second papers evoke the same paradigm or scene that underlies Herbert's lyric project, from *The Altar* to *Longing*, *Denial*, or *Obedience*, and these papers follow the same patterns of connection we see in Herbert's poems. We may identify a linkage between ideas and strategies apparently so strong that when Richardson thinks of one (silence, fragmentation), he is drawn to the other (naming, grace). The fluid relationships of *Longing* are also those of Clarissa's scraps of sense. These two versions of lyric seek to restore a battered self: what is at stake, what must be saved at all cost, is the ability of the expressive voice to provoke a response, to receive validation through an answer. Individual experience holds the potential of a solipsistic nightmare—solitude without redemption, suffering without witness.[27]

While Herbert counts on Christ's mediation between himself and his father, Clarissa has no such hope. For her, the task of reconstructing herself in fragmentation and isolation is carried out by means of a set of borrowed discourses. In these scraps of paper she writes herself into a set of patterns available to her (allegory, fable, etc.) that offer stable positions, even if these constructions are painful to apprehend. Each of Clarissa's papers can be said to represent emotion and an approach to experience by linking them with a particular style and language (similar to the way in which Herbert chooses a particular form for each poem's emotional and ideational content).[28] In Paper II, we saw the language of lament sewn to the father-child dynamic. In Paper III, reminiscence is drawn as fable; Paper VII gives us the allegorical vision of a prophet; Paper VIII shows affinities with traditional lyric outcries at betrayed love.

The variety of shapes Clarissa's papers take on demonstrates that Richardson here ranks form high among his many aesthetic or didactic concerns. Clarissa is certainly a victim of mental disorder and confusion, by her own testimony; by that of Lovelace, or of an astute reader, there is more to her expression than that: "After all, Belford, I have just skimmed over these transcriptions of Dorcas; and I see there is method and good sense in some of them, wild as others of them are" (L261, 894). Like the character she quotes in Paper X, she knows a hawk from a handsaw. We are accustomed, especially since Wordsworth, to see in poetic composition the disciplining, or at least regulation, of emotion by rule. In Herbert's lyrics, we see that emotion and idea require their own formal shapes in order to emerge on the page. Whether it is *The Pulley*, *The Flower*, or *Easter Wings*, almost all of the poems in *The Temple* show a unique verse pattern. This kind of attention to form is precisely what makes the loose, baggy monster of the novel seem insurmountably distant from its more controlled cousin.

The sprawling dimensions of Richardson's masterpiece encourage us to stop with the truism that this enormous novel could not be as a whole more distinct from one of Herbert's compact lyrics. However, when we examine the context of poetic discourse in the eighteenth century, there is reason to reconsider. The New Critical conception of a poem as a discrete entity, a formal creation bounded at top and bottom by the blankness of a page, is by no means definitive; it certainly does not define a normative reading experience at a given historical moment (it was not designed to do so). Although it is indisputable that in the eighteenth century poems were approached by readers as individual works (works which could be favorites, placed in miscellanies, quoted in letter or sermon), they were often encountered, and even designed to be encountered, as members of a series. Formal groupings like the sonnet sequence coexisted with collections like *The Temple* or Cowley's *The Mistress* (which also makes its appearance in *Clarissa*); although one would not read such collections at one sitting, these texts enforce the idea that each individual poem is part of a larger whole, a specific context which enriches and informs it. This is more than merely to say that all poems have a context beyond their first and final lines: in the case of a sequence like *The Mistress,* each piece emerges as an aspect of a given experience, a mood or time which itself can be isolated and given aesthetic being, but which receives a new level of meaning, both as statement and as representation, through its connection to its fellows.[29]

Eighteenth-century readers and writers were becoming accustomed to encountering lyric in larger non-lyric forms and with a relaxation of formal regularity: the embedded invitations and pastorals of *The Seasons* or the lamentations of *Night Thoughts*, for example. Parts and pieces also took on new importance and prose was newly opened to lyric by discoveries in biblical poetics. As we have seen, for Lowth, the emotional disarray of Hebrew poetry, "its hasty sallies and irregularities" (Elledge 2:691), marks it as poetry—in contradistinction for him to the grammatical discipline of more earth-bound prose. The British Pindaric, in its post-Cowleyan irregularity, also substitutes disorder for regulation and discipline. Fragmentariness like that of Clarissa's mad papers, in this context, suggests the power and passion of poetry, not an aesthetic or generic failure. It was perhaps the expansion of poetry through biblical modes which most directly fostered the possibilities of generic absorption or adaptation practiced by Richardson. While scholars and practitioners had long been fully aware that rhyme was not necessary to poetry, Lowth's theory of parallelism introduced a new concept. In his lectures, Lowth argues that the principle which distinguishes verse from prose in the Bible is semantic doubling: the words of the first half of a line are repeated, with some variation of intensity or diction, in the second. Meter has some importance, but not consistently so.[30] In a dramatic revolution in critical practice, verse had been found, in parts, embedded in a prose form.

When Robert Alter undertakes an analysis of this verse phenomenon more recently, he is aware that modern readers still find it strange. He begins with a statement by Barbara Herrnstein Smith: "Meter serves . . . as a frame for the poem, separating it from a 'ground' of less highly structured speech and sounds."[31] However, since poetic systems of meter postdate biblical compositions, Alter instead focuses on the idea of the "ground" for biblical poetry:

> the continuously present frame of formal structure of which Barbara Smith speaks is quite conspicuous here. To be sure, there are also certain elements of symmetry and repetition in the surrounding prose, but, set against the tight formal organization of these lines, the narrative text all around is surely perceived by reader and listener as a 'ground' of nonpoetic discourse. (6)

Smith does not suggest that the ground surrounding poetic discourse is as immediate as the frame narrative of Job or the preponderance of *Clarissa,* but the idea is useful. As we saw, Richardson goes to great lengths to separate the language of the mad papers from that of the rest of his novel—formally, these items look different on the page; rhetorically, they sound different; within the fiction they have a different history. They may not have the "tight formal organization" of semantic parallelism, but they do evince a formal particularity, and in eighteenth-century terms, then, nothing prevents their having lyric affinities.

When we encounter the series of 'poetical' fragments (Lovelace's term, again) which lets us inside Clarissa's tortured consciousness, we do well to keep such formal considerations in mind. I am not arguing that each of these fragments is a lyric, but that the strategies Richardson deploys in them are those made literary by the lyric tradition. In choosing the language of Job, whose emotive and poetic credentials were of the highest order, Richardson makes a gesture toward the lyric which should not be ignored. The emotive potential of lyric language, especially of the kind used by Job or Herbert, may well be the target of Richardson's allusions.

It is no historical or aesthetic accident that Richardson finds lyric a congenial mode, for it shares significant characteristics and moods with the epistle. Linda Kauffman reminds us that letters have great inherent flexibility: from love to business to recommendation, they may encompass almost any subject, offering a rudimentary frame for whatever content they might carry. If the letter-form is an open one, particular characteristics of expression—those of the love letter, or the letter of business, for example—tend to borrow style and mode from other, parent discourses. The demands Richardson places on the epistle lead him toward a paradigm of communication highly developed in a range of seventeenth-century poems which, like *Clarissa*'s letters, emphasize the violation of ideal modes of communication, ideals of emotional consensus.

As Tom Keymer has shown, *Clarissa* operates not so much on a belief in the transparency of familiar letters, but on a mythology of correspondence.[32] If letters are supposed to be the closest approximation of consciousness, it is never supposed that they are the real thing (*Clarissa*'s letters may be written to the moment, for example, but they are most often copied over before they are sent): true intimacy is more asymptotic than attainable. Even for those characters who believe in their own sincerity, like Clarissa or Anna, although the letter always pushes toward the ideal of free and truthful communication, it always threatens to run short. For them, the image the letter projects of its writer is always compromised—there are things one wishes to say but cannot, or things one wishes to believe or to be believed, but which ultimately are illusions. We are alone, and fallen, and writing seems only to confirm our isolation.

Here the lyric paradigm we encounter in Herbert's poetry becomes again important, for here we may discover a structural relationship (in addition to one of quotation and adaptation) between *Clarissa*'s letters and Herbert's lyric project. If Clarissa works toward a myth of the transparency of the soul in the letter, a myth against which she measures each moment of writing, Herbert has his own version of the ideal by which his attempts are scaled. When Herbert even considers the possibility of true mutuality, he hits a humbling boundary, Christ's passion. Witness *The Reprisal*:

> I have considered it, and find
> There is no dealing with thy mighty passion:
> For though I die for thee, I am behind:
> My sins deserve the condemnation.
>
> (36, ll. 1–4)
>
> Ah! was it not enough that thou
> By thy eternal glory didst outgo me?
> Couldst thou not grief's sad conquests me allow,
> But in all vict'ries overthrow me?
>
> (37, ll. 9–12)

Whatever suffering Herbert may undergo, Christ's passion has prefigured and surpassed it. Powers of sympathy pale in comparison: Christ need not suffer with, he has already suffered for. Any attempt on the poet's part to offer a medium for shared emotion is already overthrown by Christ's inimitable example. He is the ideal lyric subject, and it is against this that Herbert struggles.

Herbert's inability to attain the kind of complete identity of emotion which constitutes Christ's passion (the doctrinal fact that Christ's suffers for us, that his suffering encompasses ours) is a lyric as well as a religious dilemma. This problem of consensus (union of feeling) is represented in

The Temple in terms of silence. In many of his lyrics, as in Clarissa's letters, Herbert's voice seems too often to go unheard. *Denial* evokes Herbert's distress at appeals to God which seem to fall only into a void:

> O that thou shouldst give dust a tongue
> To cry to thee,
> And then not hear it crying! all day long
> My heart was in my knee,
> But no hearing.
>
> Therefore my soul lay out of sight,
> Untuned, unstrung:
> My feeble spirit, unable to look right,
> Like a nipped blossom, hung
> Discontented.
> (80, ll. 16–25)

Thematically and linguistically, Herbert's scene appears almost a foretaste of Clarissa's dilemma. Denied the response and protection of her own father, she hangs "like a half-broken-stalked lily," at the mercy of Lovelace, her betrayer (L256, 881).

What is particularly compelling about both Herbert's and Clarissa's constructions of denial—the absence of complete consensus, intimacy, and correspondence (in Lovelace's terms, again, a union of hearts)—is that it leads each to similar strategies of self-presentation. Surrounded by silence, Herbert's verse emerges as a physical counter, a record and indication of his search for consensus, as we see in the famous smoothness of *Denial*'s ending stanza, where the last line is finally in tune with the others:

> O cheer and tune my heartless breast,
> Defer no time;
> That so thy favours granting my request,
> They and my mind may chime,
> And mend my rhyme.
> (80, ll. 26–30)

Herbert here attempts to make use of the material potential of verse (its sound); but in addition to using the sensual properties of the poem, the resonance of meter and rhythm, he often attempts to use verse as a token, a physical link between himself and God. *Obedience* offers the most explicit instance of this strategy. There, Herbert emphasizes the poem's character as a written document:

On it my heart doth bleed
As many lines as there doth need
To pass itself and all it hath to thee.
(104, ll. 6–8)

As with Herbert's shaped verse, the poem's physical presence as much as its meaning is key to its effectiveness (or at least to the demands placed on it). These moves prefigure what Janet Altman terms epistolarity, or "the use of the letter's formal properties to create meaning."[33] Epistolarity as technique often involves a constructive emphasis on the surface of the page, with its ink, illegible script or even blots caused by tears. Typical would be the drop that falls on a note from Mrs. Harlowe to her beleaguered daughter: "This answer I received in an open slip of paper, but it was wet in one place. I kissed the place; for I am sure it was blistered, as I may say, with a mother's tear!—The dear lady must (I hope she must) have written it reluctantly" (L54, 230). Herbert's use of such techniques shows us how the demand for a lyric consensus, interrupted or foreclosed, pushes the writer to approach the epistolary condition. *Clarissa* is located at this juncture. Faced with the foreclosure of lyric consensus, Clarissa and Herbert come to occupy the same imaginative and a similar formal condition. Herbert's letters to God, we imagine, succeed no more (or no less) than any of his other prayers. Clarissa, however, has the disadvantage of merely writing to mortals; they seem perhaps harder to reach, but by using the strategies of religious verse, Richardson gains access to a powerful vocabulary of emotional union, calling on the language, imagery, and structures that mark lyric expression.[34] In generic terms, the traditional ability of poetry to move the heart and mind is what a prose form like the novel must equal if it is to be successful, if it is to be animated within its reader's consciousness; this emotive power is what is at stake in Richardson's adaptation of the lyric.[35]

Clarissa's exploration of the lyric mode intensifies as she nears death and letters become increasingly ineffective. In their stead, she crafts a self-elegy. Clarissa's tableau of emblems and verses (all taken from lyric sources in the Bible), engraved within inches of her dead body, creates a lyric voice from the manipulation and adaptation of emblems, much as do Herbert's poems.[36] Clarissa, like lyric poets before her, uses the doubleness of the emblem to create a speaking image of herself:

> The principal device, neatly etched on a plate of white metal, is a crowned serpent, with its tail in its mouth, forming a ring, the emblem of eternity, and in the circle made by it is this inscription:

CLARISSA HARLOWE
APRIL X.
[Then the year]
AETAT. XIX.

For ornaments: at top, an hour-glass winged. At bottom, an urn.

Under the hour-glass, on another plate, this inscription:

> HERE the wicked cease from troubling: and HERE the weary be at rest. Job iii.17.

Over the urn, near the bottom:

> Turn again unto thy rest, Oh my soul! For the Lord hath rewarded thee. And why?
> Thou hast delivered my soul from death; mine eyes from tears; and my feet from falling. Ps. cxvi. 7,8.

Over this text is the head of a white lily snapped short off, and just falling from the stalk; and this inscription over that, between the principal plate and the lily:

> The days of man are but grass. For he flourisheth as a flower of the field: for, as soon as the wind goeth over it, it is gone; and the place thereof shall know it no more. Ps. ciii. 15, 16. (L451, 1306).

The final emblem is taken from the image which Lovelace uses to describe Clarissa, drugged and pleading, just before he rapes her: "And down on her bosom, like a half-broken-stalked lily, top-heavy with the overcharging dews of the morning, sunk her head with a sigh that went to my heart" (L256, 881). This is an emblem whose presence speaks betrayal, but Lovelace's brutality and deception are rebuked and all but erased by the emblem's accompanying text. Clarissa may be as a flower in the field, but so is Lovelace, and with Clarissa's passing, the marks of Lovelace's brutality disappear as well: he has no triumph.

At least one of the other emblems also enacts a hidden dialogue or contest. The first ornament, "an hour-glass winged," figures the speed with which time passes; this basic signification is available to two primary interpretations within the text. The briefness of the human lifespan is one of the staple warnings of conduct books and sermons, reminding us, as does Wither in his *A Collection of Emblemes, Ancient and Moderne* (1635),

"Live, ever mindfull of thy dying; / For, Time is alwayes from thee flying" (Emblem 77).[37] However, images of time's swift passage are also linked to the *carpe diem* tradition, to the wooing lover whose desires speed him as fast as Marvell's winged chariot—to Lovelace, even if he never makes the sort of offers given by Marlowe's Shepherd or Mr. B (and he is thus spared the replies of a Nymph or a Pamela).[38] Clarissa's chosen text makes the address to Lovelace specific: there is no doubt that he is the wicked one who has troubled her most.

Through this use of emblems, Clarissa is working to create an image of the self around the dissonance of two discourses, one of her own, one of her betrayer's. George Herbert, too, uses dissonance between emblems to frame his imagined self, and to frame his particular lyric project. He is not menaced by a Lovelace; for him the danger of betrayal comes from within. Herbert's well-known dialogic strategies often involve an allegorical figure whose presence enables him to voice divisions within his own soul. This is the structure of *Hope*, where the poet stages an exchange or dialogue of emblems:

> I gave to Hope a watch of mine: but he
>   An anchor gave to me.
> Then an old prayer-book I did present:
>   And he an optick sent.
> With that I gave a viall full of tears:
>   But he a few green eares:
> Ah Loyterer! I'le no more, no more I'le bring:
>   I did expect a ring.
>
> (121, ll. 1–8)

Barbara Lewalski renders this poem less cryptic, translating these emblems into their plainer meanings:

> The speaker gives his watch (time), and receives in return an anchor (hope); he then gives an old prayer-book (his long-continued devotion) and receives an 'optick' glass (with which to see . . . heaven afar off). He responds with a 'viall full of tears' (his repentance), and is given a few 'green eares.' (203)

Herbert is waiting for God, waiting for the assurance of grace, and as Lewalski notes, the ring of the poem's last line is the symbol of a union constantly deferred. In *Hope* we see the other side of Herbert's general construction of his speaker as a child: weakness and impatience. The speaker's final retreat is subject to a lesson which his limitations do not allow him to articulate, according to Lewalski: "The point, which the reader should infer by interpreting the emblems better than the speaker, is that the business of Hope is with expectation, not fruition: the speaker must patiently wait to receive his ring hereafter" (203).

The speaker's voice and desires (as represented by the emblems he chooses) and the emblematic offerings of Hope are two alternatives with which the poet feels equal dissatisfaction. The ideal (waiting) cannot satisfy, and the infantile (wanting) cannot be sustaining. This dissonance is instructive, and Herbert's decision to present emblems as images without explication, only supported by their dialogic relation, is key to the pattern of significance. The emblems appear almost as slides—or as individual woodcuts—and the gaps between them open up not only a space for interpretation, but the time for contemplation. Each emblematic reference slows down the poem, tracks it out, gives the reader, and Herbert, time to weigh each option. Herbert is spectator of his own internal struggle, and emerges as spectator and poet simultaneously, in appearing as the consciousness which can understand the poem's "lesson" even if he doesn't get it—even if that lesson remains unprofitable. All of this happens between the poem's frames, in the time of "loitering," where and when Herbert gives the poem and himself over to interpretation.

If we return to *Clarissa*, we find a similar structure. In her self-elegy, each emblem is contested: a final meaning is reified, but not naturally so.[39] On the one hand, there is the work we have to do to interpret the tableau (this holds within the novel, as well—her aunt's tears keep her from even reading it);[40] on the other, the novel's story dramatizes the impossibility of earthly coexistence, or even supremacy, for either of the alternatives the emblems offer. Even if one discourse (that of moral rectitude) is right, it cannot withstand the temporal challenge offered by the other. Clarissa's goodness is effaced, as a flower in the field; Lovelace's wickedness ends in misery. If there is a place where this dissonance can be resolved, it is certainly elsewhere—in the hereafter, or barring that, at the lyric moment, that of confrontation with the reader.

In *Hope*, Herbert's emblems must wait for a resolution which occurs only in the imagination of the poet or informed reader, outside the poem, outside its given data, figures, and forms. If Herbert's poem is a lyric, that is, more than an accumulation of emblems (and not just because of meter or line-length), it is so because of the consciousness which is drawn around it—the poem achieves a lyric intensity when it realizes the presence of a mind which contains all the poem shows and more, the consciousness of the poet who gets the lesson the dialogue has to teach. Clarissa's set of emblems emerges as more than a conventional display for much the same reason. What makes it lyric has to do with the way the self is positioned vis-à-vis the tension around what each symbol means, with how and why the self is able to speak through. Part of the answer lies in the very sense we have of circling a self, of drawing ever closer to an invisible core whose presence we feel but which is materially or denotatively absent. Clarissa's body is hidden beneath; her soul has flown away; the record of her consciousness sits, starkly posed between these alternatives.

In exploring the resonance between Richardson's use of lyric and those of his precursors, we are able to foreground some key features of a certain version of the lyric mode. What makes Job's, Herbert's, or Clarissa's complaints poignant is the threat of the foreclosure of consensus as much as the record of their sufferings. At issue is an affective program, an attempt to frame sense and make it not just understandable, but shareable, to offer up personal experience as more than individual—as participatory. In Herbert, *Clarissa*, and Job, we see the terrible isolation in suffering which drives each to speak, and each to thoughts of death. We also witness a search for alternatives, for modes of expression and kinds of exchange which join the individual in emotional union with the world beyond.

The final question must be this: what does Clarissa, or Richardson, do to the lyric in thus adapting it? Most obviously, the integrity of form is destroyed—the lyric is dilated and diffused, its conventions spread over many pages and embedded in a new genre. In its place we find an integrity of the subject, a record of consciousness and its desire to reach outward, no matter how brutalized it may have been. Subjectivity in these terms is an ideal construction that seeks the participation of others in an imaginative intimacy (a search whose failures are as important as its successes). These alterations to the lyric are significant, in part because they suggest that lyric at this moment is seen as adaptable, absorbable, and ultimately changeable, that it is flexible, not fixed, that its language and structures are available to be adopted, like the hymn, by any and all properly disposed comers, and that generic boundaries are as open to imaginative crossings as the boundaries of personal experience.

NOTES

1. *Clarissa* (New York: Penguin, 1980), 141. All references to the novel are to this edition.

2. See, for example, Margaret Anne Doody, *A Natural Passion: A Study of the Novels of Samuel Richardson* (Oxford: Clarendon Press, 1974); and Mark Kinkead-

Weekes, *Samuel Richardson: Dramatic Novelist* (Ithaca: Cornell University Press, 1973); see also Christina Marsden Gillis, *The Paradox of Privacy: Epistolary Form in* Clarissa (Gainesville: University Presses of Florida, 1984); and Linda Kauffman, *Discourses of Desire: Gender, Genre, and Epistolary Fictions* (Ithaca: Cornell University Press, 1986).

3. "Richardson: Original or Learned Genius?" *Samuel Richardson: Tercentenary Essays,* ed. Margaret Anne Doody and Peter Sabor (Cambridge: Cambridge University Press, 1989): 188–202. There has been some debate about the extent of Richardson's knowledge of literature, but recent critics have been arguing in favor of a greater, rather than a lesser, range of learning. Michael Connaughton suggests that, even given Richardson's use of collections of quotations, Richardson's acquaintance with Herbert, for example, was more than that given by a commonplace book ("Richardson's Familiar Quotations: *Clarissa* and Bysshe's *Art of English Poetry,*" *Philological Quarterly*, 60 [1986], 191).

4. On the fluidity of generic distinctions, see Ralph Cohen, "On the Interrelations of Eighteenth-Century Literary Forms" in *New Approaches to Eighteenth-Century Literature*, ed. Phillip Harth (New York: Columbia University Press, 1974). For biblical genres, see Lewalski's *Protestant Poetics* (Princeton: Princeton University Press, 1979), cited hereafter in the text. About the debates on pastoral, see *inter alia* Pope and Johnson. The ode is canvassed by Watts, Young, and Congreve, among others. Drama, of course, offered its own range of exemplary emotional statements—both Congreve's *Mourning Bride* and Dryden's *Tyrannick Love* could provide model passionate outbursts. For the moment, it is important to note that in finding appropriate quotations for his novels, Richardson often relied on sources like Bysshe's *Art of English Poetry*, which arranged exemplary quotations under headings (often emotional categories like "Fear"). Michael Connaughton points out that whatever affinities Richardson may have felt for the drama, "only slightly over half of the quotations from *Clarissa* are from plays, and nearly all are in Bysshe. Had Richardson's objective been to recreate theatrical types, he would have been more likely to turn for help to the *Thesaurus Dramaticus* or its later version, *Beauties of the English Stage*. Even in Bysshe, moreover, he does not deliberately seek out dramatic sources" (193).

5. See Lewalski's *Protestant Poetics*; Louis Martz's *Poetry of Meditation* (New Haven: Yale University Press, 1954); Helen Vendler's *Poetry of George Herbert* (Cambridge, MA: Harvard University Press, 1975); and Anne Williams's *The Prophetic Strain* (Chicago: University of Chicago Press, 1984).

6. *Select Hymns, Taken out of Mr. Herbert's Temple, and Turn'd into the Common Metre* (1697), ed. with an introduction William E. Stephenson (Los Angeles: Augustan Reprint Society, 1962), 1, quoting the clergyman Simon Browne around 1720.

7. Robert A. Erickson, "'Written in the Heart': Richardson and Scripture," *Eighteenth-Century Fiction* 2 (1989): 17–52. Erickson first notes the Job connection, which is later analyzed closely by Jonathan Lamb in *The Rhetoric of Suffering: Reading the Book of Job in the Eighteenth Century* (Oxford: Clarendon, 1995). I strongly disagree with Lamb's assessment that "Richardson's Job, the scriptural centerpiece of *Clarissa*, is used to introduce a theodicy more akin to Pope's views

about the suppression of individual suffering than to . . . amplifications of a singular complaint" (227). Lamb's neglect of the parallels between Clarissa's coffin self-elegy and Job's projected monument is perhaps explained by his preference for a more conservative reading of Richardson's approach to individual suffering than my own.

8. All biblical quotations are from the 1611 Authorized Version.

9. Williams discusses Job's place in regard to the sublime in some depth: "Symon Patrick, bishop of Ely, remarks in his popular commentary on Job (1678) that the poetry has a 'grandeur [that] is as much above all other poetry, as thunder is louder than a whisper,' a remark quoted by Edward Young in the introduction to his own paraphrase" (60).

10. This survey is based on the LION English Full-Text Poetry Database. Job's complaint and God's response are the two most popular subjects of paraphrase. Most are in rhymed couplets, but Elizabeth Rowe's *Philomela* (1737), an expansion upon 19:26, and several hymns by Watts and Wesley are in lyric verse. The hymns use the pronouns "I" and "We," emphasizing the personal nature of suffering and complaint (even if each must be overcome). As might be expected given the general waning of the couplet, paraphrases published after 1785 (notably William Mason's and Edward Perronet's) tend to be in lyric verse.

11. Tom Keymer discusses Clarissa's meditations in great depth in "Richardson's *Meditations*: Clarissa*'s Clarissa*," in *Samuel Richardson: Tercentenary Essays*, ed. Margaret Anne Doody and Peter Sabor (Cambridge: Cambridge University Press, 1989), 89–109. My account of the facts of publication relies heavily on Keymer.

12. *Meditations*, ed. Thomas Keymer, *Samuel Richardson's Published Commentary on Clarissa* 1747–65, 3 vols. (London: Pickering and Chatto, 1998), 1:170.

13. See Norman Maclean, "From Action to Image: Theories of the Lyric in the Eighteenth Century," in *Critics and Criticism*, ed. R. S. Crane (Chicago: University of Chicago Press, 1952): 408–60. Affective claims are most important in criticism of the Pindaric ode, with Dryden's *Alexander's Feast* being a primary example of the congruence of lyric and emotion.

14. Patricia Meyer Spacks, *The Poetry of Vision* (Cambridge: Harvard University Press, 1967), 121.

15. *Eighteenth-Century Critical Essays,* ed. Scott Elledge, 2 vols. (Ithaca: Cornell University Press, 1961), 2:690.

16. *Eighteenth-Century Critical Essays,* ed. Elledge, 1:151–52.

17. Clarissa's use of the second person indicates how deeply disturbed and internally fragmented she is: not only is she completely overthrown by the experience of rape, but she has been constantly concerned about the status of her own experience throughout the novel. She is dealing here, as she puts it, with her "hated self" (L295, 974). In others of the mad papers, she does use the first person, but it is not until she faces death and composes her self-elegy (her coffin) that she is able to speak more clearly of her self through her conflicts and divisions.

18. An anonymous reader of this essay kindly reminded me that aposiopesis has other roots and connotations (especially as the traditions of sensibility coalesce).

However, here I feel that combined with a range of stylistic and other borrowings from lyric, the pauses and breaks in these papers reinforce a lyric connection. I take this opportunity to thank the two editorial readers and the editors of this volume for their extremely helpful comments and suggestions.

19. The irregularity of the Pindaric ode is an interesting analogue. As the form develops, criticism has it that irregularity is precisely what allows the Pindaric to carry more emotional weight than other forms. See, for example, Isaac Watts's comments in his preface to *Horae Lyricae*.

20. See, for example, Ian Watt, *The Rise of the Novel*, or Mark Kinkead-Weekes, *Samuel Richardson: Dramatic Novelist*. Richardson's 'plainness' is often seen in counter distinction to the floridness of romance or the epic complexities of Fielding. For an interesting counter-argument, see Irwin Gopnik, *A Theory of Style and Richardson's Clarissa* (The Hague: Mouton, 1970).

21. *The Works of George Herbert*, ed. F. E. Hutchinson (Oxford: Clarendon, 1941), 148–50. All references to Herbert's poems are to this edition.

22. Both laments rewrite Job 10:

> My soule is weary of my life, I will leave my complaint upon my self; I will speake in the bitternesse of my soule.
>
> . . . .
>
> Thine hands have made me and fashioned me together round about; yet thou doest destroy me.
>
> Remember, I beseech thee, that thou hast made me as the clay, and wilt thou bring me into dust againe?
>
> Hast thou not powred me out as milke, and cruddled me like cheese?
>
> Thou hast cloathed me with skin and flesh, and hast fenced me with bones and sinewes (10:1; 8–11).

23. Again, the extent of Richardson's familiarity with literary tradition has been the subject of considerable debate (see note 3 above). Richardson quotes from *The Temple* in a letter to Lady Bradshaigh as well as in *Clarissa*. See *Selected Letters of Samuel Richardson*, ed. John Carroll (Oxford: Clarendon Press, 1964), 91.

24. *The Family, Sex, and Marriage in England, 1500–1800* (New York: Harper Colophon Books, 1979), 124–27.

25. *The Art of Shakespeare's Sonnets* (Cambridge, MA: Harvard University Press, 1997), 2.

26. *Table Talk*, ed. Carl Woodring, vol. 14, pt. 2 of *The Collected Works of Samuel Taylor Coleridge* (Princeton: Princeton University Press, 1990), 295.

27. Perhaps this is what drew Blake to *Clarissa*. As Kinkead-Weekes points out, Blake had great respect for the novel (237 n. 1), and we may notice the similarity between Paper VII and poems like *The Sick Rose* and *The Human Abstract*. Kinkead-Weekes dismisses any connection to Blake as a misreading of Richardson's symbolism, but I disagree. His attitude is largely a result of his aims: Kinkead-Weekes is not looking to explore lyric genealogies because his concern is with dramatic ones. The Blake connection, however, suggests further consequences of

my argument which are too large to explore here—namely, that the manipulation and adaptation of lyric in Richardson has effects in the later history of Romantic poetry and the future of the lyric.

28. Not all of the papers rely on lyric models as closely as Papers II, III, or VII. The juxtaposition of standard models of lyric expression with other kinds of speech is suggestive: if we can accept that Richardson is working within a generalized concept of the lyric involving emotional expression and emotional consensus, intimacy, community, and the fragmentation of these ideals, the other papers can be seen as experiments in expanding the lyric mode beyond its received constructions.

29. We may note that the ten post-rape papers bear an analogical relationship to the traditional sonnet sequence. Like *Astrophil and Stella*, the (suggestively) epistolary *Pamphilia to Amphilanthus*, or parts of Shakespeare's sonnets, this sequence of papers reworks a range of emotions around a particular circumstance. The sonnet sequence, as a form, is perhaps best known for its ability to compartmentalize emotion and event, to separate moods and feelings for contemplation, to offer each moment up as shareable aesthetic and sensual experience (even if the pain of isolation is a theme of a given sonnet, the principle behind these expressions remains the same). As Peggy Samuels writes of the sonnet sequence:

> the sonnet has a tendency to make a definitive statement; it leans toward or ingests the epigram. However, if the sonnet is set within a sequence, the attempt at totalization or definitive statement and the closure of the individual sonnet are placed in question. One need only think of Shakespeare's sonnet sequence to feel how the mere act of beginning another sonnet retrospectively pronounces the previous sonnets on the same subject incomplete.

See her "Milton's Use of Sonnet Form in *Paradise Lost*," *Milton Studies* 24 (1988): 142–43. *Paradise Lost* offers yet another prime example of the absorption of lyric into a larger form, of course.

30. As in Anglo-Saxon verse, the number of stresses in the first half-line were often (but not always) repeated in the second.

31. Robert Alter, *The Art of Biblical Poetry* (New York: Basic Books, 1985), 6.

32. *Richardson's* Clarissa *and the Eighteenth-Century Reader* (Cambridge: Cambridge University Press, 1992), 1.

33. *Epistolarity* (Columbus: Ohio State University Press, 1982), 4.

34. Tom Keymer has argued that "the mad papers . . . open the way to new modes of composition. . . . [L]ike the rape itself, the fragmentation which accompanies it prepares Clarissa for the redefinition of self and experience in a new literary form, marking the point of a shift from realism to abstraction, and from epistolary narrative to meditation" (*Meditations,* 93–94). That new mode also evolves into a lyric one, as I argue here.

35. Anne Williams, *Prophetic Strain*, samples typical discussions of the power of poetry: "Sir Richard Blackmore writes, 'Tis in the power of poetry to insinuate

into the inmost Recesses of the Mind, to touch any Spring that moves the Heart, to agitate the Soul with a sort of Affection, and transform it into any Shape or Posture it thinks fit.' Or [Charles] Gildon: 'I think it may easily be made out, that there is nothing has a greater Power or Influence on the Heart than Poetry. . . . There is indeed no manner of Question but that true Poetry has Force to raise the Passions and to allay them, to change and to extinguish them'" (51). We should also note that Gildon was one of the early contributors to the growing epistolary craze in England.

36. Richardson also borrows from the tradition of the self-elegy we encounter in Donne and from his emblem poetry. It is beyond the scope of this essay, sadly, to explore these further connections.

37. Huston Diehl, *An Index of Icons in English Emblem Books, 1500–1700* (Norman: University of Oklahoma Press, 1986), 127.

38. Compare Pamela's updated and Christian point-for-point refutation of Mr. B's proposal to that of Ralegh's Nymph to Marlowe's Shepherd.

39. For an alternative reading of the use of emblems in *Clarissa* and the tensions around them, see Murray Brown, "*Emblemata Rhetorica*: Glossing Emblematic Discourse in Richardson's *Clarissa*," *Studies in the Novel* 27 (1995): 455–76. From a perspective different from mine, he argues that the power of Clarissa's final use of emblems comes from the reification of the deployment of emblems as mere commonplace. He maintains that part of Richardson's didactic project is to demonstrate that emblems are not merely fanciful or conventional icons, that rather they schematize truths which experience can be made to verify. Clarissa's death is one of those experiential verifications. He writes, "The emblematic commonplaces which we have been conditioned to understand with rhetorical topicality break those nominal boundaries, and we are confronted with emblems-made-actual" (457). I break from Brown somewhat in arguing that there is no simple victory in the emblematic dialogue. He writes, "Whereas Clarissa uses emblems and emblematic language to register her spiritual idealism, Lovelace appropriates these images in his attempts to facilitate and justify his agenda" (455). Lovelace abuses emblems, trying to "twist [them] into any shape he desires, but because they are not neutral counters, they do not serve him long" (456). In the end, the emblems return to their rightful meanings, according to Brown, functioning as a clear 'metalanguage' through which the text's didacticism can function.

40. This is the scene: "Her uncles looked and turned away, looked and turned away, very often upon the emblems, in silent sorrow. Mrs. Hervey [her aunt] would have read to them the inscription—These words she did read, *Here the wicked cease from troubling*: but could read no further. Her tears fell in large drops upon the plate she was contemplating, and yet she was desirous of gratifying a curiosity that mingled impatience with her grief because she could *not* gratify it, although she often wiped her eyes as they flowed" (L500, 1399). The desire to maintain such a gap between perception and interpretation is also perhaps why Richardson separates our introduction to the coffin from the emotional scene that it eventually creates (by almost 100 pages) —the textual distance gives us the time to analyze the earlier scene, and to absorb it, before the later emotional *Anschluss*.

Advertisements for Books in London Newspapers, 1760–1785

JAMES TIERNEY

The present essay is meant as successor to a paper that I delivered at the Book Trade Conference at London University in 1994, a paper that was later printed among the conference proceedings in a volume entitled *A Genius for Letters.*[1] The earlier paper drew upon years of reading book advertisements printed in mid-eighteenth-century English newspapers while working in the North Reading Room of the British Library during the 1970s and early 1980s—those wonderful days when one actually got to thumb through the original papers, not crank through microfilms. The long period of eye-straining but delightful research was a necessary undertaking while I was preparing an edition of the correspondence of the mid-eighteenth-century London bookseller Robert Dodsley.[2] (In the eighteenth-century book trade, a "bookseller" was the equivalent of a modern publisher; a "publisher," although some held copyrights, largely acted as a distributor or seller for booksellers' products or engaged in the publication of pamphlets.) Since Dodsley's correspondence was, by the nature of his business, full of references to newly published works—both to his own publications and to those of others—this plentiful fund of newspaper advertisements proved invaluable for many editorial purposes. Without them undoubtedly I would not have identified many of the authors and works referred to only obscurely in the text of the correspondence, nor would I have been able to assign dates to many undated letters. I needed only to discover the relevant announcement among the plethora of advertisements in such newspapers as the *Daily Advertiser*, the *General Advertiser*, the *General Evening Post*, and the *London Evening Post*, and immediately the mystery was solved and a footnote could be added to the letter for the benefit of future users of the edition. It was the most basic kind of literary detective work but entirely gratifying because it worked.

When I came to write the earlier paper, I was aglow with the advantages that newspaper advertisements afforded my work on Dodsley's correspondence, and I proceeded to elaborate on the specific values that newspaper advertisements offered students of book history—how advertisements are mines of information about books and the book trade itself. For instance, I explained how book advertisements frequently supply bibliographical data pertinent to individual publications—the size of a book, the quality of its paper, whether it carries illustrations and by whom, the edition number, its cost, and whether or not it is being offered by subscription—all of which, of course, are particularly significant in the case of books no longer extant. In addition, I called attention to the fact that book advertisements furnish the names of booksellers and (sometimes) printers, their shop locations, products, and services—many of whom are not recorded in existing biographical dictionaries and directories—as well as the business collaborations among these tradesmen. What's more, I noted that book trade advertisements and notices frequently reveal valuable data on persons, products, and services in such ancillary fields as bookbinding, papermaking, inkmaking, and engraving, as well as information relevant to book auctions, the opening of new book shops, the publication of periodicals, even feuds among members of the trade. All of this led me to the sweeping conclusion that the consulting of contemporary newspaper advertisements was a necessary component of any effort to produce the definitive history of the book in eighteenth-century England. I was pleased to be able to make this statement, for it was the cumulative wisdom of many years of patiently inspecting thousands of newspaper advertisements.

Yet at the same time I made that statement, something I had discovered late in my research for that paper was nagging at me, something I hadn't detected years earlier when working on Dodsley's correspondence. As already mentioned, my work with newspaper advertisements to that point had been largely confined to the period of Dodsley's publishing career, or from 1735 to 1764. During this period newspapers and newspaper advertising had been growing by leaps and bounds. For instance, just prior to Dodsley's appearance on the London publishing scene—in the 1720s and early 1730s—four of the newspapers that would dominate the advertising world for most of the century were founded: the *Daily Advertiser* (1730), the *London Daily Post and General Advertiser* (1734, a paper variously entitled the *General Advertiser* and the *Public Advertiser*), and two thrice-weeklies, the *London Evening Post* (1727) and the *General Evening Post* (1733). Concurrent with Dodsley's opening of his shop in Pall Mall in 1735, the *Daily Gazetteer* made its first appearance. The following decades of the 1740s and 1750s saw the inception of three other major book advertisers: the *Whitehall Evening Post* (1746), *Lloyd's Evening Post* (1757), and the *London Chronicle* (1757).

The numerous book advertisements in these publications clearly attest to the centrality of books to the advertising trade during these decades. For instance in 1745 the *Daily Advertiser*, although never close to the leaders in terms of the percentage of books versus other kinds of advertisements, was printing an average of fourteen book advertisements every day. In the case of the other newspapers mentioned above, the number of book advertisements far outstripped the total number of all other advertisements combined. For instance, the *London Evening Post* and the *General Evening Post*, were averaging twenty-nine and twenty-four book advertisements per issue, respectively or 54 percent and 75 percent of their total advertising complement in 1745. By 1762, the latecomers, the *London Chronicle* and *Lloyd's Evening Post*, were printing approximately sixteen book advertisements per issue, or 75 percent and 62 percent of their total advertising complement. Some of these advertisements were admittedly repeat ads (common practice allowed a special rate for running the same ad on three consecutive days), but nonetheless it is clear that, except for the *Daily Advertiser*, most of the newspapers that led the field in advertising from the 1740s through the early 1760s relied principally upon booksellers for the contents of their advertising columns.

As I say, late in my research for the former paper—when I began to examine more thoroughly newspaper advertisements at the very end of Dodsley's career in the mid-1760s—I noticed that the trend had begun to reverse itself, and that newspaper advertisements for books had begun to fall off. At the time, of course, I could only allude to the phenomenon and suggest that it was a subject for future study. But the discovery threatened my notions regarding the values of eighteenth-century newspaper advertisements for the study of book history, a subject about which I had been so confident.

Now, further research for the present essay—extending the examination of book advertisements through 1785—has mounted enough evidence to confirm those earlier suspicions. Indeed a major decline in book advertising does occur during the third quarter of the century, and, in the case of some newspapers, the reduction is quite dramatic. Although my samplings of advertisements from the period are admittedly in no way comprehensive and require more work to lay out the case in full, taken together they present evidence that seems incontrovertible. Especially convincing, I believe, is the fact that these samplings are taken from the same newspapers that I mentioned above as carrying a high percentage of book advertisements during the 1740s and 1750s—all of them leaders in newspaper advertising during the period.

Before presenting the statistics, however, I need to say something about the seasonal fluctuation in the numbers of book advertisements appearing in the newspapers. Normally, newspapers carried more book advertisements during December and early January than at any other time of the year. This phenomenon is probably due to two factors. By this time of year, booksellers' production of books had reached one of its two yearly highs. After a long, slow summer period—when both authors and booksellers took their holidays—December was the month when all the processing of the fall's harvest of manuscripts had been completed—the editing, printing, proofing, and final printing. Secondly, not unlike modern commercial practice, booksellers strove to get their products on the market and advertised by early December in order to capitalize on traditional Christmas gift-giving.

The second high-yield period of book advertisements occurred during late March through early May. Again, practical commercial factors explain the rise. Book production is once more in high gear after the Christmas holiday period. Secondly, booksellers are striving to get their books on the market before Parliament rises and before the town empties for the summer holidays. Although book advertisements certainly appeared in newspapers during other months—and occasionally in surprisingly high numbers—the pattern just outlined above pretty much holds. Only during those years when some major political, religious, or social issue gripped the country's attention—for instance, the trials of the Scottish rebels in the summer of 1746—is the pattern broken.

The reason for pausing to make these seasonal distinctions in book advertising is to assure the reader that, in the presentation of the following statistics, I have consciously avoided skewing the facts (mixing oranges and apples). That is, I have chosen to use either yearly averages of newspaper advertisements or to contrast the numbers of advertisements appearing in different years by employing statistics from the same month of those years, often the exact day of the month. The *London Evening Post*, which in 1745 was printing an average of twenty-nine book advertisements per issue or 54 percent of the paper's total advertising complement, fifteen years later in 1760 had slipped to an average of fourteen book advertisements per issue, or only 39 percent of the advertising content. By 1765, the number falls even lower: seven book advertisements per issue, or 23 percent of the total advertising content. Particularly telling is the contrast in the number of book advertisements in what should normally be the high-yield Christmas season: in the 18–20 December 1750 number, for instance, the paper carried thirty-three book advertisements, but that for 19–21 December 1765 printed only six. For some reason I have yet to detect, the numbers of book advertisements begin to rise again by 1770. In this year the *London Evening Post* was printing 15 book advertisements per issue, or 38 percent of its total number of advertisements. In 1785, the figures are about the same. However, as is clear, neither the number of advertisements nor the percentage of total advertisements even approaches those of 1745, or those of the rest of the 1740s and 1750s.

In the case of the *General Evening Post*, the slide begins a little earlier, but because I haven't been able to survey an adequate number of issues for the later century, the evidence for my thesis is not as thorough as I would like. However, the trend is certainly evident. Although, in 1744, the paper had been averaging twenty-four book advertisements per issue, or 76 percent of its advertising columns, the number of advertisements had decreased in 1759 to twenty, or 54 percent. In effect, the proportional increase in the paper's overall advertising was not matched by the rise in the number of books advertised. Significantly, the fifteen book advertisements appearing in the September 24–27, 1785 issue fall far short of the twenty-five book advertisements that had appeared in an approximate September issue of 1756. The *London Chronicle*, which a year after its inception in 1757 had been printing an average of sixteen book advertisements per issue, by 1774 shows only thirteen such advertisements per issue; by 1780, the *Chronicle* averaged only four book advertisements per issue, although 1785 shows five per issue. Its May 6–9, 1758 issue—during a high season of book production—offered twenty-four books for sale, whereas its counterpart in 1774 offered only thirteen. *Lloyd's Evening Post* seems not to have been particularly concerned with book advertisements during the early years of its establishment under Thomas Kinnersley; during 1757 and 1758, it averaged only in the single digits. By 1762 under the new management of the bookseller William Nicoll it was printing at least a dozen book advertisements per issue. By 1766, however, *Lloyd's Evening Post* had again fallen back into the single digits and would remain there through the 1770s and 1780s.

By far the most dramatic change occurred in the *Daily Advertiser*. Although the number of book advertisements in this daily paper never closely rivaled the sum total of other kinds of advertisements it carried, through the 1740s it had always advertised a respectable number of books. In 1745, for instance, it printed an average of fourteen book advertisements per issue, an average that dropped to eleven by 1760. By late 1764, the number had diminished to seven book advertisements per issue; by 1774, to five; and by 1780, to one and a half per issue. My samplings for each month of 1786 showed not a single book advertisement, even during the normally high period of book production, April and early May.

Not surprisingly, this phenomenon is reflected in the practice of the provincial newspaper as well. In her recent study of the provincial bookseller Benjamin Collins and his involvement in the newspaper trade, Christine Ferdinand devotes an entire chapter to a consideration of the advertising practices of Collins's two weekly newspapers, the *Salisbury Journal* and the *Hampton Chronicle*.[3] Significant for present purposes, she first notes the phenomenal growth of advertising in the *Salisbury Journal* from the 1730s through 1770: "The most striking difference between the *Salisbury Journal* of the 1730s and 1760s is in the *number* of advertisements—from an annual average of 296 in the 1730s, to 675 in the 1740s, 1,350 in the 1750s, to nearly 2,500 in the 1760s, and to over 3,300 in 1770." However, especially pertinent is Ferdinand's account of the drop-off in book advertisements: "The largest group of advertisements is for books and book-related material in the 1740s and 1750s, with an average of about 30 per cent of the total number [of advertisements]; real estate takes the lead in the 1760s when books drop to about 18 per cent."[4]

The most obvious reaction to this major shift in booksellers' advertising practice is to ask the question: during a thirty-year period when book production is known to have escalated, why did London's booksellers drastically cut back on the advertising of their books? The situation is certainly puzzling, since booksellers had been so comprehensive in advertising their wares earlier in the century, and since the number of advertisements for other products and services accelerates throughout the same period. Attempting to supply some answer to this question has led me to a number of speculations on contemporary market factors that may have played a role in the decline of book advertising in the period's newspapers. These considerations constitute the subject of the rest of this essay.

Probably a good starting point would be a consideration of a fundamental budgetary matter: the rising cost of placing an advertisement in a newspaper. The primary factor influencing the rising cost of advertising through the century was the government-imposed duty on newspaper advertisements. Prior to the Stamp Act of 1712, there had been no duty on newspapers nor on newspaper advertisements. The Stamp Act of this year, however, besides imposing a half-penny duty on each copy of a newspaper sold, placed a one-shilling duty on each individual advertisement appearing in each number of a newspaper.[5] Once advertising rates became stabilized in the 1730s, newspaper publishers were normally selling advertising space at the rate of two shillings for two-inches of a column in a three-column newspaper; that is, one shilling went to the government and one shilling to the publisher's coffers. When the government duty was doubled in 1757, the rate for the same advertising space was raised to three shillings. Finally, in 1780, the government added another 6d to the duty on each advertisement, and most newspaper publishers responded with an advertising rate of 3° shillings.[6] In effect, roughly over a fifty-year period, although the cost of placing a standard two-inch advertisement in a London newspaper rose 57 percent, publishers continued to earn only the one-shilling income for the same advertisement.

In light of the increases prompted by government duties, the question must be asked: did thrifty-minded booksellers and authors reconsider their advertising programs after the 50 percent rise in advertising costs in 1757 and decide that their budgets required a cut-back? Authors who preferred not to sell their copyrights to booksellers and chose to stand the expenses of publication themselves (employing a bookseller only as an agent) would, of course, be daunted by the increased cost of advertising. Even for prosperous booksellers, although a one-shilling rise in cost per advertisement may not seem like a lot, over a period of time the sum could mount up. That this rise in cost certainly had a significant impact on contemporary booksellers is evident in the fact that groups of them (as we shall see in a moment) created partnerships and began their own newspapers so that they might avail themselves of discount advertising rates.

Another phenomenon of the mid-century, the sudden growth of the book reviewing industry—marked by the founding of the *Monthly Review* in 1749 and the *Critical Review* in 1756—may also have had a hand in the cutback in book advertising. Michael Harris has suggested to me that perhaps the rather comprehensive coverage afforded in the reviewing journals inclined booksellers to feel less need to expend their resources on advertising in order to make their latest wares known to the public.[7] The suggestion makes eminently good sense: pressures on booksellers' budgets as a result of the government's doubling of the duty on advertisements in 1757 may well have tempted booksellers to allow review journals to serve as the heralds of some of their new publications.[8]

The decline in book advertising may also have resulted from a major rethinking of the entire strategy of marketing books. With the accelerating number of books coming to market each year, the rising cost of advertising, and the increasing competition with other products and services for advertising space in the most desirable daily and thrice-weekly newspapers, perhaps booksellers were forced to take a long hard look at their past advertising practices and to opt for a more sensible approach to marketing their wares. Instead of continuing to be comprehensive in the advertising of their books—advertising every book they published—perhaps commonsense economy required that they be more selective, that they advertise only sure sellers to lure customers to their shops, where potential purchasers would then be exposed to the rest of their stock. Such a marketing approach would inevitably become the mode of modern merchants, who simply can't afford to advertise everything on their shelves, and there's no reason to believe that the strategy did not occur to these shrewd, market-conscious eighteenth-century merchants.

Still another commercial consideration could have played a role in the decrease of book advertising, but it requires some prefatory explanation. All of the newspapers employed above for statistical purposes had been founded by small groups of booksellers for the purpose of advertising their own products at discount rates. Significantly, one of them, *Lloyd's Evening Post,* was founded only three weeks after the crown's concurrence (28 June 1757) with the government's doubling of the duty on advertisements.[9] Such enterprises constituted a common practice among booksellers of the age, as reflected in the statement by John Henley, editor of the contemporary periodical *Hyp-Doctor* in 1732: "One Consideration which forc'd *the Trade* to start and multiply such Papers was to contract the Expense of advertising their own Books by Partnership in public Papers of their own Property and Management where they might the most freely, commodiously, and cheaply insert their own Advertisements, and command those of the Town."[10] Because share-holding partners of these newspapers normally paid only the government duty for placing advertisements in their own papers, they were saving—at least before 6 July 1757—half of the cost of advertising by entering into these partnerships. After that date, however, when the government doubled the duty, their savings were reduced to one-third.

In time, however, as a result of the resale and frequent splitting of shares in these newspapers, the original small group of founders, by the 1760s had usually expanded to embrace a large number of shareholders. Although the evidence for ownership and for sale transactions is fragmentary, we do know that, for instance, as early as 1747, Robert Dodsley bought a 1/15 share in the *London Evening Post*, and, in 1750, a 1/26 share in the *General Evening Post* was sold. Although some of the original founders often held more than one share, extant records show that, after 1750, the *Gazetteer* had twenty owners, the *General Evening Post* about a dozen, and the *London Chronicle* about ten.[11]

Now, by the 1760s, all of these bookseller/owners could not expect to advertise all of their books in the limited advertising space that their newspapers afforded. Moreover, even if they could, a paper would be depriving itself of some lucrative income by shutting out full-price advertisements in favor of shareholders' discount advertisements. Although extant records of the *General Evening Post* in the 1730s show many entries for advertisements at one shilling (shareholders' discount rate), the records of the *Grub Street Journal* for the same period show that its owners could place advertisements at discount rates only during the slack summer season. In other cases, shareholders were required to pay full price when the advertising complement of the paper was tight, or they could place discounted advertisements only according to a certain schedule. Likewise, evidence from marked copies of the *London Daily Post* suggest that shareholders' discounted advertisements were published only during the slow months of July, August, and September.[12] In effect, it seems owner policies, drawn up at the founding of a paper and occasionally revised at general meetings, regularly reflected a concern for the loss of revenue when space for full-price advertisements was taken up by members' discount advertisements. Since this ambivalent attitude on the part of the shareholders had clearly persisted over a number of decades, in itself the attitude probably had little effect on the decrease of book advertising in the 1760s. However, perhaps because of this ambivalence, share-holding booksellers, weak of resolve in the face of additional profits to be made from full-price advertisements for other products, inevitably capitulated to the next commercial phenomenon to be considered—the rise of consumerism—and abandoned the original purpose for founding these newspapers. Once again, Michael Harris has suggested something of the same notion to me, when saying that shareholders, now selling their advertising space to others, were content with the profits and gradually moved away from advertising their own books.[13]

The rise of consumerism as reflected in newspaper advertisements of this period has not been better charted than in Christine Ferdinand's study of Benjamin Collins and the *Salisbury Journal*, mentioned earlier.[14] Although the *Journal* was indeed a provincial newspaper, Ferdinand's account of heightened and broader consumer-oriented advertising confirms my own impression of what was going on in London newspapers during the third quarter of the century. In examining the 50,000 or so advertisements in the *Journal* spanning the period 1736 to 1770, Ferdinand breaks down the ever-expanding offers of goods and products into ten categories that range from real property through medicines, books, and wines to the professional services of portrait painters, estate surveyors, and decorative plasterers. What is especially revealing in her account is the rapid growth both in the number of *Journal* advertisements and in the ever-increasing variety of products and services offered to the general public during this period.[15] Initially one might be tempted to think the expansion of advertising columns in Collins's newspaper should be attributed to the proprietor's own greed for additional income from this source, but the record shows that his subscribers increased substantially during the same period, suggesting that not only were readers not put off by the increase in advertising but that they actually demanded these products and services as much as Collins was interested in advertising them.

It is this "consumer revolution" that Ferdinand identifies that, I believe, took its toll on the advertising policy of the major share-held newspapers. Although the papers were originally set up to afford the bookseller/proprietors discounted advertising, I suggest that the extra revenue available through increasing the number of a paper's full-price advertisements seduced proprietors away from their original purpose. The savings available to each member through now limited opportunities for discount advertising probably did not match the profits to be made from a paper dominated by full-price ads. And, as consumerism grew, there was no shortage of the latter.

In so doing, the proprietors of the *London Evening Post*, the *General Evening Post*, the *London Chronicle*, and *Lloyd's Evening Post* (and doubtless others) were, to a degree, following the example of the *Daily Advertiser*, which many years earlier had caught on to the new wave of consumerism, becoming the epitome of a commercial advertiser. Although the *Advertiser* had printed a respectable number of book advertisements in the 1740s, its direction was clear by 1760 when its average number of nonbook advertisements had risen from 66 to 115 in the interim. By 1770, its desire to capitalize on the consumer craze led to the reduction of its news content to 1° columns of its total twelve columns and the introduction of almost illegible, reduced-size advertisements, both of which tactics allowed the proprietors to squeeze in an incredible average of 180 advertisements over its four pages. Although the other newspapers considered above regarded themselves as "content-oriented" publications, not simply "advertisers," doubtless their proprietors, as competing businessmen, could not ignore the *Advertiser*'s success.

Although I have emphasized consumerism as a major force affecting advertising policy, some or all of the foregoing market factors may have coalesced to reverse the fortunes of book advertising in London newspapers during the last half of the eighteenth century. Quite possibly there are other factors I've overlooked, and the study is far from complete. As in all preliminary studies, more research is required, specifically a broader survey of newspapers carrying book advertisements and an examination of all extant records of newspaper proprietors. Still, it's now clear to me that the opinion I had expressed in my earlier paper regarding the value of newspaper advertisements for the study of the history of the book must now be modified: the study of book history is better served by newspaper advertisements of the first sixty years of the century than by those of the last forty.

NOTES

1. Robin Myers and Michael Harris, eds., *A Genius for Letters: Booksellers and Bookselling from the Sixteenth to the Twentieth Century* (Winchester, Eng.: St. Paul's Bibliographies; Delaware: Oak Knoll Press, 1995), 103–22.

2. James E. Tierney, ed. *The Correspondence of Robert Dodsley, 1733–1764* (Cambridge: Cambridge University Press, 1988) and hereafter cited as *Correspondence.*

3. C. Y. Ferdinand, *Benjamin Collins and the Provincial Newspaper Trade in the Eighteenth Century* (Oxford: Clarendon Press, 1997), 180–208.

4. Ibid., 193.

5. 10 Anne, c. 19. *Journals of the House of Commons*, 16, 22 May, 27, XXVII 227, 234. The duty was part of a bill also imposing duties on soap, on various kinds of domestic and imported paper, and on imported printed linens, silks, and other kinds of cloth.

6. (1757) 30 Geo. II, c. 19. *Journals of the House of Commons*, 23 May—28 June, XXVII, 911, 916, 924; (1780) 20 Geo. III, c 28. *Journals of the House of Commons*, 22 March—4 May, XXXVII, 749, 806, 818, 835. For advertising costs, see *Correspondence*, 100–101; Ferdinand, 184–85; and Michael Harris, *London Newspapers in the Age of Walpole.* (Rutherford: Fairleigh Dickinson University Press, 1987), 59–63.

7. Michael Harris suggested this possibility in the discussion following the Book Trade Conference paper alluded to above.

8. The extent of book reviewing during the period can be gleaned from Antonia Forster's *Index to Book Reviews in England, 1749–1774* (Carbondale: Southern Illinois University Press, 1990). Forster lists 3,023 individual book reviews published in sixteen different periodicals during the period.

9. *Journals of the House of Commons*, XXVII, 924.

10. Quoted in Harris, 67.

11. *Correspondence*, 519; Harris, 74.

12. The foregoing evidence relevant to the *General Evening Post,* the *Grub Street Journal*, and the *London Daily Post* is taken from Harris, 60–61.

13. See note 7 above.

14. Ferdinand, 191–208.

15. According to Ferdinand: "There is something of a consumer revolution documented in its [*SJ*'s] advertising columns: first, in the record number of its advertisements; then in the overall greater diversity [of products and services] . . . . Services that had been considered luxuries for any but the wealthy [earlier in the century] were advertised extensively . . . Leisure activities were sold to a larger public audience; more and more goods were sold through the newspaper" (Ferdinand, 207).

Officer and Lady: Pants and Politics in Caroline de la Motte-Fouqué's *Das Heldenmädchen aus der Vendée* (1816)

ELISABETH KRIMMER

I. Hybrid Existences

The secondary literature on novels and dramas by German women writers of the eighteenth century often stresses the fact that these texts are thematically limited to the realm of home and family. Lydia Schieth, for example, maintains that "the portrayal of a reality outside of the home and of alternative life choices constitutes a taboo for novels by women writers."[1] According to Karin Wurst, neither the female protagonists nor their authors were able to "imagine adventures outside of the house."[2] Dagmar von Hoff writes that "controversy, deviation, motion, the Other" are sacrificed in dramas by women writers: "They chose confinement, final forms, stagnancy, death."[3] It cannot be denied that these analyses are adequate representations of a large number of novels and dramas by eighteenth-century women writers. But one should also keep in mind that they do not do justice to many other such texts. In historical reality as well as in fiction, women devised strategies that enabled them to expand their sphere of action and to lead—or at least imagine—a life of adventure and excitement. One such strategy was cross-dressing.

It is generally acknowledged that questions of authorship are inseparable from the gender of the writing subject. The demarcations are especially clear-cut in the eighteenth century when authorship was construed as masculine territory upon which female writers were transgressing. In writing, a woman assumed male prerogatives and lost her claim to pure femininity. Authorship thus made a hybrid of the woman writer, and this hybrid revenged itself by haunting her text in the form of a cross-dressed heroine.[4] In numerous texts by eighteenth-century women writers, cross-dressers leave behind the proclaimed values of female domesticity and conservative femininity and venture out into the murky terrain formed by the intersection of gender, aesthetics, and politics.

In the following pages, I want to focus on Caroline de la Motte-Fouqué's novel *Das Heldenmädchen aus der Vendée* [The Heroic Maiden from the Vendée] (1816), a text that features a female protagonist who dons male attire and leaves her home in order to become a soldier. In this novel—just as in Therese Huber's novel *Die Familie Seldorf* [The Seldorf Family] (1795/96)—the royalist uprising in the Vendée in the wake of the French Revolution opens up a new sphere of action for the heroine. But while the plot evolves around the Vendée events, the date of publication and letters by Fouqué suggest that the actual frame of reference for this novel is not the battles of the French Revolution but the German Wars of Liberation.

I want to begin my investigation with a brief survey of the historical events that provided the backdrop for Fouqué's text. In doing so, I intend to show that Fouqué's cross-dressed heroine is not a singular fictional creation but rather part of a long tradition of female soldiers in male attire; a tradition which teaches us that the ideal of female domesticity and compliance that we have come to associate with eighteenth-century womanhood was not as all-encompassing as we make it out to be. But in perceiving the newly gained freedom of the woman underneath the clothes, we should not overlook the masculine attire that hides her body. If a woman entered the public sphere and engaged in masculine activities, she abandoned her own gender. The adoption of the exterior trappings of the other sex is the visible manifestation of this transgression.A woman who lives free and heroically forfeits her femininity and becomes an exile from her own gender. This conflicted identity manifests itself in Fouqué's text. The second part of this paper therefore analyzes Fouqué's sophisticated argumentation. Fouqué is walking the tightrope between her heroine's unwomanly participation in the war on the one hand, and her endeavor to conform to traditional stereotypes of femininity on the other. In tracing the destiny of the cross-dressed heroine, I intend to reveal the contradictory and ultimately self-defeating interrelation between gender, politics, and aesthetics that scars this text.

II. Amazons and Heroic Virgins

Many women used the societal turmoil of the French Revolution to foray into the masculine territory of politics. Some participated in public uproars and marches, others joined the armed forces. Often, the invasion of such traditionally male realms was accompanied by the appropriation of male clothing. Théroigne de Méricourt, for example, who led the women's march to Versailles, felt that male clothing enabled women to participate in public events more directly.[5] For female Revolutionary Republicans, cross-dressing and political action went hand in hand. In red pants they assisted their male comrades, the Jacobins, in ousting the Girondists from the legislative assembly by guarding the exits with swords.[6]

Cross-dressed women also served as soldiers in the armed forces of the republic. Some women joined the National Guard as early as 1789. Female officers were among the members of the "Societé fraternelle des patriotes de l'un et l'autre sexe". According to Levy, dozens of women enlisted in the revolutionary army.[7] Often, female soldiers were not only tolerated but received a warm welcome. The sisters Félicité and Théophile Fernigh, for example, who fought along with their father at the eastern front, were widely praised for their courage in defending the fatherland. Other female soldiers whose names have come down to us are Thérèse Figueur ("Sans-Gêne"), Madame Poncet ("Breton Double") and Angélique Marie Josèphe Brulon, who joined the 42nd infantry regiment after the death of her husband and received the cross of the Legion of Honor for her courage in combat.[8]

In this shifting social climate, it is hardly surprising that spirited women demanded the implementation of laws which would institute armed service for women. On March 6, 1791, 300 women signed a petition which was brought before the French legislative assembly by Pauline Léon, the future president of the Club of Revolutionary Republicans. In this petition, the women of the Revolution demanded nothing less than the right to bear arms and to participate in warfare.[9] But as much as the male members of the national assembly supported natural rights in other instances, this petition was rejected. A similar petition by the women of the Hôtel de Ville-district, submitted on July 31, 1792, met with the same fate.

The rejection of these petitions, however, did not lead to the removal of women from the armed forces. Their presence in the army remained undiminished. As late as 1793, dozens of Parisiennes donned male clothing and enlisted in regiments. There was even a plan to form a battalion of amazons to be named after the above-mentioned sisters Fernigh. It is not clear whether this troop ever existed.[10] All these events strengthen the hypothesis that although the cross-dressed woman was welcome, the woman who insisted on her femininity while demanding masculine rights could not be accommodated within the existing gender dichotomy. Eventually, even the acceptance of the cross-dressed soldier would fade away.

The year 1793 is generally considered the turning point for women's involvement in the Revolution. Since the subsistence crisis in France was a major factor in sparking off the revolutionary uprisings, and since the female gender tended to be most concerned about the shortening of supplies, women played an important role in the early phase of the revolution, e.g., in bread marches and the like. Building on these early experiences, women succeeded in organizing themselves increasingly during the course of the Revolution. Their activity reached its peak between the spring and autumn of 1793. The ban on women's clubs which was passed in October of 1793 must be seen as an attempt to contain the growing political power of the other sex. It was also in 1793 that a law was passed which excluded all women from service in the army. This was due to a report by J. F. Delacroix, a deputy of the revolutionary government, who attributed the deplorable state of affairs of the armed forces to the presence of women, i.e., female soldiers, sutlers, and prostitutes.[11] In practice, however, this ban was inefficient in expelling women from the army. We know, for example, that Thérèse Figueur participated in battles as late as 1806 and that Angélique Brulon's retirement in 1799 was due to wounds received in combat, not to administrative instructions.[12]

Women also participated in the uprising in the Vendée which began in March 1793 and ended in July 1796. The peasant Renée Bordereau, for example, who masqueraded as a man, became known as the Vendean Joan of Arc. Francoise Després served the royal army as a messenger, provisioner, and troop leader, while the Vicomtesse Turpin de Crissé is remembered as a peacemaker.[13]

The important role that French women played in revolutionary events captured the attention of the German public. Reactions and comments were generally disapproving and apprehensive as the German intelligentsia rallied its forces to fend off the specter of the public woman. The following statement by Joachim Heinrich Campe, a German who witnessed these events first-hand during his journey to Paris, is representative of the general sentiments about women's involvement in the French Revolution. Campe thinks:

> that the women of Paris and, as it seems likely after several events in the provinces, the entire female sex in France is inferior to the male sex in terms of culture, moderation and moral, and, almost always excels in bloodthirstiness and cruelty, when violence occurs.[14]

Given such opinions, it is hardly surprising that even the few staunch German Republicans opted against the participation of women in their revolutionary activities. The Jacobins of Mainz, for example, did not accept female devotees of liberté and egalité into their circle.[15]

However, even in Germany there was a time for amazons. Interestingly, it was the service for the fatherland, not the ideals of liberty and emancipation, that provided the justification for female participation in warfare.[16] Numerous German women enlisted in the army during the Wars of Liberation against the Napoleonic rule. In the heated atmosphere of national enthusiasm, references to a woman's patriotism served as justification for her "unwomanly" conduct. The patterns of this discourse are manifest in contemporary documents, such as Rückert's poems about Eleonore Prochaska (see below) or the speech of the Prussian general Tauentzien before the senate.[17] They continued to dominate the scholarly reception until the twentieth century, as is evident in the following quote from Major Noel, the author of a book about the heroines of 1807–1815:

> What deep sorrow these simple, modest, and quiet female souls must have felt about the fatherland which is trampled upon by the enemy, that they left their household and family in order to fight for their country.[18]

Thus, rather than perceiving cross-dressed soldiers as warrior women, the Napoleonic wars gave rise to a new German conservativism that transformed patriotic warfare into a feminine activity. However, notwithstanding such celebration of female patriotism and self-sacrifice, it is also likely that the dearth of volunteers contributed to the acceptance of female soldiers.

Among the cross-dressed officers of 1807 were such impressive characters as Rosalie von Bonin, who was in command of a cavalry unit of seventy men and who captured a French general. Another amazon, the famous Anna Lühring (1796–1866), donned her brother's clothes and joined the "Lützower Jäger" as Eduard Kruse. She participated in the war against Napoleon and concealed her gender successfully. The final discovery of her womanhood was brought about by a letter by her father, not by suspicious behavior or appearance on her part. According to Cyrus, Lühring is a perfect example of "how easily one was taken for a man if one had a uniform, gun, and perky behavior."[19] Even after the discovery of her sex, Anna Lühring was accepted and well-liked in her regiment. That her position was precarious all the same is demonstrated by the fact that every document relating to her case is deeply concerned with her chastity. Obviously, virginity, i.e., the renunciation of her sexuality, was the price that the female hero had to pay.

Yet another female Lützower Jäger, Eleonore Prochaska, alias Jäger Renz, managed to hide her gender until she died. During her last battle in 1813, Prochaska seized the drum of a French drum-major and drove her comrades to attack until she herself was fatally wounded by a bullet. Her heroic death inspired numerous male contemporaries to artistic creations. Friedrich Rückert, for example, wrote a poem about her,[20] and Beethoven composed the music for the tragedy *Leonora Prochaska*, written by Friedrich Duncker, the privy councilor of Friedrich Wilhelm III.

Neither the adventures of the French cross-dressers nor those of their German successors remained unnoticed by women writers of the time. Both Therese Huber in *Die Familie Seldorf* (1796/97) and Caroline de la Motte-Fouqué in *Das Heldenmädchen aus der Vendée* (1816) wrote novels which feature cross-dressed heroines. But while both writers focus on the Vendée uprisings, the following analysis will demonstrate that in Fouqué's case the Vendée events come to stand for the German resistance against the French. It is interesting to note that Fouqué also adopts the strategy of patriotic sacrifice to justify her heroine's "unwomanly" conduct. Unlike Therese Huber's Sara Seldorf ,who fights for the republican cause, Caroline de la Motte-Fouqué's Elisabeth de la Rochefoucault fights for King, God, and fatherland.

In the following, I want to analyze Fouqué's political views in connection with her concept of femininity. I am especially interested in how her concept of gender influences her portrayal of the cross-dressed character, and how this, in turn, affects her heroine's chances of survival. I will also demonstrate how Fouqué's contradictory concept of gender and politics manifests itself in the aesthetic structure of the text.

III. An Angel for God, King, and Fatherland

In her time, Caroline de la Motte Fouqué was a widely known and well-liked author.[21] She wrote over sixty stories, twenty novels, and numerous essays on education, fashion, mythology and many other topics. She socialized with artists and writers of her time, such as Rahel Varnhagen and her husband August Varnhagen von Ense, Jean Paul, August Wilhelm Schlegel and Ludwig Tieck. Today, however, Fouqué is either forgotten altogether or remembered as an addendum to the biography of her husband Friedrich de la Motte Fouqué, the author of the well-known *Undine*-tale. It seems that Fouqué must be counted among those female authors who are subject to a twofold bias. While traditional scholarship considered her texts trivial, feminist scholarship ignored Fouqué because of the conservative agenda of her work.[22]

Fouqué's novel *Das Heldenmädchen aus der Vendée* tells the story of Elisabeth Rochefoucault, an orphan, who is staying with her uncle, the duke de la Tremouille, in the Vendée when the uprising against the republic starts. Elisabeth first remains at home with an unmarried relative, the marquise de Robillard, while her uncle and his son, the brave and radiantly beautiful prince Talmont, lead the royalist forces. But when the republicans attack the castle, Elisabeth decides to don male clothing and join the war. Together, Elisabeth and the prince go through victory and defeat as they discover their love for each other. The turning-point occurs when the Vendée troops attempt to conquer the coast in order to secure a base for auxiliary forces from England. This endeavor fails, Elisabeth is wounded, and the prince dies.

In the second part, Elisabeth goes to England in order to contact French aristocrats who are in exile there. After initial difficulties, a fleet is raised which is supposed to come to the aid of the Vendée royalists. But in spite of good preparations, the attack fails because of the egotism and thirst for glory of some of the officers. After having led the troops one last time, Elisabeth dies a heroic death under the crucifix.

The decision to feature a protagonist who belongs to the party of the historical losers casts a dark shadow over the entire novel.[23] From the very beginning, there is an atmosphere of somber resignation combined with numerous premonitions of illness and death. In addition to the certainty of defeat, the political perspective of the author gives rise to yet another failure. The royalist opposition to the revolutionary demands for freedom and equality for all runs counter to the attempt to secure the equality of the female heroine. This predicament, which remains unresolved to the end, causes multiple internal contradictions.[24] But while such contradictions are detrimental to the aesthetics of the novel, they are also a striking testimony to the author's struggle with conventional notions of femininity. One might therefore argue that it is precisely these contradictions, as well as Fouqué's futile attempts to reconcile them, that make this text so fascinating even today.

Fouqué tries to justify her heroine's warrior-like behavior with a recourse to patriarchal values. It is only the dire situation of the fatherland, along with the heart-felt wish to serve her country, which motivate Elisabeth to leave the traditional place in the house. Instead of serving one husband, Fouqué's heroine is now subordinated to God, King, and fatherland. Thus, Fouqué argues for a violation of the patriarchal order and its gender-specific division of work by a reference to this very order.[25] She takes traditional stereotypes, such as female self-sacrifice and self-denial, and instrumentalizes them for her own purpose by infusing them with patriotism. In doing so, Fouqué employs the same argumentational structure that was applied to female soldiers during the Wars of Liberation. In destroying the enemies of God and the King, Elisabeth hopes to annihilate the "unwomanliness" of her own transgression. It is a sign of Fouqué's sophisticated strategy that she has a male character—Elisabeth's uncle, the duke—explain the connection between female self-sacrifice and patriotism in his eulogy to Elisabeth after the first battle:

> Thus, he praised the women and their pure self-denial, and how this heavenly shield laid itself on their breast so firmly and protectively that they defy grievous danger without particular efforts. Certainly, he added full of emotion, their weapons are not from this world.[26]

Through religious stylization and a reevaluation of her combative behavior as sacrifice, Elisabeth's militancy is simultaneously confirmed and negated. Even when Fouqué portrays battle scenes, Elisabeth is never directly involved in any kind of violent or aggressive behavior. She is reduced to the status of symbolic figurehead rather than being acknowledged as equal participant in the fight. She may carry a sword and a pistol, but she must not use it. Furthermore, in participating in the war, Elisabeth is not acting according to her own volition and strength but as an instrument of "higher" powers:

> Not conscious of herself, neither thinking nor wanting, Elisabeth had seized the white flag from one who stopped beside her. Like an arrow she divided the lines. Magnetically, she was drawn to where the plume of the prince waved back and forth in the throng . . . Do not leave your flag, people from the Vendée, she shouted with her pure angelic voice. Save the honor of France.[27]

Fouqué emphasizes Elisabeth's purity and her "angelic voice" in order to set her apart from the self-interested fighters. Elisabeth becomes an empty vessel whose pure nature is able to guarantee the precarious bond between the troops and their aristocratic leaders. This bond was endangered because the prince—unlike his affable and popular father, the old duke—is alienated from the crowds. It is precisely this rift between troops and officers which again and again is cited as the cause for the inferior combat strength of the royalist forces. Without leadership, Fouqué argues, these troops—which consist mostly of peasants—are disorderly and weak-willed. An inept leader, even though better than no leader, will not succeed in mobilizing his followers. Only perfect harmony between feudal lord and vassal can guarantee the victory. And who better to provide such harmony than Elisabeth? Her eyes directed towards the prince while calling the Vendée forces to battle, Elisabeth functions as "missing link" between the duke and his people. Thus, Fouqué has her readers convinced that it is woman's participation in the war that makes victory possible.

Fouqué's double speak which tries to normalize her heroine's transgression as a necessary consequence of her "true feminine" nature, inevitably gets caught up in the traps of her own argumentation. For in a society where the adoption of masculinity can never be justified, the donning of male clothing becomes a breaking test. As Elisabeth puts on the "unfamiliar clothes that repel her unwillingly," "her new dreadful attire" (I: 88), she suffers a dizzy spell, she trembles, her knees give in. But although Fouqué stresses that Elisabeth is now "an entirely different being, a stranger to herself" (I: 89), she also mentions her "tender, undeniable femininity" (I: 90) that shudders at the thought of her new task.

The instability of Elisabeth's new identity is evident in the permanent shift of gender identifications. Unlike Sara Seldorf in Therese Huber's novel, Elisabeth is never fully recognized as a man. She is a boy, a beautiful youth, a young sir with the face of a girl, or simply the poor little one. If she is not categorized as boy, i.e., not yet a man, she is not categorized at all. Often Elisabeth is seen as a neuter entity, as "appearance" or "youth" per se. More often, however, her femininity is discovered altogether. It is of note that it is only after her separation from the prince that her underlying gender is frequently unveiled. It seems that her love for the prince functioned as a guarantee of her femininity. In other words, so long as becoming the mate of a powerful man is a woman's highest goal, her femininity remains unquestioned and transgressive actions may be excused. After the death of the prince, however, the pressure on Elisabeth to live up to the requirements of the traditional gender roles increases. In this respect, Fouqué's novel differs from Therese Huber's portrayal of a cross-dressed heroine. For whereas Sara Seldorf's utterly convincing performance of masculinity establishes gender as a social construct rather than as "natural" fact, Fouqué insists on the natural femininity of her cross-dressed protagonist.

In addition to Fouqué's reluctance to transgress against traditional gender stereotypes, her political logic also undermines her heroine's adoption of masculinity. Elisabeth's flirt with that which is opposed to her nature threatens to discredit Fouqué's political agenda by unwittingly likening her protagonist to the republicans. This dilemma results from Fouqué's attempt to ground her critique of the republican party in the latter's "unnatural" behavior. Especially with respect to Robespierre, but also in connection with Charlotte Corday and the Gironde, Fouqué stresses repeatedly that, in order to perform their sinful crimes, these revolutionaries act against their own blood, and even against their own nature. Barbaroux, for example, a member of the Gironde, disguises himself as a crippled beggar, and his companion Cornelius dresses up as an old woman in order to escape persecution. Thus, the fact that Elisabeth, too, acts against her own female "nature" by cross-dressing, obfuscates the political message that Fouqué intends to convey. Since the sole differentiation between the royalist and the republican party is the latter's predilection for disguise and deceit, Elisabeth's own disguise constitutes an unwanted closeness to her ideological opponent. Such unwanted similarities between the pure heroine and the depraved Cornelius make it necessary to stress Elisabeth's virtue and femininity over and over again. But since the heroine's transgression is an indispensable element of the plot, the contradiction cannot be resolved but must be glossed over through the repetition of the same old stereotypes. It is this repetition that is most likely perceived as aesthetic failure by a reader whose training is based on canonical texts by male authors. It is therefore reasonable to assume that the gender discrimination that lies at the heart of this conflict has a negative impact on the aesthetics of this text.

One strategy that is employed to cover over the contradiction between the heroine's phallic presumption and her "natural" femininity, is the introduction of a twofold structure in which every attempt at dominance and authority is immediately followed by a revocation of all demands. It is symptomatic that, in starting her new life as a soldier, Elisabeth acquires pistols and a sword but never actually uses them. Although initially Elisabeth joined the army out of patriotism, by the end of part I her presence in combat has become redefined as an ardent wish to be with her beloved prince. Throughout the entire novel, Elisabeth has no authority, and, even though an officer, is never in command. But again, the reader wonders whether Elisabeth's lack of authority can also be interpreted as a sophisticated strategy on Fouqué's part. When the troops of the exiles land on the coast of France, the victory is forfeited by individual leaders' desire for glory while Elisabeth's wise insights and plans are ignored. We may assume that victory would have been possible, had Elisabeth been consulted. In this context it is also important to note that the English take Elisabeth for a German.[28] If we remember again that *Das Heldenmädchen* was written in close proximity to the Wars of Liberation, the novel can be read as testimony to Fouqué's conviction that German women should be included in patriotic endeavors.[29]

Caroline de la Motte-Fouqué herself certainly took a lively interest in political events. She contributed by donating money and jewelry to the campaign for the fatherland organized by Princess Wilhelm. Her literary activities also attest to her interest in the patriotic cause. Fouqué composed a *Ruf an die deutschen Frauen*, in which she encouraged her female compatriots to sacrifice for the fatherland. How much the Wars of Liberation preoccupied her is also evident in a letter to Varnhagen in which the author exclaims: "I think of nothing but this great fight" (145).

However, in spite of such attempts to influence the course of events, Caroline de la Motte-Fouqué's realm of agency was severely limited when compared to that of the protagonist of her novel. While her imaginary heroine participates in the war and enjoys the company of her beloved prince, Fouqué remained at home by herself. Her husband Friedrich enlisted in 1813 and fought in the famous "Völkerschlacht" at Leipzig in October of 1813. Fouqué's two sons also joined the army. While they were engaged in battle, all Caroline de la Motte-Fouqué could do was wait for their safe return. In 1813, French troops took up their quarters in the Fouqué family estate in Nennhausen. In addition to worrying about her loved ones, Caroline now also feared for her own safety, as she tells Varnhagen in a letter from November 1813:

> Often we were threatened here, and only recently the Mark was almost ravaged. . . . During that time I have lived through hours of such despair as nobody can imagine.[30]

De la Motte-Fouqué's desperation and immobility set her apart from her fictional heroine. They do, however, remind the reader of another female character in the novel. Aphrodise, the sister of the Parisian carpenter Duplair—in whose house Elisabeth's relative, the marquise Robillard, finds shelter—suffers from periodically occurring paralysis. From the morning hours until noon, she is mute and paralyzed and yet fully conscious. Aphrodise is the only person to recognize Robespierre's depravity—the latter also a resident in the Duplair household—yet her knowledge remains without consequence. When Aphrodise is briefly liberated from her paralysis, she admonishes St. Just, Robespierre's companion, to speak the truth. But even this last and only action before she dies remains without consequence. Unlike in Elisabeth's case, there is no need to stress Aphrodise's feminine virtues. Her paralysis, however, illustrates drastically the price she pays for her conformity to traditional gender roles.

Although Fouqué's inability to act as she is waiting for news from her husband and sons reminds one of Aphrodise's paralysis, and though imagining the feats of a fictional heroine may have helped Fouqué to cope with this situation, her intellectuality and vivid interest in the political events of her time are mirrored in the character of the marquise. Just like the author herself, the marquise de Robillard, a single relative of Elisabeth, is a femme de lettres. She reads the newspaper and is in correspondence with numerous contemporaries. But far from being portrayed sympathetically, the marquise represents Fouqué's fear of female intellect. The marquise's persistent efforts to convince others of her analysis of the political situation, and her repeated attempts to direct the actions of the male protagonists, are in stark contrast to her utter helplessness in practical matters. Her impracticality is demonstrated at the very beginning of the novel when the inhabitants of the castle prepare to leave their residence. The marquise, while ruling entire states in her mind, allows herself to be overwhelmed by trifles. Under her direction her coach is loaded with so many mirrors, cases full of essences, a cage for a parrot, and her pet pugs, that there is no more room for Elisabeth, who ends up riding. The marquise's solemn vow never to give way to the enemy is forgotten as soon as hostile forces appear at the castle's gate. Her cowardice and helplessness are carried to such extremes that it is only with greatest efforts that she is finally saved by her people. Once exiled from the castle, she becomes completely dependent on her old servant Anna.

Furthermore, not only is there an unbridgeable gap between the marquise's theoretical insights and her practical abilities, but her theories themselves are also proven wrong. Due to her limited understanding, the marquise becomes an instrument in the hands of the Gironde. The more she is entangled in their plans, the more she resorts to fainting fits and illnesses until she finally goes mad.

In spite of this negative portrayal, there are also instances where the marquise succeeds in mobilizing the masses. Her call to free Paris from the revolutionaries and to save the queen is answered by loud cheering (I: 34), and her attempt to rouse the masses against her persecutor Cornelius leads to the death of the latter:

> Ha! She cried, rushing to the armed crowd, a traitor! Citizens, the mercenary of the convent is in your midst! In a wild embrace she kept hold of Cornelius, and violently pulling him, she repeated: a traitor! Beat him to death, a perjured traitor. Momentarily, a thousand fists were clenched against Cornelius... and before he could move his smooth tongue, he lay dead on the ground.[31]

It is undeniable that her demagoguery brands the marquise as a fury. But even though she corresponds to the stereotype of the "female hyena" of the "Goethezeit," in Fouqué's eyes she is fighting for a good cause. Her goal of freeing Paris and saving the monarchy is shared by the positive figures in the novel. Furthermore, her opponent Cornelius must be counted among the most depraved characters of the novel. His punishment and death are justified within the logic of the text. One might also add that the marquise is the only main character in the novel who sees Napoleon and recognizes in him the future emperor of France. The fact that she dies immediately after she is granted this insight might be interpreted as absolution. As different as these three female characters are, they all share one common fate. Unlike Therese Huber's Sara Seldorf, Aphrodise, the marquise de Robillard, and Elisabeth are dead at the end of the novel. The central contradiction of the novel—the portrayal of "natural" femininity combined with a demand for male agency—can only be reconciled through the death of the female heroine. Elisabeth, already an angel during her lifetime, is transfigured into a supernatural being. In the end, Sombreuil witnesses her appearance as an angel.

IV. Conclusion

In *Das Heldenmädchen aus der Vendée*, Caroline de la Motte-Fouqué imagines a heroine who dons male attire and leads the life of a soldier. In choosing as her setting a period of political and social turmoil, Fouqué makes use of the fact that a time of radical changes—such as the French Revolution of 1789 and the Wars of Liberation against Napoleon—often brought about greater independence for women and facilitated transgressions against traditional gender codes. Furthermore, in portraying a heroine who not only participates in the war, but actually makes a vital contribution to the success of the military enterprise, Fouqué makes an argument for including women in the patriotic effort.

Fouqué's explicit adherence to the patriarchal structure of feudal lord and vassal is coupled with her adoption of traditional gender stereotypes. She justifies Elisabeth's unfeminine participation in warfare by reinterpreting it as female self-sacrifice in the service of the fatherland. Ultimately, however, the traditional gender roles prove too inflexible and the reconciliation with Elisabeth's new power fails. "Natural" gender can only be restored through the death of the cross-dressed heroine. Given this, it seems justified to assume a connection between the author's political stance and her ideal of femininity. Fouqué's static concept of society, which assigns every individual to his or her "natural" place, does not tolerate exceptions. Not even Elisabeth's privileged position in the social hierarchy can provide an excuse for her violation of gender norms. Fouque's attempt to justify transgressions against patriarchal gender norms with a recourse to these very norms can only go so far. However, even if we concede that there is little freedom to be gained from doing it for daddy, we should not ignore Fouqué's historical situation or the fact that Fouqué herself as a woman author was transgressing against gender norms. It remains to be hoped that *Das Heldenmädchen aus der Vendée* will find readers who will not condemn it because of its ideological conservatism, but who will attempt to understand it within its context, and with all its contradictions.

NOTES

1. Lydia Schieth, *Die Entwicklung des deutschen Frauenromans im ausgehenden 18. Jahrhundert: Ein Beitrag zur Gattungsgeschichte* (Frankfurt a.M.: Lang, 1987), 220.

2. Karin A. Wurst, ed., *Frauen und Drama im achtzehnten Jahrhundert* (Köln: Böhlau, 1991), 54.

3. Dagmar von Hoff, *Dramen des Weiblichen: Deutsche Dramatikerinnen um 1800* (Opladen: Westdeutscher Verlag, 1989), 71.

4. Among the female authors who invented cross-dressed characters are Bettina Brentano-von Arnim, Karoline von Günderrode, Friederike Helene Unger, Karoline Paulus, Therese Huber, Dorothea Schlegel, Charlotte von Stein, Caroline von Wolzogen, and Benedikte Naubert.

5. Cf. Viktoria Schmidt-Linsenhoff, ed., *Sklavin oder Bürgerin? Französische Revolution und neue Weiblichkeit 1760–1830* (Frankfurt a.M.: Jonas, 1989), 471; Méricourt was one of the most ardent supporters of a female battalion, as is demonstrated in her speech of 1792 before the "Société fraternelle des patriotes de l'un et de l'autre sexe," cf. Darline Gay Levy et. al., *Women in Revolutionary Paris 1789–1795* (Urbana: University of Illinois Press, 1980), 104.

6. Cf. Darline Gay Levy and Harriet Branson Applewhite, "Women of the Popular Classes in Revolutionary Paris," *Women, War, and Revolution*, ed. Carol R. Berkin and Clara M. Lovett (New York: Holmes & Meier, 1980), 9.

7. Cf. Levy, *Women in Revolutionary Paris*, 221.

8. Cf. O. P. Gilbert, *Women in Men's Guise* (London: Jarrold & Sons, 1932), 1–92.

9. "Yes, we lack weapons, and we want to ask for your permission to equip us with them . . . . We want to be able to defend ourselves. You must not reject us, and society must not refuse a right which was given us by nature," qtd. from Ursula Geitner, "Die eigentlichen Enragé ihres Geschlechts: Aufklärung, Französische Revolution und Weiblichkeit," *Grenzgängerinnen: Revolutionäre Frauen im 18. und 19. Jahrhundert: Weibliche Wirklichkeit und männliche Phantasien.*, ed. Helga Grubitzsch, Hannelore Cyrus and Elke Haarbusch (Düsseldorf: Schwann, 1985), 205.

10. Cf. Claudia Opitz, "Der Bürger wird Soldat—und die Bürgerin? Die Revolution, der Krieg und die Stellung der Frauen nach 1789," *Sklavin oder*

Bürgerin? Französische Revolution und neue Weiblichkeit 1760–1830, ed. Viktoria Schmidt-Linsenhoff (Frankfurt a.M.: Jonas, 1989), 46.

11. Cf. Claudia Opitz, "Die vergessenen Töchter der Revolution—Frauen und Frauenrechte im revolutionären Frankreich von 1789–1795," *Grenzgängerinnen: Revolutionäre Frauen im 18. und 19. Jahrhundert*, ed. Grubitzsch, Cyrus, and Haarbusch (Düsseldorf: Schwann, 1985), 292.

12. Cf. Julie Wheelwright, *Amazons and Military Maids: Women Who Dressed as Men in the Pursuit of Life, Liberty, and Happiness* (London: Pandora, 1989), 91.

13. For more information on the role of women during the Vendée uprisings see Marilyn Yalom, *Blood Sisters: The French Revolution in Women's Memory* (New York: HarperCollins, 1993), 191–209.

14. "daß die Weiber in Paris und, wie es nach verschiedenen Vorfällen in den Provinzen das Ansehn hat, das ganze weibliche Geschlecht in Frankreich dem männlichen an Cultur, an Mäßigung und Sittlichkeit nachsteht, und, so oft es zu Grausamkeiten kommt, sich fast immer durch Blutdurst und Grausamkeit auszeichnet," qtd. from Geitner, "Enragé," 192.

15. Cf. Schmidt-Linsenhoff, *Sklavin oder Bürgerin*, 498.

16. The women of 1848, who participated in barricade fighting in 1848, were also received with distrust and suffered from denunciations. This is further evidence for the assumption that, although service for the fatherland justified a violation of gender roles in Germany, fighting for the republic did not.

17. "not a predilection for independence nor fancy but ardent love for the fatherland and the sublime mind who awakened all over Germany so miraculously and to whom it owes its freedom, has led them [these women] to the ranks of the defenders of the fatherland" (Tauentzien before the senate on January 22, 1815), qtd. from Major Z. D. Noel, *Die deutschen Heldinnen in den Kriegsjahren, 1807–1815* (Berlin: Julius Köppen, 1912), 87.

18. "Welch tiefes Weh müssen diese einfachen, bescheidenen und stillen Frauenseelen über das vom Feinde mit Füßen getretene Vaterland empfunden haben, daß sie ihre häuslichen und Familienbeziehungen aufgaben, um für ihr Vaterland zu kämpfen," Noel, *Die deutschen Heldinnen*, XIV.

19. Helga Cyrus, "Von erlaubter und unerlaubter Frauenart, um Freiheit zu kämpfen: Freiheitskämpferinnen im 19. Jahrhundert und die Freie Hansestadt Bremen," *Grenzgängerinnen: Revolutionäre Frauen im 18. und 19. Jahrhundert*, ed. Grubitzsch, Cyrus, and Haarbusch (Düsseldorf: Schwann, 1985), 33.

20. "Ich müßte mich schämen, ein Mann zu heißen / Wenn ich nicht könnt' führen das Eisen / Und wollte Weibern es gönnen / daß sie es führen können // Wer ist der Geselle, so fein, so jung? / Doch führt er das Eisen mit gutem Schwung. / Wer steckt unter der Maske? / Eine Jungfrau, heißt Prochaska. // Wie merkten wir's nur nicht lange schon / Am glatten Kinn, am feinen Ton? / Doch unter den männlichen Taten / Wer konnte das Weib erraten? // Aber es hat sie getroffen ein Schuß! / Jetzt sagt sie's selber, weil sie muß. / Wundarzt, geh beileibe / Nicht unsanft um mit dem Weibe! // Zum Glück traf Dich die Kugel nicht eh'r, / als bis Du dir hattest genügliche Ehr' / Erstritten in Mannesgebärden, / Jetzt kannst Du ein Weib wieder werden. // Doch ich müßte mich schämen ein Mann zu heißen, /

Wenn ich nicht wollte führen das Eisen, / Und wollte Weibern es gönnen, / daß sie es führen können" (qtd. from Noel, *Die deutschen Heldinnen*, 53–54). Auguste Krüger alias August Lübeck, who received the Iron Cross, was also the subject of a poem by Rückert.

21. Caroline de la Motte Fouqué was born in 1775 in Nennhausen in Havelland. She was a member of the old aristocratic von Briest family. In 1789 she married the officer Rochus von Rochow whom she left after the birth of two sons and one daughter. The divorce was already on its way when Rochus shot himself, probably because of gambling debts. Very soon afterwards Caroline married the writer Friedrich de la Motte Fouqué. This marriage is generally described as happy. Caroline died in 1831. For more detailed information about her life see Jean T. Wilde, *Caroline de la Motte Fouqué: The Romantic Realist*, (New York: Brookman Associates, 1955) and Vera Prill, *Caroline de la Motte-Fouqué* (Berlin: Kraus, 1933).

22. To my knowledge, the only detailed analyses of the novel are to be found in Birgit Wagenbaur, *Die Pathologie der Liebe: Literarische Weiblichkeitsentwürfe um 1800* (Berlin: Erich Schmidt, 1996), 260–67, and in Todd Kontje, *Women, the Novel, and the German Nation, 1771–1871: Domestic Fiction in the Fatherland* (Cambridge: Cambridge UP, 1998).

23. The Vendée insurrection lasted from March 1793 to May 1795 when the Vendée was obliged to recognize the Republic. For more information see Yalom, *Blood Sisters,* 191–209.

24. An analysis of Therese Huber's novel *Die Familie Seldorf* shows that support for the goals of the Revolution also led to internal contradictions because of the implicit identification of "human" and "male." The structure of the conflict, however, is different.

25. Even Elisabeth's decision to join the army is supervised by patriarchal authority: absorbed in ardent prayer in front of the crucifix, Elisabeth decides to don male attire and proceeds to fight for the fatherland, cf. Caroline de la Motte Fouqué, *Das Heldenmädchen aus der Vendée* (Wien: Haas'sche Verlagsbuchhandlung, 1816), I: 77.

26. "So pries er die Frauen in ihrer reinen Selbstverleugnung, und wie dies Himmelsschild sich so stark und schirmend auf ihre Brust lege, daß sie der ernsten Lebensgefahr ohne sonderliche Anstrengung trotzen. Gewiß, setzte er gerührt hinzu, ihre Waffen sind nicht von dieser Welt" (Fouqué, *Heldenmädchen*, I: 137).

27. "Sich selber nicht bewußt, weder denkend noch wollend, hatte Elisabeth einem neben ihr Haltenden die weiße Fahne aus der Hand gerissen. Wie ein Blitz theilte sie die Reihen. Dorthin, wo der Federbusch des Prinzen im Gedränge hin und wieder wankte, zog es sie magnetisch. Ihre Hand zitterte nicht, sie konnte den Schaft, an welchem das Panier befestigt war, hoch in die Luft schwingen. Verlaßt Eure Fahne nicht, Vendéer, rief sie mit klarer Engelsstimme. Rettet die Ehre Frankreichs" (Fouqué, *Heldenmädchen*, I: 131).

28. Note also that the regiment of the heroic aristocrat Sombreuil received its training in Germany (cf. Fouqué, *Heldenmädchen*, II: 60).

29. The parallel is even more obvious if one keeps in mind that Fouqué's second husband Friedrich belonged to the dynasty of the de la Motte Fouqué which formed part of the Vendée aristocracy.

30. "Wir sind hier oft bedroht worden und noch neuerlich war es nahe daran, daß die Mark verheert ward ... Damals habe ich Stunden der Verzweiflung verlebt, von der ich niemand ein Bild machen kann," qtd. from Karl August Varnhagen von Ense, *Biographische Porträts* (Leipzig: F. A. Brockhaus, 1871), 145.

31. "Ha! Schrie sie, in den bewaffneten Haufen stürzend, ein Verräther! Bürger, ein Besoldeter des Conventes mitten unter Euch! Sie hielt Cornelius wild umschlungen und ihn gewaltsam hervorziehend, wiederholte sie: ein Verräther! Schlagt ihn tod, ein meineidiger Verräther. Im Augenblick ballten sich tausend Fäuste gegen Cornelius . . . und ehe er die geschmeidige Zunge rühren konnte, lag er . . . todt am Boden" (Fouqué, *Heldenmädchen*, II: 163–164).

Spying, Writing, Authority: Eliza Haywood's *Bath Intrigues*

JULIETTE MERRITT

In 1755, the year before her death, Eliza Haywood published *The Invisible Spy*. It was her final piece of spectatorial fiction, a form that had become popular in England following the translation in 1687–94 of Giovanni Paolo Marana's *L'Espion turc* (1684),[1] a text to which Haywood herself had turned from time to time throughout her long career. Haywood's own texts frequently feature an invisible or unnoticed observer. The narrator of Haywood's *Memoirs of a Certain Island Adjacent to the Kingdom of Utopia* (1725) is taken up by Cupid into a cloud where he can observe but cannot be seen, for example, because "Fate . . . had made choice of him to be the Discoverer of Secrets, to which the greater part of the world were wholly Strangers."[2] In her *Memoirs of a Certain Island*, a scandal chronicle, Haywood followed most directly Delariviere Manley's *New Atalantis* (1709) where Astrea (goddess of Justice), Virtue, and Intelligence visit the earth and "pass unknown and unregarded among the crowd of mortals."[3] Where the observing eye of *Memoirs of a Certain Island* gathers material for a scandalous discourse, Haywood's more polite and respectable periodical *The Female Spectator* (1744–46), has instead a reformist agenda. The Female Spectator, who alerts us to a network of spies which brings her back intelligence, intends to make her readership "acquainted with other People's Affairs" so that they may learn "to regulate their own."[4] Whether scandalous or reformist (the distinctions are not always clear), the spectatorial text creates its discourse out of the connection between seeing and writing. In Haywood's *Bath Intrigues* (1725), a relationship among the concepts of spying, authorship, and satire is assumed. In four letters to his friend Will, J.B., at his friend's request, relates a series of sexual escapades he has witnessed while visiting Bath. He is puzzled, however, as to why Will has selected him for an "Intelligence" who has "neither Wit enough to set up for an Author, nor Ill-nature for a Satyrist."[5] This essay will examine Haywood's use of this relationship, a use in which J.B.'s doubt regarding his suitability becomes the first gesture towards an interrogation of the observer's discursive authority.

In one of her dedications, Haywood claims for herself a "tolerable Share of Discernment."[6] The apparent modesty of this profession is somewhat misleading. As one of the leading tropes of rationality in the seventeenth and eighteenth centuries, "discernment" was an essential component of judgement and reason. For Haywood to value herself on possessing such an attribute (even a "tolerable Share" of it) is an assertion of her intellectual abilities. "Discernment" is also a visual trope of perception and observation; to invoke it underlines the importance of visual authority in her writing, and also signals Haywood's desire to colonize the privileged position of the spectator, a position conventionally regarded as male territory. In *The Female Spectator* Haywood consciously followed Addison and Steele's *Spectator* in constructing a discursive position based on the discerning spectator.[7] Underlying this rhetorical strategy is an unquestioned confidence in the legitimate and unquestioned authority of vision. However, in *Bath Intrigues*, where the voyeuristic aspects of spectatorship are foregrounded and the ethical uncertainty of the spy's role is emphasized, Haywood interrogates this assumption. She adopts the figure of the observer/writer as her strategy for acquiring the authorial position. But given the notorious reputation of the spy, whose impulses are so often prurient and voyeuristic, there are certain risks in adopting such a persona as the basis for a public voice. As Virginia Swain emphasizes, the philosophical and social repercussions to the seventeenth-century developments in optics included the fact that "the role of the spectator [became] highly ambiguous." Over the course of the seventeenth and eighteenth centuries, "viewing and voyeurism tend to merge":

> the rethinking of God's design which accompanied the new discoveries, and the new uncertainties surrounding the place of humankind in the natural order which followed from this rethinking, also made sight an instrument of self-doubt. Was the gaze intruding where it did not belong? The penetration of the gaze where it is unexpected and perhaps unwelcome becomes a frequent literary and artistic theme.[8]

This is certainly true of *Bath Intrigues* where the primary subject is female sexual (mis)behavior. The author, J.B., is a sexual voyeur who, in order to "obey the dictates of a present Curiosity," (1) hides himself to witness the seduction of Lady Bellair, and pretends to be drunk in order to overhear the lovemaking of another woman and her lover, to name only two examples of his invasive looking. As he becomes more deeply implicated in his activity as a spy, he crosses over from being a detached observer to being an actual participant in "Intrigue." This participation he also relates for Will's pleasure, becoming, as a result, an object of his own scandalous discourse. *Bath Intrigues* is highly self-reflexive, not only critical of the voyeurism out of which its satiric discourse is created, but also self-conscious that the relationship between spectatorship and discursive authority is a contentious one. Addressing the problems, even contradictions, attending Haywood's project exposes the uncertain nature of authority itself, contributes to ongoing efforts to analyze the specific rhetorical strategies women writers develop in order to participate in public discourse: to advance, in Susan Lanser's phrase, their "project of self-authorization."[9]

It is in *The Invisible Spy* that Haywood articulates most clearly her critical understanding of the two forms of authority, visual and linguistic, that underpin the discursive position she seeks. In this late text, a Magus provides two items which assist the Spy's voyeurism: a "Belt of Invisibility . . . renders the party invisible to all human eyes," and "The Wonderful Tablet . . . receives the Impression of every Word that is spoken, in as distinct a manner as if engrav'd." The two are, as the Magus attests, "concomitant" because "the satisfaction that either of them would be able to procure, would be incompleat without the assistance of the other."[10] Initially, this concomitance of Belt and Tablet appears simply to suggest a mutually beneficial relationship between two distinct but equal activities—seeing and writing. In completing one another, they work together to produce the Spy's text. However, the Tablet's creation of a visual, documentary record which the author's "too defective" memory is unable to produce is intended to overcome the questionable veracity of reported speech. Thus, it is not mere gossip and hearsay that the Invisible Spy relates. Although there appears to be a distinction made between a visual order, signified by the Belt, and a linguistic order, created by the Tablet, the Tablet's provision of an "engrav'd" visual record ensures that it is a *visual* regime which produces and guarantees the text's discourse.[11]

This tension, then, between the visual and the linguistic[12] reveals doubts about the spoken word, doubts Haywood had already revealed much earlier in *The British Recluse* (1722). This story of seduction and betrayal voices at the outset suspicions regarding speech: "Of all the Foibles Youth and Inexperience is liable to fall into," the narrator begins, "there is none, I think of more dangerous Consequence, than too easily giving Credit to what we hear . . . If we cou'd bring our selves to depend on nothing but what we had Proof for, what a world of Discontent shou'd we avoid!"[13] The narrator does not reveal what would constitute proof, but linguistic ambiguity is foregrounded to warn women of the rhetoric of seduction. The Invisible Spy's Tablet, however, argues for the veracity of the written, visual, text. As such, it works to establish the hegemony of vision as the basis for discursive authority.

Similar doubts regarding speech were already apparent in Addison and Steele's *The Spectator.* Mr. Spectator's voluntary "Resignation of Speech" is a strategy designed to affirm his visual authority. It is through his silence, specifically, that his enhanced vision is produced:

> It is remarkable that those who want any one Sense, possess the others with greater Force and Vivacity. Thus my Want or rather Resignation of Speech, gives me all the Advantages of a dumb Man. I have, methinks, a more than ordinary Penetration in Seeing; and flatter my self that I have looked into the highest and lowest of Mankind, and made shrewd Guesses, without being admitted to their conversation, at the inmost Thoughts and Reflections of all whom I behold.[14]

By placing himself on the margins of social life, the Spectator creates the distance between viewer and viewed required by the Cartesian subject position. As a result, he can applaud his ability to "discern the Errors in the Oeconomy, Business, and Diversion of others, better than those who are engaged in them; as Standers-by discover Blots, which are apt to escape those who are in the Game"(1: 4–5). Although he can remove the obstacle which impairs perception—participation in the "Game" of life—he cannot escape the irony that much of his written discourse derives from overheard conversations. The knowledge he purports to acquire, even though confirmed by vision, is inevitably mediated by the Spectator's own language.

The Invisible Spy's and Mr. Spectator's anxious attempts to buttress vision against an apparent anxiety regarding speech are overdetermined—such strategies reveal the very uncertainty that plagues visual authority. And it is Haywood's awareness of this ambiguity that underlies her deployment of vision in *Bath Intrigues*. From the beginning, J.B appears ill at ease with his role as an "Intelligence," and the reader is alerted to the work's meta-critical impulse through J.B.'s misgivings about being a purveyor of sexual gossip: "I find it is but giving a willing Ear to Scandal, and a thousand Tongues are ready to oblige you, especially in such a place as this"

(16). J.B. rationalizes his participation in a practice he condemns by appealing to a higher ideal—the obligations of friendship. "I assure you," he writes to Will,

> there is nothing affords me less Satisfaction, than the finding out Failings of this kind; and the exposing them, is yet more ungrateful . . . But since I have promis'd it . . . will not now pretend to make any Arguments how far it may or may not be agreeable to my own Inclinations; 'tis sufficient I do you a pleasure, which, my dear *Will*, you must give me leave to assure you, shall always be the first thing is view. (34)

Beyond the attempt to obfuscate the dubious aspects of his spying, J.B. purports to define and limit the extent of his own pleasure; if his desire has any scopic aspect at all, it is merely that he has his 'eye' on Will's specular pleasure. A chain of seeing defines this relationship between writer and reader. Just how ironic J.B.'s attempts at justification are will become more clear as he develops in his role and discovers the true nature of his "Inclinations."

Not only does he disavow any personal benefit or pleasure, he also makes an argument for his essential asexuality:

> You expect, perhaps, I should entertain you with some Amours of my own, but I can tell you, Example has no effect on me; and I can be told my Friends are employ'd in their several Intrigues, without envying their Happiness, or wishing to partake it.—If ever I knew what an amorous Inclination was, since my coming to the *Bath* it was for the Wife of a *French* Merchant, and I believe should have made a tryal how far Fortune would have befriended me, if I had not discovered, an intimate Friend had been before-hand with me, and took off all the stock of Love that Lady had on her hands. (28)

J.B.'s disingenuity expresses the ambiguity inherent in a discursive position based on the claims of a voyeur, claims which in this particular instance are clearly contradictory. He denies that he is amorous (an indifference suited to his role as a spy), yet he is aroused by the wife of a French merchant. Contrary to his assertion that he is impervious to "Example," he is aroused by what he sees, and does not remain a disinterested spy. In *Bath Intrigues*, "Example" produces a pornographic text, but the literature of "Example"—the cautionary tale or awful warning—is a form of representation which has, in other contexts, a didactic function. It is frequently distinguished from "precept" as being more likely to educate and reform readers. *Bath Intrigues* is an unlikely marriage between a pornographic and a cautionary text, designed both to arouse and improve.

J.B. is first aroused by what he sees while on an excursion to gain "Intelligence" for Will. He falls into a "Debauch" when, under the cover of drunkenness, he has "the opportunity of observing every thing, without being suspected of being capable of observing any thing" (34). Drunkenness is a means of invisibility, of hiding out in the open. When the company had "grown in all appearance *Non Compos Mentis,*" he observes, or, more accurately, overhears a friend's wife and her lover:

> You know, dear *Will*, I am not very amorous, but the luscious Conversation I listen'd to, the Beauty of the Woman, who is certainly one of the finest Creatures in the World, and the great quantity of Wine I had drank, altogether inflamed my Blood, and I began to wish myself in my Friend's place. (35)

Despite the disclaimer, it is a wish he must fulfill. To do so he blackmails the woman, threatening to expose her unless she grants to him the "same Favour." The success of this extortion he also relates for Will's pleasure: "She led me into the garden, and in a little Arbour compleated my Desires in as riotous and full a manner as I could wish, and far beyond my hope"(37). That J.B. overhears rather than actually sees the two lovers is significant. Although Haywood explores the connection between seeing and sex, to avoid the more explicit pornography of a pictorial description, only certain aspects of the visual can be represented. It is more accurate to say, therefore, that J.B. is aroused by what he hears, a "luscious Conversation," rather than by what he sees. To recognize this is to focus our attention on the relationship between language and desire, but it may also, recalling the Invisible Spy's Tablet, cast doubts on the accuracy of J.B.'s report precisely because it is overheard rather than visually witnessed, and because it is reproduced from memory.

Yet J.B. also exposes himself: opportunistic and unscrupulous, he readily extorts sexual favours to satisfy a desire created by the lure of sexual voyeurism. As a voyeur and then as a participant, his sexuality is inextricable from the sexual activity of others. He requires a mediator or conduit—another man—in order for his desire to be aroused. This is consistent with his role as a spy/writer because he mediates between the reader and the private world he reveals to the reader's gaze (or suggests to the reader's imagination). He is both the witness at the centre of information and the messenger, yet he is not the disinterested, reluctant observer he claims to be.

The leap J.B. makes from spectator of amorous intrigues to a scandalous figure himself dissolves the subject/object distinction which, according to convention, structures the scopic regime and creates spectatorial authority. In becoming an object of our (and Will's) voyeuristic gaze, he loses any privilege his position as a disinterested spectator may give him. Although Haywood insists on tarring J.B. with his own brush, neither can the reader of scandal sheets avoid the taint of voyeurism. We are an important link in the chain of seeing, and we are invited to participate in the specular pleasure of Will and J.B. It is this point Haywood insists on making—producer and consumer are complicit, and neither can claim an authoritative or even neutral position. In Simon Varey's estimation, *Bath Intrigues* is a "good, if unedifying, example of popular English scandalous fiction of the period" (viii). Scandal narratives often evoke this kind of ethical criticism, but to regard *Bath Intrigues* as "unedifying" is, to some degree, understandable as the reader is unavoidably implicated in J.B.'s voyeurism, and we may feel discomfort at our own position at the keyhole.[15]

So where does this leave Haywood's "project of self-authorization" which is based upon the link between spectating and writing? In erasing the distinction between spectator and object, and completely discrediting the spectator himself, Haywood throws questions of authority—where it resides, how one possesses it—into debate. If spectatorship can be the means of achieving a "voice," what are we to make of this ironic undermining of its terms of authority? Haywood foregoes the position of moral superiority that the critical text usually constructs for its persona. In *Bath Intrigues*, the "satirist" (J.B. himself) is as much under attack as anyone else.[16]

Such a Scriblerian impulse is made absolutely clear in *The Invisible Spy*, where no attempt is made to mitigate the spy's voyeurism. On the contrary, in the second volume a letter from Scriblerius expresses astonishment at the Spy's undertaking :

> I am shock'd and scandalized beyond measure at your title . . . What but the very Devil incarnate can have tempted you to assume one so ungracious to all degrees of people? . . . human prudence has taught us to elude the scrutiny of all known examiners; but who can guard against what they do not see? . . . you may explore all the necessary arts and mysteries of our several avocations, without our having it in our power to bribe you to secrecy. (2: 8–9)

Scriblerius simultaneously challenges the Spy's project and acknowledges the Invisible Spy's two sources of power. First, in possessing a scrutiny which is unknowable and unavoidable, where the object of sight cannot return a challenging look, the Spy cannot be made a spectacle as J.B. can. Second, invisibility precludes the offer of a bribe—neither can the Spy be silenced. Either way, a spy's power is the power to instill fear. Samuel

Johnson expressed his interest in this form of power through the exemplary story of Nugaculas in *Rambler* 103. Nugaculas applies his natural inquisitiveness to the seemingly worthy endeavour of discovering the "various motives of human actions." Although his friends "could not deny that the study of human nature to be worthy of a wise man," the unfortunate result of Nugaculas' project is that he unwittingly becomes a scandal chronicler: "He is, by continual application, become a general master of the secret history, and can give an account of the intrigues, private marriages, competitions, and strategems of half a century." Thus, although not "ill-natured" himself, he is hated and feared because "he is considered by great numbers as one that has their fame and their happiness in his power, and no man can much love him of whom he lives in fear."[17] Although Johnson's story points to the dangers of a natural yet unregulated curiosity, he also defends Nugaculas' laudable, even benign, aims—to understand human nature and motivation. Johnson's defense would be understood by eighteenth-century readers who, through frequent exposure, were familiar with a central trope in the exploration of human psychology. The desire to uncover the mystery of human motivation is a trope which was, in fact, employed by Haywood in *The Female Spectator* to lend further credibility to her discourse. In addition to her project of reform, the Female Spectator also seeks to discover the "Secret Springs" behind human action. However, Johnson's defense of Nugaculas' perhaps excessive curiosity would not have been extended to the female writer of scandal, to a Manley or a Haywood.

The question of the Invisible Spy's authority or right to criticize arises in another letter, this time from a woman. She writes to ask, "who set you up for a Censor of your Neighbours actions?—By what Rule do you pretend to judge what is deserving Reproof, and what is not so?" (4: 4–5). The Invisible Spy does not respond to the woman's query; it is enough, apparently, that the issue of authority is stated and left open for the reader to ponder. The source of the Spy's power is clear—an unhindered gaze—but the issue of moral authority, the "Rule" normally required of one who presumes to be critical of others, is sidestepped.

If *The Invisible Spy* and *Bath Intrigues* undermine the authoritative position of their personae, certain questions regarding the efficacy of Haywood's satiric agenda may be raised. Underlying Scriblerius' amazement at the Spy's boldness are certain common assumptions regarding the figure of the spy: he or she is always untrustworthy. We cannot, with any confidence, be certain that a spy has a firm allegiance to ideological or political authority. Spies, therefore, have the potential to be extraordinarily subversive (the 'double agent' comes to mind). They are marginal figures, yet, as witnesses, central to the production of, in this case, scandalous discourse. It is more accurate to say that the Spy has power rather than authority, because the latter term suggests a critical, moral or political legitimacy. Haywood's spies make no such claim. This distinction Haywood makes between power and authority, however, points to a route left open for those on the margins of discourse: women may be excluded from the institutions of authority, but they do exercise forms of power. For a writer like Haywood, whose lurking iconoclasm is never far from the surface of her texts, the disruptive spy is a logical figure to deploy in her own bid for authorship.

In discrediting J.B., however, does Haywood discredit her own project as well? Not necessarily, if we consider more fully J.B.'s function. Despite the pervasive irony of her work, the objective of Haywood's feminist discourse can be found in her insistence that women make the crucial distinction between self-display and self-regard. J.B. may discredit himself as a moral authority of the kind we normally associate with satire, but he is an effective vehicle for Haywood's critique of female "Mismanagement."

To this end, his role is to demonstrate how vulnerable women are to a gaze that perpetually seeks them out; *Bath Intrigues* alerts women to the presence of this gaze and its social effects. In making women the predominant focus of sight in her work, especially as providers of voyeuristic pleasure, Haywood may exploit a scopic regime thoroughly oppressive to women. I would argue, however, that Haywood represents the dominating male look in order to teach women the necessity of evading it. Furthermore, the hegemonic power of the male gaze is also challenged and demystified by making, for example, J.B.'s "Inclinations" the focus of our sight. His credibility may be destroyed, but not his utility—he is an "awful warning" indeed of the importance of sexual privacy for women. Women are viewed—openly and covertly—in a visual culture which regards them as sexual objects. Yet this very act of sight, of women on display, is also the focus of Haywood's concern and criticism. Her texts demonstate the need for women to avoid public scrutiny, especially in sexual matters. In a later scene, J.B. witnesses another pair of lovers, Lady Bellair and "a Gentleman of the long Robe." As they leave the garden,[18] he scrambles up a tree; what he sees from this perspective provokes his condemnation:

> it not being very dark, [I] saw them go into the House, stopping every two or three Paces, to renew their Vows, and seal them with a Kiss.—This Indiscretion in a Woman of that Lady's Character, surpriz'd me no less than her Fall from Virtue had done; because, as there were several Lodgers both in the House I was in, and that she went into, she could not be certain but that someone, agitated by the same Curiosity I was, might observe their Behaviour—But when that little Devil, *Cupid*, has once taken possession of the Senses, there is seldom any room for Prudence. (13–15)

The twin themes of prudence and indiscretion are fundamental to Haywood's exploration of sexual and social politics. She does not (or rarely does) condemn women's sexual behaviour on moral grounds. For Haywood, it is a matter of how a woman conducts herself in public in order to protect her reputation. Lady Bellair neglects to perceive her behaviour as the censoring public will see it. Blind to her own self-interest, she exposes herself to J.B.'s scrutiny and criticism. Yet what Haywood frequently demonstrates in her writing is the impossibility for women to escape this penetrating male gaze—there is no real private space for women where they can screen themselves from eyes that are intent upon finding them out. The garden, frequently a place for contemplation, (indeed, J.B. has retired to the garden to indulge reflection), is a setting where women are especially vulnerable. In Haywood's texts, seductions are frequently accomplished in a garden—*Bath Intrigues* is no exception.

J.B. reiterates his "Wonder" at indiscreet conduct in the case of Lady R——'s unfortunate "amorous League with a young Fop, who makes it his business to boast of the Favours he receives from her" (26). In addition to his bragging, he has shown her letters in public, documentary evidence of her sexual activity. In "A Discourse on Writings of this Nature" (1724), Haywood urges caution to women when expressing themselves on paper. Letters, ostensibly private forms of discourse, are potentially public acts and, therefore, hold certain dangers for women. Haywood warns, "Letters often live longer than the Person who wrote them—they may by some Accident be lost!—may miscarry—somebody must be trusted to convey 'em, and the Fidelity of such sort of People is not much to be depended on."[19] As Karen Hollis has recently noted, "the disruption of correspondence is so pervasive in Haywood's work that it discredits the connection between letters and female sexual or interpretive agency promoted by many of her predecessors."[20] Haywood further adds: "Paper cannot blush, and our Thoughts, in spite of us, will often take a greater Liberty in expressing themselves that way, than the natural Bashfulness of Virtue will permit 'em to any other." Currently, female self-expression of various forms in enthusiastically applauded, but in this very interesting text women's participation in certain forms of discourse is regarded ambivalently; Haywood consistently recognizes the risks of public speech for those disconnected from power.

Lady R——, furthermore, is complicit in her own self-exposure:

> she toys with him, is jealous of him, falls in Fits if she sees him but barely civil to any other Woman, and all this without regard who observes her Behaviour, or what may be conjectur'd by it.—The truth is, I believe,

> some Women glory in their Amours, and think it a greater Honour to be thought *amiable* than *virtuous*; if it were not so, we should not have half the Subject for that *just* Satire which we now abound in. (26–27)

Their indiscretion is further compounded by his railing wife "so that between the Husband's Vanity, and the Wife's Jealousy, nothing that passes between them is a Secret" (27). A woman's propensity to flaunt her sexual indiscretions rather than conceal them bespeaks a lack of proper self-regard and is, in Haywood, a problem of female "Mismanagement." Her position is a conservative one—self-regard so often entails self-censorship—but as earlier critics have already noted, Haywood's feminism is fundamentally pragmatic, her writings designed to "aid women in their struggle for survival within existing social structures."[21]

In terms of strategies for "self-authorization," Haywood's objective cannot be to derive the privileges of authorship from an ethical or even neutral posture. And if there is no basis for J.B.'s moral authority, neither is his visual authority secure because the eyes of a third party, the reader, are also present. Triangulating the gaze is not, however, the only way scopic power can be rendered uncertain; the dyadic gaze of viewer and viewed is also subject to challenge.

This possiblity is explored in one of several *Spectator* papers dealing with the problem of "Starers." In No. 20, a woman writes to complain of the Spectator's "Imitators":

> Ever since the SPECTATOR appeared, have I remarked a kind of men, whom I chuse to call *Starers*; that without any regard to Time, Place, or Modesty, disturb a large Company with their impertinent Eyes. (1: 86)

The letter writer belongs to a congregation, made up chiefly of women, who suffer from the impertinence of such a Starer:

> very lately one whole Isle has been disturbed with one of these monstrous Starers; He's the Head taller than any one in the Church; but for the greater Advantage of exposing himself, stands upon a Hassock, and commands the whole Congregation, to the great Annoyance of the devoutest Part of the Auditory; for what with Blushing, Confusion, and Vexation, we can neither mind the Prayers nor Sermon. (1: 86)

The women experience the discomfort of being openly scrutinized but, as the letter writer points out, the Starer also makes an object of himself; he forces the congregation to look at him, and in "exposing himself" draws the woman's criticism. In fact, by becoming a spectacle, the Starer has inverted the structure by placing himself in the feminine position. In doing so, he loses the scopic advantage the "Looker-on" has as long as his looking remains concealed. The Starer can be confronted—'stared down'—but only by another man. The Spectator, in reply, rules out any other option:

> a Fellow that is capable of shewing an impudent Front before a whole Congregation, and can bear being a publick Spectacle, is not so easily rebuked as to amend by Admonitions. (1: 86)

Rather, his friend Will Prosper, armed with his own Hassock and the Spectator's directions "according to the most exact Rules of Opticks," will confront the "Starers Eyes whereever he throws them" in order to make him "feel a little of the Pain he has so often put others to, of being out of Countenance" (1: 86–87). Women cannot meet the eyes of a Starer directly. Modesty demands that they keep their eyes averted, for a woman's bold stare is the sign of a brazen sexuality. If the women in church look at all, it is because their glance has been extorted from them: "While we suffer our Women to be thus impudently attacked, they have no Defence, but in the End to cast yielding Glances at the Starers" (1: 87). Yet, what will happen when Will Prosper climbs upon his hassock? Will he, too, become a spectacle and be robbed of the power of his gaze? Quite possibly, for the spectator is always potentially a spectacle in the eyes of another. As a result, scopic power can be transferred or given up in an endless process of the creation and dissolution of the subject/object structure.

The Spectator himself is aware of the threat a returning look can pose to his scopic power. In order to fulfill his "Pleasures [which] are almost wholly confin'd to those of Sight," it is essential that he be the one who looks, for he admits that "the greatest Pain [he] can suffer, is . . . being talked to, and being stared at" (1: 6). He must avoid the confrontation of a returning stare because his position as an autonomous subject can be challenged by the look of another.

That the Spectator attempts to circumvent this fact – to remove himself from the world's look – is part of the playful fiction of his persona. He goes so far as to claim a kind of public invisibility: "I can very justly say with the antient Sage, *I am never less alone that when alone* . . . I am insignificant to the Company in public Places" (1: 19). So insignificant is he that although his person is well known, he is routinely referred to as "Mr. what-d'ye-call-him" (1: 19). He occupies an ambiguous position as both seen but nameless, as present but taken little notice of. While this may be a function of his speechlessness, it is also his method of appearing to reside only on the subject side of the look, to derive "power from absence."[22] The rhetorical device of deriving discursivity from marginality, is a strategy which hopes to exploit a perceived connection between unhindered observation and knowledge, but whatever his claims to the contrary, Mr. Spectator does not exist as an autonomous subject and is always in danger of becoming a spectacle, a reversal he is anxious to avoid. Full spectatorial power, in any of its aspects—epistemological, social, sexual—is an illusion. Spectatorial fiction, in fact, consistently demonstrates that the subject/object structure is inherently unstable.

Addison and Steele clearly (if unwittingly) show in *The Spectator* that retaining scopic power is problematic and uncertain. Although the Spectator would like to count on his "Penetration in Seeing" and distinguish his activity from the "Impudence" of mere "Starers," his is a dubious activity. If, as a reformer of manners and morals, the "Correction of Impudence" falls within his purview because it is an "Offence committed by the Eyes," how is this "Impudence" different from the Spectator's own looking? When he and Will debate the merits of the various women presented to their view one evening at the theatre (No. 4), does he think it "Prudence" to look away because he might be caught staring himself? The woman's complaint against "Starers" makes the connection, implying that the Spectator has set a trend which is now being copied. Yet it is true that the Starer's exhibitionism makes him a mere "awkward Imitator" (1: 86), a debased practitioner of the art of looking. He is, in fact, a ridiculous or comic copy; as an exhibitionist, he wants to be seen rather than to see. The Spectator, on the other hand, knows when to look away. Although his secretiveness enhances the privilege of his position, he cannot entirely avoid the taint of voyeurism, especially since the object of his looking is often a woman, scrutinized not only in order to confirm male scopic power but for her value as a desirable object. As Will and the Spectator rhapsodize over "Beauty . . . chastised by . . . Innocence," (1: 20) we might be distracted from the voyeuristic nature of their activity, yet a sexual return on their looking is clearly registered. So while the Spectator does not tell us why it is "Prudence" to look away, his statement is significant for this gap; we suspect that we do not have full knowledge of the Spectator's specular motives. Despite his disarming irony and gentility, he may be no more than an "impudent Starer" himself.

The foregoing discussion shows how the privileges of Cartesian vision are uncertain even in a text such as *The Spectator* which so carefully (yet ironically) constructs an apparently autonomous observer, protected from the returning stare which would put his scopic advantage in jeopardy. The consequence of the public nature of J.B.'s letters (we are never told how they came to be published) is that he stands as exposed before us as the women he satirizes. This is oddly appropriate given that letters are personal documents whose true subject is often their author. Quite possibly,

J.B., rather than the women he beholds, is the primary object of scrutiny and Haywood's satire. Furthermore, another woman of *Bath Intrigues* suggests a strategy, other than avoiding exposure, by which women might improve their specular position: Lady Leer demonstrates that they themselves might return the gaze. Regina Schwartz argues for such an approach. In drawing upon Lacan's view of he way in which the subject is constituted by the gaze, she states:

> If subjects and objects are constituted by the act of seeing—the subject sees and the object is the focus of sight—what happens when the watching subject is watched and the object of sight looks back? Such questions push psychoanalysis, willingly or not, into the realm of politics, where insights into the complexities of the gaze could enable women to reclaim their gaze instead of leading to another patriarchal dead end, "the male gaze."[23]

As her name suggests, Lady Leer embodies a distinct application of the female look:

> her eyes invite almost as many as look on her, her Tongue refuses Encouragement to none: but I believe the Man is yet unborn who can boast of any more than these Superficial Favours; — yet she has a way peculiar to herself, of keeping them all in hopes, and cheats them so handsomely, that when they find themselves impos'd upon, they have not the power of complaining. (39)

She is an unsuitable subject for scandalous discourse because she manages her conduct with admirable skill. If she avoids "Intrigues," there is no suggestion that she does so on the grounds of virtue; rather, she prudently manipulates specular relations to her advantage. She maintains her role as sexual object, inviting the male look, but never becomes subject to it. On the contrary, her name tells us that she is an agent of the look, and of the most sexual looks at that. Lady Leer is therefore a complex figure and J.B.'s observations reveal that he does not fully comprehend her. Sexuality is for her pure performance, an act that literally never takes place. She is, in fact, compared to a famous actress, the "once celebrated Mrs. Bracegirdle:"

> Always easy, never kind,
> When you think you have her sure;
> Such a Temper you will find,
> Quick to wound, slow to cure. (40)

Ultimately her power is accounted for by her superior intellect; "she has certainly an Understanding superior to what most of her Sex can pretend to, or her Designs could never be carried on with . . . Smoothness and Success" (40). But included in her "Designs" is "the Management of her Sister's Fortunes, who tho' they have Husbands, still permit her to be their Trustee" (40). Lady Leer may, in the form of role-playing, pretend to fulfill her sexual function, yet her real advantage lies in the appropriation of two important forms of male power: scopic and economic privilege. And her real focus is money the material basis of power.

Hence *Bath Intrigues* and *The Invisible Spy* expose both the ethical uncertainty the role of the "Looker-on" entails and the fundamental ambiguity of subject/object relations. In *Bath Intrigues*, the voyeuristic aspects of spectatorship are emphasized, including the voyeur's tendency for exhibitionism. In *The Invisible Spy*, the spectator's invisibility does not permit the same deconstruction of the spectator/spectacle dichotomy; instead, Haywood concentrates on issues of authorship, power and the interplay between visual and moral authority. As Scriblerius, the writer to the Invisible Spy, reminds us thirty years after the publication of *Bath Intrigues*, "human prudence has taught us to elude the scrutiny of all known examiners" (2: 8). It is this Haywood would have women understand—the need for a pragmatic management of their visibility. That the visible field is complex and difficult to navigate Haywood makes clear, but that women must attempt to master it is also clear, and they must do so despite the double bind a voyeuristic male sexual economy creates for them. Women are enjoined to be objects on display, yet they are chastised for their vanity and exhibitionism. She uses scandal fiction to criticize female indiscretion—making public what ought to be kept private—yet it is undeniable that in doing so she exploits for commercial ends the titillation provided by women's scandalous sexual behaviour.[24] It must also be admitted in the figures of J.B. and the Invisible Spy, we also see the difficulty of keeping prying eyes out of private places.

NOTES

1. Jerry C. Beasley, *Novels of the 1740s* (Athens: University of Georgia Press, 1982), 46.

2. Eliza Haywood, *Memoirs of a Certain Island Adjacent to the Kingdom of Utopia* (London: n.p., 1724–25), 3.

3. Delariviere Manley, *The New Atalantis*, ed. Rosalind Ballaster (London: Penguin Books, 1992), 13.

4. Eliza Haywood, *The Female Spectator*, 7th ed., 4 vols. (London: T. Gardner, 1771), 1: 3.

5. Eliza Haywood, *Bath Intrigues in Four Letters to a Friend in London*, ed. with an introduction by Simon Varey (Los Angeles: Augustan Reprint Society, 1986), 1. All further parenthetical references are to this edition.

6. Eliza Haywood, "Dedication" to William Yonge in *The Fatal Secret; or, Constancy in Distress*, 2nd ed. (London: J. Roberts, 1724), 3.

7. For a discussion of spectacle and spectatorship in Haywood 's writing see my unpublished dissertation "Beyond Spectacle: Eliza Haywood's Female Spectators" (diss., McMaster University, 1998); and also my article "'That Devil Curiosity Which Too Much Haunts the Minds of Women': Eliza Haywood's Female Spectators," *Lumen: Selected Proceedings from the Canadian Society for Eighteenth-Century Studies*, 16 (1997): 131–46.

8. Virginia Swain, "Lumieres et Vision: Reflections on Sight and Seeing in Seventeenth-and Eighteenth-Century France," *L'Esprit Createur* 27 (1988): 8.

9. Susan Lanser, *Fictions of Authority: Women Writers and Narrative Voice* (Ithaca: Cornell University Press, 1992), 7. The rhetoric of authorship is also the subject of Catherine Gallagher's *Nobody's Story: The Vanishing Acts of Women Writers in the Marketplace, 1670–1820* (Berkeley: University of California Press, 1994), and Tina Krontiris's *Oppositional Voices: Women as Writers and Translators of Literature in the English Renaissance* (London and New York: Routledge, 1992).

10. Eliza Haywood, *The Invisible Spy*, 4 vols. (London: T. Gardner, 1755), 2:13. All further references are to volume and page number of this edition.

11. Haywood's interest in, even preoccupation with, sight and seeing has not gone unnoticed. Two recent articles, Kathryn King's "Spying upon the Conjuror: Haywood, Curiosity, and 'The Novel' in the 1720s," *Studies in the Novel* 30 (1998):178–93, and Barbara Benedict's "The Curious Genre: Female Inquiry in Amatory Fiction," *Studies in the Novel* 30 (1998): 194–210, both regard curiosity as one of the early novel's formative energies. Both essays build on J. Paul Hunter's work on the (sub) literary influences on the early novel, specifically his view that from its inception the novel was an inquisitive genre. See *Before Novels: The Cultural Contexts of English Fiction* (New York: W.W. Norton, 1990). For Peter Brooks forms of ocularity are also central to novelistic discourse because they contribute to the revelation of the body as an object of desire and knowledge. See also his *Bodywork: Objects of Desire in Modern Narrative* (Cambridge, MA: Harvard University Press, 1993).

12. For a history of the tension between these two orders, the visual and the linguistic, see Martin Jay's *Downcast Eyes: The Denigration of Vision in Twentieth-Century French Thought.* (Berkeley: University of California Press, 1993), esp. chap 1, "The Noblest of the Senses: Vision from Plato to Descartes," 21–82.

13. Eliza Haywood, *The British Recluse*; *or, The Secret History of Cleomira, Supposed Dead*, in *Secret Histories, Novels, and Poems*, 3rd ed., 4 vols. (London: A. Bettersworth, C. Hitch, D. Browne, T. Astley, and T. Green, 1732).

14. Joseph Addison and Richard Steele, *The Spectator*, ed. Donald F. Bond, 5 vols. (Oxford: Clarendon Press, 1965), 1: 19–20. All further parenthetical references are to volume and page number of this edition.

15. John Richetti expresses a similar distaste for scandal fiction in his *Popular Fiction Before Richardson: Narrative Patterns 1700–1739* (London: Oxford University Press, 1969), 119.

16. Dustin Griffin's view of satire supports my argument here. His stated purpose is to reintegrate the Menippean tradition into theories of satire and to argue that "satire is problematic, open-ended, essayistic, ambiguous in its relationship to history, uncertain in its political effect, resistant to formal closure, more inclined to ask questions than to provide answers, and ambivalent about the pleasure it offers." See his *Satire: A Critical Reintroduction*. (Lexington: University Press of Kentucky, 1994), 5.

17. Samuel Johnson, "The Rambler" in the *Yale Edition of the Complete Works of Samuel Johnson*, 16 vols., eds. W. J. Bate and Albrecht B. Strauss (New Haven: Yale University Press, 1969), 4: 188–89.

18. For a discussion of the garden as erotic setting see April London, "Placing the Female: The Metonymic Garden in Amatory and Pious Narrative, 1700–1740," in *Fetter'd or Free? British Women Novelists, 1670–1815*, eds. Mary Anne Schofield and Cecilia Macheski (Athens: Ohio University Press, 1986), 101–23

19. Eliza Haywood, "A Discourse Concerning Writings of this Nature," appended to *Letters from a Lady of Quality to a Chevalier* (London: T. Chetwood, 1724), 5–6.

20. Karen Hollis, "Eliza Haywood and the Gender of Print," *The Eighteenth Century* 38 (1997): 45.

21. Marilyn Williamson, *Raising Their Voices: British Women Writers, 1650–1750* (Detroit: Wayne State University Press, 1990), 239. See also Ann Messenger, *His and Hers* (Lexington: University Press of Kentucky, 1986).

22. Scott Paul Gordon, "Voyeuristic Dreams: Mr. Spectator and the Power of Spectacle," *The Eighteenth Century* 36 (1995): 12.

23. Regina Schwartz, "Rethinking Voyeurism and Patriarchy: The Case of *Paradise Lost*," *Representations* 34 (1991): 86.

24. I am indebted to Felicity Nussbaum for reminding me of this seeming inconsistency in Haywood's scandal fiction. Haywood's attempt to blend the cautionary tale with the scandal chronicle, a genre that often uses women for pornographic effect, does suggest that there are contradictory impulses at work in her writing. Yet it is the same dilemma created by her amatory fiction, where representations of seduction, those infamous 'warm scenes' for which she is well known, are intended as warnings of the dangers of giving way to passion. For the most extensive discussion of Haywood's amatory novels to date, see Rosalind Ballaster, *Seductive Forms: Women's Amatory Fiction from 1684–1740* (Oxford: Clarendon Press, 1992).

"Is He No Man?" Toward an Appreciation of Male Effeminacy in English Dance History

JOHN BRYCE JORDAN

> Up until the nineteenth century in Europe, prejudices against the male dancer did not exist.
>
> —Ramsay Burt, *The Male Dancer* (1995)

The male dancer has been an enduring source of anxiety in the United States and England to varying degrees throughout the twentieth century.[1] This anxiety derives from the pervasive attitude that dance is somehow not appropriate for men and the concomitant suspicion that men who dance are in some way not fully masculine. With the male dancer's compromised masculinity, or effeminacy, inevitably also comes the expectation of his homosexuality, given the conflation of these two terms and their mutual implication in modern Western society.[2] This essay investigates the history of the perceived connection between dance and male effeminacy by examining portrayals of male dancers in three dramatic comedies from the English Restoration period. These examples shed light on one stage in the history of effeminacy and demonstrate the importance of dance to the construction of the effeminate man as a recognizable type in English culture. By focusing on examples from the seventeenth century, this essay also challenges certain assumptions common in the dance community, which has typically treated the issue of effeminacy in relation to male dancers as a stereotype of more recent origin. It will be helpful therefore to first address the ramifications of the perceived effeminacy of male dancers on the dance community at large and the consequent treatments of the male dancer typical in popular and scholarly writings on dance as one important context for this investigation.

Although rarely articulated explicitly in polite or scholarly contexts, the widespread expectation of effeminacy among male dancers has nonetheless profoundly shaped the dance community, helping to produce a professional dance world of choreographers, dancers, and audience members disproportionately composed of women.[3] The limited number of men in dance has also created something of a seller's market for male dancers, with lower levels of technical expertise required of men than of women at the entry level, and resulting in relatively more opportunity for men in professional companies.[4] Accompanying this gender imbalance, and at least partly in response to the perceived short supply of skilled male dancers, a tradition has developed of encouraging men to dance, and with it a set of arguments explaining why dance *is* appropriate for men and why the so-called stereotypes about male dancers are incorrect. For instance, dance writers frequently cite the physical demands of ballet as evidence of the male dancer's virility, and the spectacular, athletic dancing of Rudolf Nureyev, Edward Villella, Mikhail Baryshnikov, and others is often treated as a tacit argument for the masculinity of these dancers, and by extension, of male dancers more generally.[5]

This line of reasoning is sometimes supplemented by other arguments which, rather than refute the specific content of the prejudice against the male dancer, instead attempt to reframe it as local and small-minded. One version of this relies on cross-cultural examples to persuade readers that dance is intrinsic to many other societies around the world and should therefore be part of our own.[6] These examples often prominently feature men dancing, implicitly arguing for the importance of male dancers to a healthy, unrepressed society. A different, but related strategy turns instead to history, drawing upon the cultural prestige of the European aristocracy to argue that dance and masculinity are not opposed. The standard dance historical narrative traces ballet's origin to the Renaissance courts of Italy, where dance served to celebrate the prince and to impress visiting dignitaries. It next follows the tradition to France, where the technical foundation of classical ballet was first elaborated. The dance form developed at the French court then spread throughout Europe, until as one dance writer puts it, "Every monarch and princeling from St. Petersburg to Paris and Stockholm to Naples had his ballet."[7] These past aristocratic patrons and participants are recounted to establish the higher status of dance and of male dancers in previous eras, positioning present day ballet and modern dancers as the heirs to a distinguished tradition. Both the historical and the cross-cultural arguments function in a similar way. They attempt to isolate the disparaging twentieth-century Western attitude towards male dancers as the exception to larger global or historical patterns. In so doing, prejudice against men dancing is reinterpreted as ethnocentric or uneducated, and critics of male dancers are portrayed as parochial and unsophisticated.

Lest these sort of pronouncements about male dancing be assumed to be confined to outdated dance texts, one could cite Ramsay Burt's 1995 book *The Male Dancer*, in which the author attempts to address the place of male dancers and the choreographic representations of masculinity in Western art dance, including to a limited degree the issues of effeminacy and homosexuality. Even in this recent book, Burt's argument still tries to confine these issues to the nineteenth and primarily the twentieth centuries, stating that "up until the nineteenth century in Europe, prejudices against the male dancer did not exist" (10). Intentionally or inadvertently, Burt perpetuates a historical narrative which treats the seventeenth and eighteenth centuries as periods of uncomplicated acceptance of dancing for men, and which uses the supposedly recent development of negative attitudes toward male dancers as a tacit rebuttal to such prejudices. The recurrence of this type of argument, whether explicit or implicit, in many surveys of Western dance history calls for a more critical re-examination of the historical evidence, as well as a reassessment of the motives and strategies underlying such apologies for male dancers. Specifically, the broad-sweep histories of popular dance books, which are sometimes also reproduced in more scholarly books such as Burt's, are intended to combat the notion that dancing is unmasculine, and this is necessarily connected to a discomfort with the prevalence of homosexuality among male dancers. The stated desire to increase the number of men in dance is thus in part a desire to increase the number of straight men in dance by downplaying the perception and anecdotal evidence that a large percentage of male dancers are gay and/or effeminate.

In response to these attitudes and approaches to this topic, I would like to propose as an alternative a history of dance which does not apologize for or minimize the associations of Western dance with male effeminacy and homosexuality over the last one hundred and possibly three hundred years, and which instead is interested in further uncovering and examining that relationship, whether factual or only perceived. This would be a history which does not attempt to gloss over the negative attitudes expressed toward male dancers in earlier periods, but which instead examines the purpose and functions of such attitudes in their particular social moments and in the longer development of modern gender and sexual categories. As one step in this critical revision, this essay examines three English Restoration comedies for their portrayals of men who dance. In these accounts it is only a kind of effeminacy and not same-sex desire which is foregrounded in relation to the male dancer, however the sexual desires of the men are called into question in other ways. The examples do nonetheless clearly establish the existence of negative attitudes toward men who dance in a period much earlier than has typically been acknowledged in dance scholarship.

This essay focuses on the English Restoration period in part because of the importance given to the late seventeenth century in traditional narratives of Western dance history, particularly the role of dance at the court of Louis XIV.[8] In standard accounts, this was a time when important people not only respected dance, but danced themselves, giving them a highly informed eye for appreciating the dancing of others. These highly skilled amateurs mingled with professionals in dance-centered spectacles, with no costs spared for costumes and scenic effects. Dance histories inevitably also emphasize the serious political ends served by these danced performances at court. The spectacles were carefully choreographed to glorify the French King, reinforcing his position as the absolute ruler of his country while helping to establish the French court as the cultural center of Europe. Louis' court was widely imitated, often and significantly through the importation of French dances and dancing-masters. Aristocrats throughout Western Europe and England studied French noble style dance, along with the French language and French fashions, in their efforts to emulate *Le Grande Monarque* and the glory of the French court. The centerpiece of this dance-historical utopia was Louis himself, the "Sun King," dubbed so after dancing the role of the sun and dispelling the chaos of night in one of these allegorical spectacles.[9] Proverbially taking a dance lesson every day of his life, Louis' involvement established dance as not just an entertainment for kings to observe passively, but worthy of a ruler's active study and participation. Louis and his courtiers have thus served as reassuring examples both of the eminent place of dance in Western history and the important role of male dancers in that history. As an activity of kings and a social requirement for important men of the past, dance could be refigured as an acceptable—even noble—accomplishment, and despite contemporary appearances to the contrary, a preeminently masculine one. It is not enough, however, to cite the example of Louis' court for historical evidence of dance's past importance and the prominent participation of men without also acknowledging differences in the status of dance in different national contexts. While the dance practice developed at the French court did spread to become popular across Europe, including in England, the specifics of that popularity bear a closer examination. The analysis offered here focuses on the gendered connotations of the dance form as it spread to the English environment. The examples from English dramatic comedy demonstrate that the royal patronage of dance in France in this period did not foreclose other, more critical appraisals of dance in England, and indeed may have been an important motivation for these satirical attacks.

In many surveys of dance history, the English dance tradition seems pale in comparison to its French counterpart. While Paris and Versailles glittered at the center of an elaborate and evolving dance performance genre, England seemingly made few forays into dance innovation before resigning itself to imported artists and a second-hand performance tradition.[10] Though some dance historians point to a vital domestic dance culture during the English Renaissance, broad-sweep dance histories have typically depicted England in the eighteenth and nineteenth centuries as effectively devoid of notable choreographers, performers, and dance writers, with England dropping out of many accounts until the twentieth century.[11] The one important exception in this overview narrative is John Weaver, a dancing-master of the early eighteenth century included in virtually all dance histories. Weaver translated the new French system of dance notation into English and authored his own theoretical and historical treatises on dance.[12] He is most famous, however, for his early choreographic efforts combining dance with pantomime into self-contained dance dramas. Though surveys of dance history sometimes give the impression that Weaver was an anomalous exception to an otherwise limited or non-existent dance tradition in England, such a view is misleading. Weaver was but one of many dance professionals working in London and elsewhere in England in the early eighteenth century, some of whom also published their choreographies in notation.[13] And this community of dance professionals did not, of course, arise suddenly at the turn of the eighteenth century but grew out of an earlier group of teachers and performers; Weaver's father, for instance, was also a dancing-master.[14] Part of the work of this essay then, is to add to our understanding of Weaver's position within this longer trajectory of English dance history by further examining the decades prior to his famous publications and choreographic experiments.

To be sure, a few more focused treatments of English dance history have already begun to uncover a more detailed history of dance in England in the late seventeenth and early eighteenth centuries. One of the most important of these is *Famed for Dance,* a small collection of essays discussing dance in England between 1660 and 1740.[15] But as its title suggests, in an effort to demonstrate the importance of dance in English history, *Famed for Dance* avoids any extended discussion of negative attitudes toward dance or male dancers, concentrating instead on celebrated choreographers, performers, and performances, particularly those at the English court. It thus participates in the same strategy discussed earlier, using an association with the European aristocracy to portray dance as a serious, important, and implicitly masculine activity. Another valuable source, Carol Marsh's "French Court Dance in England, 1706–1740," also focuses much needed attention on this period through close analysis of the dancing manuals and collections of notated dances published in England in the early eighteenth century.[16] But while the efforts of Marsh and other dance scholars have contributed enormously to modern reconstructions of these dances, analysis of the notation sources does not necessarily tell us much about the meaning or reception of the dance form, or about the connotations its performers might have carried in this period. For this sort of information, the dancing manuals need to be supplemented with accounts in other types of sources.

Restoration comedy offers one avenue for investigating these aspects of English dance history, providing clues to understanding England's charged relationship with French dance culture, the changing characteristics of masculinity, and the history of dancing as either a masculine or non-masculine practice. While they do not provide a realistic depiction of the everyday, the comedies do, nonetheless, reference upper-class behavior and comment on it through their satirical portrayals. Thus while the particular extravagances of comic characters like James Howard's Frenchlove or George Etherege's Sir Fopling Flutter may be ridiculously exaggerated, the repeated inclusion of characters like them who adopt French styles does suggest an actual vogue for similar goods and behaviors. And more specifically, the frequent inclusion of dance as one component of these early depictions argues for the popularity of French dancing, at least among a segment of London's upper class, to which the plays were satirically responding. A few examples will serve to demonstrate the existence of this early form of bias against male dancing expressed through its relation to French culture and male effeminacy. Within this context, Weaver's work can be better understood as one outcome of more than forty years of English curiosity about and importation of French dance practices and their gradual assimilation into a thriving domestic dance establishment. This process was not without its resistors and detractors, however, and most interesting for the purposes of this essay is the important role played by notions of masculinity and effeminacy in expressing resistance to this importation of the French dance style.[17]

The English Mounsieur (1663)

Almost immediately after the reopening of the London theaters with the Restoration of Charles II in 1660, a new type of character was introduced onto the English stage. In him, English national identity is contrasted with the French, not through a representation of someone from France, but through an English character who has gone to France and returned to London enamored with French goods and customs. James Howard's *The English Mounsieur* is one of the first plays to incorporate this comic figure, establishing a pattern which would be repeated again and again in later comedies. Frenchlove, the English monsieur of the play's title, is described by the other characters in the first scene as "an effected [*sic*] English man translated into a ridiculous French man," describing not only Frenchlove's comic sin of affectation, but also an English attitude toward French custom in general as itself ridiculous. Both elements are important in understanding the reception of French noble style dance as it began to be introduced into England in the seventeenth century.

A ball scene provides one of the many opportunities used in the play to debunk Frenchlove's frequently expressed belief in the superiority of French goods and customs. An association between affected male characters and dance was to prove popular with audiences, becoming a common feature of English comedy during the first two decades of the Restoration. It's use in *The English Mounsieur* suggests that as early as the 1660s, the relationship between Englishmen and dance was already complicated by issues of gender and national identity. In this play, Frenchlove arrives at a ball as the musicians are beginning to play. After making a formal entrance bow, he immediately attempts to assert his French sensibility and judgment with respect to the dance music. The stage directions indicate that "he beats the time of the Corant false," and his rhythmic mistakes precipitate an argument with the lead musician.[18] Frenchlove is eager to find fault with the English musicians and excuse his own error by claiming a distinction between French and English "time" or rhythm. When the musician protests the non-difference, Frenchlove threatens to speak to the King and have the musician sent to France to study with the King of France's Violins, "to teach you the French way of play" (20). This dialogue associates Frenchlove with both the King of France and, notably, the King of England, implicitly relating Frenchlove's Francophilia to Charles II's own French-influenced sensibilities. Within the play, Frenchlove's threat serves as an example of his overly high self-opinion, in that he presumes an influence at court, while for audiences it served as a reminder of Charles II's recent exile in France and the King's subsequent promotion of many aspects of French culture. That French style is the butt of this and many subsequent plays' satire gives some indication of the nationalist resistance King Charles faced when attempting to introduce or reintroduce aspects of French court practices and tastes in England.

After Frenchlove's argument with the musician, a female character invites Frenchlove to dance a courante, but he resists, still complaining about the musicians.

> Lady Wealthy: Come Mr. Frenchlove, will you dance a Corant?
>
> Frenchlove: Withall my heart Madam, if these fiddlers could play the right French time.
>
> Lady Wealthy: Let them try.
> *(They play, and he takes L. Wealthy by the hand as to begin, but finds fault with their playing and will not dance.)*
>
> Frenchlove: Madam, excuse me 'tis impossible to dance to their playing.
>
> Lady Wealthy: *(aside)* This fool cannot dance, and so puts it off (20).

The courante is one of the only specified dances in early Restoration plays, arguing for its popularity with London audiences, or at least their familiarity with the dance type. The courante's association with Frenchlove also suggests that it sometimes functioned as a sign of Frenchness. Interestingly, in this case it is the English Lady Wealthy who proposes the dance and who seems prepared to dance it with Frenchlove, although presumably she suggests it with the expectation that it would appeal to his French tastes. She is also the one to voice the play's critical assessment that Frenchlove is using the musical disagreement to hide the fact that he cannot actually dance. Her familiarity with the courante and her willingness to perform it, however, are in contrast to the other characters present, particularly the men, who, despite their presence at the ball, do not participate. The male lead, Welbred, enters the room following Frenchlove's failure to dance, and chastises Frenchlove and the others for not dancing: "What are you all mad good people, to have music and no dancing, why, how now Mr. Frenchlove won't you let those ladies see your rare quality" (20). Though Welbred feigns dismay at the lack of dancing at the ball, the complete lack of effort at dancing by him or anyone else suggests that dancing, and in particular the courante, was one of the practices associated with

French culture that audiences would have expected only someone like Frenchlove to attempt. To have Welbred or Comely or one of the other male characters dance a courante would have worked against the comic contrast the play constructs between Frenchlove and these other "regular" Englishmen. As with other examples of Frenchlove's supposed refinement, the play takes a patriotic delight in displaying his actual inability and lack of perceptiveness, undercutting Frenchlove's self-aggrandizing claims about the exceptional quality of French goods and practices and the superiority of his own Francophile tastes.

These early intersections between dance, gender and nationality are reinforced at the end of the play when two of the women characters perform identifiably English dances. Despite often having little or no motivation from plot events, ending a comedy with dancing was to become a very common formula in Restoration theater. In this case, the play ends with two solo dances by women. The first is a jig, which the dancing character identifies as her town jig, and which Frenchlove dismisses as "English." Then another woman, who had been masquerading as a Francophile, reveals her true English identity to Frenchlove by dancing "like an Englishwoman." Both of these instances, the only actual dancing in the play, underscore the position of dance in relation to issues of both gender and national identity. This scene, taken in tandem with the earlier ball scene where Lady Wealthy was the only character actually prepared to dance, suggests that a positive or at least neutral relationship between women and dance was already in place in the early 1660s. In this very early play, while English men do not even consider dancing unless they are comically Frenchified, English women are able to dance for others without negative consequence or commentary. Though some other early plays were organized around anti-Puritan sentiments, which allowed male dancing to be on the side of more sympathetic, non-Puritan characters, as the French-affected character grew in dramatic importance, male dancing became less tenable apart from satirical portrayals and became primarily a performance of foreign affectation and foolishness.[19] Female characters, however, largely escaped these negative associations, and so were more likely to be featured and accepted as dancers, as they are in the conclusion to *The English Mounsieur*.

The Gentleman Dancing-Master (1672)

William Wycherley's *The Gentleman Dancing-Master*, provides another clear case of male dancing belittled through its association with a foolish character affected with French tastes and manners.[20] The play begins with the young heroine, Hippolyta, scheduled to marry her cousin, Monsieur Parris, a match decided not by her but by her father. Predictably, Hippolyta is not interested in Parris or his French ways, and she devises a scheme to have him unwittingly introduce her to Gerrard, the desirable male in the play. When her suspicious father catches Hippolyta with Gerrard in her room, she has Gerrard pretend to be a dancing-master sent by her Frenchified fiancé to prepare her to dance a courante at their wedding. These faux dancing lessons serve as the main plot device and give the play its title.

The play makes clear that Hippolyta had previously studied dancing at the Hackney School, a girl's academy.[21] Thus the "lessons" depicted in the play are to help her brush up on her technique before the wedding. The association of dancing with a girls' school again suggests that French noble style dances such as the courante were already somewhat gendered as a woman's activity, or at least that such dancing skill was not considered ridiculous or inappropriate for young women. This is decidedly in contrast to the male characters in the play, for whom dancing ability serves as a mark of foreignness and deficient masculinity. Though the fiancé, Monsieur Parris, never has the opportunity in the play to actually perform a dance, he does on two occasions offer to dance, and other situations also associate dancing with Parris's Francophile tastes.[22] The most important of these is perhaps Hippolyta's attribution of the idea of her dancing lessons to him. Though the ruse is actually Hippolyta's idea and is carried out by Gerrard, the plan is made believable to the father by being attributed to Monsieur Parris. Parris also highlights dance when he inadvertently provides a catalog of his own tastes in response to Hippolyta's request for a description of Gerrard. After allowing that Gerrard is handsome, witty, brave, and of good sense and judgment, Parris still cannot give him an enthusiastic endorsement. When pressed why, he gives many examples of Gerrard's supposed failings, including, "Then for being well-bred, you shall judge: first, he can't dance a step, nor sing a French song, nor swear a French oate [*sic*], nor use the polite French word in his conversation" (1.1.127–29). Notably Parris begins this list of important qualities with dance. Gerrard's inability to dance, (or sing or speak in French) are signs of Gerrard's lack of good breeding in Parris's eyes, and so implicitly speak well of Gerrard to Hippolyta and the audience. Grouped as it is with these other ridiculed skills, dancing is marked as something extraneous to an English gentleman's training and something he is better off without.

After some initial hesitation, Hippolyta's father, Don Diego, agrees to let the dancing lessons continue. Though generally approving of the dancing lessons as part of the wedding preparations, Diego states that he would prefer a Spanish sarabande to a French courante because he is as enamored of all things Spanish as Parris is in love with things French. From the English perspective, Spanish and French characters were diametrical opposites, providing several comic opportunities to pit Parris and Don Diego's tastes against each other.[23] The sarabande is one of a number of dance and music forms believed to have its origin in the Western Hemisphere and to have been introduced to Europe via the Spanish as a result of their colonization efforts in the Americas.[24] It was thus a logical dance type to be associated with Don Diego. This international exchange of dance forms is referenced again later in a scene between Gerrard and Parris. By this point Don Diego has insisted that Parris renounce his French speech and fashions and instead adopt a Spanish wardrobe or be forbidden to marry Hippolyta. While in this new Spanish dress, Parris meets up with Gerrard, and knowing of Gerrard's disguise as a dancing-master, teases him, saying, "Poor angry dancing-master. Prithee match my Spanish pumps and legs with one of your best and newest sarabands. Ha ha ha! Come—" (5.1.70–74). This scene re-emphasizes the Spanish association of the sarabande, however it also foregrounds Parris's attention to both clothing and dancing, as he identifies his new persona in relation to his shoes, leggings, and willingness to dance in the Spanish style. Gerrard, of course, does not comply with the taunting request for a dance tune, and instead angrily draws his sword and lunges at Parris, making him dance out of the way. Parris begins to fight back, but then decides against it, and this unwillingness to fight aligns him with other affected males from the comedies, who are often portrayed as cowards.[25] Meanwhile, Gerrard's heroic manliness benefits from his macho display of anger and willingness to fight, heightening the dramatic contrast between the two men. Gerrard's characteristics, as those of the attractive male lead, represent the desirable qualities in an English gentleman at this moment. And complementary to Gerrard's obvious willingness to fight and his skill with a sword is his demonstrated unwillingness and inability to dance. His disguise as a dancing-master provides multiple occasions when it would be helpful to dance at least a little to carry off the deceit, and his complete lack of knowledge forces Hippolyta to make up excuse after excuse to her father. Gerrard's incapacity and frequent protests work to distance him from what must have been very inappropriate skills for an appealing male character. Dance in the French noble style, while now portrayed as part of an ordinary upper-class girl's education, is still held at arm's length from the male hero, and it is his inability in this area which marks him as masculine and desirable.

Monsieur Parris, on the other hand, who repeatedly proclaims his dance skill, is explicitly emasculated. This is apparent from the first scene when he is discussed in a dialogue between Hippolyta and her servant Prue. They are complaining about being shut indoors and forbidden any contact with men, when Hippolyta reconsiders for a moment: "But . . . what do we make of . . . my husband elect . . . ? We have had his company these three days. Is he no man?" Prue replies, "No faith, he's but a *monsieur*. But you'll resolve yourself that question within these three days, for by that time he'll be your husband" (1.1.29–35). Playing on what must have already been an established joke disparaging the masculinity of the French-affected Englishmen, the straight-talking servant woman doesn't hesitate to discount Parris's manhood, calling him a "monsieur" as if this were a self-explanatory insult. She even suggests that he is impotent or otherwise sexually compromised in claiming that Hippolyta will discover his deficiencies once married. Later the play further relates Parris's concern with French fashion to a diminished interest in women. When Don Diego first demands that he give up his French clothes, Parris protests saying, "I am ruinne den, undonne. Have some consideration for me, for dere is not the least ribbon of my garniture but is as dear to me as your daughter, jarni" (3.1.255–57). Like other similar French-affected characters in the comedies, Parris seems more oriented towards French style than toward romantic or sexual liaisons with women, valuing the decorations on his clothes as much or more than his intended bride. Though not obviously marked as sodomitical, his limited interest in women and his avoidance of fighting, both of which are implicitly related to his fascination with French fashions including dance, all work to mark Parris as "no man," and locate him within, to paraphrase Wayne Koestenbaum, the compelling saga of male effeminacy.[26]

The Man of Mode; or, Sir Fopling Flutter (1676)

Though clearly indebted to earlier characters like Frenchlove and Monsieur Parris, Sir Fopling Flutter is perhaps the best known representative of the French-affected Englishman, as well as of a certain model of effeminate aristocratic excess, thanks to the enduring popularity of Etherege's play. And even more than in the two comedies discussed already, dance in the French noble style is here explicitly tied to the French-affected male. This is evident from the start of the play when Fopling is first referenced by the other characters. After several devastating descriptions mocking Fopling's various affectations, one of the men reports Fopling's own self-description, which he reportedly called a "catalogue of his good qualities, under the character of a complete gentleman." The list includes to "dress well, dance well, fence well, have a genius for love letters, and agreeable voice for a chamber, be very amorous, something discreet, but not overconstant."[27] Just as in *The Gentleman Dancing-Master,* dance takes a prominent place on this mocked list of skills. Fopling's high opinion of dance returns to comic effect a number of times in the play. The next is at a social gathering at one of the other character's homes. Fopling, hearing music, crashes the party on his way home. He arrives with a group of masked dancers who are acting as his footmen and whom he describes as "A set of balladines, whom I picked out of the best in France" (4.1.267). They eventually perform a dance for the assembly, allowing the inclusion of a dance for six men in the French noble style within the play. This type of performance within a performance was one of the common devices for including dance on stage. This particular dance is largely designed for comic effect, with Fopling talking over the performance to criticize the one English dancer in his troupe:

> To an English dancer, English motions! I was forced to entertain this fellow, one of my set miscarrying. —Oh, horrid! Leave your damned manner of dancing and put on the French air. Have you not a pattern before you?—Pretty well! Imitation in time may bring him to something (4.1.303–308).

While no other record of the choreography is preserved in the text, one can imagine a figured choreography for six, five of whom gracefully intertwine, precisely marking out the dance rhythm in counterpoint to the music, while the sixth awkwardly stumbles and casts about for his place in imitation of the others. Unlike the two previously discussed plays, which mostly reference French dance without actually including much of it, *The Man of Mode* allows this performance of French noble style dancing, albeit still mediated through humor. Similar to the ambivalence expressed elsewhere in the play about clothes and other French fashions, this danced scene would offer the audience an opportunity to enjoy French dancing while maintaining a degree of distance thanks to the bumbling of the English dancer. Nevertheless, this higher degree of inclusion points to a growing acceptance of French dancing among London audiences, even if still not whole-hearted.

In the mid-1670s of *The Man of Mode*, however, it is explicitly French noble style dancing which is held at a distance, not dance understood more generally. The sympathetic characters can take part in a dance, and thereby perform it for the audience of the play, but it is English country dances which they are allowed to perform. These were social dances for groups of six or more people in which participants were paired with a partner of the opposite sex. These dances first began to be collected and published in

1651 by John Playford under the title *The English Dancing-Master*, which continued to be reprinted in updated form well into the eighteenth century. Though new choreographies continued to be created, the dancing was treated as a traditional English form. The dances became a common feature of theatrical comedies of the 1670s and after, often performed at the happy conclusion of a play. At the time of *The Man of Mode*, English country dance was established enough for the sophisticated urbanites of the play to be depicted taking part in it while avoiding any critical commentary. In contrast, the French dancing style of Fopling was still new enough to be kept at arm's length, placed on the foreign bodies of his servants and on the self-consciously Frenchified Fopling himself. Similar to *The English Monsieur* where Frenchlove's dancing is contrasted to wholesome English jigs, here the patriotic role is taken by the country dances. But Fopling is not appalled by the English dances as was his predecessor Frenchlove, and Fopling may even participate in the final celebratory dance of the play, typically a country dance. Also significant, the other characters watch and presumably enjoy Fopling's troupe of French dancers, with no disparaging comments being made about them, further suggesting an increased interest in the French form as long as it is performed by non-English bodies.[28]

When Fopling introduces his group of "balladines," the heroine, Harriet, goads Fopling on to dance himself. Fopling resists the woman's entreaties, though not without making excuses, and in the process brags about his abilities. Claiming fatigue, he says,

> I have sat up so damned late and drunk so cursed hard since I came to this lewd town that I am fit for nothing but low dancing now—a *courante*, a *bourrée*, or a *menuet*. But St. André tells me, if I will but be regular, in one month I shall rise again (4.1.286–90).

He then "endeavors at a caper" and curses "debauchery" for his (implied) failure. His excuses provide the opportunity for Fopling to show off his knowledge, naming three dance types of the French noble style and categorizing them as low dances. Fopling thereby expands the number of French dances named in English comedy beyond just courantes and sarabandes to include bourrées and minuets, demonstrating their growing familiarity to English audiences. The audience is also expected to recognize the name of St. André, a noted French dancing-master who had recently worked in England. Fopling drops the name of St. André, just as he does the names of French wig and clothing makers elsewhere, in a (failed) attempt to present himself as fashionable and sophisticated.[29] To further encourage Fopling's boasting, another character claims to have heard Fopling's dancing commended, to which he responds with characteristic immodesty, "It had the good fortune to please in Paris. I was judged to rise within an inch as high as the basqué in an entry I danced there" (4.1.293–95).[30] Fopling, claiming to have performed an "entry" or *entrée*, a figured choreography in the French style, ends by making a boast about the height of his jumps. It is important to see in this bragging Fopling's attempt to shore up his masculinity with claims of physical prowess, as well as the play's refiguring of this claim as ridiculous and inappropriate. Whether because he is not able to actually produce the claimed feat, or because of the perceived absurdity of such tests, it is obvious that the play does not value his supposed jumping ability. Masculinity in this context is dependent on something this man lacks, and his claims of dancing prowess do not convince anyone otherwise. Instead, they only further contribute to his belittlement. Later in the play, Fopling announces his intention to perform a ballet, which is both in tension with, and a tool of, his attention to women. One of the characters asks Fopling why he doesn't go after Mrs. Loveit, a woman who has scorned him, and Fopling replies, "An intrigue now would be but a temptation to me to throw away that vigor on one which I mean shall shortly make my court to the whole sex in a ballet" (5.2.339–41). Though his plan to mount and star in a ballet principally serves as yet another opportunity to expose Fopling's absurdly high opinion of himself, the scene also reasserts the specific link between Fopling and French dance, as well as drawing attention to his peculiar relationship to women.

In *The English Mounsieur*, *The Gentleman Dancing-Master*, and other Restoration comedies, affected male characters are typically portrayed as less sexually motivated than the sympathetic male leads. Frenchlove disdained all English women, regardless of attractiveness, simply because they weren't French, and Monsieur Parris begged to keep his French clothes claiming to love each ribbon more than his fiancée.[31] Fopling reveals a similar attitude when he renounces his interest in Mrs. Loveit, saying, "No one woman is worth the loss of a cut in a caper" (5.2.343). But Fopling specifically describes his intentions in mounting a ballet as a way to "court the whole sex," complicating the easy interpretation of Fopling as uninterested in women. In fact, from the first time Fopling is introduced, he is said to be "brisk upon the ladies" (1.1.361), and several times in the play he is described or shown actively socializing with women, with at least the formal pretext of some romantic interest. Like previous French-affected characters, Fopling does seem more strongly motivated by his obsession with things French than by sexual or romantic attractions. But unlike them, his interest in women is never so opposed to his love of France. For instance, he describes his French clothes as made "to make my court to you ladies" (4.1.301–302). Also, unlike those previous characters, Fopling seems to actively seek out women's company. But while Fopling understands these interactions as part of courtship, the play subtly casts them in a different light. And as subsequent plays will make even more explicit, a male type is being mapped out here: one who enjoys women's company, but who does not take advantage of that familiarity for sexual ends. Rather Fopling and the women share certain tastes and interests, including an attention to personal appearance and a catty evaluation of the appearance of others, all of which only serves to throw his masculinity further into question. Rather than being interested in women, Fopling is portrayed as having a woman's interests, or at least interests and enthusiasms incompatible with masculinity, including French noble style dance. And it is these interests which help paint him as deserving of the play's ridicule.

In light of these findings, the assertions of Ramsay Burt and other dance historians need to be reassessed. This research strongly suggests that negative attitudes toward male dancing did not arise for the first time in England in the nineteenth century as has usually been assumed. Already in the seventeenth century, dramatic depictions align dance, particularly French noble style dance, with the most ridiculous male figures. These characters' interest in dance is part of their larger fascination with French culture, and with that interest comes an expectation of a kind of male effeminacy. This is most obvious in Monsieur Parris being called "no man," but even earlier in *The English Mounsieur*, the affected male character's sexual motivation is subordinated to his Francophile tastes. This diminished sexual interest in women, along with an aversion to fighting, and later, a preference for socializing with women over men, all contribute to the portrayal of these male characters as deficiently masculine or effeminate. These portrayals thus demonstrate that a connection between effeminacy and male dancing was in circulation in England at least as early as the 1660s and 70s. The particular relationship of the English to French dance demonstrated here also offers an important additional perspective on the value and status of dance at the time of Louis XIV. Though dance may have served important political purposes as part of Louis XIV's absolutist strategies, this was no guarantee that dance was held in equal regard in other national contexts. And while English Kings and Queens may have attempted to imitate Louis' use of dance as part of their political self-representation, the satirical treatments of French dance in these plays should serve as a reminder that such danced displays would not necessarily be received by everyone as glorious and ennobling.

Despite these early satires of dance and male dancers, however, subsequent comedies suggest a growing interest in and acceptance of French dance over the Restoration period by English audiences. In some plays, such as Thomas Shadwell's *Bury Fair* (1689) and George Farquhar's *The Constant Couple* (1699), dance begins to shift its allegiance away from the ridiculed affected male characters and instead becomes more closely aligned with the male protagonists. In other comedies, such as Aphra Behn's *The Emperor of the Moon* (1687) and William Congreve's *The Old Bachelor* (1693), more elaborate danced scenes begin to be included either as interruptions to or congruous with the dramatic plot. Dance appears to have become more acceptable for men to participate in and more popular as a feature of stage entertainment, both of which contributed to the support of a relatively large number of dance professionals working in London and surrounding areas.[32] Appreciating this changing English relationship to French dance allows us to better understand the work of John Weaver. Rather than the seemingly isolated and anomalous example of dance theory and practice described in many surveys of dance history, his work can be better understood as part of a burgeoning English dance culture, itself the direct result of at least forty years of English interest in French noble style dance. Seen in this light, the early adopters of French noble style dance in England take on a new importance, and we can perhaps find in Frenchlove and Sir Fopling the trace of those early English gentlemen originally responsible for the importation and promotion of French dancing in England. Though intensely disparaged as effeminate, self-aggrandizing, and of poor judgment, the Restoration men who served as models for, and who were lampooned in, the portrayals of Frenchlove, Monsieur Parris, and Sir Fopling, helped lay the groundwork for the integration of dance and other elements of French style into English aristocratic culture that took place at the end of the seventeenth century. Weaver and the other early eighteenth-century English dancing-masters can be seen as owing a debt to these earlier Francophiles, condemned as effeminate, whose enthusiasm, participation, and patronage helped make possible the flowering of dance in England in the first half of the eighteenth century.

By attending to the issue of effeminacy as it is articulated in relation to the dancing man, this work also participates in a recent trend in scholarship on the history of sexuality which has broadened the scope of study beyond a narrow focus on sex practices to include other components relevant to modern sexual identities.[33] In this more genealogical approach, elements which may or may not have been directly related to same-sex desire in their own period are nonetheless of interest for their importance to later identity constructions. In the case presented here, prior to the more explicit link between male same-sex desire and various effeminate characteristics which was to become so prominently articulated in the eighteenth century, there were already in circulation in the seventeenth century ideas about a class of effeminate men with a particular relationship to Frenchness.[34] This earlier category of effeminate men is of central importance to later constructions of the effeminate male sodomite in the eighteenth century, which in turn has a more distant, but still significant relationship to the classification of the sexual invert in the nineteenth century, and ultimately to gay and queer identities in the twentieth. Though the affected man of the seventeenth century was not identical to and did not function in the same way as these later typologies, the earlier figure is nonetheless an important contributor to subsequent constructions of sexual and gender categories as they evolved in the eighteenth century. And interestingly, although perhaps not so surprisingly, dance plays a significant role in at least some of these early formations.

NOTES

1. In the discussion that follows I am principally concerned with the place of the male dancer in ballet, modern dance, and their historical predecessors. Men in some Western dance forms, particularly tap dance, have to a certain degree avoided the stereotypes that affect male dancers in other styles. Though an analysis of why some dance forms are less affected by anti-male dancer prejudice than others is beyond the scope of this study, I would predict that even men in tap and other popular dance styles have been affected to some extent by the attitudes discussed here.

2. For one study of the modern interrelation of these ideas from the perspective of English literature see Joseph Bristow, *Effeminate England: Homoerotic Writing After 1885* (New York: Columbia University Press, 1995).

3. Ramsay Burt cites a 1969 report by the Arts Council of Great Britain indicating that seventy-five percent of ballet audiences in Great Britain were female. See *The Male Dancer: Bodies, Spectacle, Sexualities* (London: Routledge, 1995), 200 n. 3. A more recent study in the United States reports that seventy-three percent of the choreographers surveyed were female. See Dick Netzer and Ellen Parker, *Dancemakers: A Study Report Published by the National Endowment for the Arts* (Washington, DC.: National Endowment for the Arts, 1993), 16.

4. For a reference to the limited supply of male dancers, see Lincoln Kirstein and Muriel Stuart, *The Classic Ballet: Basic Technique and Terminology* (New York: Alfred A. Knopf, 1952), 8, and for the resultant decreased competition that male dancers face, see Thalia Mara, *So You Want to Be a Ballet Dancer* (New York: Pitman Publishing, 1959), 24. For the relatively lower levels of technical skill among male dancers in Britain, see Mary Clark and Clement Crisp, *Dancer: Men in Dance* (London: British Broadcasting Corporation, 1984), 173.

5. For example, see Mary Clark and Clement Crisp, *Understanding Ballet*, (New York: Harmony Books, 1976), 12, 15, 20; and Camilla Jessel, *Life at the Royal Ballet School*, (New York: Methuen, 1979), 41, 45.

6. See, for example, Ted Shawn, *The American Ballet* (New York: Henry Holt and Company, 1926), 88–98; Curt Sachs, *World History of the Dance*, trans. Bessie Schönberg (New York: Seven Arts, 1952); José Limón, "The Virile Dance" in *The Dance Has Many Faces*, 2d ed., ed. Walter Sorell (New York: Columbia University Press, 1966); Erick Hawkins, "Why Does a Man Dance, and What Does He Dance, and Who Should Watch Him?" in *The Dance Experience: Readings in Dance Appreciation*, ed. Myron Howard Nadel and Constance Nadel Miller (New York: Universe Books, 1978); and Jamake Highwater, *Dance: Rituals of Experience*, rev. ed. (New York: Alfred van der Marck Editions, 1985).

7. Peter Brinson, "The Social Setting" in *The Ballet in Britain: Eight Oxford Lectures* (London: Oxford University Press, 1962), 19. Other examples include Walter Sorell, *Dance in Its Time* (Garden City, NY: Anchor Press, 1981); Selma Jeanne Cohen, *Dance as a Theatre Art: Source Readings in Dance History from 1581 to the Present* (New York: Harper and Row, 1974), 6–9; and Ivor Guest, *The Dancer's Heritage: A Short History of Ballet* (New York: Macmillan, 1961), 1–11. For examples overtly emphasizing the role of men, see Walter Terry, *Great Male Dancers of the Ballet* (Garden City, NY: Anchor Books, 1978), 10–19; Alexander Bland and John Percival, *Men Dancing: Performers and Performances* (New York: Macmillan, 1984), 10–16; and Clarke and Crisp, *Dancer*, 7–18.

8. For examples assigning special importance to the court of Louis XIV in dance history, see Mary Clarke and Clement Crisp, *Ballet: An Illustrated History* (New York: Universe Books, 1973), 28–30; Alexander Bland, *A History of Ballet and Dance in the Western World* (London: Barrie and Jenkins, 1976), 48–49; Sandra Noll Hammond, *Ballet Basics* 2d ed. (Palo Alto, CA: Mayfield Publishing Company, 1984), 11–15; Lincoln Kirstein, *Four Centuries of Ballet: Fifty Masterworks* (New York: Praeger Publishers, 1970; New York: Dover, 1984), 86–87; Highwater, *Dance: Rituals of Experience*, 67–70; and Ferdinando Reyna, *A Concise History of Ballet* (New York: Grosset and Dunlap, 1965), 53–57. A more recent example, albeit with different theoretical objectives, is Norman Bryson's "Cultural Studies and Dance History," in *Meaning in Motion: New Cultural Studies of Dance*, ed. Jane C. Desmond (Durham, NC: Duke University Press, 1997), 55–77.

9. Bland, *A History of Ballet and Dance,* 48.

10. For instance, Lincoln Kirstein's ubiquitous, if venerable, *Dance: A Short History of Classic Theatrical Dancing* (New York: G. P. Putnam's Sons, 1935) concludes, "In fact the English, except for their Anti-Masque, have always kept aside from the main course in the development of theatrical dancing. . . . [T]here have been very few (if any) great English dancers, and only recently has a contemporary national ballet been able to hold audiences which have always been more than eager to acclaim French or Russian dancers" (176).

11. For discussions of dance during the English Renaissance, see Arnold Haskell, "The English School of Ballet," in *The Ballet in Britain*, 31; and Peter Brinson,

"The Social Setting," in the same volume. See also Skiles Howard's more recent work, *The Politics of Courtly Dancing in Early Modern England* (Amherst: University of Massachusetts Press, 1998).

12. Weaver's collected works are reprinted in facsimile in Richard Ralph, *The Life and Works of John Weaver* (New York: Dance Horizons, 1985).

13. Other English dancing-masters whose work survives in notation include Mr. Isaac, John Essex, and Kellom Tomlinson. For a list of extant English dance publications from the early eighteenth century, see Wendy Hilton, *Dance and Music of Court and Theater: Selected Writings of Wendy Hilton* (Princeton, NJ: Princeton Book Company, 1981; Stuyvesant, NY: Pendragon Press, 1997), 338–341.

14. Ifan Kyrle Fletcher, "Ballet in England, 1660–1740," in Ifan Kyrle Fletcher, Selma Jeanne Cohen, and Roger Lonsdale, *Famed for Dance: Essays on the Theory and Practice of Theatrical Dancing in England, 1660–1740* (New York: New York Public Library, 1960), 14.

15. Ibid.

16. Carol Marsh, "French Court Dance in England, 1706–1740: A Study of the Sources" (Ph.D. diss., City University of New York, 1985).

17. The type of dance most important to this discussion is known today as baroque dance or dance in the French noble style. Both a social dance and, with the addition of more complex steps and technical flourishes, a theatrical performance form, the French noble style is a demanding dance form in which participants mark out a visual rhythm in counterpoint to the musical phrasing through the regulated raising and lowering of the body. Rather than conforming the body's parts into geometric shapes as in nineteenth-century ballet, the baroque dancer traces geometric paths through the room, while maintaining a graceful poise and noble bearing. The baroque dancer most typically moves in dynamic relationship to a partner, whose physical size and movement style produce a unique expanse of movement across the dance area. A successful performance requires each dancer to precisely and symmetrically match his or her partner's scale of movement and thus produce a harmonious whole. Based on the extant repertoire of notated dances, the vast majority of which are for a man and a woman, the style's principal focus is the cross-gendered couple. Several other standard, though less common variations were also performed, however, including versions for same gender couples, solo dances for men and women, as well as a small number of group works. The social form provided an opportunity for both men and women of high birth to demonstrate and reinforce their noble status through a performance of grace and nonchalance under the strain of being observed by King and fellow aristocrats, who, as dancers themselves, were well qualified to appreciate the challenges of the dance form and the marks of a particularly successful performance. These observers were necessarily also well qualified, and perhaps sometimes even eager for the opportunity, to perceive one another's missteps.

The three examples below focus particular attention on the French noble style either in isolation or in contrast to other English styles of dance both because of the French form's foreign origin and the relative newness of the form to English audiences. Over the succeeding several decades, French dancing, as it was known in the period, was to become increasingly popular, with the social dance form becoming a standard component of upper- and sometimes middle-class English social life, while the essentially similar but more virtuosic theatrical form became a featured entertainment on English stages. The comedies of the 1660s and 1670s preserve some of the initial English reactions to this new and highly demanding dance style which was to spread across Europe in the early eighteenth century and eventually develop into modern ballet technique. For an extensive analysis of this form from the perspective of dance reconstruction, see Hilton, *Dance and Music of Court and Theater.* For an exhaustive catalog of the choreographies which have survived in notation, see Meredith Little and Carol G. Marsh, *La Danse Noble: An Inventory of Dances and Sources* (New York: Broude Brothers, 1992).

18. James Howard, *The English Mounsieur*, Augustan Reprint Society Publication, nos. 182–83 (Los Angeles: William Andrews Clark Memorial Library, University of California, Los Angeles, 1977), 20.

19. For one early example of French dancing treated more sympathetically, see John Tatham, *The Rump; or, The Mirrour of the Late Times,* in *The Dramatic Works of John Tatham* (1871; New York: Benjamin Blom, 1967), 270–72.

20. Jennifer Kaye Lowe Martin has also discussed the dancing in Wycherley's play in "The English Dancing-Master, 1660–1728: His Role at Court, in Society and on the Public Stage" (Ph.D. diss., University of Michigan, 1977).

21. William Wycherley, *The Gentleman Dancing-Master*, in *The Country Wife and Other Plays,* ed. Peter Dixon (Oxford: Oxford University Press, 1996), 2.2.457–60.

22. When Don Diego demands to see how the dance lessons are progressing, Monsieur offers to dance with Hippolyta since Gerrard, unable to dance, refuses (4.1.678–79). See also Monsieur's request for a sarabande, discussed below.

23. For the English understanding of the French and Spanish as having opposite characters, see *Gentleman Dancing-Master*, 424 n. 146.

24. Betty Bang Mather and Dean M. Karns, *Dance Rhythms of the French Baroque: A Handbook for Performance* (Bloomington: Indiana University Press, 1987), 291.

25. See, for example, the characters Vapor and Slander in Robert Howard and George Villiers, 2d Duke of Buckingham, *The Country Gentleman* (1669), or the title character in John Crowne, *Sir Courtly Nice* (1685).

26. Wayne Koestenbaum's *The Queen's Throat: Opera, Homosexuality, and the Mystery of Desire* (New York: Vintage Books, 1993) first suggested to me the importance and the little studied nature of the history of effeminacy: "The falsetto is part of the history of effeminacy—a compelling saga yet to be written" (164–65).

27. George Etherege, *The Man of Mode; or, Sir Fopling Flutter* ed. W. B. Carnochan (Lincoln: University of Nebraska Press, 1966) 1.1.365–67.

28. The two old-fashioned characters are, however, somewhat taken aback, the man mistaking the dancing for a "mumming," an out-of-date term for a masked performance, and the woman worrying about who might be hiding behind the masks (4.1.309–13).

29. St. André was a French choreographer and dancer who was brought to London to direct the dances in a production of *Psyche* at the Duke's theater in 1674. He may have been named as Master of the Compositions for Ballets by Charles II (Fletcher, "Ballet in England," 8–9).

30. Significantly, one important Englishman who did actually dance an entrée in Paris with St. André was James Crofts, Duke of Monmouth, the illegitimate son of Charles II. According to Fletcher, in 1672 King Charles II aided Louis XIV in his battles against Holland by sending British troops under Monmouth's command. That same year Monmouth danced with St. André in a performance at the French court, and Monmouth subsequently persuaded St. André to return with him to England ("Ballet in England," 7–9). Given the similarities, the depiction of Fopling is perhaps intended in part as a lampoon of Monmouth and his interest in French dancing.

31. *English Monsieur*, 5, and *Gentleman Dancing-Master* 3.1.255–57.

32. For a list of dancing-masters working in England in the early eighteenth century, see Marsh, "French Court Dance in England," 289–299.

33. Two very different examples of scholarship exploring more than the sexual in the history of sexuality include George Haggerty, *Men in Love: Masculinity and Sexuality in the Eighteenth Century* (New York: Columbia University Press, 1999) and Kevin Kopelson, *The Queer Afterlife of Vaslav Nijinsky* (Stanford: Stanford University Press, 1997).

34. Scholarship arguing for a new association between sodomy and effeminacy in eighteenth-century English culture, including the apparent development of a subculture of effeminate sodomites or "mollies" in London at the turn of the eighteenth century, includes Randolph Trumbach's influential essay "The Birth of the Queen: Sodomy and the Emergence of Gender Equality in Modern Culture, 1660–1750" in *Hidden from History: Reclaiming the Gay and Lesbian Past*, ed. Martin Duberman, Martha Vicinus, and George Chauncey, Jr. (New York: Meridian, 1989); and Alan Bray, *Homosexuality in Renaissance England* (London: GMP, 1982). Cameron McFarlane's more recent work raises important questions about the theory of a radical shift in the understanding of sodomy in relation to effeminacy as articulated by Bray, Trumbach, and others. See *The Sodomite in Fiction and Satire, 1660–1750* (New York: Columbia University Press, 1997). Nevertheless, the hypothesis of a significant shift in understanding in England between the Restoration and the eighteenth-century remains suggestive and is at least not contradicted by the examples discussed here. None of these three portrayals of effeminate men from the comedies include any discussion or obvious implication of sodomitical behavior.

Lancashire Spiritual Culture and the Question of Magic

DAVID PAXMAN

The last chapter of Fielding's *Tom Jones* reports that Mr. Blifil, the novel's chief hypocrite, has gone "to one of the northern Counties, about 200 Miles distant from *London*," where he has "turned Methodist, in hopes of marrying a very rich Widow of that Sect."[1] The narrator doesn't name Blifil's destination, but 200 crow miles north northeast of London would land him in Lancashire, between Manchester and Lancaster, while 197 road miles would place him smack in Manchester. Fielding chose Blifil's destination carefully: Lancashire had a reputation for strong religious zeal of the kind he despised, and he meant to link it to Blifil's hypocrisy. Literature links both strong Catholicism and Protestant dissent to Lancashire. Shakespeare biographers now fill in some of his missing years by tracing him to "Catholic Lancashire," where he may have worked in the household of Thomas Hoghton as a tutor and secretary. Moll Flanders' Catholic friends in that county introduce her to Jemmy, her Lancashire husband of whom she was especially fond, and a Catholic priest performs the marriage rites. Defoe's Colonel Jack is also married in Lancashire by a disguised Catholic priest, of whom "there are many in that Part of the Country."[2] In the nineteenth century Elizabeth Gaskell's *Mary Barton: A Tale of Manchester Life* (1848) is distinguished by Gaskell's desire to offer Christian conduct as a solution to the economic and political strife brought by industrialization.

In addition to evangelism and Nonconformity, Lancashire had a reputation for occult phenomena such as magic, conjuring, and prophesying. Heywood and Broome's *The Late Lancashire Witches* (1634) and Thomas Shadwell's *The Lancashire Witches, and Teague o Divelly the Irish Priest* (1681) both recall occurrences of witchcraft. Shadwell depicts the witches as mischief makers in whom only the most ignorant and illiterate characters believe, and the Irish priest as a fraud. However, the satirical thrusts are complicated by an irony.[3] The level-headed and skeptical Hartford jeers at any belief in witches, even while the plot actually features witches gathering in his house. Joseph Addison's comedy *The Drummer* (1716), also set in Lancashire, is more single-minded. It depicts the efforts of a suitor to a wealthy, beautiful widow to drive out a rival suitor by disguising himself as a ghost and haunting the house. Sham love equates with sham spirits.

Clearly, Lancashire was home to unusually strong religious zeal as well as to belief in the occult. This essay aims to examine magic and spiritualized religion as a regional response to trends in eighteenth-century English religion. Under the influences of latitudinarian leadership, natural religion, and skepticism, the Established Church was turning its back on enthusiastic, spiritualized religion, yet Lancashire seemed always to welcome the latest revival, reform, or spiritual call and to host the largest bazaar of occult exotica. Mainstream Protestants viewed Lancashire's spiritual practices as religion distorted to accommodate the unbridled and fantastic volitions of the zealous. Lancashire Nonconformists viewed any religion shorn of its charismatic and inspirational elements as a religion cut to human dimensions. We can view its spiritual culture as a dissenting voice in a more general discourse regulating the boundaries between types of knowledge and power that properly or improperly transcended ordinary human limits.

This study will first substantiate the claim that Lancashire fostered an unusual spiritual culture. It will then show that controversy over the two poles of northern spiritual culture—spiritualism and magic—reveals general and recurring problems of defining legitimate and non-legitimate spirituality. Magic and conjuring declined, but attention to them increased in times of political crisis as polemicists sought to discredit heterodox viewpoints. More important, spiritualism comprised a middle ground and battle ground between legitimate and nonlegitimate religion as conjuring, spells, and magic fell into disrepute. Controversial writers used figures of magic to discredit spiritualist religion; however, defenders of the spiritual were keen to point out that in doing so the attackers blurred the boundaries by which they defined the legitimacy of their own religious activities.

I

Although Lancashire's reputation spread widely partly because metropolitan commentators exploited stereotypes made easy by distance, Lancashire also earned its reputation. Robert Halley observes: "More distinctly than any other county, Lancashire has a religious history of its own. Its Puritanism has been remarkable for many peculiarities: its Nonconformity has been, in many respects, unlike the Nonconformity of the other parts of England." Halley notes that Lancashire had unusually strong parties of Catholics and Puritans, had its own rules for Sabbath diversions, and had a legally established Presbyterian Church. Also, under Elizabeth, Puritanism was encouraged there while persecuted elsewhere.[4] Even before seventeenth-century religious and political upheaval fanned Lancashire spirituality into flame, the county was seen as a wilderness harboring a great but uncultivated spiritual potential. Some blamed the Established Church for failing to fill the vacuum left there when Catholic monasteries and chapels were closed. In 1590 a group of Lancashire clergy petitioned the Church to remedy the area's ignorance and superstition.[5] James I, on a progress through Lancashire on his way from Scotland to London in 1617, found the county infested by Puritans and Papists.[6] In a pamphlet published in London, "An Exhortation to his Dearely beloved Countrimen" (1641), George Walker spoke of Lancashire as a "rough, untilled barren desert, over-runne with ignorance, superstition, and poperie."[7] He noted that Lancashire had not shared in the spiritual or material prosperity of the rest of England as it should have, given that its people surpassed their countrymen generally:

> For wee are not to deale with a stubborne, brutish ill natured people like the wild Irish. . . . The people of our native Country are generally of another constitution, and of a contrarie but farre better naturall disposition; although they are most constant in their resolutions, while they conceive and imagine them to be just, good and godly, and doe follow that course of religion and life, which they have embraced for the best with strong affection and zeale; yet naturally they are so ingenious, and so reasonable and tractable, that when good reason is shewed to them for the contrary, they are ready as to conceive and understand it, so to yeild unto it generally and for the most part. (11–12)

Indeed, the "head-strong blind zeale" found there results from ignorance and lack of preaching, not a reprobate disposition.

Local pride no doubt tainted Walker's reliability, but history bore out his assessment of the region's religious potential. Lancashire welcomed many religious movements. In a 1698 tour Celia Fiennes observed of Rochford, "These parts religion does better flourish than in places where they have better advantages."[8] Catholicism was particularly strong. Even after the dissolution of the monasteries, the Dominican order in Lancashire remained intact.[9] In a 1687 visitation the vicar-apostolate John Leyburne recorded 8,958 confirmations performed during his Lancashire sojourn.[10] A century later Bishop Petre documents the strength of the Catholic population, with 14,000 in Lancashire and 1,500 in neighboring Yorkshire. John Macky wrote in 1724 that "there are more of the Roman Catholick Religion in this County, than in any three others in England."[11] John Bossy estimates that in 1700 a tenth of the Lancashire population was Catholic,[12] and that with 16,000 to 18,000 recusants, "there were more Catholics in this relatively small area than in the rest of the North put together."[13] They were not a marginal, powerless community; Bossy states that "most of the larger landowners in the county seem to have been Catholics."[14]

Protestant Nonconformity began to grow during the Civil War, but the causes of the rapid rise of dissent in the region remain something of a puzzle. Lancashire's distance from London, its landscape of isolated dells, and its location at the crossroads of Ireland, Scotland, Wales, and England may explain some of its propensity for uncommon religious movements. Bossy conjectures that the Quakers "successfully filled the vacuum created by the geographical and social indrawing of Catholicism during the seventeenth century."[15] Turning to another group, W. A. Shaw observes, "In no county of England did so large a proportion of the clergy become convinced and aggressive Presbyterians as in Lancashire, and in few counties was there less antecedent cause, either in the form of episcopal persecution or of actual Presbyterian propaganda."[16] To explain the transition, Shaw guesses that the clergy in Lancashire were either readily compliant with Parliament or saw the advantages of the Presbyterian system to their selfish clerical instincts, but his conjectures merely substitute political self-interest for the less tangible but equally plausible religious motives. After the Restoration, numerous ministers who could not accept the terms of the 1662 Act of Uniformity found themselves, with many of their congregations, Nonconformists. After 1689 and the accession of William and Mary, a large number of Lancashire clergy who could not alter their oath to James II found themselves banned from their pulpits as nonjurors. Their strength contributed to the uncertain loyalty of Lancashire during the1715 and 1745 Jacobite uprisings and explains why Prince Charles raised his standard there.

Many groups were drawn to this region and tapped its devotional readiness. A historian of Nonconformity in Lancashire has said, perhaps overstating the case, that Quakers may "almost be called a Lancashire sect, as the earliest and most successful labours of their founder were in that county and its neighbourhood."[17] George Fox began his ministry in Lancashire, preaching publicly for the first time in 1647. A 1652 journey brought him to Pendle Hill. On the summit, in the same neighborhood where the Lancashire witches had lived, Fox had one of the instigating visions of his ministry. He recorded: "We came near a very great high hill, called Pendlehill, and I was moved of the Lord to go up to the top of it; which I did with much ado, it was so very steep and high. When I was come to the top, I saw the sea bordering upon Lancashire. From the top of this hill the Lord let me see in what places he had a great people to be gathered." After retiring to an inn and preaching, Fox had another vision in which he saw "a great people in white raiment by a river side, coming to the Lord."[18] At Swarthmoor, which became the spiritual home of Friends in the region, he converted and eventually married Margaret Fell.

The Moravians entered Lancashire in 1743 and at nearby Fulneck, in the West Riding of Yorkshire, established a "second Herrnhut" (the homeland of the Moravians in Germany).[19] Methodism took deep hold in Lancashire, also. In the middle and late eighteenth century, when many Nonconformist congregations had become Unitarian and the Church of England had reached a low point as a spiritual force, the Methodists, states Shaw, "saved, nay even created, popular religion in Lancashire."[20] John Wesley preached at Manchester in 1738. Strong Methodist centers of influence took hold in Manchester, Warrington, Bolton, and Wigan. By the early nineteenth century "few parts of the Methodist connexion commanded the same substantial support and vast resources as the large societies in South Lancashire."[21] By 1830 Lancashire had over nine percent of the Britain's Wesleyan membership.[22] The Shaker movement, or the United Society of Believers in Christ's Second Appearing, originated in Manchester in 1747 when its founders, James and Jane Wardley, broke away from other churches to seek greater purity and cultivate spiritual gifts that included ecstatic trances, convulsions, singing, and dancing. Ann Lee joined in 1758, and in 1770, while in prison for her beliefs, received a vision in which she was instructed that sex caused Adam and Eve's expulsion from Eden. In accordance with a 1772 vision she led the group to New England to found a community of abstinence and simplicity. Another American religion had its first large-scale success outside North America in Lancashire in 1837. Elders of the Church of Jesus Christ of Latter-day Saints converted 1,500 in nine months in Preston and the Ribble valley. Heber C. Kimball felt an impression regarding area's unusual spiritual readiness while near the village of Chatburn, in the shadow of Pendle Hill: "I was constrained to take off my hat, for I felt that the place was holy ground. The Spirit of the Lord rested upon me and I was constrained to bless that whole region of country."[23]

II

Alongside its flourishing Nonconformity, Lancashire produced a stream of bizarre, paranormal, occult, and magical phenomena worthy of *The X Files*. The taxonomy used in Jessica Lofthouse's study of north-country folklore suggests the almost unclassifiable variety that sprang from the fecund spiritual borderlands. She mentions fairies, boggarts, bogeys, barguests, dobbies, trolls, ghosts, wizards, witches, giants, treasures, spells, astrologists, prophets, conjurors, and other manifestations of the demonic,[24] to which we might add exorcism, specters, witch stones, child wonders, learned pigs, musical dogs, charms, healings, rumblings, and magic wells.

Let's start with the Lancashire witches. Tried in 1612, seven females and one male were eventually executed for witchcraft. The whole affair came to official notice when one of the group was apprehended for theft and began making allegations against her friends. With the help of the only contemporary, factual account, Thomas Potts's *The Wonderful Discoverie of Witches in the Countie of Lancaster* (1612), we can see that senility, ignorance, and deprivation account for many of the actions of which the perpetrators were accused, and to which they readily confessed. In 1634 a new set of charges brought four more women to London for interrogation and provided the occasion for a hasty production of Heywood and Broome's *The Lancashire Witches*, based on the 1612 incident, to capitalize on London's fascination for sensational spiritual irregularities. Curiously, even though witchery occurred throughout Britain, the Lancashire connection held on while other regional incidents were forgotten.

Child wonders and prophets sprang up in the region. Four tracts of 1679 record the story of Charles Bennett of Manchester, who at age three and without instruction could speak Latin, Greek, and Hebrew and answer difficult questions on scripture and theology. One day his father misread aloud a sentence from the Bible. The child told him there was no such passage in scripture. The father checked; the child was right. While still three he told his parents that he must speak to the king at London. At Coventry, magistrates and ministers who repaired to him admired his learning. In one version of his story he actually visited the king, refused to discuss their interview, but prophesied that he, the child, would die in nine days.[25] The most notable prophet of the region, the Cheshire prophet, Robert Nixon, requires us to step out of county boundaries. Note, however, that an early eighteenth-century chronicler explained Nixon by proximity to Lancashire.

"Lancashire, which is not far off, has been famous for witches, and I am afraid Cheshire is a little infected by its neighbourhood."[26] Nixon, a near-idiot given employment by Thomas Cholmondley of Vale Royal in the very late 1500s and early 1600s, uttered prophecies that had wide-ranging political import, such as the following:

> When a raven shall build in a stone lion's mouth on the top of a church in Cheshire, then a King of England shall be driven out of his kingdom and never return more.
>
> When an eagle shall sit on the top of the house, then an heir shall be born to the Cholmondley's family; and this heir shall live to see England invaded by foreigners, who shall proceed so far as a town in Cheshire; but a miller, named Peter, shall be born with two heels on one foot, and at that time living in a mill of Mr. Cholmondley's, he shall be instrumental in delivering the nation. . . . A young new set of men of virtuous manners shall come, who shall prosper, and make a flourishing church for two hundred years. (6)

Even though the prophecies were spoken a century earlier, interest in them peaked in the early 1700s when no less than five short books were issued.[27] One of these, by John Oldmixon in 1714, reached a fifteenth edition in the eighteenth century, if we can believe that edition's title page, and even saw reprints in the nineteenth century.

III

Quizzical prophets, illiterate witches, and boy wonders serve little purpose when set alongside the type of spiritualism that influences ethical conduct by producing inner change. The historical problem was to disentangle them. One way to separate them is to note that, while Lancashire's religious and magical cultures both drew on nonmaterial forces for protection and strength and existed side by side in the seventeenth century, they were, for the most part, generally incompatible in their aims and were practiced by different people. On the occult side, in *Religion and the Decline of Magic*, Keith Thomas emphasizes the interrelatedness of magic, astrology and witchcraft as parallel and even rival explanatory systems. They all offered the means by which people could take control of forces usually beyond their understanding and influence. Magic and witchcraft accomplished this end by direct intervention in the secret forces of nature, astrology by anticipating events and comprehending their causes.[28] These practices could rival each other, as when astrologers claimed to be the only sure discoverers of witchcraft (632), and they often appealed to different classes of people. For example, astrology's elaborate technical basis attracted educated people (635), whereas witchcraft and certain types of magic were known to attract the illiterate.

Thomas argues that to some extent, religion, astrology, and magic had "parallel functions" because "they all purported to help men with their daily problems by teaching them how to avoid misfortune and how to account for it when it struck" (631). However, Thomas drives a strict distinction between religion and magic, astrology, and witchcraft. Following Malinowski's lead, Thomas says, "Religion refers to the fundamental issues of human existence while magic always turns round specific, concrete and detailed problems." Popular magic in England

> provided protection against witchcraft, and various remedies for illness, theft, and unhappy personal relationships. But it never offered a comprehensive view of the world, an explanation of human existence, or the promise of a future life. It was a collection of miscellaneous recipes, not a comprehensive body of doctrine. Whereas the faith of the Christian was a guiding principle, relevant to every aspect of life, magic was simply a means of overcoming various specific difficulties. It is true that magic could sometimes have its expressive aspect. Its rituals for curing the sick or identifying thieves might involve the enactment of satisfying little dramas, not unlike the ceremonies of the Church. The intellectual magician might even have Faustian dreams in which magic became the key to existence. But it remains true that at the popular level magic's role was much more limited than that of religion. (636–37)

Thomas shows that the rise of mainstream, institutionalized religion coincided with the decline of magic, which survived mainly in less urban and less educated precincts. Lancashire is such a precinct. Even there, magic mostly died out in the eighteenth century. Almost all references to it by then are satirical or dismissive.[29] However, Lancashire religion goes counter to the assertion that generally, insofar as religion outlived magic, it did so by banning spiritual gifts, individual inspiration, and other divine interventions as well. Thomas remarks, "When the Devil was banished to Hell, God himself was confined to working through natural causes" (639); therefore, when religion triumphed over magic, "it was religion with a difference" (640). I'm not sure George Fox, John Wesley, and their Lancashire converts would agree. Quakers and Wesleyans never valued ritualistic and mechanical means of exorcizing life's problems. Lancashire's unusual numbers of Nonconformists, Methodists, and nonjurors were simply not satisfied with the kind of religion Thomas defines as the rule in the eighteenth century.

When Thomas says that religion differs from magic because it offers a comprehensive view of life and an explanation of human existence, we need to note that what people accepted as a comprehensive view of life changed over time. A brief review of two texts will help expose the moving boundaries involved in defining the spiritual nature of Christianity and relating it to a larger explanation of life. Many other texts could serve, notably of Dryden, Locke, Swift, Toland, and Boyle; however, the two below will suffice to characterize a shift in thinking and show its consequences for regulating spiritual involvement. James I's *Daemonologie* (1597) has its eye mostly on Scotland; however, the issues, together with Scotland's proximity to Lancashire, make it relevant. In its attack on witchcraft, the document helps us see the appeal of magical interventions, their relation to a broader understanding of all that exists, and the sources of instability that accrue in defining the limits between the legitimate and illegitimate. James observed that three passions draw ignorant people to occult powers: "Curiositie in great ingines: thirst of revenge for some tortes deeply apprehended: or greedie appetite of geare, caused through great poverty."[30] Learning provides no sure cure because the apparent rewards of learning, understanding, and mastery seem so pale and unfruitful when measured by the great investment of effort and time. Hence the learned, too, are seduced by a desire to overcome limitations that seem too constrictive:

> For divers men having attained to a great perfection in learning, and yet remaining overbare (alas) of the spirit of regeneration and frutes thereof: finding all naturall things common, as well to the stupide pedants as unto them, they assay to vindicate unto them a greater name, by not only knowing the course of things heavenlie, but likewise to climb to the knowledge of things to come thereby.[31]

James believed in witches and wrote to an audience that saw them as a dangerous influence. The occult had its greatest power when people could not abide the limitations implicit in human knowledge. James estimated that magical practices continued to thrive because people wanted more than quotidian reality could give them. Yet religion by its nature took people beyond quotidian reality.

John Collier, an eighteenth-century Lancashire writer hostile to spiritual enthusiasm and Dissent, captured the contrast from James I's day to his own. He was one of many to voice the suspicion that Christian ministers promoted belief in witchcraft and magic in order to bolster their own spiritual authority. He says of a contemporary of James, "Witches and daemons, he thought were as common as old women and crows. . . . He made no baulks of believing the stories and prophecies of the *Ten Sybils*; though a genius of small penetration might see they were the offspring of over zealous Christians, written on purpose to knock down heathenism, and prop Christianity." "All these, and many more such boyish trumpery, were the dreams of our primitive fathers, and the monks, their heirs and successors; and vanished, in great measure, with that most high, and mightily-conceited James the first."[32] As we follow the change from boyish trumpery to skepticism, we should alert ourselves to inherent risks the transition brought to religion. What if religion, too, were stripped of its individual and particular powers of transcending the ordinary and calling on divine powers during the crises of life? What if it asked only patient reform of character, steady compliance, and reasonable effort?

Archbishop Tillotson tried to accomplish within religion what James had attempted in the occult, that is, to restrict spiritual beliefs and practices to their proper sphere. Seeking to emphasize the ethical and minimize the ritual aspects of religion, Tillotson depicted much popular Christianity as essentially a species of conjuring. In one of his most famous sermons he maintained that most people will do anything to please God—short of actually improving their character. He observed that as ancient Israel "were well enough content to offer up anything else to God . . . provided he would not oblige them to become better," so in his own day people "hate to be reformed; and for this Reason, they will be content to do any Thing, rather than be put to the Trouble of Mending themselves; and God may have any Terms of them, so he will let them be quiet in their Sins, and excuse them from the real Virtues of a good Life.[33]

In the transition from James's *Daemonologie* to Tillotson's sermon, we see the shift Thomas has defined. Religion moves away from particular divine interventions—with good and evil spirits competing to provide them—and toward general principles coupled to an emphasis on character and conduct. Both James I and Tillotson tried to reduce the appeal of spiritual practices that too readily complied with the passions of the weak. Yet their assumptions about what exists and how such powers connect with the human will are a world apart. James I believes in devils and witches and discredits them by showing how dangerous they can be. Tillotson has nothing to say of them. They operate only in the background as fully discredited versions of the spiritual manipulations many Christians still practice, notably anything smacking of Catholic ritual and mystery—what Tillotson would call the external parts of religion. By this contrast he reduces the universal appeal of sacrifices, rituals, and vows by showing that those who mistake them for religion discredit both God and themselves. They placate God by manipulation and are superior to conjuring only in that they address good rather than evil powers, but they have no place in a world where conjuring has disappeared. However, in leaving behind the charismatic, ecstatic, and vitalizing individual involvement with transcendent forces, the institutionalized, ethical religion that Thomas describes lost an element that some Christians considered necessary: a spiritually vitalizing, immediate, personal contact with God. In Quakerism, Methodism, and Nonconformism generally, that element survived. Those who followed these sects sought within religion the particular involvement with supernatural forces and self-confirming emotional charge that magic, conjuring, and sorcery had provided its practitioners. Spiritualism mediated the religion of general principles—The Thirty-Nine Articles, the Book of Common Prayer, and the hierarchical organization of the Church of England—and the religion of the individual who felt a need to stand, even if only occasionally, on something more tangible than principle, to stand on the brink that divides the everyday world and the world of infinity.

I don't argue that strong religious feelings disappeared from Anglicanism, but they were often subjected to constraints that virtually eliminated the traditional operations of the spirit in favor of more generalized feelings of love and reverence. Enthusiasm had an honored place, particularly of the sort endorsed by Shaftesbury. We must note the difference between the positively valenced Shaftesburian type and the types exhibited by zealous Nonconformists, however. Shaftesburian enthusiasm excludes any popular fury, prejudice, mystic frenzy, pessimism, threat, "horrors of a superstitious kind,"[34] or an imagination so fired that it burns up reason and judgment. The latter, incidentally, were the marks of the French immigrants of 1707 who sought refuge in England. Shaftesbury condones divine inspiration; however, because it produces some of the same effects as bad enthusiasm, the great problem is to differentiate it from the frenzy that many mistake for divinely instigated experience. To separate the seemingly irregular but heavenly gifts from various kinds of mental distemper requires that one know oneself, be capable of judgment, pay attention to the evidence of the senses, and apply the tests of good humor, ridicule, and purpose. Hence Shaftesburian enthusiasm is carefully hedged to include love and other feelings produced by ideas of greatness and exclude the expression of particular states such as visions, prophecy, and promptings.

IV

Spiritualism's middle ground between superstition and legitimate religion meant that it could be characterized as witchcraft in the dress of religion or as religion breaking the shackles of rationalism and compromise.

Therefore it will be no surprise that magic and spiritualism spilled over onto each other when religious or political factions made use of the differences between them to stigmatize and polarize. As a part of this rhetorical instability, those out of the political and religious mainstream were most likely to see divine portents, and those in the mainstream to equate such portents with conjuring. Equally, both sides were vulnerable during crisis to being denounced by those who professed secret spiritual insight into their neighbors' activities. Once we see the rhetorical use of the boundaries between religion and magic as a pattern, we will not be surprised that political and religious strife triggers the periodic renewal of interest in the paranormal. Crises focused attention on conjuring, witchcraft, and other black arts as those locked in controversy searched history for unusual events, augurs, figures, and parallels useful against their opponents. The underlying assumption seemed to be that abnormalities coincident with upheaval have similar signs and can be traced to similar causes.

Most of the prodigies and occult practices I reviewed earlier either had, or could be given, political overtones. The 1612 Lancashire witch trials came at a time when it was feared that Catholicism might be staging a comeback in the North. The hanging of witches who hardly professed any religion might seem unrelated to efforts to control Catholicism, but a shrewd county official under James I might conceivably believe witch trials a prudent, if indirect, warning shot. Roger Nowell, who prosecuted the witches in Lancaster, had powerful uncles in the Church, and his family had benefitted greatly under Elizabeth. In her study of the trials, Rachel Hasted reasons that the witchcraft accusations "may be seen as an astute political move. Such a prosecution showed that the magistrates were diligently seeking out the king's enemies and imposing religious conformity. It served as a warning to ordinary people that drastic punishment awaited those who clung to old customs and beliefs."[35] The trial of another Lancashire sorcerer, one Richard Dugdale, ended without conviction in 1689. The Reverend Zachary Taylor of Wigan could see that the allegations were a tissue of superstition and deception. Interestingly, however, he "insisted that the whole affair was an artifice of the Nonconformist ministers, in imitation of the pretended miracles of the Catholic priests."[36] The logic is worth exploring. Even though most Nonconformists denounced any magic or conjuring, their preachers, Taylor reasoned, would benefit from superstition in the same way Catholic priests supposedly benefitted from the belief in miracles. Put cynically, it is easier for those seeking spiritual authority to dupe those who already give credit to superstitions and magical folkways. Put more sympathetically, anyone who believes that divine powers can dramatically intercept the individual will likely believe that evil powers can do so, too.

The spate of books on the prophet Nixon coincided with the Jacobite uprising of 1715. Regional interest would have been strong because of Nixon's proximity in Cheshire and also because Lancashire had a powerful Jacobite faction, many of whom were brutally punished at the "bloody assize" in Lancaster, even after surrendering peacefully to royalist troops at Preston. Joseph Addison devoted Number 24 of his *Freeholder* paper to the Jacobites, making the interesting allegation that the disenfranchised are most inclined to believe in supernatural assistance. The Jacobites, he said, "are reduced to the poor comfort of prodigies" and "begin to see armies in the clouds, when all on earth have forsaken them. Nay, I have been lately shewn a written prophecy that is handed among them with great secresy, by which it appears their chief reliance at present is upon a Cheshire miller that was born with two thumbs upon one hand."[37] Oldmixon's account of Nixon seems to favor sheer fascination with the prophecies, although one can detect an anti-Jacobite in the seeming detachment. He finds "as little imposture in it as the Jacobites pretend there is in the person it seems to have an eye to; but whether they are both impostures alike or not, I leave the reader to determine."[38] Later he adds, "For my own part, I build nothing on this or any other prophecy, only there is something so very odd in the story, and so pat in the wording of it, that I cannot help giving it as I found it" (8). He reports that in Budworth parish, an eighteen year old boy now lives with three thumbs, and a miller with two heels on one foot is living in Nagginshire Mills, but, says Oldmixon, "I find he does not intend to make use of them, for he is a bold Briton, and a loyal subject to King George, zealous for the Protestant succession" (9). Oldmixon concludes with this facing-both-ways endorsement: "Those that will not believe our prophecy, may leave it alone; but if hope is a good help to faith, I shall not long be among the incredulous" (16). Fielding revives interest in Nixon's prophecies in *Tom Jones* through the mouth of that credulous Jacobite, Partridge. It will be remembered that the novel unfolds during the 1745 Jacobite invasion and that Tom is headed north to join the army against it. When Partridge alludes to the prophecy of a miller with three thumbs, Tom Jones replies, "With what stuff and nonsense has thou filled thy head? . . . Monsters and prodigies are the proper instruments to support monstrous and absurd doctrines."[39]

Lancashire newspapers, during times of crisis, also played on the county's reputation for legitimate and fringe religion, drawing national events on a backdrop of the local and familiar. This was particularly true following the rebellion of 1745. Once again, as in 1715, Lancashire found its political loyalties in doubt when Prince Charles marched into the area and raised his standard at Preston. Manchester had the distinction of being the only town in England to give its name to a rebel regiment. The crown stationed troops at Manchester to suppress any residual support of Prince Charles from the town's numerous nonjurors and Catholics. The *Adams's Weekly Courant* of February 24, 1746, when Prince Charles was collecting troops in Scotland for an invasion, contains a poem that seems ominously to link the town's spiritual and political hubbub:

> We Manchester Men are so stout, or so righteous,
> It is not one Demon or two that cou'd fright us.
> * * * *
> That Lucifers Agents here swarm in the Street,
> You need only ask the first Non-Con you meet;
> He'll swear there's such Crowds, and they make such a Riot,
> That Folk cannot go to the *Meeting* in Quiet.

The December 30, 1746 *Adam's Weekly Courant* carried two items linking political events with the spiritual fringe. It reported that in Liverpool, guards upon the watch saw "apparitions of several lately executed there, stalking about, with their Heads in their Hands." A letter assuring citizens that republicans were almost nonexistent in Manchester brought this reply: "If it be true, it is a very sudden Conversion, something like the Instantaneous one of the Methodists."

Rival papers exploited similarities between the area's role in the rebellion, the beheading of Charles I, and events surrounding the Rump Parliament.[40] The November 25, 1746 *Manchester Magazine* insinuates that Manchester has become a refuge for nonjuring priests. A letter in the December 1 *Adams's Weekly Courant* expresses the vulnerability and fear in those who realized that they could be easily charged, somewhat like a witch, of treason. The writer commends the wonderful advances in science whereby even the illiterate, without pains or study, could exactly discern the political sentiments of those who disagreed with them, yet without any risk of being charged as conjurors. In a similar vein, a piece in 1747 humorously argues for more attention to auguries and fortune telling. The writer then proposes that "a College of Augurs and Soothsayers be founded for the constant service of the State, sitting Members for which might be draughted out of our numerous Clergy."[41]

Nonjurors, in that liminal zone between legitimate and nonlegitimate religion, sometimes expressed their vulnerability to misinterpretation. Shortly after the 1745 Jacobite rebellion, the nonjuring Manchester priest Thomas Deacon published a lengthy catechism on the doctrines and institutions of true Christianity and, by implication, flaws in the doctrines and practices of the Church in Deacon's day. *A Full, True, and Comprehensive View of Christianity* (1747) has this pithy New Testament phrase on the title page: "By evil report and good report: as deceivers, and yet true,"[42] with the implication that disciples and their actions would often be construed as false. Interestingly, Deacon discussed exorcism as one of the neglected priestly powers. It is, of course, a rite that makes sense only in a world of active evil spirits. Perhaps in Lancashire he had seen the need for exorcism. The Presbyterian Josiah Owen sarcastically retorted, "a poor contemptible devil it is, to be blown out of his dominion by the breath of a nonjuring priest."[43] Note that what Owen condemns is not the belief in devils—on the contrary, he seems to see the devil as strong and resilient—but Deacon's power to cast the devil out.

V

Figures of witchcraft, conjuring, and other demonic practices lent themselves to exploitation and reply, but spiritual religious practices, such as spiritual (not political) prophecy, visions, and other manifestations of a holy spirit were much more difficult to handle in polemical discourse. It was one thing to accept the scriptural warrant, another to establish the credibility of contemporary instances. For those locked in controversy, these instances required discussion, yet discussion often made it more difficult to sustain the difference between mainstream, legitimate religion and the spiritually suspect.

Those who circulated wonders, prodigies, and prophecies often tagged them with religious significance to lend credibility and give meaning to what otherwise would appear to be random and weird events. Think of Nixon's prophecy of virtuous manners and a flourishing church. In reporting the boy wonder who spoke Latin and Greek, writers remarked that such occurrences showed the existence of a God who could work miracles, however insignificant they appeared. On the other side, there are also hints that well meaning but ignorant Christian stewards, especially in the sixteenth and early seventeenth century, actually promoted attention to witches, spells, and ghosts, reasoning that a belief in debased spiritual forces would prepare the inhabitants to believe in a potent but benevolent spiritual being. Yet, as Keith Thomas points out, attacks on magic, witchcraft, and divination could be read as indirect attacks on spiritualized religion. Thomas reports that "when the transcript of John Dee's conjuring sessions with the spirits was published in 1659, many Puritan divines suspected it as a partisan attempt to discredit religious enthusiasm."[44]

Writers who defamed religious heterodoxy frequently cast it in the figures of magic and divination. One survey of heretics and schismatics observed of the Fifth Monarchy Men that "in their lectures and chief conventicles you might have heard such raptures that you would have thought it were a reading on astrology."[45] George Keith, one of the most dogged opponents of the Quakers in the early eighteenth century, made this comment on those who accounted for, or tried to influence, events by resorting to spiritual powers: "these have all the same result, that they bring about the end of thinking."[46] This fascinating but problematic allegation leads to my final point, that branding religious viewpoints as magic could actually create problems for orthodoxy and expose the uneasy resolution that mainstream Anglicans accepted to the religious turmoil of the seventeenth century.

Adherents of reformist and dissenting creeds who saw their beliefs defamed as magic turned the aspersion to their advantage, often by showing that those who attacked them favored similar beliefs in their own religion, however far below the surface teachings. I will need to broaden my geographical limits to pursue this, but I will do so because I think it illuminates what Lancashire's spiritual culture meant in the national context. Gerard Croese's *The General History of the Quakers* (1696) begins by noting how often Christians, confronted with heterodox opinions, want to scoff, then persecute, then afflict, then turn to fire and sword, racks and torments.[47] His book was written to allay cruel persecution and to remedy one of its causes, the fact that many viewed Quakers as followers of "Old Wives Tales" and as "Prodigies and Monsters of Mankind."[48] One of the most tenacious opponent of the Quakers, George Keith, warned in *The Magick of Quakerism* (1707) that Quakerism was a less superstitious but more dangerous type of enchantment and divination. He was answered by George Whitefield in 1708 and 1712. Against Keith's charge that the inner light doctrine is pure magic, Whitefield replied:

> He has therein contradicted his own Churches Confessions and Prayers in their Liturgy, as well as the best of their Authors and Reformed Protestants; by whom, both the Divine Light, the Seed of Eternal Life, and the Spirit of Truth, Divine Inspiration of the Holy Ghost, the Holy Aid and Help thereof . . . are largely Confessed and Prayed for, even in their own Liturgy.[49]

Under such pressure, the term *magic* began to lose the very connotations which Keith hoped to exploit. Challenged by Whitefield to show that Quakers in fact practiced the type of hellish science implied by the term *magic*, Keith clarified that he didn't mean Quakers practiced diabolical magic, exactly, but a more common kind. Keith said that his attack had tried to "plainly distinguish the Magick of Quakerism, from that which is Demoniacal; and I call the Magic of Quakerism Natural." He defined *natural* this way: "What impulse men have to do, Speak, or Write, that is not Malicious or Sinful, but Indifferent, it is but Natural; and such sort of Natural Impulses, are very frequent and common amongst all sorts of Men." To which Whitefield replied, that if Quakers follow the natural and common magic as defined, then the same charge must also be laid at door of the Established Church.[50]

Even while denying the more extreme connotations of magic, Keith implied that Quakers had by mysterious influence caused the death of a Lancashire minister on whom they had passed judgment. Whitefield merely wanted to know who had been persecuting whom, and whose influence had caused the death. Could it not have been God Almighty, he asked?[51] Whitefield's epigram from Numbers 23:23 had already implied the point: "Surely there is no Inchantment against Jacob, neither is there any Divination against Israel." In other words, properly founded religion had nothing to fear from spirits and dark powers.

Opponents of the Quakers would not even yield them use of the term *spiritual*. One very early pamphlet charged that the "seemingly spiritual" merely cloaked the more subtle means by which the devil's ministers had in later times "transformed themselves into Apostles and Ministers of Christ."[52] In a pamphlet called *A Northern Blast,* directed at Lancashire's neighbor Yorkshire, the phrase "spiritual Quaker" becomes increasingly pejorative as it is linked to a fascination for one's inner thoughts, lack of respect for masters and ministers, disregard for scripture, and "wilfullnesse rather than a religious willingness." This type of spirituality, the pamphlet avers, is a hazard. Like a strong wind it "violently turnes about the Windmill of our affections." The writer illustrates with the case of one Brother Collins, "who had a spiritual Revelation, (as he reported) to stand naked on the Kerby-Moor side Market Crosse."[53] Spiritualism, like James I's demons, could cater to the will of those not satisfied by the normal limits to their power and knowledge.

VI

The existence or nonexistence of spiritual forces, demonic or benign, had enormous consequences. Contests over such issues involved not only the transcendent but the frame of political, social, and religious knowledge according to which English society was organized and governed. The discourse of two kinds of spirituality formed part of various attempts in English politics and religion to draw the boundaries between the supernatural and the natural, between inspiration and imagination, between socially useful and socially disruptive faculties, between legitimate and nonlegitimate sources of power, and between valid and invalid interpretations of human activity achieved by importing types of knowledge of the unknown into the commonplace. For the theologian, the controversy related to the nature and relative power of the forces outside nature but governing it. For those in or out of power, the controversy centered on who countenanced whom and who was able to practice spiritual intervention—the appointed priest, the inspired individual, or the self-appointed wise man. It also involved what type of coercion to use against people who were reported to use occult powers. For those watching political alignments, the controversy involved complicated parallels between religious and political opinion. For the religious, it involved the godly versus ungodly means of fulfilling human desires within proper versus improper bounds. For the humanist and moralist, it involved the relationship between humane laws and measures for regulating a fictitious if commonly believed power.

Fielding's *Tom Jones* illustrates the interconnectedness of these issues. The novel endorses the impulses of the good heart, constrained by prudence and religion. These impulses bind society together and are ultimately linked to a benevolent providence. As his satirical treatment of Methodists and Quakers indicates, by "religion" Fielding did not mean spiritual gifts or enthusiasm. His Deistic-leaning Anglicanism had no place for spiritual tendencies that were prone to fantasy and unbridled volition. Fielding sends Mr. Blifil to Lancashire because up there hypocrisy can find a snug home among the Jacobites, Methodists, prophets, and other spiritual and political cranks who, lacking the goodness of heart to regulate their conduct, prey on each other. Lancashire's dual heritage in spiritual zeal and the occult serves to remind us that some in England, and certainly many in the North, missed the particular, individualized, and even unpredictable spiritual dimension by which religion transcended a set of general principles regulating conduct on life's journey to a far destination.

Keith Thomas's *Religion and the Decline of Magic* distinguishes between religion as a comprehensive view of life and magic as particularized and concrete means for solving immediate problems. Lancashire's dual heritage in both realms helps us see that the transition to mainstream, institutionalized religion of the eighteenth century left out just that particular, individualized aspect that made earlier religion appear, if admittedly strange, at least conformable to the individual's particular experience before the divine. English reform movements such as Anglican evangelism and Methodism show that mainstream Anglicanism did not satisfy everyone's yearning for contact with the divine through religion. Lancashire's openness to ecstatic and spiritualized religion is a more pronounced and localized version of that desire, and the discourse of spiritual religion demonstrates the unresolved conflicts in defining and regulating the desire for particular, individual transcendence.

NOTES

1. Henry Fielding, *The History of Tom Jones, a Foundling*, ed. Martin Battestin, Wesleyan Edition of the Works of Henry Fielding (Middleton, CT: Wesleyan University Press, 1975), 979–80.

2. Daniel Defoe, *The History of the Most Remarkable Life and Extraordinary Adventures of the Truly Honourable Colonel Jaque*, Shakespeare Head Edition, 2 vols. (Oxford: Shakespeare Head Press, 1927; rpt. London: W. Clowes, 1974), 2: 78.

3. Robert Hume has noted the "incongruous irony" in *The Development of English Drama in the Late Seventeenth Century* (Oxford: Oxford University Press, 1976), 358.

4. Robert Halley, *Lancashire: Its Puritanism and Nonconformity*, 2d ed. (Manchester: Tobbs and Brook, 1872), v.

5. Rachel A. C. Hasted, *The Pendle Witch Trial 1612* (Preston: Lancashire County Books, 1993), 5.

6. Edward Baines, *History of the County Palatine and Duchy of Lancaster*, 4 vols. (London, 1836), 1: 621.

7. George Walker, "An Exhortation to his Dearely beloved Countrimen, all the Natives of the Countie of Lancaster, inhabiting in and about the Citie of London; tending to perswade and stirre them up to a yearely contribution, for the erecting of Lectures, and maintaining of some godly and painfull preachers in such places of that Countrie as have most neede, by reason of ignorance and superstition there abbounding: composed by George Walker, Pastor of St. John the Evangelist in Watling Street in London" [Circa 1641], ed. and intro. Charles W. Sutton, in The Chetham Society's *Remains Historical and Literary Connected with the Palatine Counties of Lancaster and Chester,* New Series 47 (1902), 1.

8. *The Journeys of Celia Fiennes*, ed. Christopher Morris (London: Cresset Press, 1949), 222.

9. Wilfred Parkin, *The Friars Preachers in Lancashire 1260–1990* (London: Excalibur Press, 1991), vii.

10. W. A. Shaw, "Ecclesiastical History," *A History of Lancashire*, ed. William Farrer and J. Brownbill. The Victoria History of the Counties of England (1908; rtd. London: University of London Institute of Historical Research, 1966), 2: 93.

11. John Macky, *A Journey through England*, 2 vols. (1724), 2: 144.

12. J. Bossy, "Catholic Lancashire in the Eighteenth Century," in *Essays Presented to Michael Roberts* ed. J. Bossy and P. Jupp (Belfast, 1976), 54.

13. J. Bossy, *The English Catholic Community, 1500–1850* (London, 1975), 92.

14. J. Bossy, "Catholic Lancashire," 59.

15. J. Bossy, *English Catholic Community*, 393.

16. Shaw, "Ecclesiastical History," 63.

17. Halley, 258.

18. George Fox, *A Journal or Historical Account of the Life, Travels, Sufferings, Christian Experiences and Labour of Love . . .* , 5th ed., 2 vols (Philadelphia, 1808), 1:173.

19. Shaw, "Ecclesiastical History," 81.

20. Ibid., 82.

21. D. A. Gowland, *Methodist Secessions: The Origins of Free Methodism in Three Lancashire Towns: Manchester, Rochdale, Liverpool* (Manchester: Chetham Society, 1979), 20.

22. Ibid., 20.

23. Stanley B. Kimball, *Heber C. Kimball: Mormon Patriarch and Pioneer* (Urbana: University of Illinois Press, 1981), 52.

24. These are some of the types discussed by Jessica Lofthouse in *North-Country Folklore in Lancashire, Cumbria, and the Pennine Dales* (London: Robert Hale, 1976).

25. The four tracts are "The Lancashire Wonder, or the Miraculous Child of Manchester . . . To the Tune of, *In Summer Time*, or *The Godly Maid of Padstow*;" "Strange and Wonderful News, or the full and true relation of the Miraculous Inspiration of Charles Bennet; . . . With many other Circumstances most Wonderful and Strange to Relate" (London, 1679); "The Miraculous Child, or Wonderfull News from Manchester. A most true and Certain Account how one Charles Bennet, a Child but Three Years Old, doth speak Latine, Greek, and Hebrew . . . " (London, 1679); and "Strange News from West-Smithfield, or: the Man-Child of Manchester: being a true and impartial Account of the prodigious Knowledge and Elocution of a Male-Infant, of three years of age, . . . " (London, 1679). These are collected and reprinted in William A. E. Axon, "The Wonderful Child. Tracts issued in 1697 relating to Charles Bennett of Manchester, alleged to speak Latin, Greek, and Hebrew, when three years old without having been taught," *Remains Historical and Literary Connected with the Palatine Counties of Lancaster and Chester* (for The Chetham Society) new series 47 (1902). Axon investigated birth records to confirm the existence of Charles Bennet and found "no local corroboration of the wonderful narrative" (ix). However, he notes a birth recorded on June 22 1676 of Charles Bent. I wonder if Bent is not a variant spelling of Bennet.

26. John Oldmixon, *Nixon's Cheshire Prophecy at Large; Published from the Lady Cowper's Correct Copy, with historical and political remarks and Several Instances wherein it is Fulfulled* (London, 1714). In William A. E. Axon, ed., *Nixon's Cheshire Prophecies, Reprinted and Edited from the best sources, including a copy of the prophecy from an unpublished manuscript, with an introductory essay on popular prophecies* (Manchester: Heywood & Son, 1878), 16.

27. *The Strange and Wonderful Predictions of Mr. Christopher Love . . . . Also, Nixon's Cheshire Prophecy* (London [1701]); *Nixon's Cheshire Prophecy at Large . . . , by* John Oldmixon, Esq. (London, 1714); *The Cheshire Prophesy with Historical and Political Remarks* (London, 1713); *The Life of Nixon, the Cheshire Prophet; containing several surprising passages of His Life and Prophecies, Never before Printed, In a letter from a Gentleman at Namptwich to his Friend in London* (London 1714); and *Nixon's Prophecy: Containing Many Strange and Wonderful Predictions* (Liverpool, 1715).

28. *Religion and the Decline of Magic: Studies in Popular Beliefs in Sixteenth- and Seventeenth-Century England* (New York: Oxford University Press, 1971), 631–33.

29. An example is John Collier's "The Prickshaw Witch Blown Up; Or, The Conjuror Out-Conjured" (1752), in *The Miscellaneous Works of Tim Bobbin, Esq.*

Containing His View of the Lancashire Dialect, with large Additions and Improvements; and a Glossary; Also, his Poem of The Flying Dragon and the Man of Heaton. Together with other Whimsical Amusements, in Prose and Verse. To which is added, A Life of the Author, by Richard Townley, Esq. (London: for J. Allman; and for Wilson and Sons, York, 1818), 156–66.

30. James I, *Daemonolgie, in Forme of a Dialogue* (Edinburgh, 1597; rpt. Amsterdam: Theatrum Orbis Terrarum, 1969 as no. 94 of The English Experience), 8.

31. Ibid., 10.

32. "To T. P., Esq.," in *The Miscellaneous Works of Tim Bobbin*, 172–73.

33. John Tillotson, "Sermon I," *Eighteenth-Century English Literature*, ed. G. Tillotson, P. Fussell, M. Waingrow (New York: Harcourt, Brace, 1969), 205–6.

34. "Letter Concerning Enthusiasm to My Lord *****," in *Characteristics of Men, Manners, Opinions, Times* (1711), ed. John M. Robertson, 2 vols. (Gloucester, MA: Peter Smith, 1963), 1: 13.

35. Hasted, 10.

36. Edward Baines, *History*, 1: 615.

37. Joseph Addison, *The Freeholder*, ed. James Leheny (Oxford: Clarendon, 1979), 141.

38. John Oldmixon, *Nixon's Cheshire Prophecy*, 5.

39. *Tom Jones*, 440.

40. See the letters in *Adams's Weekly Courant* of Cheshire and the *Manchester Magazine* in December 1746 and January 1747.

41. *Adams's Weekly Courant* Dec. 15, 1747.

42. The passage is from 2 Cor. 6:8.

43. Quoted in Halley, *Lancashire: Its Puritanism and Nonconformity*, 478.

44. Thomas, 638.

45. Ephraim Pagitt, *Heresiography, or A Brief Description and History of the Hereticks and Sectaries Sprang up in these Latter Times*, 6th ed. (1662), 282. Qtd. in Thomas, 638.

46. As quoted in George Whitefield, 10.

47. "Epistle Dedicatory" of Gerard Croese, *The General History of the Quakers: Containing the Lives, Tenets, Sufferings, Tryals, Speeches, and Letters of All the Most Eminent Quakers, Both Men and Women* (London, 1696); an English translation from Croese's 1694 Latin work.

48. Ibid., 3.

49. George Whitefield, *Light and Truth Triumphant: Or George Keith's Imagined Magick of Quakerism Confirmed, Utterly Confounded* (London, 1712), 5.

50. Ibid., 11.

51. Ibid., 14.

52. *A Faithful Discovery of the Trecherous Design of Mystical Antichrist Displaying Christs Banners, Containing an Examination of many Doctrines of the People called Quakers in Yorkshire* (London, 1653), iii.

53. George Emmot, *A Northern Blast, or the Spiritual Quaker Converted: Being Soul-saving Advice to the giddy People of England, who are running head-long to Destruction . . . in Yorkshire* (London, 1655), 13–15.

Parallel Forces: Identity and Authority in *Roland Barthes* and *Tristram Shandy*

KATHARINE M. MORSBERGER

Despite Roland Barthes' insistence that the author is dead, Laurence Sterne, surely, is still very much alive.[1] There are striking similarities between Roland Barthes' *Roland Barthes* and Laurence Sterne's *The Life and Opinions of Tristram Shandy, Gentleman*. Despite their separation in time, the two works share certain common elements of language, form, and structure, and also a number of parallel concerns and concepts. When the life and opinions of Sterne's fictional hero are compared to the life and opinions of Roland Barthes as revealed in *Roland Barthes*, Sterne emerges as not only alive and well, but flourishing, and headed for the twenty-first century in all directions. Barthes' own concept of the death of the author reveals, paradoxically, that as an author Sterne may be said to be more alive, in the sense of remaining vital, than even Barthes himself.

Roland Barthes' analysis of the author's dead hand is convincing when applied to the fictional and critical nineteenth-century texts he discusses. For the most part, these novels are written from the omniscient author's point of view and present a given world and world-view not to be questioned.[2] In addition much nineteenth-century criticism is focused as much on the author's life as it is on his (almost invariably his) text, and tends furthermore toward uncritical hagiography of the canonized author.[3] During the eighteenth century, however, the definition of the author and the form of the text were considerably more fluid. The extended prose narrative, in particular, as a relatively new genre, its very name proclaiming its novelty, was as yet an area of experimentation in language and in form. The realistic novel or more precisely the narrative of closely observed middle-class life, was only one of the many types of extended prose narrative current during the eighteenth century.[4] Indeed the concept of what Michel Foucault called the "author-function"[5] was itself still being defined during the long eighteenth century and afterwards.[6]

In explaining his concept of the author in *The Pleasure of the Text*, Barthes distinguishes the text of pleasure from the text of bliss.[7] The text of pleasure, the classic or readerly text, is defined as a fixed entity to be approached with reverence and as the definite product, statement, and intention of an Author whose personality is indelibly stamped upon the text, from which readers and critics are to absorb a definite and intended meaning or truth. The Author's critics, as Barthes goes on to say in *Criticism and Truth*, reinforce this meaning as "what goes without saying,"[8] but these "'evident truths'" "imply a preexisting code as a structural model" (*CT* 39). The Author must therefore die in order that the reader may have access to the text. Barthes perceives the authoritarian author as "the epitome and culmination of capitalist ideology."[9] Indeed the dominant realism of the nineteenth-century novel often portrays middle-class actuality in terms of business and finance. Barthes contrasts the authoritarian text with the text of bliss, or *jouissance*, the open-ended text, the text as pure language, a text which is part of a larger text, a text without a fixed meaning. Language is free-flowing, meaning is open-ended, and the reader becomes a participant in writing, that is, in creating a meaning for the text.

A number of eighteenth-century extended prose narratives are by this definition, writerly texts, texts of bliss or *jouissance*. In particular, Sterne's *Tristram Shandy*, (1759–1767), Jonathan Swift's *A Tale of a Tub* (1704), and Denis Diderot's *Jacques le Fataliste* (1796) are all texts in which the author jettisons—or attempts to jettison—his "author-ity" (Barthes' pun) by means of a variety of stratagems, most notably departures from form, whose dominant authority, rather than that of the author, was increasingly challenged during the century.[10] Other stratagems include the use of a fluid and variously-defined narrator, one whose voice shifts in person and tone; a text self-conscious of its own textuality, a textuality often evidenced by means of typographical devices, illustrations, and verbal descriptions of the manuscript;[11] a narrative movement emphasizing a structure not immediately evident rather than a conventional plot; and a frame of "factual fiction" (Lennard J. Davis's term) in which the fact, actuality, or reality of the narrative are both established and called into question.[12] Even the epistolary novel's illusion of actuality was hilariously satirized in Cleland's

Fanny Hill, in which "writing to the moment" occurs at most improbable moments, and in Sterne's more deft—and more philosophical—treatment of the time sequences and other difficulties involved in "writing a life." Whatever or whoever the author is in the eighteenth century, he, or often she, is not the monolithic Orwellian voice of the nineteenth-century Author.

The factual nature of the fiction was an important element in establishing the authority of the narrative because fiction was still often equated with lying, an attitude prevalent in Puritan thought.[13] Thus, paradoxically, the author had to assert his identity by denying it, to challenge the dominance of form by disappearing along with the form, in masquerade, disguise, or even suicide. Samuel Richardson offered a particularly convoluted explanation of the difficulty of attempting to present his readers with a convincing "true history" while at the same time maintaining that the narrative was fiction in speaking of *Clarissa*: "I could wish that the *Air* of Genuineness had been kept up, tho' I want not the letters [in *Clarissa*] to be *thought* genuine: and this for fear of weakening their influence where any of them are aimed to be exemplary; as well as to avoid hurting that kind of Historical Faith which Fiction itself is generally read with, tho' we know it to be Fiction."[14] In practical terms, Richardson was attempting to present Clarissa as a realistic moral exemplar and Lovelace as a fictional villain not to be imitated. But the sophisticated eighteenth-century reader would readily recognize the fiction. With his usual trenchant perceptiveness, Samuel Johnson wrote to Richardson (26 September 1753) objecting to his pose as the "editor" of the letters: "Of what use is disguise by which nothing is concealed?"[15] The problem has not entirely disappeared. As Barthes has observed, "'Literature' does not tell the truth, but truth is not to be found only where there are no lies."[16] A similar but reverse problem of factual fiction occurs in the twentieth century where fictions are presented as news—most notably on television, which has assumed the authority of print. Barthes himself, in *Mythologies* and elsewhere, was among the first to call attention to the fictions and "codes" (his term) embedded in the various media.

There are of course significant differences between eighteenth-and twentieth-century texts but also common points of origin. As Barthes observed, "the erotics of the new began in the eighteenth century" (*PT* 40).[17] The commonalities and similarities between Sterne's and Barthes' texts are a case in point. Both approach their life and opinions as a work of fiction, Sterne through his alter egos Tristram and Yorick, and Barthes through what he calls "the fiction of style" (*RB* 43). Barthes' narrator is variously *I*, *he*, and *RB*; the reader, often addressed as *you*, *one*, or occasionally *we*, becomes a narrator as well. Sterne's narrator also has multiple voices, and addresses the reader in different ways. Their affinities include an extensive use of graphic resources to supplement the inadequacy of language, combined with vivid verbal images; a questioning of the perceived nature of time and chronology; a questioning of subjectivity, related to both language and time; an unconventional form and narrative technique; a concern with the author's role and its relationship to the reader; and a sense of play or *jouissance* which is ultimately serious and often ends in the contemplation of death. It is perhaps more accurate to speak of these commonalities and similarities as "parallel forces," borrowing Barthes' own term (*PT* 20), rather than to seem to imply that Sterne is to be considered a neo-structuralist, a neo-post-structuralist, a neo-modernist, or a neo-postmodernist. To do so would be to reverse both cause and effect and chronology.[18] As Clement Hawes writes, "What gives Sterne imaginative leverage over novelistic conventions is not some precocious modernity or postmodernity, but rather his emergence at a pivotal moment, before such conventions had been fully consolidated and naturalized."[19] Neither Sterne nor Barthes is easily pigeonholed (Barthes' term: *RB* 49).

Roland Barthes was a novelist manqué and he regarded his texts as novelistic, that is, as like a novel "minus the characters" (*GV* 176; also 222, 223).[20] His autobiography *Roland Barthes* is preceded by an epigraphic disclaimer: "It all must be considered as if spoken by a character in a novel" (*RB* 1). As a factual fiction the "Roland Barthes" of *Roland Barthes* is no more or less real for the reader than the "Sterne" of *Tristram Shandy*. (I use "Sterne" and "Barthes," without quotation marks, as a convenient shorthand for "the person ultimately producing the text," a cumbersome locution.)[21] Barthes in fact pointed out the irony of our supposed objectivity in criticizing dead authors when he noted that "it is at the very moment when the work becomes mythical that we are supposed to regard it as a precise phenomenon" (*CT* 76). Autobiography as novel, novel as autobiography, life and opinions, or opinions with a certain amount of life added, are all, in the final analysis, texts and only texts. They may have a certain intertextuality, which might include such factual or historical documents as letters, diaries, and memoirs; and these may be as Barthes says "perhaps continuously one single text."[22] In *Tristram Shandy* and *Roland Barthes*, the boundaries between life and opinions, between fiction and nonfiction, and creative/literary writing and criticism are fluid. Insofar as characteristics of these texts seem to be a response to parallel forces in their respective cultures, they may be not isolated oddities (as indeed *Tristram Shandy* was for some time considered), but extremes of a continuum which may provide insight into the dynamics of other texts of their respective time periods.

Sterne and Barthes both exploit graphic resources. Their narrators often resort to gesture or diagram when they find words inadequate, or to emphasize a point. Sterne satirizes his own narrative method with a series of diagrams, wildly convoluted lines in contrast to the standard linear plot. Barthes includes doodles, "or the signifier without the signified," (*RB* 187) as well as some cartoons.[23] Sterne and Barthes are both deeply concerned with the body, both as creating the text and being created by the text, inscribing their own bodies into the text. Both, in fact, were burdened with tubercular bodies.[24] Sterne's race with death was ambiguously won or not won in the text he may/may not have finished at his death. Barthes' tubercular body kept him from military service (which consequently denied him certain status and privileges later). But in their "real" lives they can treat their bodies in their texts with an offhand *jouissance*. Sterne compares his to a brokenwinded horse; Barthes casually tosses an amputated tubercular rib out the window. Sterne gives us many glimpses of the writer in action—and in death, with morbid glee recording Yorick's death in black page and epitaph early in the novel, and then as gleefully bringing him back to life throughout the text. Tristram leads death a merry dance across France. In *Roland Barthes*, after the opening series of family pictures, captioned in italic type as a way of distancing the narrator, the text's progress from the mind of the writer to handwriting which is an extension of the body, to the writing implement, to the typescript, to the printed page (we often refer to the "body" of the text as opposed to notes or periphery) to the mind and body of the reader, is documented and elaborated, including even his workspace and his choice of writing implements.

It is not without significance that both Sterne and Barthes painted, that Barthes played the piano and that Sterne was an expert viol player and also wrote songs. As William Freedman points out, eighteenth-century music in general and Sterne's chosen instrument in particular required constant improvisation within certain fixed boundaries.[25] Yorick's sermons are a variation on the theme. He has annotated them with musical terms to indicate how they are to be read, terms which puzzle "Tristram" (VI, xi, 428). The digressions can thus be interpreted as the embellishments typical of eighteenth-century music, and, one might add, of visual art. (Interestingly enough, Jo Alyson Parker defines Sterne's work in terms of chaos theory, represented graphically by random ellipses within a certain defined perimeter.[26]) Barthes and Sterne were thus probably much more aware of the relationships among the visual, the auditory, and the verbal than many writers.[27] This is not to invoke the real author's "authority" in Barthes' sense, but rather as another indication that there is a physical continuum from the "hand that writes" to the reader of the text. Barthes' epigraph can be taken quite literally, for the text appears in both Barthes' hand (in French) and in italic type (*RB* 1), an image of "the hand that writes" (*RB* 4). *Roland Barthes*' text is full of graphic images: photographs, facsimiles of his notes, music ("graphic bliss" *RB* 57) and self-caricaturing cartoons augment the words. These images function as extensions and explications of text as body, most explicitly in the hospital chart as "a farcical way of writing one's body within time" (*RB* 5) and "Anatomie," a two-headed skeleton of nerves, in a style reminiscent of the illustrations in Diderot's *Encyclopédie* or eighteenth-century caricatures of the actual body beneath the finery, or an animal's head atop such finery (*RB* 181).[28] Sterne's suggestive descriptions of his characters' body language recall the many eighteenth-century texts on gesture and "painting the passions" written for the use of actors and painters, an indication of the contemporary association between the verbal and the visual. In like manner, Barthes includes midway through his text a "photomontage" of language, a series of images from the past, italicized as were the photograph captions but perhaps also to assert the power of word over photographic image (*RB* 107–9).

Sterne also includes fragments of his travel books, inset stories and manuscripts, including supposed authorities quoted in Latin and French, with accompanying slightly off-kilter translations, and in later editions a musical score among his juxtapositions of verbal and visual. Sterne uses, exaggerates, and departs from the conventions of eighteenth-century typography to create a language of graphic gesture and voice, blending into and reinforcing his use of gesture as a theme in the novel. Voice and gesture blend with the verbal in Trim's reading of the sermon, one of the two scenes Hogarth illustrated.[29] Trim must adjust the language of his body to harmonize with the reading, bending into a simulacrum of Hogarth's "line of beauty" (and also alluding by gesture to the many manuals of instruction for preaching a sermon).[30] Body and text are constantly interrelated. Throughout *Tristram Shandy*, gestures are described in minute detail: "My father shut the book,——not as if he resolved to read no more of it, for he kept his forefinger in the chapter:——not pettishly,——for he shut the book slowly; his thumb resting, when he had done it, upon the upper-side of the cover, as his three fingers supported the lower-side of it without the least compressive violence" (V, xxxiv, 394). By exaggerating them, Sterne shows the artificiality of the established conventions for gesture. Yet the appropriate gesture is more revealing and speaks more eloquently than words.[31] The most striking instance is Trim's flourishing of his stick as he says "When a man is free . . . ," followed by a gracefully convoluted serpentine line, which "said more for celibacy" than "a thousand of my father's most subtle syllogisms" (IX,v, 604).

One of the most striking of Sterne's graphic reinforcements is the black page (I, xii, 33–34: both sides are black) marking Yorick's death, in William Holtz's words a "monstrous period marking a biological as well as a syntactical full stop."[32] Further, the epitaphs in more conventional typography which precede it have already marked Yorick's end, making the emphasis all the more pronounced. Sterne's text is filled with vocal gestures, many of them indicated by typography. By reproducing a passage with and without the dashes, Holtz demonstrates the energy and quality of speech given by the punctuation.[33] In addition to the black page and the blank pages, there is the marbled page (III, xxxvi, 227–28). It is both a "motley emblem of my work" and a challenge to the reader: "for without *much reading* . . . *much knowledge*, you will no more be able to penetrate the moral of the next marbled page (motley emblem of my work!) than the world with all its sagacity has been able to unravel the many opinions, transactions and truths which still lie mystically hid under the dark veil of the black one" (III, xxxvi, 226). In most modern texts the page appears in black-and-white, giving it an emphasis similar to that of the other graphic devices. In the first and in early editions, the page was in color, handmade by a special process and tipped into each copy. Since Sterne had the original edition of the first two volumes printed at his own expense, the page, though not unprecedented, was unusual enough to throw a great deal of emphasis on both emblem and mystery.[34] It is a second and even more striking emphasis on the sudden elision of digression and comedy into seriousness and death. This "motley emblem" may be an emblem as well for the abdication or suicide of the author. No matter how frantically the author's pen races ahead, he knows that all lives and opinions end in death.

Both authors upend chronology, Sterne much more thoroughly. Since according to Barthes language is "both finite and perpetual" (*RB* 162), there is a sense in which the work is both always finished and never finished. Barthes asks himself "How will I know that the book is finished?" (*RB* 162). Sterne's critics have asked if *Tristram Shandy* is finished, differing in their answers as to whether it contains an ending. Wolfgang Iser raises an even more pertinent question: "Does *Tristram Shandy* have a beginning?"[35] Iser reads *Tristram Shandy* as a search for the beginning of the novel, and as a challenge to the teleological nature of the standard conventional novel's (or of "history's") beginning, its ending being contained in and implied by the beginning. Barthes complained that the text "dispossesses me of my narrative continuity" (*RB* 4). But Sterne quite deliberately not only dispossesses but undermines his narrative continuity as well. The preface is only found well into the third volume (III, xx, 192), and the narrative is correspondingly out of sequence. A second dedication appears at the beginning of Volume V. The constant return to the question of Tristram's conception and to his birth, the constant digressions from and return to origins, all ultimately end back in the parlor where the narrative began, and which it may psychologically never have left, no matter how far the characters have actually progressed in space and time during the course of the narrative.[36] Self-definition intersects with time: "I am this month one whole year older than I was this time twelve-month; and having got, as you perceive, almost into the middle of my fourth volume——and no farther than to my first day's life—'tis demonstrative that I have three hundred and sixty-four days more of life to write just now, than when I first set out . . . It must follow . . . that the more I write, the more I shall have to write . . . " (IV, xiii, 285–86). Sterne jokingly or possibly not so jokingly relates his life to the life of the text. "It will do well for me; and was it not that my OPINIONS will be the death of me, I perceive I shall lead a fine life of it out of this self-same life of mine; or, in other words, shall lead a couple of fine lives together" (IV, xiii, 286). Death is "to be interrupted in a story" (VII, i, 479), he tells us, adding that "every letter . . . tells me with what rapidity Life follows my pen" (IX, viii, 610).

Perhaps for both Barthes and Sterne the emphasis on beginnings could be read as an avoidance of endings, of death. The text is both always finished and never finished. Yorick's death occurs early in the novel (I, xii, 30–32), but with the narrator's constant return to beginnings and avoidance of time Yorick is present as a living character for most of the novel. His death occurs again briefly in Volume VI (xi, 426–30) in connection with the inserted narrative of Le Fever's death (VI, vii–xi, 419–39). From this point on, there are many more references to death (452, 459–62), and the sentimental tone becomes more dominant. Volume VII begins with the narrator's being interrupted by Death knocking at the door. Though the narrator (or rather his "spirits") greets him "in so gay a tone of careless indifference" that he "doubted of his commission" (VII, i, 479), the "sentimental journey" to France becomes a flight from Death, before he is even "born" (VII, xlii, 534).

Roland Barthes begins with its end. The images (mostly photographs of family, friends, and the author) at the beginning of the text are "the author's treat to himself, for finishing the book" (*RB* 3). The real beginning of the author's life is his "productive life" (*RB* 4), which begins when he leaves the sanatorium, even as Yorick also returns to life and Tristram is constantly being born. Barthes' texts are "links in a chain of meaning . . . unattached. Who will fasten it? . . . Time perhaps: to collect old texts in a new book is an attempt to question time, to solicit time to give its answer to the fragments which come from the past; but time is double—the time of writing and the time of memory—and this duplicity evokes in its turn a subsequent meaning: *time itself is a form*" (*CE* xi; emphasis mine). Time is indeed the "form" of *Tristram Shandy*, a form constantly curving and turning back on itself, a pattern shown graphically in the text (VI, xi, 473–74).[37] Writing is a challenge to conventional notions of time; linguistic time is freed from the tyranny of objective time,[38] a tyranny represented by the straight line which Tristram sets up as a mock goal for his narrative. The straight line represents the "right line,——the pathway for Christians to walk in! say divines," "The emblem of moral rectitude! says Cicero," the progress from beginning to inevitable end, "which men of wit and genius have all along confounded . . . with the line of GRAVITATION" (VI, xl, 474–75). The straight realistic narrative, the readerly text, and the wayward open-ended text, are parallel forces; the straight line is never able to meet, though it may traverse, the wayward line of the open-ended text.

Both Barthes and Sterne challenge concepts of subjectivity, of the self and its identity. Sterne approaches the question by way of Locke. Locke questions subjectivity and the identity of the self over time, maintaining that the self, rather than being an unchanging identity, is defined by ideas and language and subject to change. The concepts were greatly debated after the publication of *An Essay on Human Understanding* in 1690. One indication of the writerly nature of Sterne's text is the lack of critical consensus as to just how much Locke influenced Sterne, whether or not *Tristram Shandy* is in fact a satire of Locke's concepts, or whether Locke was even still being seriously debated by 1759.[39] Whether satirically or not, Sterne carries both the association of ideas and the train of ideas to their logical limits and beyond. The world of *Tristram Shandy* is a verbal Babel or Bedlam. Toby Shandy, with his hobby-horse of fortifications, and Walter Shandy with his hobby-horse of noses, names, and eloquence depict what in Locke's *Essay* is in fact a minor point, the notion of the association of ideas as an irrational linking of unrelated concepts, with the resultant behavior being equally illogical. No matter what subject is introduced, Toby manages to associate some aspect of fortifications with it, and go galloping away on his hobby-horse. More significant is the idea of the self as fluid, defined by thought and language, the latter not to be trusted. Sterne stretches this concept of self-definition to its logical limits as well. Combining self-definition and the association of ideas, Walter insists that a major determinant of character is the name given to a child, an hypothesis that Toby questions: would he not have fought as bravely no matter what his name? Language in Sterne is most often confused and fluid, a series of misunderstandings, most inventively in the dialogue between Toby and the Widow Wadman.

Concerned to know just how seriously incapacitating Toby's wound in the groin might be, she inquires solicitously about it. "You shall see the very place, Madam," Toby responds. "Mrs. Wadman blush'd——look'd towards the door——turn'd pale——blush'd slightly again——recovered her natural color——blush'd worse than ever; which for the sake of the unlearned reader, I translate thus——

> "*L—d! I cannot look at it——*
> What would the world say if I look'd at it?
> I should drop down, if I look'd at it——
> I wish I could look at it——
> There can be no sin in looking at it.
> ——*I will look at it*" (IX, xx, 623).

Whereupon Toby sends Trim to fetch the map of the battlefield and fortifications, so that he may point to the exact spot where he was wounded. Gesture, language, typography, and the narrator's voice unite to produce a masterly depiction and dramatization of complete cross-purposes in communication.

Barthes raises the salient question: "Do I then exist *before* my language?"(*CT* 52) We are born into language and into a cultural code. Though the basic assumption is diametrically opposed to Locke's concept of the *tabula rasa*, as Barthes observed, "language contains more uncertainties than people are prepared to admit" (*CT* 71).[40] For Barthes, the idea that "one never owns language" (*GV* 78) has particular force because of the French Academy's codification of language. Official definition of language in this encoded form was one thing Sterne did not have to contend with. The freedom of language is the freedom of the writerly text. The characters in *Tristram Shandy* each speak a unique language. With each one operating on his or her own symbolic wave-length, collision is inevitable. Deprived of language, modern man and woman, especially in dialogue with each other, are either on a collision course or hopelessly adrift. Barthes dramatized this kind of deprivation: "If I had to imagine a new Robinson Crusoe, I would not place him on a desert island but in a city of twelve million people where he could decipher neither speech nor writing." (*GV* 122). Confronted with the Widow Wadman, Toby is equally lost in *terra incognita*.

Self-definition is also questioned by the very nature of the narrative technique. There are at least two narrative voices in Sterne, those of Tristram and the narrator. Their voices sometimes blend and sometimes do not. Often both voices are drowned in the Babel created by other voices in the text. Tristram's birth becomes one grand cacophony. Dr. Slop tries frantically to unknot the strings of his bag of instruments while Tristram's mother is groaning in labor and Uncle Toby is whistling "Lillabullero" (III, x, 168–170). Latin text and English translations of a ritual condemnation, Walter's and Dr. Slop's imprecations against Obadiah, who has tied the knot, Toby's "Lillabullero" (III, xi, 171–79) continue the din. Susannah and Dr. Slop collide with mutual recriminations (III, xiii, 184). The greatest moments of cacophony occur in France, beginning with the shipboard scene and the narrator's violent seasickness (VII, ii, 481–82), when "Tristram" is on the Grand Tour while the narrator simultaneously is on his "sentimental journey." The text becomes noisier and noisier. The entirety of Volume VII is a chaos of increasing cacophony, with the flight through France, the inset stories piled one on top of each other, all mixed with extensive quotations from guidebooks, abruptly interrupted with typography and sound. Finally Tristram and the narrator, who also seems to have become a different person, are wrenched apart: "I am at this moment walking across the market-place of *Auxerre* with my father and my uncle *Toby*, in our way back from dinner——and I am this moment also entering *Lyons* with my post-chaise broke into a thousand pieces—and I am moreover this moment in a handsome pavillion built by *Pringello*, upon the banks of the Garonne, which Mons. *Sligniac* has lent me, and where I now sit rhapsodizing all these affairs. ——Let me collect myself, and pursue my journey" (VII, xxviii, 515–16). Time as form becomes so convoluted as to stretch beyond logic to a point at which language, time, form, and authority collide.[41] With the advent of Death, the narrator's self-definition splits as well. The narrator addresses his "spirits" as "ye," and it is these "spirits" who "bade him come in" and who answer Death with such humor and confidence (VII, i, 479).

Other voices occasionally pick up the narrative, and in several instances the narrator's voice seems momentarily to disappear, in the way the playwright's voice apparently disappears into the voices of his characters. In a like manner, the multiple readers addressed by the narrator, who may or may not actually be Tristram—*Sir*, *Madam*, *the public*, *Garrick*, *Eugenius*, *Jenny*, *my dear girl*, though they are themselves incorporated into the novel as quasi-characters—rather than invent the reader as a part of the fiction, permit, or even invite, the writerly reader to participate in the game, rather than to accept the authority of the author.[42] The text is open and writerly to the extreme, a text open in all directions and headed in all of them at once, its elements so closely related that a consideration of one inevitably leads to the others in a most wayward line. The most literal example is the blank page, upon which the reader is invited to draw h/er image of the Widow Wadman.

Barthes' concept of self and identity in *Roland Barthes* is even more complex. The impact of Freud and of subsequent writers influenced by his ideas, notably Lacan, raised questions of the very existence of the self, emphasizing, in Lacan's case, the idea of the "mirror stage" and the "imaginary," the self defined in relation to others and to the Other.[43] Sterne deals with the confusion as multiple individual perceptions of the world collide. In Barthes, multiple selves collide—and not just momentarily, as those of Tristram and the double narrators do in France. There are at least four identities in Barthes' text: "I," "he," "you," and "R.B.," and, further, "this 'my' is no longer 'the self'" (*RB* 68). All these pronouns "can be reversed": "the 'I' might not be 'me'"; "I can say to myself 'you' . . . in order to detach within myself . . . the producer of writing from the subject of the work (the Author)" (*RB* 168) who is also a presence. "He" can mean either "*I am He who does not speak about himself*" or that he is speaking about himself "*as though I were more or less dead* " (*RB* 168, Barthes' emphasis). Finally there is "the mockery of all this, 'he' gives way to 'I' under the simple effect of a syntactic confusion . . . , 'he' can refer without warning to many other referents" (*RB* 169). "You" in *Roland Barthes* can also be the indefinite, mutual, complicit or implicating you, in which the self-referential you is projected onto the person addressed. Barthes observes, clearly speaking of himself, that "tuberculosis projects you into a minor ethnographic society" (*RB* 35), implying that this will also be the case should the person addressed contract tuberculosis, and thus immediately drawing the reader willy-nilly into his experience. The same sort of *you* appears in the form of a hypothetical dialogue with the person addressed: "'But I never looked like that!' — 'How do you know?' What is the "you" you might or might not look like?'" (*RB* 36) The implicating *you* is akin to the editorial "we" and to the custodial "we" of nurses and distantly related to the neutral, passive, or imperial "one," which appears in juxtaposition with "we" in a paragraph of confusion about identity and writing about oneself. "Can one—or at least could one ever—begin to write without taking oneself for another?" (*RB* 99)[44]

To write about himself, the writer must in effect commit a kind of suicide, or at least castration.[45] Sterne's use of the castration motif is likewise related to identity. The nose, along with the name, is one of the major determinants of identity, since a man is composed of sexual organ and language. Castration is one result of lack of communication or miscommunication: the most outstanding example is Tristram's castration or circumcision (which one is ambiguous) by the abruptly descending window (V, xvii, 376). (Trim has taken all the leads out of the window-sashes to use for Toby's fortifications and has neglected to mention this.) Writing is one way to transcend castration, to reintegrate the self in language, to achieve mastery of language in order to arrive at an "impersonality (not to be confused with the castrating objectivity of the realist novelist), to reach that point where only the language acts 'perform,' and not 'me'" (*IMT* 143). Instead of self-description, one says "I am writing a text, and I call it *R. B.*" (*RB* 56).

Barthes above all others was quite aware of the difficulty of creating the perfect writerly text, admitting that "he himself does all he can to manipulate the reader, and that in fact he will never renounce an art of *effects*" (*RB* 102). No more could Sterne, but is this quite the same as dead "authority"? Is not manipulation a game between writer and reader, a game to see who can out-write the other? Does this not perhaps bring these mirror-image scriptors into a mutual complicity against the status quo? Does the factual fiction not perhaps draw these two (or more? whom/what/where else does one encounter in the open text?) participants in the text into a mutual fictionality? If the "person writing" is not the same as the actual person, does the "person reading," especially the person reading a writerly text, not take on a fictionality? "Can one write [read]—or at least could one ever—begin to write [read] without taking oneself for another?" (*RB* 99) If the death of the author means the "birth of the reader" (*IMT* 148), does not the reader then become a fact of the fiction? Does not the reader also find identity in writing/reading the text? As Philippe Sollers observed, the text which seems incomprehensible to the reader forces him to "come to terms with his own unintelligibility vis-à-vis himself."[46] Identity and language or writing merge: "to think is to write . . . , to read is what we are" (Sollers 77). Or as Sollers quotes Mallarmé as having said, "to think is to write without accessories" (Sollers, 66). In the writerly text, "scriptor and reader are on the same side of the fictive screen" (Sollers 79), a prescient image. Barthes notes that when the reader becomes writer and then tries to communicate by writing his impressions, he in turn becomes author. Presumably if the critic in the process creates a writerly text, he will become a scriptor among other scriptors, perhaps what Barthes had in mind when he said that literature may return to the Middle Ages, when much writing was one vast commentary.[47]

According to Barthes, the refusal to attribute "an ultimate meaning" is "an anti-theological activity [and] truly revolutionary since to refuse to fix meaning is . . . to refuse God and his hypostases—reason, science, law" (*IMT* 147). Although for Barthes the closed readerly text creates, in Kaja Silverman's words, "an Illusory sense of liberation—illusory because through that closure his or her subjectivity has been reconfirmed,"[48] his is a subjectivity that has been defined by the doxa. The status quo and the *doxa* (Barthes' term for "received opinion" and "what goes without saying") are reinforced by the readerly text; the straight line form is confirmed. The straight line leads from beginning to end, from birth to death. Language and the ludic, the comic convoluted line away from the tyranny of time, challenge death in all its aspects, challenge the readerly, the status quo. Play with language and form can thus become subversive. Sterne recognized this aspect of the subversive, introducing diagrams that mock his own text.[49] Barthes' "signifier without signified," in a similar fashion, mocks contemporary linguistic theories, as does an interpolated cartoon.[50] Milan Kundera's analysis of the way this subversion works is worth quoting at length: "No novel worthy of the name takes the world seriously. But what does 'taking the world seriously' actually mean? What it most definitely does mean is: believing what the world wants us to believe. . . . It could be objected that a novel can refuse to believe what the world wants us to believe while at the same time keeping faith with its own truth; it can refuse to take the world seriously, but still be serious itself. But what is this 'being serious'? Serious is what someone is who believes what he makes others believe. This is really *not* the case with *Tristram Shandy*; the book . . . is non-serious throughout; it doesn't make us believe in anything: neither in the truth of the characters . . . the author . . . the novel as a literary genre: *everything* is put in question . . . in doubt, *everything* is a game . . . *everything* is entertainment (with no shame at being entertaining)."[51] The writerly response to this liberating form of subversion can at once be entertainment and serious engagement with the text.

Barthes cites the Marx Brothers' *A Night at the Opera* as "the emblem of the logical subversions performed by the Text" (*RB* 81). *Tristram Shandy* has the same sort of dramatized comic chaos. Sterne's narrative method has often been compared to that of the drama. But it is even more like that of film, a manic silent film with wildly punctuated and interminable title cards. Scene after scene is followed by "title cards"—the narrator's comments—abrupt and emphasized cutting back and forth, as Bobby's death is received upstairs and in the servant's hall; freeze frames: Mrs. Shandy left in an awkward posture at the keyhole for several chapters, Walter and Toby left for several chapters on the stairs; closeup, as the Widow Wadman's forefinger follows Toby's across the map.[52] Many scenes are, in fact, constructed like those in *A Night at the Opera*, Barthes' ideal comic "textual treasury," in which "the wild mechanics of the text-on-a-spree explodes," manifesting the subversive nature of the "*preposterous*" (*RB* 80–81). *Tristram Shandy*, after all, was considered a most inappropriate work to come from a clergyman's pen, but mainly on grounds of bawdry. Its deeper possible implications of subversion apparently passed unnoticed.[53] As expressing the unorthodoxy of refusing to assign "an ultimate meaning," Sterne's open, circuitous ending could be perceived as deeply subversive of the orthodox straight-line perception of life. At the same time, it could be an affirmation of eternity and resurrection triumphing over earthly time: Yorick re-emerges from the black page. Sterne questions and flees from death, a viewpoint diametrically opposite to the acceptance and resignation accompanying Le Fever's death, or Joseph Addison's ostentatiously humble, "See in what peace a Christian can die."[54] Yorick's is a most unorthodox "resurrection."[55]

Language on a spree can be similarly subversive. One whole chapter of *Tristram Shandy* is nothing but onomatopoetic imitations of sound, a gradual buildup of noise interrupted with the slyly irreverent comment: "Your worships and your reverences love musick——and God has made you all with good ears—and some of you play delightfully yourselves——trut-prut,——prut-trut" (V, xv, 371–72). Sterne plays with the alphabet in a series of ludicrous definitions of love (VIII, xiii). Barthes also plays with language and the alphabet, using alphabetical order to randomize the order of the definitions that form much of the text of *Roland Barthes*, and then randomizing the alphabet itself when it threatens to become form.

However subversive both Sterne and Barthes are, they each have their own doxas, in Barthes' sense of the term, the values implicit or explicit in their texts. In addition, they share a lingering though paradoxical attachment to the very codes they repudiate. Barthes's ideal solution to the politics of the self "would be to transport into a socialist society certain *charms* (not *values*) of the bourgeois art of living" (*RB* 60). For Sterne the dead hand of the past was reason, as encoded in the lingering dominance of Scholasticism; and even Lockean reason, attempting to do away with outworn concepts of language and self, was at best ambiguous. Sterne's response was equally ambiguous; he could both be influenced by and at the same time satirize Locke's theories. The refuge he sought from reason was the irrational sentiment or comic madness. The narrator/Sterne opts for sentiment, while Tristram ends back in the comic. Sterne oscillated between the two, but ends with the ludic, the "cock and bull story" which is as far as we may come to solving the mystery of the marbled page. For Barthes, the dead hand of the past was the emotionalism of doxa-bound critics, the doxa of "Public Opinion, the mind of the majority, petit bourgeois Consensus, the Voice of Nature, the Violence of Prejudice" (RB 47).

Of the two writers, Barthes actually assumes more author-ity, since he resists the concept but finds that he is nonetheless enmeshed in it (*RB* 48). The logical and ideal development would be for critic and creator to merge, bound by their mutual concern with language (*TW* 134). *Roland Barthes* is his most novelistic text, the one where he assumes the least authority. Paradoxically, it is the text in which the many selves of "Roland Barthes" become most vivid, not as authority but as the perpetrator of a kaleidoscope of texts, images, and selves, of a series of seemingly random observations adding up to a semi-coherent but open-ended perspective on many different aspects of life and literature, and all the while bringing a great deal of play, even *jouissance*, for the writerly reader. The same description could apply to *Tristram Shandy*, with the further enrichment of characters and plot (such as it is). Sterne's headlong *tour de force* is ultimately the more writerly text. Sterne keeps the game up to the end, leaving the reader still beset on all sides, as Tristram says, by life's mysteries and riddles.

From our present age of commentary we may be headed off in all directions again, just as the eighteenth century was, rather than being *en route* to a new Middle Ages, as Barthes supposed.[56] Contemporay narrative in all its manifestations integrates the visual and the verbal by means of techniques unavailable to Sterne, and to a large extent also unavailable to Barthes.[57] Further, the comic book has graduated to the status of the graphic novel, as evidenced by Art Spiegelman's *Maus* (1986) and *Maus 2* (the latter winning a Pulitzer prize), Gary Trudeau's *Doonesbury*, and Martin Rowson's renditions of both *The Waste Land* and *Tristram Shandy* itself, the latter drawing on images from Piranesi to Oliver Stone.[58] The novel in verse has re-emerged with Vikram Seth's *The Golden Gate*, in Pushkin stanzas (1986) and W. S Merwin's *The Folding Cliffs* (1999). Salman Rushdie acknowledged Sterne's influence on *Midnight's Children*, a complex and thoroughly twentieth-century novel in form and content.[59] Film has now become the dominant narrative form, crossing national and cultural barriers, and film may have been where narrative has been headed all along.[60] Eighteenth-century narrative was already much influenced by the theater, after all, and director Tony Richardson, in 1963, quite deliberately used early film techniques to translate the eighteenth-century narrative of *Tom Jones* and its authorial voice to the screen. From this perspective *The Life and Opinions of Tristram Shandy, Gentleman* becomes not an eccentric text from the past but a chaotically lucid guide to twenty-first century narrative written by someone still very much alive.

NOTES

1. Roland Barthes, "The Death of the Author," *Image, Music, Text*, trans. Stephen Heath (New York: Farrar, Straus, and Giroux, 1977), 142–48. All references are to this edition and are hereafter cited in the text. I would like to thank Carole-Anne Tyler, in whose theory seminar this paper originated; Carola Kaplan, who read all the subsequent versions with insight and encouragement; and the helpful reader for *Studies in Eighteenth-Century Culture* whose suggestions for revision considerably strengthened the final text.

2. In France, of course, this concept of criticism and interpretation was reinforced by the institution of the French Academy and the concept of an official standard for literary language.

3. On this point more generally, and especially on the changing interpretations of authors' lives in response to political and social as well as literary considerations, see further Kevin Pask, *The Emergence of the English Author* (Cambridge, England: Cambridge University Press, 1996).

4. For accounts of the novel's development see the standard and invaluable texts, Ian Watt, *The Rise of the Novel* (Berkeley and Los Angeles: University of California Press, 1957); Michael McKeon, *The Origins of the English Novel, 1600–1741*, 1987 (Baltimore: Johns Hopkins University Press, 1991); J. Paul Hunter, *Before Novels* (New York and London: W. W. Norton, 1990); John J. Richetti, *Popular Fiction before Richardson: Narrative Patterns, 1700–1739* (Oxford: Clarendon Press, 1969); and Janet Todd. *The Sign of Angellica* (New York: Columbia University Press, 1989).

5. For reasons of space, I have confined my discussion to Barthes. Michel Foucault addresses some of the same issues, but he is more concerned with the emergence of the author in relation to political and social factors. See his "What Is An Author?" trans. Donald F. Bouchard and Sherry Simon, in *Contemporary Literary Criticism*, ed. Robert Con Davis and Ronald Schleifer (New York and London: Longman, 1989), 262–75.

6. Although I am here concerned primarily with the relationships between author, text, and readers, the author's self-perception and definitions of authorship in its legal, social, and political aspects, were of course significant elements in these relationships. As Brean Hammond argues, literary property and authorial renumeration were primary issues in authorial definition, issues complicated by the co-existence of the patronage system and the fees publishers paid to writers for the rights to their texts (*Professional Imaginative Writing in England, 1670–1740* [Oxford: Clarendon Press,] 1997). Alvin B. Kernan discusses the influence of the media on the development of both the literary profession and the classification of knowledge (*Printing Technology, Letters and Samuel Johnson* [Princeton, New Jersey: Princeton University Press, 1987]). Frank Donoghue (*The Fame Machine* [Stanford, California: Stanford University Press, 1996]) emphasizes the influence of reviews and reviewers in relation to high and low culture. Donoghue also analyzes Sterne as an author who shaped his image in response to critical response, and who represented the evolution of the author from patronage to self-support (keeping in mind the fact that subscription publication itself was a form of patronage.) Kevin Pask examines the importance of literary biography, in particular its effect on the development of the canon, which in turn influenced literary biography (*Emergence of the English Author).* And, as Hammond and others have observed, the theater was an important element in the development of both the author-publisher and public response relationships. All of these issues continued to be redefined and re-interpreted over a considerable period of time. Issues of authorial remuneration, for example, continued to evolve from the Licensing Act of 1707 to the establishment

of the royalty system in the 1860's. Clement Hawes, Madeline Descargues, and Carol Watts question some major assumptions about eighteenth-century "modernity" or "post-modernity" in relation to our assessments of literary history in, respectively: "Introduction," *Christopher Smart and the Enlightenment*, ed. Clement Hawes (New York: St. Martin's Press, 1999), 1–26; "Sterne, Nabokov, and the Happy (Non)Ending of Biography," *Laurence Sterne in Modernism and Postmodernism*, ed. David Pierce and Peter de Voogd (Amsterdam and Atlanta, Georgia: Rodopi, 1996), 167–78; and "The Modernity of *Tristram Shandy*, *The Shandean* 6 (November 1994), 99–118.

7. Roland Barthes, *The Pleasure of the Text*, trans. Richard Miller (New York: Hill and Wang, 1975). All references are to this edition and are hereafter cited in the text.

8. Roland Barthes, *Criticism and Truth*, trans. Richard Howard (Evanston, Illinois: Northwestern University Press, 1972), 35. All references are to this edition, hereafter abbreviated *CT* and cited in parentheses in the text.

9. Barthes, *Image, Music, Text*, 143. All references are to this edition, hereafter abbreviated *IMT* and cited in parentheses in the text.

10. For example, see Hammond's discussion of the relationship of the mock-heroic to this process (*Professional Imaginative Writing*, 105–44).

11. Graphic devices are often used for comic effect, or simply as neutral markers in the text. In Samuel Richardson's *Clarissa*, however, graphic devices resemble Sterne's black page, and almost invariably are a deathly serious underscoring of the text's moral significance.

12. Lennard J. Davis, in *Factual Fictions: The Origins of the English Novel* (New York: Columbia University Press, 1983), develops the latter point at some length, documenting the blurred lines between "news" and "fiction" from the late sixteenth century down through most of the eighteenth century. Elsewhere Davis notes that Sterne "was painfully aware . . . that to write a novel one had to perpetrate all kinds of distortions upon reality in the name of reality" (*Resisting Novels* [New York and London: Methuen, 1987], 151).

13. The Puritan concept of imaginative writing and the nature and extent of its influence is quite paradoxical and complex. See Leopold Damrosch, Jr., *God's Plot and Man's Stories* (Chicago and London: University of Chicago Press), 1985.

14. From his letter to William Warburton (19 April 1748) discussing the preface to *Clarissa*. Samuel Richardson, *Selected Letters of Samuel Richardson*, ed. John Carroll (Oxford: Clarendon Press, 1964), 85.

15. Samuel Johnson, *The Letters of Samuel Johnson*, ed. R. W. Chapman, 3 vols. (Oxford: Clarendon Press, 1952), 1: 50.

16. Roland Barthes, *The Grain of the Voice: Interviews, 1962–1980*, trans. Linda Coverdale (New York: Hill and Wang, l985), 237. All references are to this edition, hereafter abbreviated *GV* and cited in parentheses in the text.

17. Barthes, in a number of texts, discusses the breakdown of Scholastic philosophy, the attempts to restore order, and the works that escaped this attempt. The "New" is "not a fashion, but a value," he writes (*PT* 40), an attempt to escape the dead hand of the "Old."

18. As did Jean Hyppolite, saying (for rhetorical effect) that Hegel was "doing some Barthes before the fact." Jean Hyppolite, *The Languages of Criticism and the Sciences of Man: The Structuralist Controversy*, ed. Richard Macksey and Eugenio Donato (Baltimore and London: Johns Hopkins University Press, 1979), 162.

19. Clement Hawes, "Leading History by the Nose: The Turn to the Eighteenth Century in *Midnight's Children,*" *Modern Fiction Studies* 39 (Winter 1993): 155. I would suggest that by Sterne's time, novelistic conventions had become sufficiently established that his narrative method was enough of a departure from convention to engender either admiration or outrage among his readers.

20. It is a pity that Barthes did not write a novel, or at least more texts filled with verbal images like his captions, more vivid than the accompanying photographs: "*On such a path, a gradual descent toward the Poterne (0dors) and the center of town. Here one encountered some lady of the Bayonnaise bourgeoisie walking back up to her Villa des Arènes, a little package of Bon Goût in her hand*" (*RB* 7).

21. Sterne identified with "Shandyisms"and self-consciously used the style in his letters. Donoghue argues that this was an element in Sterne's growing perception of himself as author (*Fame Machine*, 64–65).

22. In speaking of the work of Georges Bataille (*IMT* 157).

23. "Structuralist fashions," a cartoon by Maurice Henry, depicts Barthes with Michel Foucault, Jacques Lacan, and Claude Lévi-Strauss, all clad only in grass skirts, seated under palm trees. Barthes is made to say "a kind of collective 'id' replaces the image I thought I had of myself" (*RB* 147).

24. There are striking physical resemblances between the two men: both have classically slightly elongated oval faces, long and prominent noses, broad brows, and in the case of the cover photograph for *RB* and the Joseph Nollekens bust of Sterne, even similar hair styles. (See photograph of the bust [1766] in Melvyn New, *Tristram Shandy, A Book for Free* spirits [New York: Twayne Publishers, 1994], vi: 1766. Barthes and Sterne, in the cover photograph and Reynolds' 1760 portrait, strike similar poses. René Bosch ("'Character' in Reynolds' Portrait of Sterne," *The Shandean* 6 [November 1994]) convincingly demonstrates the varying accuracy of Sterne likenesses, citing the Nollekens bust as a particularly accurate likeness. See also Kenneth Monkman, "The Skull," *The Shandean* 7 (November 1995): 45–79.

25. William Freedman, *Laurence Sterne and the Origins of the Musical Novel* (Athens: University of Georgia Press, 1978), *passim.*

26. Jo Alyson Parker, "Spiraling Down 'the Gutter of Time': *Tristram Shandy* and the Strange Attractor of Death," *Weber Studies* 14 (Winter 1997): 102–14. See also Stuart Sim, "All that exist are 'islands of determinism': Shandean Sentiment and the Dilemma of Postmodern Physics," in *Laurence Sterne in Modernism and Postmodernism*, ed. David Pierce and Peter de Voogd (Amsterdam and Atlanta, Georgia: Rodopi, 1996), 109–22.

27. The music for Toby's "Lilliburlero" was included in later editions (*TS* 70). Barthes includes a page of sheet music, his composition on a poem by Charles d'Orleans, signed and dated 1939, with the caption, "Graphic bliss: before painting, music" (RB 55).

28. "To write the body. Neither the skin, nor the muscles, nor the bones, nor the nerves, but the rest: an awkward, fibrous, shaggy, raveled thing, a clown's coat" (*RB* 181).

29. The other is Tristram's christening. See Laurence Sterne, *The Life and Opinions of Tristram Shandy, Gentleman*, ed. James A. Work (Indianapolis and New York: Odyssey Press, 1940), II, xvi, 121; IV, xv, 289). All references to this edition are hereafter cited in parentheses in the text: Sterne's volume and chapter divisions are given in Roman numerals, followed by the page number in Work's edition. The most recent and definitive edition of *The Life and Opinions of Tristram Shandy, Gentleman* is published by the University Presses of Florida (ed. Melvyn New and Joan New, 3 vols. [Gainesville, 1978]).

30. As Donoghue points out, Sterne's sermons were "occasionally prefaced with a list of 'dramatis personae,' and were originally to be published under the title, *The Dramatic Sermons of Mr. Yorick*" (*Fame Machine*, 68). There were, however, relatively few "dramatic" or "Shandean" sermons (Melvyn New, ed., *The Sermons of Laurence Sterne*, vols. 4 and 5, The Florida Edition of the Works of Laurence Sterne [Gainesville, Florida: University of Florida Press, 1996], 5: 8.) Despite his playful presentation of the sermon in *Tristram Shandy*, Sterne, as Melvyn New demonstrates, took his sermons seriously (New, *ibid.*, 5: vii–xx; and 5: 1–55) Published in 1760, the first two volumes of sermons included Sir Joshua Reynolds' portrait (New, *ibid.*, 5: 1). Further, Sterne considered Sermon II one of his best. Though it opens with a witticism, the rest is a serious explication of Ecclesiastes vii. 2, 3: "It is better to go to the house of mourning, than to the house of feasting" (New, *ibid.*, 68; for the text of the sermon, see 4: 12–20).

31. Similarly, Barthes uses a diagram of a gesture in order to illustrate a novelistic technique (*IMT* 103).

32. William Holtz, "Typography, *Tristram Shandy*, the Aposiopesis, etc.," *The Winged Skull: Papers from the Laurence Sterne Bicentenary Conference at the University of York*, ed. Arthur H. Cash and John M. Stedmond (Kent State University Press; London: Methuen, 1971), 250.

33. Ibid., 252. It is worth observing here that Sterne's sermons were often punctuated with long dashes, and that words and passages appear in italics, and, occasionally, block capitals. As Roger Chartier demonstrates, when dramatic texts in England were printed with "formal mechanisms . . . borrowed from French published theatrical works," such as act and scene divisions, stage directions, and lists of dramatis personae, they acquired a new and elevated status. See his *Order of Books*, trans. Lydia G. Cochrane (Stanford: Stanford University Press, 1994), 53.

34. W. G. Day, in "*Tristram Shandy* :The Marbled Leaf," *The Library* 27 (1972): 143–45, describes the process of printing, pointing out that some later eighteenth-century editions omitted the marbled page or printed it in black and white.

35. Wolfgang Iser, *Laurence Sterne: Tristram Shandy*, trans. David Henry Wilson, Landmarks of World Literature (Cambridge: Cambridge University Press, 1988), 1.

36. As Work observes, the narrative's "veritable chronology" of dates and events is actually the "most obvious structural device" ("Introduction," *TS*, xlviii). The

physical "life," the action, moves in space and time; the "opinions," the interior life, constantly reverts to Tristram's conception and birth — or to his or the narrator's death.

37. As Victor Shklovsky notes: "By violating the form, he forces us to attend to it; and, for him, this awareness of the form through its violation constitutes the content of the novel" ("Sterne's *Tristram* Shandy: Stylistic Commentary," *Russian Formalist Criticism*, trans. and ed. Lee T. Lemon and Marion J. Reis [Lincoln: University of Nebraska Press, 1965], 30–31, 55–56). Shklovsky considers Sterne's diagrams as evidence of this awareness.

38. Roland Barthes, "To Write: An Intransitive Verb?" *Language of Criticism and the Sciences of Man*, ed. Macksey and Donato, 136–38.

39. Sterne's relationship to Locke is a complex one. Melvyn New briefly discusses the issue in his introduction to the notes for the Florida Edition of *Tristram Shandy*, referring the reader to studies by John Traugott, Kenneth MacLean, Ernest Tuveson, Arthur Cash, and Helen Moglen. See the notes to *Tristram Shandy,* ed. by Melvyn New with Richard A. Davies and W. G. Day (Gainesville: University Presses of Florida, 1984), 3: 7 n. 8; and 3: 16–17. John Vignaux Smyth's *A Question of Eros: Irony in Sterne, Kierkegaard, and Barthes* (Tallahassee: Florida State University Press, 1986) is a persuasive argument for Sterne's satire of Locke. Christopher Fox (*Locke and the Scriblerians* [Berkeley, Los Angeles, London: University of California Press, 1988]) lucidly summarizes the issues raised by Locke's views of subjectivity. Given Locke's extensive influence in areas of thought ranging from epistemology to education to economics, I would argue that by mid-century his major ideas, like Freud's in the twentieth century, were part of the basic cultural assumptions even among those who had not actually read him.

40. As did Locke. The Widow Wadman episode could be read as a comic gloss on *An Essay concerning Human Understanding* III. ii. in which Locke says that "*words in their primary or immediate Signification, stand for nothing, but the* Ideas *in the Mind of him that uses them . . . .*" (*An Essay concerning Human Understanding*, ed. Peter H. Nidditch [Oxford: Clarendon Press, 1975, rpt. 1990]: II. ii. 2. 405, original emphasis). Locke goes on to point out the "unavoidable Obscurity and Confusion into their signification, whenever we make them stand for any thing, but those *Ideas* we have in our own minds" (II. ii. 5. 407).

41. The epistolary novel shares this paradox, but attempts to mask it, presenting the narrative and letters as happening in real time.

42. For a different reading, see Betty Rizzo, "'How Could You, Madam, be so inattentive': Tristram's Relationship with the Reader," *Approaches to Teaching Sterne's* Tristram Shandy (New York: The Modern Language Association of America, 1989), 67–71. See also Donoghue (*Fame Machine*, 56–58) for Sterne as author in relation to his readers. Eighteenth-century readers often rewrote or attempted to rewrite texts. There were numerous satires of and additions to *Tristram Shandy*. While leading his readers a merry chase, Sterne actually modified the content of the final books according to readers' responses, moving from satire to sentiment after sales declined (*Fame Machine*, 75). Richardson on the other hand was bombarded with requests to save Clarissa, and even with drafts of possible endings, but resisted his readers to the end.

43. Lacan's is a more sophisticated interpretation, but "man is a social animal," both formed by and reflecting h/er society, was a commonplace among eighteenth-century thinkers.

44. For further analysis of the effect of pronouns on content, see Hawes, *Smart*, 202–5. As Hawes points out, the analysis of pronouns' effect on reader response, in this case the effect of the sublime made by changing from singular to plural, or vice-versa, goes back to Longinus *On the Sublime*.

45. See Barthes' analysis of Honoré de Balzac's *Sarrasine* in *S/Z*, 1974, trans. Richard Miller (New York: Hill and Wang; Noonday Press, 1974). Norman Simms documents the prevalence of anti-Semitism in England in relation to circumcision fantasies as a threat to gentile males ("The Missing Jews and Jewishness in *Tristram Shandy*," *The Shandean* 4 [November 1992]: 135–52).

46. Philippe Sollers, "Literature and Totality," *Writing and the Experience of Limits*, ed. David Hayman, trans. Philip Barnard with David Hayman (New York: Columbia University Press, 1983), 76. All further references are to this edition and hereafter cited in parentheses in the text. "Literature and Totality" was first presented in one of Roland Barthes' seminars, November 1965.

47. Barthes has a number of references to Aristotle's system of rhetoric and to the medieval approach to rhetoric and literature. One of the most extensive discussions is in "To Write: An Intransitive Verb" in *The Languages of Criticism and the Sciences of Man: The Structuralist Controversy* (Baltimore and London: Johns Hopkins Press, 1970), hereafter cited in parentheses as *TW*.

48. Kaja Silverman, *The Subject of Semiotics* (New York: Oxford University Press, 1983), 245.

49. Sterne could here be asserting the untidiness of actual life rather than challenging the ideal of the straight line. The wayward text might thus be read as a commentary on human fallibility, making a point about the paradoxical nature of Christianity as well as his own erratic narrative. See New's discussion of Sterne's essential orthodoxy (*Sermons*, 5: 27–35).

50. One of Johnny Hart's *BC* cartoons, with the caption "The History of Semiology," in which a character riding a stone unicycle passes a sign saying "sign ahead," which, when it appears, reads simply "sign" (*RB* 128).

51. Milan Kundera, "Introduction to a Variation," *Jacques and His Master* (1981), trans. Simon Callow (London and Boston: Faber and Faber, 1986), 13. Tim Parnell challenges Kundera's argument, saying that though both Sterne and Kundera "deploy sceptical rhetoric for dogmatic ends," Sterne uses the "rhetoric of scepticism in the service of embattled Anglican orthodoxy" ("Sterne and Kundera: The Novel of Variations and the Noisy Foolishness of Human Certainty," in *Modernism and Postmodernism*, 155).

52. I am indebted here to Tony Richardson, who suggested a similarity between the eighteenth-century novel and silent film techniques in filming *Tom Jones*. John Osborne wrote the script. See further Osborne, *Tom Jones: A Film Script* (New York: Grove Press, 1964).

53. The critical reception of the novel is concisely summarized in Alan B. Howe's introduction to *Sterne: The Critical Heritage* (London and Boston: Routledge & Kegan Paul, 1974), 1–36.

54. Edward Young, "Conjectures on Original Composition," in *Eighteenth-Century English Literature*, ed. Geoffrey Tillotson, Paul Fussell, Jr., and Marshall Waingrow (New York: Harcourt, Brace, & World, Inc., 1969), 888.

55. Sim argues that *Tristram Shandy* expresses a deterministic "metaphysics of catastrophe" (*Islands*, 120) but that would make it more subversive of traditional doctrine than I believe it to be. Because determinism challenges free will, an essential element in the Christian scheme of salvation, if *Tristram Shandy* is indeed deterministic, it is to that extent theologically subversive. Rather, I tend to agree with New that Sterne's "riddles and mysteries" are part of a long Christian tradition in which God's plan is obscure to humanity (4: xii.; 4: 293).

56. See Chartier's discussion of "the return of the author" (op. cit., 70).

57. Though both Sterne and Barthes may well have appreciated Mark Salzman's recent "Viva La Resolucion: Music and the Novel." Salzman combined the oldest form of narrative technique with music available well before the twentieth century, narrating "a story with a similar emotional arc to Bach's Cello Suite No. 3 in C major—while playing the suite." Salzman's rationale was that "the struggle to create narrative coherence and resolution in music and in fiction cannot be separated from our struggle to find narrative coherence and resolution in our lives" (Los Angeles *Times*, "Weekend," Thursday, June 22, 2000, 5).

58. For examples of Rowson's interpretation, see Martin Rowson, "Hyperboling Gravity's Ravelin: A Comic Book Version of *Tristram Shandy*," *The Shandean* 7 (November 1995): 62–88.

59. See Clement Hawes, "Leading History by the Nose," 147–68. There are of course numerous other examples of thematic and formal variety in late twentieth-century narratives, for example, authors such as Italo Calvino (in particular his *If on a winter's night a traveler* [1979]) or Jorge Luis Borges, and entire genres such as magic realism and science fiction.

60. Addison commented that landscapes in motion, produced by the camera obscura, were an art form more closely resembling nature than any other representations (Joseph Addison, Richard Steele, et. al., *The Spectator*, ed. Donald F. Bond, 5 vols. [Oxford: The Clarendon Press, 1965], *Spectator* 414, 3: 550–51 and ibid., n. 2; *Spectator* 31, 1: 128–29, n. 5). As Fredric Jameson asks, "Did human nature change on or about December 28, 1895? Or was some cinematographic dimension of human reality always there somewhere in prehistoric life, waiting to find its actualization in a certain high-technical civilization? (and thereby now allowing us to reread and rewrite the past now filmically as the philosophy of the visual?)." See his *Signatures of the Visible* (New York and London: Routledge, 1992), 5.

Addison's Aesthetics of Novelty

SCOTT BLACK

The history of eighteenth-century British aesthetics has been written mainly as an explication of two terms, the beautiful and the sublime, with critics generally taking as their starting point Burke's disqualification of "novelty" as a separate category of analysis. Only recently have some begun to account for the historical fact of this category before the *Enquiry* (1757).[1] In this paper I examine "novelty," not to correct Burke or to defend the pleasures of novelty, but to offer an account of its significance as one of three terms—great, beautiful, novel—in Addison's "Pleasures of the Imagination" (1712).[2] I argue that novelty is the central category of the "Pleasures," offering a self-reflection of both the *Spectator* itself and the dynamics of the civil society that the periodical essay was instrumental in articulating.[3]

For the last sixty years, Addison has been read as a precursor of the romantic sublime.[4] Clarence DeWitt Thorpe (1937) concludes his study of novelty by saying that Addison helped "open the way to . . . phases of romantic critical philosophy," while Robin Dix more recently (1986) suggests that the category was a starting point for attitudes that were "more firmly established, and more fully developed, by the Romantic theorists."[5] Neil Saccamano challenges the teleology of the sublime that underwrites such work, offering instead a discussion of the sublime's "logic" and "dynamics" in the "Pleasures."[6] For all the rigor with which he resists the telos of a sublime history, though, Saccamano structures his account by its terms, reading Addison with reference to Burke: "Unlike Burke, Addison neither defines a distinct aesthetic pleasure (delight) to cover this negative category [fear], nor considers terror the predominant sublime pleasure."[7] But what Addison didn't do does not fully explain what he did do, and what he did do is perhaps best understood by entertaining his own terms. For instance, Saccamano says "the 'pleasing Astonishment' felt in surveying the infinite universe after reading the 'Theories' of 'the new Philosophy'" is "one of the moments entitling the 'Pleasures' to its place in histories of the Kantian natural sublime."[8] In the paper to which this refers (S #420), Addison does write of things that will be explained by the sublime, but I don't think he writes of them in sublime terms: "The Understanding, indeed, opens an infinite Space on every side of us, but the Imagination, after a few faint efforts, is immediately at a stand and finds her self swallowed up in the immensity of the Void that surrounds us" (S, 3:576). Addison's response to this gap between the understanding and imagination is to wonder if the reason for "this Defect of Imagination" might be that there is not enough "room in the Brain for such variety of Impressions" (S, 3:577)—an empirical question that refers to a Lockean problematic.

The sublime offers one model of reflection, but not the only one in the history of eighteenth-century aesthetic thinking. Discussing an example of Locke's imagery of the infinite, Jules David Law notes "there is no aesthetics of the sublime here; the sensation of failure (constitutive of the 'confused' comparative idea or the attempt to comprehend the negative as a positive idea) does not present itself as a dramatic solution to the tension between the knowable and the unknowable. We might say that the difference between Locke on the one hand and Burke or Kant on the other is that Locke refuses to *thematize* failure."[9] I think something similar is going on in Addison's explicitly Lockean aesthetics. Law describes such "empiricist reflection" as "a self-critical procedure, in which perpetual correction and revision (of impressions, of language, and of judgments) are more important that the establishing of permanent categories or conditions of knowledge."[10] This equally describes the method of essay writing, and I argue that Addison develops the category of novelty in order to explain the effects of the essay. Novelty theorizes the pleasures of essays, and this offers an alternative to an aesthetics organized by the sublime.

Michael McKeon has argued that aesthetics emerged as a field by "replacing" theology.[11] Rather than being the medium through which controversy is decided, theology became a participant in debate, one category of explanation among others.[12] McKeon describes aesthetics as "the last refuge of transcendent spirit, the discourse of literary and artistic experience."[13] But sometimes there is new wine in new bottles, and with "novelty" Addison's aesthetics provided a mode of reflection that did not merely explain what theology explained (making transcendence a function of art rather than God), but rather explained what theology explained in a different way, offering new explanatory structures along with new explanations. The desire for transcendence is explained by its mechanics—desire—not its object—God. The challenge of Addison's aesthetics is that it does not *replace* theology so much as *displace* it, not just offering new ways of theorizing transcendence, but also providing the terms for a different kind of abstraction: the "Method" that "the Essay Writer must practice."[14]

With the "Pleasures of the Imagination" Addison provides terms for understanding the effects of the periodical essay. The pleasures of the imagination occupy a middle area between "Sense" and "Understanding," a virtuous way to "Step out of Business" without stepping into "Vice or Folly" (S #411, 3:537, 3:539). Echoing his earlier suggestion that the press be used to "unbend the Mind from its more severe Employments with innocent Amusements" (S #124, 1:507), Addison says the imagination allows "a gentle Exercise of the Faculties," a break from the "serious Employments" of the understanding without the "Negligence and Remissness" of "sensual Delights" (S #411, 3:539). The imagination "serves as a kind of Refreshment, and takes off from that Satiety we are apt to complain of in our usual and ordinary Entertainments" (S #412, 3:541), and when Addison begins to categorize the pleasures of the imagination (great, beautiful, and novel), "novelty" names such diversion and variety:

> Every thing that is new or uncommon raises a Pleasure in the Imagination, because it fills the Soul with an agreeable Surprise, gratifies its Curiosity, and gives it an Idea of which it was not before possest. . . . whatever is new or uncommon contributes a little to vary human Life, and to divert our Minds, for a while, with the Strangeness of its Appearance: . . . It is this that recommends Variety, where the Mind is every Instant called off to something new. (S #412, 3:541)

With the category of "novelty," Addison theorizes the pleasures of the *Spectator*, and so provides an aesthetics for the emerging urban and urbane public space defined by the periodical essay.

"Wrought into a World": Creation and the Aesthetics of Novelty

The pleasures of the imagination, as Addison stresses in the first paper in the series (S #411), are specifically pleasures. They are not substitutes for understanding, but refreshments that allow the mind to relax after the labor of thinking:

> the Pleasures of the Fancy are more conducive to health, than those of the Understanding, which are worked out by dint of Thinking, and attended with too violent a Labour of the Brain. Delightful Scenes whether in Nature, Painting, or Poetry, have a kindly Influence on the Body, as well as the Mind, and not only serve to clear or brighten the Imagination, but are able to disperse Grief and Melancholy, and to set in motion the Animal Spirits in pleasing and agreeable Motions. For this reason Sir *Francis Bacon*, in his Essay upon Health, has not thought it improper to prescribe to his Reader a Poem or Prospect, where he particularly dissuades him from ["]knotty and subtile Disquisitions["], and advises him to pursue ["]Studies, that fill the Mind with splendid and illustrious Objects, as Histories, Fables, and Contemplations of Nature["]. (S, 3:539)

As part of his project to bring learning out of the closet and into the public (S #10, 1:44), Addison routinely peppers his papers with quotations, which he usually carefully attributes. Here he quotes Bacon's "Of Regiment of Health." The actually quoted lines (which I have indicated) surround a sentence of Bacon's that is of central significance for the "Pleasures" but that is withheld until the next number. Here is Bacon's text, with Addison's quotations marked:

> As for the passions and studies of the mind, avoid envy, anxious fears, anger fretting inwards, *subtle and knotty inquisitions*, joys and exhilarations in excess, sadness not communicated. Entertain hopes, mirth rather than joy, variety of delights rather than surfeit of them, wonder and admiration (and therefore novelties), *studies that fill the mind with splendid and illustrious objects (as histories, fables, and contemplations of nature)*.[15]

I read Addison's "Grief and Melancholy" as a gloss on Bacon's "sadness not communicated." Melancholy is the unsocial humor, the disease of the solitary scholar, and for both Addison and Bacon the imagination is the means to return from the closet of study to the world of conversation. Between the knotty and subtle investigations of the melancholy scholar and the cure for this in "splendid and illustrious objects" that relieve the mind from envy, anxiety and anger, Bacon suggests the moderating influence of "variety," "wonder and admiration," and grounds these in "novelties," which in turn serve to introduce those splendid objects that correct the diseases of solitary study. Novelties, for Bacon, bring the scholar to communication, offering relief from the isolated passions of the study, as they return one to wonder, the motive that grounds the modern method of natural philosophy.[16]

Several reasons could account for Addison's elision of Bacon's passage. If, as I argue, the most important thing Addison takes from Bacon is the one elided, one could suppose an anxiety of influence. But the source is not suppressed; Bacon is named, and named as an authority, one of those "Polite Masters" Addison wants to credit as a source and exemplar of polite writing (S #421, 3:577). Or perhaps in writing about novelty Addison wants to be new, to exemplify the content by the form. The novelty of the observation (and so the suppression of the old text) would provide the effect Addison wants to claim for the concept as the reader's affective response will demonstrate the truth of what he says. But there is only the faintest gesture of elision, indeed the text is announced, and even recommended. Addison's delayed introduction of "novelty," then, seems an effect neither of anxiety nor cleverness, but part of a strategy of emphasis by deferral. In citing Bacon, Addison relies not only on what is directly quoted, but on the passage in its entirety. If a diligent reader had looked up Bacon, she would find that what Addison had omitted today hints at what's to come tomorrow. The ellipses serve as an invitation. What Bacon mentions becomes a central point Addison makes about the efficacy of the pleasures of the imagination, and by allowing the reader to find "novelty" for herself, Addison involves her in one of the activities analyzed under the category of novelty.

Addison uses Bacon to suggest that the imagination resocializes the solitary (dispersing melancholy) and returns the scholar to wonder (clearing and brightening the mind). But in strategically quoting him, Addison leaves out of this introductory paper the precise means by which Bacon says the imagination accomplishes its tasks. Explicating this means becomes a central purpose of the "Pleasures," and Addison returns to it as he begins his analysis of the imagination, introducing novelty as the category of aesthetic pleasure that explains the attraction of the whole series of papers. When he announced the "Pleasures," Addison promised to offer more than the "Mechanical rules" of criticism and rather "shew . . . the several Sources of that Pleasure which rises in the Mind upon the Perusal of a noble Work." This is meant to correct the "Gothic taste which has taken Possession among us," a taste that has "no manner of Influence, either for bettering or enlarging the Mind" (S #409, 3:530). Aesthetics is a method of self-knowledge; a study of the effects of reading will make better, more self-aware readers. Echoing Bacon, Addison says the motivating force of knowledge is the pleasure of novelty: God "has annexed a secret Pleasure to the Idea of any thing that is *new* or *uncommon*, that he might encourage us in the Pursuit after Knowledge, and engage us to search into the Wonders of his Creation"; such pleasure "serves as a Motive to put us upon fresh Discoveries" (S #413, 3:545). Novelty explains the practice of aesthetics as a "Pursuit after Knowledge" that will exercise and "enlarg[e] the Mind" by motivating this "search into the Wonders of . . . Creation."

In the "Pleasures" such wonders are represented by Ovid. Addison uses Homer to exemplify the pleasures of the great, Virgil the beautiful, and Ovid the novel: "When we are in the *Metamorphoses*, we are walking on enchanted Ground, and see nothing but Scenes of Magick lying round us" (S #417, 3:564). Ovid "describes a Miracle in every Story, and always gives us the Sight of some new Creature" (S, 3:565). Magic becomes miracle, and the gesture towards the divine is fulfilled at the end of the paper when the "strange" (or "novel") in *Paradise Lost* is exemplified by "the Creation of the World," along with the rebellious angels' metamorphoses (into devils) and Satan's "Search after Paradise" (S, 3:566).[17] Ovid's magical and miraculous re-creations (metamorphoses) are sacralized in Milton's "Creation of the World," the consummate act of novelty, the originary making of something new. This suggests a change in Addison's thinking. Earlier he had characterized both "the Battel of the Angels, and the Creation of the World" as "great Actions" (S #267, 2:540). Here, while still calling the battle of angels "great," he calls Creation "novel." Turning to another example of the novelty of *Paradise Lost* will help flesh out the implications of this realignment of creation with novelty. (I return to Ovid and Virgil at the end of the paper.)

Addison's third example of novelty in Milton, Satan's "Search after Paradise" (S, 3:566), refers back to an earlier discussion of *Paradise Lost*. In #315, he had written:

> Satan's Walk upon the Outside of the Universe, which, at a Distance, appeared to him of a globular Form, but upon his nearer Approach, looked like an unbounded Plain, is natural and noble: As his roaming upon the Frontiers of the Creation, between that Mass of Matter, which was wrought into a World, and that shapeless unform'd Heap of Materials, which still lay in Chaos and Confusion, strikes the Imagination with something astonishingly great and wild. (S, 3:143–44)

Here is the passage Addison refers to:

> Meanwhile upon the firm opacous Globe
> Of this round World, whose first convex divides
> The luminous inferior Orbs, enclos'd
> From Chaos and the inroad of Darkness old,

> Satan alighted walks: a Globe far off
> It seem'd, now seems a boundless Continent
> Dark, waste, and wild, under the frown of Night
> Starless expos'd, and ever-threatening storms
> Of Chaos blust'ring round, inclement sky.[18]

Addison describes the passage's movement as two-fold, with two specific effects generated by it. He refers to the first half as "natural and noble," and I take the phrase "enclos'd / From Chaos" as the key moment in this phase, while the "great and wild" effect of the second half is exemplified by "Chaos blust'ring round." Addison's commentary on the passage's two movements (first in "From Chaos" and then out to "Chaos blust'ring round") is summarized by the "globular Form" (Addison adds the "Form" to Milton's "Globe") and its opposite, the "unform'd Heap of Materials." In this earlier paper on *Paradise Lost*, "Chaos and Confusion" and "a globular Form" exemplify respectively the great and the beautiful (the natural corresponds to the beautiful), but in the "Pleasures" the passage illustrates novelty.[19] The novelty of the passage seems to be the movement of Satan from the unwrought to the wrought. This is the activity of creation, and in the passage, Satan—and Milton's reader—do what creation does, move from chaos to form, while discovering for the first time, creation, the new world itself. Creation is the original transformation, and this passage enacts that first look at the original novel thing, "that Mass of Matter, which was wrought into a World." Characterized by Ovid's metamorphoses and Milton's Creation, novelty describes the pleasures of bringing form to chaos, the pleasures of creation as well as recreation.

As the *Spectator* developed, Addison realigned his categories, and by the time of the "Pleasures" novelty is distinctly dynamic. Whereas earlier Addison said Homer's characters have "a certain Dignity as well as Novelty" (S #273, 2:562), in the "Pleasures" epic dignity serves as foil for the dynamism of novelty. The greatness of *Paradise Lost* is exemplified by its epic qualities, but now these are confined, like Homer, to static actions and preformed characters, the battle of angels, the majesty of the messiah, and the stature of Satan (S, 3:566).[20] The beautiful likewise is inactive. Addison had earlier described Milton's Paradise as "the Scene of the principal Action," a "picture of Still-Life," one of "the weak unactive Parts of the Fable" (S #321, 3:170); in the "Pleasures" it is featured as one of the beautiful aspects of *Paradise Lost*, along with heaven, the angels, Adam and Eve. The beautiful describes the stages on which the action happens and the created beings who act these ordered dramas on something approaching human scale.[21]

Homer's "great" is "Savage," "uncultivated," and "mis-shapen," while Virgil's "beautiful" is "well-ordered" (S #417, 3:564).[22] What's unformed is great, what's formed is beautiful, but the activities of metamorphoses and creation are novel. In #321, Satan's "transforming himself into different Shapes" gives "an agreeable Surprize" (S, 3:172), a phrase that is later repeated as one of the effects of novelty (S, 3:541). The category of novelty articulates the pleasures of change and creation, the pleasure taken in the movement from the unformed to form (or, for pagans like Ovid, from form to form). Addison returns to this in the concluding paper of the series when he says the imagination has "something in it like Creation" (S #421, 3:579). The analogy between this faculty of the mind and divine creation suggests that the pleasures the imagination takes in novelty are the pleasures of its own powers of creation. For Addison, novelties bring the mind to a recognition of its own active power, and through his Miltonic expansion of Ovid, he connects this with the power of creation, the activity of participating in Creation.[23]

If the mind recognizes its own powers through the experience of novelties, novelties also stimulate further mental activity. The "new Principle of Pleasure" that Addison discusses as the secondary pleasures of the imagination—"the Action of the Mind" in comparing copies with even unpleasant originals such as dunghills (S #418, 3:566–67)—should be understood as an aspect of novelty.[24] Novelty names the mind's delight in moving between representations and the natural world. And reversing this process, returning refreshed to the study from which novelty first rescued one, activates the processes discovered by novelty (the mind's powers of representation)—bringing one from aesthetic appreciation to the activity of copying, now not after the truths of nature, but the truths of the understanding.

Some turn like this seems necessary to explain the cryptic lines in the final, summary paper on the imagination (#421):

> The Pleasures of the Imagination are not wholly confined to such particular Authors as are conversant in material Objects, but are often met with among the Polite Masters of Morality, Criticism, and other Speculations abstracted from Matter; who, though they do not treat directly of the visible Parts of Nature, often draw from them Similitudes, Metaphors, and Allegories. By these Allusions a Truth in the Understanding is as it were reflected by the Imagination; we are able to see something like Colour and Shape in a Notion, and to discover a Scheme of Thoughts traced out upon Matter. And here the Mind receives a great deal of Satisfaction, and has two of its Faculties gratified at the same time, while the Fancy is busy copying after the Understanding, and transcribing Ideas out of the Intellectual World into the Material. (S, 3:577)

The "Pleasures of the Imagination" opened by discussing the relaxing uses of aesthetic pleasure. As a break from the work of the understanding, the imagination refreshes the mind by contemplating novelties. As Addison develops the category of novelty, it becomes the effect through which we recognize the imagination's power of representation. The final paper opens by suggesting that the pleasure of recognizing this very power of re-creation is the source of morality, criticism, and abstract speculations. What makes the abstractions of the understanding communicable (what brings the work from the study to other people) is the power of fancy to bring its ideas into material, to give shape and form to thought. Intensifying this in the same way as he did his earlier *Paradise Lost* criticism, Addison says the imagination "has something in it like Creation; It bestows a kind of Existence . . . It makes Additions to Nature, and gives a greater variety to God's Works" (S #421, 3:579). From the pleasures of variety to the creation of more variety, Addison has moved from recreation to creation, and he finally describes the activity of the imagination in the register of novelty, as creation and variety.

Periodical essays, then, are novel objects. In them, the imagination makes sense of the understanding, gives shape to ideas, and orders chaos. Earlier, Mr. Spectator had described the process of composing the *Spectator* as forming it from a mess of notes he described as "my Speculations in the first Principles, that (like the World in its Chaos) are void of all light, Distinction and Order" (S #46, 1:196). Novelty explains the pleasure we take in finding "Form" in "that shapeless unform'd Heap of Materials, which still lay in Chaos and Confusion," and so also describes Mr. Spectator's method. In this way Addison lightheartedly connects essay writing to creation: both exemplify the activity of forming that makes the human world human, the world in which we live beyond the limits of the natural world by copying the creative act that made it.

Such freedom, though, is ambiguous and seems to threaten Addison as well as excite him. He writes: "It is this Talent of affecting the Imagination, that gives an Embellishment to good Sense, and makes one Man's Compositions more agreeable than another's" (S #421, 3:578). But the ability to reform readers is based on the possibility of deforming them as well: "how great a Power then may we suppose lodged in him, who knows all the ways of affecting the Imagination, who can infuse what Ideas he pleases, and fill those Ideas with Terror and Delight to what Degree he thinks fit? . . . he can so exquisitely ravish or torture the Soul through this single Faculty, as might suffice to make up the whole Heaven or Hell of any finite Being" (S, 3:580). At the end of the "Pleasures," Addison returns to *Paradise Lost*, echoing the proud comment of Satan, "The mind is its own place, and in itself / Can make a Heav'n of Hell, a Hell of Heav'n."[25] Satanic pride in the autonomy of the mind figures the danger of affecting others through the imagination. Precisely because they give pleasure in diverting the mind from understanding, such compositions can also distract it, remaking the world into another, sinister, creation.

This Satanic ending of the "Pleasures" characterizes the abuse of the imagination as a sin of pride, an error of enthusiasm.[26] If that's the case on Thursday (#421), on Friday (#422) Steele addresses such fears by analogizing writing and conversation: "What has been said to be the mark of a good Writer, will fall in with the Character of a good Companion. The good Writer makes his Reader better pleased with himself, and the agreeable Man makes his Friends enjoy themselves, rather than him, while he is in their Company" (S, 3:583–84). Politeness moderates the vulgarity of pride (here a "Raillery" that disturbs "Conversation"), and discovers in others, as novelty discovers in things, what may be concealed, even to themselves. Steele is referring back to the opening of the "Pleasures": "A Man of Polite Imagination . . . looks upon the World, as it were, in another Light, and discovers in it a Multitude of Charms, that conceal themselves from the generality of Mankind" (S #411, 3:538). The imagination mediates politeness through the promise of novelty—a new world, a world seen "in another Light"—but likewise politeness answers the abuse of the imagination by transferring its mechanism from texts to other people.

A week later Steele asserts that the "new world" at the center of the "Pleasures of the Imagination" is not Milton's Creation but the world of the *Spectator*. The "Pleasures" conclude on July 3, and on July 11 Steele asks for contributions to the *Spectator*, promising his readers:

> a great Harvest of new Circumstances, Persons, and Things from this Proposal; and a World, which many think they are well acquainted with, discovered as wholly new. This sort of Intelligence will give a lively Image of the Chain and mutual Dependence of Humane society, take off impertinent Prejudices, enlarge the Minds of those, whose Views are confin'd to their own Circumstances. (S #428, 4:6–7)

The self-awareness of this polite and commercial public will be mediated by the pleasures of novelty, "a World, which many think they are well acquainted with, discovered as wholly new." In Steele's application of Addison's aesthetics of novelty, the mundane associations of the modern world become the content of the knowledge learned through the pleasures of the imagination, and this way of understanding the social becomes the condition of its reproduction, the guarantee of its very existence. It is in the terms of novelty that the polite imagination of the "Pleasures" explains and reproduces a public bound together by commercial dependencies.

"Taking the Hint": The Aesthetics of the Middle Style

Behind Steele's use of an image of mundane association as a means of explaining and reproducing civil society lies Addison's aesthetics of novelty, and behind "novelty" lies Addison's project of reclaiming the middle style. Novelty theorizes the effects of the middle style, offering a way to understand human relations as based neither on the language of reason nor on the language of poetry, but rather on writing that, in C. S. Lewis's phrase, "stand[s] on the common ground of daily life and deal[s] only with middle things."[27] In the "Pleasures," Addison complicates the *Spectator*'s initial critical emphasis on the great and the beautiful in order to return the middle style to its proper position—to make the overlooked "middle style" the basis of a polite prose that could challenge the enthusiasm of the sublime, or what he calls the "Gothic."[28] The *Spectator*'s project of instilling a taste for polite writing can be understood as a prescription for the moderate and tempered style of the Georgics as the proper discourse of urban relations.[29]

When Johnson famously describes Addison's prose as "the model of the middle style," he is being exact.[30] In his "Essay on Virgil's Georgics," Addison had argued for a rehabilitation of the Georgics' "Middle stile," and claimed to be correcting a critical oversight: "the *Georgics* are a subject which none of the Critics have sufficiently taken into account."[31] Forecasting the terms of novelty in his description of georgic, Addison contrasts it to pastoral: Both deliver "precepts," but pastoral gives "plain and direct instruction," while georgic gives them "with the address of a Poet," and "raises in our minds a pleasing variety of scenes and landscapes, whilst it teaches us; and makes the dryest of its precepts look like a description" (E, 2:4). The pleasures of novelty—surprise, mental activity, and discovery—are the characteristics of georgic: Virgil "took notice of the effect which had the most surprise, and by consequence the most delight in it" (E, 2:6). Such surprise and delight are presented as the motives of learning, tied—as they will be in the "Pleasures"—to the pleasures of discovery:

> Virgil . . . loves to suggest a truth indirectly, and without giving us a full and open view of it, to let us see just so much as will naturally lead the imagination into all the parts that lie concealed. This is wonderfully diverting to the understanding, thus to receive a precept, that enters as it were through a by-way, and to apprehend an Idea that draws a whole train after it. For here the Mind, which is always delighted with its own discoveries, only takes the hint from the Poet, and seems to work out the rest by the strength of her own faculties. (E, 2:6)

In the georgic, as in the *Spectator*, an "indirect" and broken form surprises the reader, activating her own thinking, which in turn causes delight in her mind's new "discovery" and "the strength of [the mind's] own faculties"—a dynamic exemplified by the selective citation of Bacon I discussed above.

However, in the "Pleasures" Virgil is the exemplar of the beautiful not the novel, and between the essay on the Georgics (1697) and the "Pleasures" (1712), Addison adjusts his account of the middle style in terms of Ovid, the exemplar of novelty. In the "Notes on Ovid," appended to his translations from the *Metamorphoses* (1704), Addison repeats his complaint of the lack of critical appreciation of the middle style: "There are few books that have had worse Commentators on them than *Ovid's Metamorphosis*."[32] Remedying this, Addison defends Ovid against those "who run [him] down in the gross, for a low middle way of writing" (N, 1:134). Praising Ovid's descriptions as "simple and unadorn'd," and "always wonderfully easie and natural" (N, 1:134, 136), Addison justifies the middle way of writing by pointing to Ovid's graceful mastery of style, his matching a variety of styles to a variety of things: "There is so great a variety in the arguments of the Metamorphoses, that he who would treat of 'em rightly, ought to be a master of all stiles, and every way of writing. Ovid indeed shows himself most in a familiar story, where the chief grace is to be easie and natural" (N, 1:139). These comments define the *Spectator*'s practice as well, and its own self-conscious variety and emphasis on the surprising charm of the familiar are finally theorized in terms of the Ovidian pleasures of novelty.

For Addison, Ovid is the poet of novelty and the nature of the everyday is the condition of his poetry. Addison couples "Ovid's copiousness of invention" and "great insight into nature" (N, 1:142), while discussing Virgil's poetry as supernatural: "the genius of each Poet discover[s] itself in the language of the Nurse: *Virgil's Iris* could not have spoken more majestically in her own shape; but *Juno* is so much altered from her self in *Ovid*, that the Goddess is quite lost in the Old Woman" (N, 1:143). Virgil's language shows the divinity concealed in the everyday—his goddess is always a goddess, always majestic—while Ovid's language, like his goddess, fully assumes its human role. Virgil's style, which makes dung graceful, expresses his majestic genius turning everything—like Iris—into its own shape.[33] This is the language of the beautiful, referring to an order beyond the ordinary. In contrast, Ovid's style is mundane, and the effect of his metamorphoses depends on the goddess becoming the nurse. While beauty shows the divinity behind the everyday, novelty offers the pleasure of watching the divine become ordinary—not finding the divine *through* the ordinary but finding what had been divine *as* the ordinary.

Virgil, Ovid, and "The Language of the Nurse"

Addison reads the two scenes of nurses as examples of "the genius of each Poet discovering itself in the language of the nurse," as allegories of their respective poetics. As Ovid and Virgil exemplify for Addison the novel and beautiful, I will look at these representative scenes to flesh out some of the implications of the distinctions made in the "Pleasures." The category of novelty absorbs the Ovidian, theorizing the pleasures of Ovid's poetics, while the "beautiful" explains Virgil's. The novel and the beautiful are assigned different ends by Addison—novelty serving as the motive of learning, and beauty the motive of worship—and the conditions for this distinction are established in Addison's earlier criticism of the two poets.[34] I will argue that Ovid's poetics suggest a model for the teleology of the aesthetic pleasure he exemplifies, and suggest that the aesthetics of novelty offer, as an alternative to an aesthetics of the beautiful, a mode of understanding organized by the mundane world.

Virgil's nurse is in book 5 of the *Aeneid*.[35] Juno's messenger, Iris, is sent down to Sicily in the form of an old woman in order to stir up the Trojan women into burning their ships and so stopping the men from their seemingly incessant roaming. But the impersonated nurse fails because, as Addison notes, she sounds so majestic. Virgil's language adapts its subject to itself, not itself to its subject, and Iris can only amaze the women: "Wrap'd in amaze, the matrons wildly stare" (A, 5:840). Her spell is broken because it doesn't ring true: "No Beroe this, tho she belies her face: . . . Behold a Goddess in her ardent Eyes" (A, 5:843, 845). As allegory, the language of beauty raises even sick old women to the status of goddesses by showing a superhuman beauty in the poetry their language is able to form. Virgil's Beroe can't help being divine, can't help showing the superhuman through her beauty, a beauty that points beyond itself and even seems to deny itself. Such divine beauty is figured as that which is beyond language. When the Trojan women don't believe her, Iris abandons the disguise and assumes her proper shape, a rainbow, which does what even the most beautiful of speeches couldn't do. The women are "seiz'd with Rage Divine" (A, 5:856), enthralled enough to serve as pawns in Juno's game, moved to be more than themselves, and mad enough to burn the ships. This Virgilian allegory imagines the beautiful as something beyond language, beyond argument, finally beyond passion itself—a moment of divine inspiration that points beyond the human.

Whereas the beautiful orders in both senses (showing an order that compels), novelty offers a way to think of effects without reference to anything beyond the human. In Addison's Ovid episode, Juno is jealous of Semele because Semele is pregnant with Jove's child, and the goddess appears before the woman in the shape of Beroe.[36] After talking of many things, the topic of Jove comes up and Beroe warns the young woman to beware of lying lovers who claim they are gods in order to seduce young innocents.[37] She advises Semele to demand evidence and make Jove prove his love by giving her a taste of his divinity:

> But if he be indeed the thundering *Jove*,
> Bid him, when next he courts the rites of love,
> Descend triumphant from th' etherial sky,
> In all the pomp of his divinity;
> Encompass'd round by those celestial charms,
> With which he fills th' immortal *Juno*'s arms. (N, 114, lines 355–60)

Semele gets Jove to do this and she dies as a result. (Jove tries to moderate his "celestial charms" to save his lover, but cannot.)

I think Addison singled out this scene because it contains an Ovidian critique of Virgilian poetics. Virgil's goddess can't help being a goddess, can't really disguise the fact. Virgil's Iris does what Ovid's Juno wants Jove to do, she descends "in all the pomp of [her] divinity." For Ovid, though, such things are impossible. The very effectiveness of Juno's scheme depends on her completely counterfeiting the human, the better to "ensnare" Semele.[38] This of course is ironic. In her demand for Jove to show his divinity, to prove his divine love by loving her like a god, Semele allegorizes the limit of representation in the Ovidian world. Where Juno is cruel in her disguise, Jove is kind, as the consequence of Juno's impersonation proves. Juno is disguised in order to get Jove to remove his disguise, and Semele is put in the doubly mistaken position of trusting the consistency of appearances but distrusting their necessity. By trusting the disguised Juno, Semele commits herself to distrusting disguises. She confuses verisimilitude with truth and truth with love, when actually what seems true is a lie and what seems a lie is love. She dies to prove the impossibility of both appearance and truth. Though convinced by the false Beroe to be destroyed by the true Jove—dying for the truth—Semele was also able to love only because of Jove's falsity, his disguise. For Ovid, love is possible because truth isn't.

Such exchanges work only one way: gods become human but can't go back to being gods. The logic of the story, moving from Juno's becoming human to Jove's reluctant return to divinity, suggests that once lost the divine is not accessible again. And so, as Addison says, Ovid directs his attention to the "language of the nurse," to what is left after the goddess disappears. The loss of access to an unmediated real, the kind of truth divinity guaranteed, is the cost of Semele's loving Jove; she can love him because she doesn't fully get him. Allegorically, such poetry (the poetry of love) is possible because language loses its divine reference and becomes always and only a medium. In Addison's account, such mediated language shows Ovid at his most Ovidian. And if at first this means that Ovid doesn't fly as high as Virgil, the conclusion of the episode proves such moderation to be necessary.[39]

Ovid's story warns against the Virgilian conception of representation. This allegory of inspiration gone wrong wryly comments on poetry that seeks what it can't really want. In Ovid mediation is necessary: Semele, wanting to touch the god—to have contact with the divine—is "Consum'd amidst the glories she desired" (N, 1:115, line 394), a cruelly literal version of inspiration that suggests the loss of divinity requires a *necessary* moderation. The literal loss of the goddess (Juno disappears into Beroe) figures the allegorical loss of the gods—an erasure of the divine as a ground of explanation which makes the gods, like Jove here, into figures that narrate the effects of passions. In these terms, the nurse's goading of Semele to demand her lover fully inhabit the passion he claims is shown to be dangerous not because lightning will strike her down but because passion, even love, will burn her up. Without gods, Ovid offers an account of the passions—their effects and consequences—as the ground of, and the primary mode of, explanation in a post-theological world, a world of goddesses disappeared into old women. Unable to adapt herself to the human, Virgil's Iris turns to painting the sky to convince her auditors, but Ovid's Juno realizes her end by insinuating her message rather than overpowering her auditor. Novelty requires the reader's activity (her curiosity, desire, and pleasure) to produce its effects. What we find, or make, for ourselves in reading a novel text works better than a text that commands our attention with its pre-ordered performance. Granting the burden of proof to the reader in this way requires perhaps that we assist in our own destruction, but also consequently that we participate in our own salvation, or at least in our own judgment. Rather than becoming gods, heightened to the point of self-destructive madness by the claim to inspiration, novelty implies a trust in the hesitancy of belief and a witting refusal of the temptations of certainty, even at the cost of doubt.

Like Ovid's poetics, an aesthetics of novelty—the aesthetic pleasure, as Steele suggests, appropriate to the mundane, transactional world of the *Spectator*—offers a world of mediated, perhaps compensatory, pleasures. The divine is lost as divine but available as pleasure of a more visceral kind. For Ovid pleasure points not beyond itself but to itself, and offers the labors of passion, sex, and poetry as the conditions of understanding. The pleasures of the beautiful and the great *act on* us, producing our passive responses, our subjecthood. The pleasures of novelty describe *our activity*, demanding an active response, and explaining how we make the world we live in. The emphasis on making, on activity, on curiosity and desire, keeps the major emphasis (but not all) of Addison's aesthetics on this side of the divine, in the mundane and civil spheres where passions provide most of the motivation, and moderation is necessary not to spite but to save such passion.

Beyond the Virgilian divinity that well-ordered figures express, the Ovidian emphasis on everyday—in which the divine *becomes* human—studies the activities and changes, the passions and movements, of the human world. I take the "novelty" of the "Pleasures" to offer terms for an extra-theological knowledge, a mode of human knowledge grounded in the practices of the social. Rather than studying the moral agent in terms of her experience of a divine good, a rule, or law, Addison's aesthetics of novelty provide terms for studying the moral agent in terms of her experience of human goods, a mode of understanding structured by a civil sphere known through the "Pleasures of the Imagination."

If, as McKeon says, the condition of aesthetics is bracketing the sphere of the religious (defining it *as* a sphere), then aesthetics depends on developing a discourse that can discuss what theology used to explain. In these terms, the Ovidian discourse of the passions would have been newly significant in the development of a discourse of aesthetics. Addison's "Pleasures" theorize both a Virgilian response and an Ovidian one, but by offering an aesthetics of the divine at all, he points towards the absorbing of Virgil's pieties into Ovid's passions. Placing an aesthetics of human passions alongside one organized by the divine order, Addison provided a way to understand human desires without reference to the divine.

While Addison certainly should not be understood as anti-religious, he did introduce terms that, by finding a way to avoid religious controversy (aesthetics serving as the tub of the tale), eventually displaced what he had tried to moderate.[40] Aesthetics was both a condition and effect of civil society, one of the discourses by which a public sphere was constituted, a discursive site in which disagreements over theology could be bracketed in the interests of peace—a peace guaranteed by a shared commitment to a discourse of politeness, the object of an aesthetics of novelty. Premised on the restless and extensive activity of human desire (the desires we have for each other) an aesthetics of novelty offers an alternative to the intensive and enthusiastic activities of extrahuman desire (the desire we have for something else). This provides a way to see the interaction of human desires, not a disinterested abstraction from them, as a defining condition of understanding the human world.

NOTES

1. Edmund Burke, *A Philosophical Enquiry into the Origin of our Ideas of the Sublime and the Beautiful*, ed. Adam Phillips (1757; New York: Oxford Univ. Press, 1990), 29. Section 1, part 1 opens: "The first and simplest emotion which we discover in the human mind, is Curiosity. By curiosity, I mean whatever desire we have for, or whatever pleasure we take in novelty" (29). Here simplicity is given an ontogenetic value—the pleasures of novelty are childish—instead of the methodological significance given in the second preface: "In considering any complex matter, we ought to examine every distinct ingredient in the composition, one by one; and reduce every thing to the utmost simplicity" (4). Ronald Paulson discusses novelty as the central category of the "Pleasures" in chapter 3 of *The Beautiful, Novel, and Strange: Aesthetics and Heterodoxy* (Baltimore: Johns Hopkins Univ. Press, 1996).

2. The "Pleasures of the Imagination" appeared in the middle of the *Spectator*'s run (March, 1711–December, 1712), #411–#421 (June–July 1712). Addison and Steele, *The Spectator*, ed. Donald F. Bond, 5 vols. (Oxford: Oxford Univ. Press, 1965); hereafter cited parenthetically in the text and abbreviated S.

3. In the first claim I follow Paulson, who suggests that novelty theorizes the *Spectator*'s practice (53). For the context of the second claim, see Scott Black, "Social and Literary Form in the *Spectator*," *Eighteenth-Century Studies* 33 (1999), where I argue that the *Spectator* was instrumental in articulating terms with which to understand a distinct and semi-autonomous sphere of relations—a sphere that will be political economy's object of study and one that we (its heirs) call a social, not a political or a religious, order. I explain this as developing at the nexus of the technology of the press, the social space of the city, and the adaptation of the literary form of the essay.

4. The *locus classicus* for such critics is Samuel Monk, *The Sublime: A Study of Critical Theories in Eighteenth Century England* (New York: MLA, 1935). Two standard Monk-based accounts of Addison's aesthetics are Marjorie Hope Nicholson, *Mountain Gloom and Mountain Glory: The Development of the Aesthetics of the Infinite* (Ithaca: Cornell Univ. Press, 1959), 300–23, and Lee Andrew Elioseff, *The Cultural Milieu of Addison's Literary Criticism* (Austin: University of Texas Press, 1963), 95–120.

5. Clarence DeWitt Thorpe, "Addison and Some of His Predecessors on 'Novelty,'" *PMLA* 52 (1937), 1129. Robin Dix, "Addison and the Concept of 'Novelty' as a Basic Aesthetic Category," *British Journal of Aesthetics* 26 (1986), 389.

6. Neil Saccamano, "The Sublime Force of Words in Addison's 'Pleasures,'" *ELH* 58 (1991), 84–86.

7. Saccamano, 95.

8. Ibid., 101.

9. Jules David Law, *The Rhetoric of Empiricism: Language and Perception from Locke to I. A. Richards* (Ithaca: Cornell Univ. Press, 1993), 70. Law notes:

"Whereas for Burke and Kant the failure of comprehension or the inadequacy of sensuous intuition to rational idea produces something distinct and interesting, for Locke such a failure is undramatic and simply prompts a return to more limited investigations" (70).

10. Law, 14.

11. Michael McKeon writes of "the 'replacement' of religious by literary spirituality" ("Politics of Discourses and the Rise of the Aesthetic in Seventeenth-Century England," *Politics of Discourse*, ed. Kevin Sharpe and Steven N. Zwicker [Berkeley: Univ. of California Press, 1987], 36): "The rise of the aesthetic consists in the assumption by 'art' of those tasks that traditionally were performed by religious belief and experience" (49). He summarizes his argument: "The decline of religion . . . is not only coincident with but also a function of the rise of the aesthetic" (37).

12. "The crucial element is the categorical self-consciousness itself . . . Religion exercises its authority by tacit dominion" (McKeon, "Politics," 35).

13. McKeon, "Politics," 49–50.

14. "An Essay Writer must practice in the Chymical Method, and give the Virtue of a full Draught in a few Drops" (S #104, 1:506). See Black, "Social and Literary Form," 31–32.

15. Francis Bacon, "Of the Regiment of Health," *Essays*, ed. John Pritcher (New York: Penguin, 1985), 156.

16. In Aphorism 80 of *The New Organon* (1620; ed. Fulton H. Anderson [New York: Macmillan, 1960]), Bacon complains that "natural philosophy" has only been "a passage and a bridge to something else"—not undertaken for its own sake, for the sake of curiosity and the desire for knowledge—"unless it were [by] some monk studying in his cell, or some gentleman in his country house" (77). Bacon distinguishes his natural philosophy from the solitudes of either religion or the country, suggesting it's organized by secular, urban, and communicative practices.

17. See Paulson for an account of the "strange," which "houses" "the genre of the pastoral" and is located in the country (68). I think this can be distinguished from the georgic form and urban locus of novelty.

18. John Milton, *Paradise Lost, Complete Poems and Selected Prose*, ed. Merritt Y. Hughes (New York: Macmillan, 1957), 3:418–26.

19. The natural lines up with the beautiful. In S #321, Addison refers to the propriety of Adam and Eve's sentiments and speech as "natural" (S, 3:176), while in this paper Adam and Eve are called beautiful.

20. This is not of course to say that such actions or characters don't move, but that they don't change, they don't metamorphose. The thrill of reading battles between supernatural beings is awe, not curiosity about the outcome.

21. I stress "approaching" as Addison points out that one of the beauties of Milton is that Adam and Eve "take a Tincture" from Paradise, "their Thoughts are always *Paradisiacal*" (S #321, 3:171).

22. This would explain why the devils are great and the angels beautiful. The angels as formed are beautiful, while the devils are deformed by rebellion, having returned to unshaped chaos by denying the ordering law.

23. I see this as a Lockean project. Locke writes: "Bodies, by our Senses, do not afford us so clear and distinct an *Idea* of *active Power*, as we have from reflection on the Operations of our Minds" (*Essay concerning Human Understanding*, ed. Peter H. Nidditch [New York: Oxford Univ. Press, 1975], bk. 2, ch. 11, §4; p. 235).

24. Paulson remarks that "the *Spectator* itself embodies the secondary imagination" (73).

25. Milton, *Paradise Lost*, 1:254–55.

26. Locke says that enthusiasm "takes away both Reason and Revelation, and substitutes in the room of it, the ungrounded Fancies of a Man's own Brain, and assumes for them a Foundation both of Opinion and Conduct" (*Essay*, bk. 4, ch. 19, §3; p. 698).

27. C. S. Lewis, "Addison" (1945), *Selected Literary Essays*, ed. Walter Hooper (New York: Cambridge Univ. Press, 1969), 167.

28. Addison's aesthetics are an extension of his previous critical essays (S #409, 3:530), a means to combat what is called in the wit papers, "Monkish Ignorance" (S #60, 1:253) and "Gothic Taste" (S #62, 1:268; S #409, 3:530). For Addison, the sublime names the problem of Gothic "Extravagencies of an irregular Fancy" (S #62, 1:268) as the excesses of the "disordered" imagination (S #421, 3:579) that he argued should be reformed by "the beautiful Simplicity" of the Greek and Roman classics (S #62, 1:268; S #409, 3:530).

29. For Cicero, the orator of the middle style is "moderate and tempered" [*modicum et temperatum*] (*Orator*, trans. H. M. Hubbell [Cambridge: Loeb, 1938], 376). For Cicero's discussion of the middle style, see 91–96. In his *Lectures on Poetry* (trans. William Bowyer, 1742; Menston, Yorkshire: Scolar Press, 1973), Joseph Trapp distinguishes the sublime style from the "Humble, which has its Elegance as it is used in its proper Place. It is proper, when we would describe, in a familiar and easy Manner, the common Concerns of Life" (87–88). The "Humble" includes both the middle and low styles, "the former [in georgic] represents common Life, and more especially as it appears within the City; the latter [pastoral] draws all its Images from the Country" (88). These lectures were originally published as *Praelectiones Poeticae*, 3 vols. (1711, 1715, 1719).

30. Samuel Johnson, "Addison," *Lives of the Poets*, ed. G. B. Hill, 3 vols. (Oxford: Clarendon, 1905), 3:149.

31. Addison, "Essay on Virgil's Georgics" (1697), *Miscellaneous Works*, ed. A. C. Guthkelch, 2 vols. (London: G. Bell and Sons, 1914), 2:3; hereafter cited parenthetically in the text and abbreviated E. The essay prefaced Dryden's translation, and opens by discussing Virgil's introducing to Rome, in imitation of the Greeks, three kinds of poetry, each with its peculiar style: the "sweetness and rusticity" of the pastoral, the "majesty" of the heroic, and "the Middle stile" of the georgic.

32. Addison, "Notes on Ovid" (1704), *Miscellaneous Works*, 1:134; hereafter cited parenthetically in the text and abbreviated N.

33. Virgil "delivers the meanest of his precepts with a kind of grandeur, he breaks the clods and tosses the dung around with an air of gracefulness" (E, 2:9).

The way Addison will describe the secondary pleasures of the imagination—"the Action of the Mind" that compares representations with dunghills (S #418, 3:566–67)—seems to refer back to this Virgilian dynamic.

34. God "has annexed a secret Pleasure to the Idea of any thing that is new, or uncommon, that he might encourage us in the Pursuit after Knowledge" (S #413, 3:545); God "has made so many Objects appear beautiful, that he might render the whole Creation more gay and delightful. . . . So that it is impossible for us to behold his Works with Coldness or Indifference" (S #413, 3:546). For Addison, greatness teaches us to see ourselves vis-à-vis the extra-natural world; beauty, to see ourselves vis-à-vis the natural world; and novelty, to see ourselves vis-à-vis the human world.

35. Virgil, *Aeneid*, trans. John Dryden, volumes 5–6 of *Dryden's Works*, ed. William Frost and Vinton A. Dearing (Berkeley: University of California Press, 1987), lines 5:791–865; hereafter cited parenthetically in the text and abbreviated A.

36. Ovid, *Metamorphoses*, book 3, trans. Addison, *Miscellaneous Works*, 1:112–15.

37. "Talking of many things" translates literally, *ubi captato sermone diuque loquendo* (*Metamorphoses*, ed. and trans. Frank J. Miller [Cambridge: Loeb, 1977], 3.279), but Addison emphasizes his interpretation of Ovid in his translation: "Much did she talk about love" (N, 113, line 347). This certainly makes sense: Semele's lover's name comes up, so surely the topic of love would have been part of the general gossip. Nevertheless, Addison extrapolates "talk of love" from "many things," and I suspect this has to do with what Addison takes to be Ovid's genius discovering itself in the language of the nurse.

38. "Ensnare" is Addison's translation (N, 114, line 361) of "*formarat*" (*Metamorphoses*, 3.288), which can be more exactly but perhaps less forcefully rendered as "molded."

39. Addison cites the passage of Jove's moderation of his glory, an attempt to save Semele, as particularly indicative of Ovid: "*Jupiter* makes a very majestick figure with his Thunder and Lightning, but it is still such a one as shows who drew it; for who does not plainly discover *Ovid*'s hand in [the passage about Jupiter using a "Temper'd" second rate lightning bolt]" (N, 1:143, lines 380–89). Either the love at the core of power, or the way power is moderated by love, or simply the fact of a "lesser mould and lighter weight" (N, 1:114, line 383; *saevitae flammaeque minus, minus addidit irae* [304]) distinguishes a "lesser" Ovidian poetics from the power and height of Virgil's.

40. McKeon points to this important dynamic: "the secularizers themselves often are more likely to see their sponsorship of the political, the historical, and the material as fully consistent with the continued health of the religious realm" (35).

Contributors to Volume 30

A. Owen Aldridge is Professor Emeritus of Comparative Literature at the University of Illinois, Urbana. He was the founder of the journal *Comparative Literature Studies* and was among the founders of ASECS. Among his many books, those most pertinent to the present essay are *Early American Literature: A Comparatist Approach* (Princeton, 1982) and *Thomas Paine's American Ideology* (Delaware, 1984). Three collections of essays have been gathered in his honor, *Deism, Masonry, and Enlightenment* (Delaware, 1987), *Aesthetics and the Literature of Ideas* (Delaware, 1990), and *Crosscurrents in the Literatures of Asia and the West* (Delaware, 1997).

Scott Black is Assistant Professor of English at Villanova University. He is currently working on the development of the essay as a genre in the contexts of eighteenth-century aesthetics and the emergence of a sphere of social relations.

Jenny Davidson is an Assistant Professor of English and comparative literature at Columbia University. Former managing editor of *The Yale Journal of Criticism,* she is currently completing a manuscript titled "Hypocrisy, Politics, and Politeness, 1688–1814." She is also writing a historical novel about Jonathan Wild.

John Bryce Jordan, a doctoral candidate in dance history and theory at the University of California, Riverside, studies and performs postmodern and eighteenth-century dance. He is the assistant editor of *Continuous Replay: The Photographs of Arnie Zane,* edited by Jonathan Green (MIT Press, 1999).

Elisabeth Krimmer is a Visiting Assistant Professor of German at Mount Holyoke College. She received her doctoral degree from the University of Massachusetts. Her research interests focus on eighteenth- and nineteenth-century German women writers. She has published articles on Annette von Droste-Hülshoff, Bettina Brentano von Arnim, Charlotte von Stein, Sophie La Roche, Frederike Helene Unger, and Leontine Sagan. She is currently finishing a book on cross-dressing in eighteenth-century literature and culture.

Laura Laffrado is Professor of American Literature and Director of Graduate Studies at Western Washington University. She is the author of *Hawthorne's Literature for Children* (Georgia, 1992). She is currently at work on a book on gender and genre in early American literature.

Juliette Merritt is a Lecturer of English at McMaster University in Hamilton, Ontario. Her article on Eliza Haywood was originally presented at the 1998 ASECS meeting. An earlier essay on Haywood, "'That Devil Curiosity which Too Much Haunts the Minds of Women': Eliza Haywood's Female Spectators" was published in *LUMEN* (1997). Both articles form part of the book she is revising for publication, "Beyond Spectacle: Eliza Haywood's Female Spectators."

Katharine M. Morsberger is an independent scholar living in Claremont, California, who has published numerous articles and reviews on topics ranging from John Locke to John Steinbeck, from Dryden's and Pope's translations of Chaucer to Christopher Isherwood's and Don Bachardy's teleplay *Frankenstein: The True Story.* With Robert E. Morsberger, she is the author of a biography, *Lew Wallace: Militant Romantic.* Her doctorate is from the University of California, Riverside.

Mitzi Myers teaches at the University of California, Los Angeles. She has published extensively on Mary Wollstonecraft, Hannah More, Maria Edgeworth, and historical children's literature and pedagogy. As co-editor of the twelve-volume edition of Maria Edgeworth's selected works, she has assumed special responsibility for the volumes treating of the adult novel *Belinda* (1801) and *Practical Education* (1798) as well as the tales for children and young adults. She recently edited a special issue of *Eighteenth-Century Life* titled *Ireland 1798–1998: From Revolution to Revisionism and Beyond* (1998).

David Paxman, an Associate Professor of English at Brigham Young University, has published on eighteenth-century British poetry, aesthetics, prose fiction, and intellectual history in *Eighteenth-Century Studies*, *Philological Quarterly*, *Modern Philology*, *Journal of the History of Ideas*, and *Restoration*. He is currently studying regional literary cultures in England.

Cynthia Richards is an Assistant Professor of English at Wittenberg University in Springfield, Ohio. Currently working on a book entitled "Radical Collaborations: Mary Wollstonecraft and Her Contemporaries," she has previously published on Aphra Behn and Eliza Haywood.

G. Gabrielle Starr is Assistant Professor of English at New York University. She is at work on a book of genre history, "The Novel and the New Lyricism," and is also collaborating on a multidisciplinary project on aesthetics and the brain.

Heather I. Sullivan is an Assistant Professor of German at Trinity University in San Antonio. She has published several interdisciplinary articles on literature and the earth sciences around 1800, and is currently working on a book project on this topic. She is also the author of *The Intercontextuality of Self and Nature in Ludwig Tieck's Early Works* (Lang, 1997).

James Tierney, Professor of English at the University of Missouri-St. Louis, edited *The Correspondence of Robert Dodsley, 1733–1764* and has published widely on aspects of publishing history, especially on newspapers and periodicals. He is currently involved in the long-term project, "A CD-ROM Subject Index to Pre–1800 English Periodicals."

Executive Board 1999–2000

For information about the
American Society for Eighteenth-Century Studies, please contact:

ASECS
P.O. Box 7867
Wake Forest University
Winston-Salem, NC 27109-7867
Telephone: (336) 727-4694
Fax: (336) 727-4697
E-mail: asecs@wfu.edu
Web Site: http://www.press.jhu.edu/associations/asecs

Patron Members 1999–2000

Paul Alkon
Mark S. Auburn
James G. Basker
Barbara Becker-Cantarino
R. Bernasconi
Theodore E. D. Braun
Peter M. Briggs
Patricia Brückmann
Michael Burden
Joseph A. Byrnes
Brian A. Connery
Louis Cornell
Margaretmary Daley
Marlies K. Danziger
Joan DeJean
Roland Desne
William F. Edmiston
Frank H. Ellis
Clarissa C. Erwin
Timothy Erwin
Roger J. Fechner
Jan Fergus
Charles N. Fifer
Dustin H. Griffin
Joan R. Gundersen
Phyllis Guskin
Wolfgang Haase
Roger Hahn
Steve Holliday
Robert H. Hopkins
Robert D. Hume
Lynn A. Hunt
Margaret C. Jacob
Regina Mary Janes
Annibel Jenkins
Gary Kates
Shirley Strum Kenny
David H. Koss
Thomas W. Krise
Colby H. Kullman
Susan Lanser
J. Patrick Lee
Meredith Lee
Nancy M. Lee-Riffe
Elizabeth Liebman
H. W. Matalene
Marie E. McAllister
Helen Louise McGuffie
Alan T. McKenzie
Donald C. Mell, Jr.
John H. Middendorf
Earl Miner
Dennis Moore
Frank Palmeri
Jane Perry-Camp
R. G. Peterson
J. G. A. Pocock
John Valdimir Price
Ralph W. Rader
John Radner
Ronald C. Rosbottom
Linda H. Roth
Treadwell Ruml II
Roseann Runte
Harold Schiffman
William C. Schrader
Richard Sher
Kazuko Shimizu
English Showalter
John Sitter
Patricia Meyer Spacks
Susan Staves
Ann T. Straulman
Masashi Suzuki
Mika Suzuki
Ruud N. W. M. Teeuwen
Diana M. Thomas
Linda Veronika Troost
Raymond D. Tumbleson
Bertil VanBoer
David F. Venturo
Howard D. Weinbrot
Byron R. Wells
Karin E. Wolfe
James Woolley
William J. Zachs
Lisa M. Zeitz

Sponsoring Members 1999–2000

Paula Backscheider
Joseph F. Bartolomeo
Jerry C. Beasley
David Blewett
Carol Blum
Thomas F. Bonnell
Martha F. Bowden
Gay W. Brack
O. M. Brack, Jr.
Leo Braudy
Leslie Ellen Brown
Judith Colton
Thomas M. Columbus
Michael J. Conlon
Brian Corman
Howard J. Coughlin, Jr.
Patricia B. Craddock
Robert De Maria
Jo Lynn Edwards
A. C. Elias, Jr.
Antoinette Emch-Dériaz
David Fairer
Robert Folkenflik
Bernadette Fort
Brandon Brame Fortune
Christopher Fox
Jack Fruchtman, Jr.
Parme Giuntini
Diana Guiragossian-Carr
Basil Guy
Karsten Harries
Phillip Harth
Donald M. Hassler
Julie C. Hayes
Daniel Heartz
Charles H. Hinnant
J. Paul Hunter
Adrienne D. Hytier
Malcolm Jack

Thomas Jemielity
Loftus Townshend Jestin
Sarah Jordan
Frederick M. Keener
Charles A. Knight
Gwin J. Kolb
Catherine Lafarge
John E. Larkin, Jr.
April London
David D. Mann
Robert Markley
John A. McCarthy
David McNeil
Shirley McNerney Rendell
Linda E. Merians
Kathryn Montgomery
Dewey F. Mosby
Maureen E. Mulvihill
Malcolm H. Murray
Nicolas H. Nelson
Mary Ann O'Donnell
John H. O'Neill
Hal N. Opperman
Douglas Lane Patey
Virginia J. Peacock
Ruth Perry
Stuart Peterfreund
James Pollak
Adam Potkay
Thomas R. Preston
Ruben D. Quintero
Thomas J. Regan
Cedric Reverand II
Walter E. Rex
John Richetti
Albert J. Rivero
Betty Rizzo
Raymond Rizzo
Peter Sabor
J. T. Scanlan
Mona Scheuermann
Barbara B. Schnorrenberg
Gordon J. Schochet
Donald T. Siebert
Stephen Soud
Joan Koster Stemmler
Damie Stillman
A. G. Tannenbaum
Randolph Trumbach
Jack Undank
Peter Wagner

Institutional Members 1999–2000

American Antiquarian Society
Brown University–John Carter Brown Library
University of California–Science Library
University of California
Carleton University Library
Case Western Reserve University–Kelvin Smith Library
University of Connecticut–Homer Babbidge Library
University of Chicago Dept. of Art History–CWAC
Emory University–Robert W. Woodruff Library
University of Evansville Library
Florida Atlantic University–Wimberly Library
Fordham University Library–Periodicals
Fordham University–History Dept. Chairman
Georgia State University–William Russell Pullen Library
Harvard College Library
Holy Cross College–Dinand Library
Indiana University Library
Johns Hopkins University–Milton S. Eisenhower Library
University of Kansas Libraries
University of Kentucky–Young Library
McMaster University Library
Metropolitan Museum of Art–Thomas J. Watson Library
University of North Carolina–Davis Library
Northwestern University Library
University of Notre Dame Library
University of Notre Dame–Institute for Scholarship
Ohio State University–Library Serials Division
Omohundro Institute of Early American History–Kellock Library
University of Pennsylvania Library
University of Rochester Library
Rutgers University–Alexander Library
SUNY at Binghamton Library
Smith College–W. A. Neilson Library
Smithsonian Institution Library
University of Southern California
Stanford University–Green Library
University of Tennessee Library
University of Texas at Austin–General Library
Towson State University–English Dept.
University of Tulsa–McFarlin Library
University of Victoria–McPherson Library
Washington University–Olin Library
William Andrews Clark Memorial Library
University of Wisconsin at Madison–Dept. of English
Yale Center for British Art–Reference Library
Yale University–Sterling Memorial Library
York University–Scott Library

Index

Every effort has been made to include references to all identifiable persons living before or during the long eighteenth century, as well as to often cited twentieth-century critics and commentators, and to provide a selective listing of relevant concepts and keywords. Readers may also wish to consult the endnotes of each essay for more comprehensive information.